Novell® Certified Linux Professional (Novell CLP)

Study Guide

Emmett Dulaney

Novell
PRESS™

Novell®

800 East 96th Street, Indianapolis, Indiana 46240 USA

Novell® Certified Linux Professional Study Guide

International Standard Book Number: 0-672-32719-8

Library of Congress Catalog Card Number: 2004109384

Printed in the United States of America

First Printing: December 2004

07   06   05   4   3   2

Trademarks

All terms mentioned in this book that are known to be trademarks or service marks have been appropriately capitalized. Novell Press cannot attest to the accuracy of this information. Use of a term in this book should not be regarded as affecting the validity of any trademark or service mark.

Novell is a registered trademark; and Novell Press and the Novell Press logo are trademarks of Novell, Inc. in the United States and other countries. All brand names and product names used in this book are trade names, service marks, trademarks, or registered trademarks of their respective owners.

Linux is a registered trademark of Linus Torvalds.

Warning and Disclaimer

Every effort has been made to make this book as complete and as accurate as possible, but no warranty or fitness is implied. The information provided is on an "as is" basis. The author and the publisher shall have neither liability nor responsibility to any person or entity with respect to any loss or damages arising from the information contained in this book.

Bulk Sales

Pearson offers excellent discounts on this book when ordered in quantity for bulk purchases or special sales. For more information, please contact

> **U.S. Corporate and Government Sales**
> 1-800-382-3419
> corpsales@pearsontechgroup.com

For sales outside of the U.S., please contact

> **International Sales**
> international@pearsoned.com

Acquisitions Editor
Jenny Watson

Development Editor
Mark Cierzniak

Managing Editor
Charlotte Clapp

Project Editor
Matt Purcell

Copy Editor
Margaret Berson

Indexer
Ken Johnson

Proofreader
Kathy Bidwell

Technical Editor
Warren Wyrostek

Publishing Coordinator
Vanessa Evans

Designer
Gary Adair

Page Layout
Heather Wilkins

Contents at a Glance

Table of Contents

Chapter 4 Working with Files   133

Chapter 5 Basic Linux Administration   157

About the Author

Emmett Dulaney is the author of several Linux, Unix, and certification titles. The Certification columnist and reviewer for UnixReview, he teaches the business of technology at Anderson University. He holds, or has held, 17 different vendor certifications and is a former partner in Mercury Technical Solutions.

Dedication

This book is dedicated to my family. Were it not for their patience, contributions, and understanding, I would not be able to accomplish a fraction of the little I do.

Acknowledgments

A great many people worked behind the scenes on this book, but it would not have been possible without the help of Warren Wyrostek. Though he is listed in the front as the Technical Editor, he served as far more on this title than that—as he does on most books that include him. Without his going above and beyond the call of duty, this title would have never come to be, or would be a dim shell of what it currently is.

A great deal of thanks is owed to Jenny Watson for giving me the opportunity to write this book. I appreciate her confidence and encouragement to step out from the Development Editor role once in a while.

Thanks also belong Matt Purcell, the Project Editor for this book. His ability to keep the book on track proved to be the impetus needed every now and then to stay up late at night.

Margaret Berson and Mark Cierzniak rounded out the team and added valuable contributions on every page.

We Want to Hear from You!

As the reader of this book, *you* are our most important critic and commentator. We value your opinion and want to know what we're doing right, what we could do better, what areas you'd like to see us publish in, and any other words of wisdom you're willing to pass our way.

You can email or write me directly to let me know what you did or didn't like about this book—as well as what we can do to make our books better.

Please note that I cannot help you with technical problems related to the topic of this book and that due to the high volume of mail I receive, I may not be able to reply to every message.

When you write, please be sure to include this book's title and author as well as your name and email address, or phone number. I will carefully review your comments and share them with the author and editors who worked on the book.

Email: feedback@novellpress.com

Mail: Mark Taber
          Associate Publisher
          Novell Press/Pearson Education
          800 East 96th Street
          Indianapolis, IN 46240 USA

## CHAPTER 1

The NCLP Certification Process and Planning Your Approach

This book is in your hands for a reason. The title on the cover reads "NCLP Study Guide," not "Twenty-Seven Keys to Pool Maintenance," so we can only assume that the reason why you are holding this book is that you want to become a Novell Certified Linux Professional (NCLP). If this is the case, you've made a wise choice.

This book walks you through the process of obtaining that certification, and gives you a good start toward the Certified Linux Engineer (CLE) certification, if you want to continue on your journey beyond CLP.

Although Novell does not have prerequisites for this exam, it is highly recommended that prior to attempting to become certified at the NCLP level, you pass two other exams:

1. LPI 101 from the Linux Professional Institute
2. LPI 102, also from the Linux Professional Institute

These exams are focused on generic Linux—topics that apply whether you are using SuSE, Red Hat, or any other Linux implementation. Not only will these exams assist you with your studies for the NCLP, but as an added bonus to your journey, after you pass these two exams, you become LPIC Level–certified by the Linux Professional Institute.

Taking exams is not something that most people anticipate eagerly, no matter how well prepared they may be. In most cases, familiarity helps ameliorate test anxiety. In plain English, this means you probably won't be as nervous when you take your fourth or fifth certification exam as you will be when you take your first one.

Whether it's your first exam or your tenth, understanding the details of the exam (how much time to spend on questions, the environment you'll be in, and so on) and the exam software used will help you concentrate on the material rather than on the setting. Likewise, mastering a few basic exam-taking skills should help you recognize—and perhaps even outfox—some of the tricks and gotchas you're bound to find in some of the exam questions.

This chapter describes some proven exam-taking strategies that you should be able to use to your advantage.

The Exam Situation

When you arrive at the testing center where you scheduled your exam, you'll need to sign in with an exam coordinator. He or she will ask you to show two forms of identification, one of which must be a photo ID, and both should have your signature. After you've signed in and your time slot arrives, you'll be asked to deposit any books, pagers, cell phones, bags, or other items you brought with you. Then, you'll be escorted into a closed room. Typically, the room will be furnished with anywhere from one to half a dozen computers, and each workstation will be separated from the others by dividers designed to keep you from seeing what's happening on someone else's computer.

You'll be furnished with a pen or pencil and a blank sheet of paper, or, in some cases, an erasable plastic sheet and an erasable felt-tip pen. You're allowed to write down any information you want on both sides of this sheet.

Most test rooms feature a wall with a large picture window. This permits the exam coordinator standing behind it to monitor the room, to prevent exam takers from cheating. The exam coordinator will have preloaded the appropriate certification exam and you'll be permitted to start as soon as you're seated in front of the computer.

All certification exams allow a certain maximum amount of time in which to complete your work. Although this may sound quite simple, the questions are constructed not only to check your mastery of basic facts and figures about SuSE and Linux technologies, but they also require you to evaluate one or more sets of circumstances or requirements. You might be asked to select the best or most effective solution to a problem that can be tackled in a number of different ways. Taking the exam is quite an adventure, and it involves real thinking. This book shows you what to expect and how to deal with the potential problems, puzzles, and predicaments.

As you're taking the exam, keep working on each question until you're certain you have done the task thoroughly.

With a traditional multiple-choice exam like LPI, you're better off guessing at a solution than leaving a task untackled if you start running out of time. Time management on a practicum exam, though, is even more critical as you must complete the steps fully and completely. You either get a 100% or a 0% on the practicum. There is no variation.

Exam-Taking Basics

The most important advice about taking any exam is this: Read each question, task, or assignment carefully. Some wording is deliberately ambiguous, some questions use double negatives, and others use terminology in incredibly precise ways.

Here are some suggestions on how to deal with the tendency to jump to an answer too quickly:

▶ Make sure you read every word in the question. If you find yourself jumping ahead impatiently, go back and start over.

▶ As you read, try to restate the question in your own terms. If you can do this, you should be able to pick the correct answer(s) much more easily.

▶ When returning to a question after your initial read-through, read every word again—otherwise, your mind can quickly fall into a rut. Sometimes, revisiting a question after turning your attention elsewhere lets you see something you missed, but the strong tendency is to see what you've seen before. Try to avoid that tendency at all costs.

▶ If you return to a question more than twice, try to articulate to yourself what you don't understand about the question, or what appears to be missing. If you chew on the subject for a while, your subconscious might provide the details that are lacking or you might notice a "trick" that will point to the right answer.

Above all, try to deal with each question by thinking through what you know about the operating system—its characteristics, behaviors, and facts. By reviewing what you know (and what you've written down on your information sheet), you'll often recall or understand things sufficiently to determine the approach to take to the question.

Exam-Handling Strategies

The NCLP exam is a hands-on practicum.

This means that you won't be answering multiple-choice questions about who created Linux. Instead, you're much more likely to be adding a new user to the system. In other words, the test centers on performing tasks.

The tasks assume that you understand the inner workings of Linux utilities inside and out. If your knowledge in these areas is well grounded, it will help you cut through many otherwise confusing questions.

Time management has been mentioned before, and it cannot be stressed enough. With five minutes left in the exam, you should be simply checking that everything is working correctly, or you have already failed.

Planning Your Approach

When pursuing a certification, it is best to approach it as you would any other large undertaking.

Becoming an NCLP requires a significant investment on your part. Not only does the price of this book cancel out a reasonable dinner for four (or two, with drinks), but there is also the cost of the exam to consider as well as the sizable amount of time that you are going to spend reading, studying, and taking the test. You should endeavor to get as much out of this investment as you can.

To this end, I encourage you to apply yourself wholly to this enterprise. Sure, you can read a chapter every now and then and skim and skip around as I did with the Bill Clinton autobiography. You can skip topics that you're familiar with or that you've had limited experience with before, but are you really pursuing the best tactic when you do this?

This exam is aimed at the same audience level as LPI, RHCA, and similar exams. It is, however, focused *only* on SuSE Linux. When studying for this test, you can forget all about how things work in Red Hat or Debian and think only in terms of the one Linux flavor that you are hopefully most familiar and comfortable with.

There are three courses that Novell recommends you have the knowledge from before taking this exam. You do not need to sit through the courses—in other words, that is not a mandatory prerequisite—but you do need to know the topics. The three courses in question are

▶ Linux Fundamentals (3036)

▶ Linux Administration (3037)

▶ Advanced Linux Administration (3038)

Table 1.1 lists the topics and objectives from course 3036, and where they are covered in this book.

Topics and Objectives of Course 3036
TABLE 1.1

TOPIC	OBJECTIVE	CHAPTER(S) COVERING
Understanding the Linux Story	The History of Linux	2
	Identify the Components of SLES 9	2
	Understanding the Mulituser Environment	2
Using the Linux Desktop	Overview of the Linux Desktop	2
	Using the KDE Desktop Environment	2
	Using the GNOME Desktop Environment	2
	Accessing the Command Line	3
Locating and Using Help Resources in the Linux System	Accessing and Using man Pages	13
	Using info Pages	13
	Accessing Release Notes and White Papers	13
	Using GUI-based Help in the Linux System	13
	Finding Help on the Web	13
Administering Linux with the YaST2 Management Utility	Introduction to YaST2	12
	Managing User Accounts with YaST2	12

Table 1.1 Continued

TOPIC	OBJECTIVE	CHAPTER(S) COVERING
	Installing a Printer in the Linux System	9, 12
	Understanding the YaST2 Software Management Feature	12
	Obtaining Hardware Configuration Information from YaST2	12
Working with the Linux Shell and Command Line	Introduction to Command Shells	3
	Understanding Command Syntax and Special Characters	3
	Executing Commands at the Command Line	3
	Common Command Line Tasks	3
	Piping and Redirection	3
	Managing User Accounts	5
	Executing RPM Package Related Operations	10
	Using the Basic Linux `mail` Command	10
Managing Directories and Files in the Linux System	Understanding the File System Hierarchy Standard (FHS)	8
	Identify File Types in the Linux Systems	8
	Changing Directories and Listing Directory Contents	3
	Creating, Viewing, and Appending Files	3
	Copying and Moving Files and Directories	3
	Creating Directories	3
	Deleting Files and Directories	3
	Finding Files on Linux	13
	Using `grep` to Search File Content	3
	Understanding Regular Expressions	3

Table 1.1   Continued

TOPIC	OBJECTIVE	CHAPTER(S) COVERING
	Archiving Files with `tar`	5
	Compressing and Uncompressing Files with `gzip` and `bzip2`	5
	Managing File Permissions and Ownership	4
Using Linux Text Editors	Introduction to Linux Text Editors	3
	Using Command Line Editors to Edit	3
	Using Desktop Editors to Edit Files in the Linux System	3
Understanding and Viewing Processes in the Linux System	View Processes from the GUI and the Command Line Interface	3
	Understand the Runlevel Concept	7
	Multiuser Processes and Multitasking in the Linux System	3
Managing the Network Configuration	Managing the Network Configuration from YaST2	12
	Introduction to Network-Related Command Line Commands	11

Table 1.2 lists the topics and objectives from course 3037, and where they are covered in this book. You will notice that there is some overlap between topics in this course and the preceding one.

Topics and Objectives of Course 3037   **TABLE 1.2**

TOPIC	OBJECTIVE	CHAPTER(S) COVERING
Introduction to Managing the SuSE Linux Enterprise Server	Describe SuSE Linux Enterprise Server 9	2
	Update the SLES 9 Installation	2
	Monitor Your SLES 9 System	10

Table 1.2 Continued

TOPIC	OBJECTIVE	CHAPTER(S) COVERING
Manage User Access and Security	Describe Basic Linux User Security Features	4, 5
	Manage Linux Users and Groups	5
	Manage and Secure the Linux User Environment	5
	Secure Files and Directories with Permissions	4
	Configure User Authentication with PAM	5
	Implement and Monitor Enterprise Security Policies	4
Manage the Linux File System	Select a Linux File System	8
	Configure Linux File System Partitions	8
	Configure a File System with Logical Volume Management (LVM)	8
	Configure and Manage a Linux File System	8
	Set Up and Configure Disk Quotas	4
	Back Up and Restore the File System	5
Manage Software for SuSE Linux Enterprise Server	Manage RPM Software Packages	10
	Verify and Update Software Library Access	10
	Manage Software Updates with YaST Online Update Server (YOU)	12
Manage System Initialization	Describe the Linux Load Procedure	7
	Manage Runlevels	7
	Manage the Kernel	10
	Manage the GRUB Boot Loader	7

Table 1.2   Continued

TOPIC	OBJECTIVE	CHAPTER(S) COVERING
	Modify System Settings	7
Manage Linux Processes and Services	Manage Processes	2
	Describe Startup Shell Scripts and Services	7
	Schedule Jobs	13
	Use System Logging Services	5
Connect the SuSE Linux Enterprise Server to the Network	Configure Your Network Connection	11
	Configure and Manage Routes	11
	Test the Network Interface	11
Enable Infrastructure Services	Configure and Manage Network Printing Services	9
	Configure Network File Systems	11
	Manage Resources on the Network	11
Enable Internet Services	Configure SuSE Linux Enterprise Server Time	5
	Enable a Web Server (Apache)	11
	Enable the Extended Internet Daemon (`xinetd`)	11
	Enable an FTP Server	11
Manage Remote Access	Prove Secure Remote Access with OpenSSH	11
	Enable Remote Administration with YaST	12
	Configure a Network Installation	11

Table 1.3 lists the topics and objectives from course 3038, and where they are covered in this book. Again, you will notice some overlap between topics in this course and the preceding ones.

Novell Certified Linux Professional Study Guide

TABLE 1.3 **Topics and Objectives of Course 3038**

TOPIC	OBJECTIVE	CHAPTER(S) COVERING
Install SLES 9	Perform the SLES 9 Base Installation Step	2
	Perform the SLES 9 Configuration Step	2
	Troubleshoot the Installation Process	2
Configure the Network Manually	Understand the Linux Network Terms	11
	Set Up Network Devices with the IP Tool	11
	Save Device Settings to a Configuration File	11
	Set Up Routing with the IP Tool	11
	Save Routing Settings to a Configuration File	11
	Configure Host Name and Name Resolution	11
	Test the Network Connection with Command Line Tools	11
Configure Network Services	Deploy OpenLDAP on a SLES 9 Server	11
	Configure an Apache Web Server	11
	Configure a Samba Server as a File Server	11
Secure a SLES 9 Server	Create a Security Concept	10
	Limit Physical Access to Server Systems	10
	Limit the Installed Software Packages	10
	Understand the Linux User Authentication	5
	Ensure File System Security	10
	Use ACLS for Advanced Access Control	4

Table 1.3   Continued

TOPIC	OBJECTIVE	CHAPTER(S) COVERING
	Configure Security Settings with YaST	12
	Be Informed About Security Issues	10
	Apply Security Updates	10
Manage Backup and Recovery	Develop a Backup Strategy	5
	Back Up Files with `tar`	5
	Work with Magnetic Tapes	5
	Copy Data with `dd`	5
	Mirror Directories with `rsync`	5
	Automate Data Backups with `cron`	13
	Troubleshoot the Boot Process of a 9 System	7
	Configure and Install the GRUB Boot Loader	7
Develop Shell Scripts	Use Basic Script Elements	6
	Use Variable Substitution Operators	6
	Use Control Structures	6
	Use Advanced Scripting Techniques	6
	Learn About Useful Commands in Shell Scripts	6
Compile Software from Source	Understand the Basics of C Programming	13
	Understand the GNU Build Tool Chain	13
	Understand the Concept of Shared Libraries	13
	Perform a Standard Build Process	13
Monitor a SLES 9 Installation	Monitor the Operating System	5, 13
	Monitor the File System	8, 13

Table 1.3   Continued

TOPIC	OBJECTIVE	CHAPTER(S) COVERING
	Monitor Processes	3
Manage Hardware and Component Changes	Understand the Differences Between Devices and Interfaces	2
	Understand How Device Drivers Work	2
	Understand How Device Drivers Are Loaded	7
	Understand the `sysfs` FileSystem	7
	Understand How the SLES 9 Hotplug System Works	7
	Understand the `hwup` Command	7
	Add New Hardware to a SLES 9 System	10

Now that you know the lay of the land, there is no reason not to start the journey toward the NCLP certification. Tomorrow is good, but today is better! So put aside a few hours and turn to the next chapter, where the focus is on just what SuSE Linux Enterprise Server (SLES) truly is.

CHAPTER 2

Understanding SuSE Linux Enterprise Server

This chapter serves as an introduction to SuSE and Linux. It provides a historical overview building up to where the product is today, and looks at related topics needed to prepare you to start using SLES 9 and be ready to tear into the chapters that follow. This chapter covers the following course objectives:

1. The History of Linux (3036)

2. Identify the Components of SLES 9 (3036)

3. Understanding the Multiuser Environment (3036)

4. Overview of the Linux Desktop (3036)

5. Using the KDE Desktop Environment (3036)

6. Using the GNOME Desktop Environment (3036)

7. Describe SuSE Linux Enterprise Server 9 (3037)

8. Update the SLES 9 Installation (3037)

9. Manage Processes (3037)

10. Perform the SLES 9 Base Installation Step (3038)

11. Perform the SLES 9 Configuration Step (3038)

12. Troubleshoot the Installation Process (3038)

13. Understand the Differences Between Devices and Interfaces (3038)

14. Understand How Device Drivers Work (3038)

Introducing Linux

Course Objectives Covered

1. The History of Linux (3036)

3. Understanding the Multiuser Environment (3036)

In days of old, when knights were bold, operating systems were mostly proprietary in nature. This means that they were owned by a company and that company charged a licensing fee for every implementation of the operating system on a machine—be it a desktop, laptop, or other device.

In 1991, Linus Benedict Torvalds, a Finnish student, decided to try to create an open version of Unix for the PC platform. It originally began as a hobby and he was able to create the heart of the operating system, which is known as the *kernel*. The kernel is responsible for all the low-level tasks within the computer; it delegates work to all the system peripherals, such as video cards and hard drives. The kernel handles all the filesystem requests and even processes requests through the TCP/IP stack. Without the kernel, there would be no operating system. To this day, Linus Torvalds is still responsible for the kernel and oversees all modifications to it.

Kernel numbers take the form of `linux-x.y.z`, where *x.y.z* is the version number. The highest even number is the latest stable version, whereas the highest odd number is considered a test version.

Because Linux is an open, nonproprietary system, others are free to contribute to Linux and enhance it. Developers from all over the world have taken over the job of creating the applications, binaries, and utilities that make Linux the operating system that it is today.

The operating system is also *multiuser*, *multitasking*, and *multithreading*. Being multiple user merely means that more than one user at a time (concurrently) can access and interact with the operating system; a separate shell is used to interface with each user.

Because the operating system is multitasking, it can do more than one thing at a time. It can read a file from the hard drive at the same time that it is sending a report to the printer, and so on. The tasks can often be divided into threads—the smallest elements of each task. Because Linux is multithreading as well, it can do various parts of a task simultaneously, allowing it to finish the task much faster than if it had to synchronously wait for one item to finish before starting another.

Introducing SLES 9

Course Objectives Covered

2. Identify the Components of SLES 9 (3036)

7. Describe SuSE Linux Enterprise Server 9 (3037)

SuSE Enterprise Linux Server 9 (known as SLES 9) is a robust enterprise Linux server marketed by Novell. It is an evolutionary advancement from previous versions of servers products from SuSE, acquired when Novell purchased that company.

SLES 9 is built around the 2.6 kernel and as such supports the following:

- ▶ Hyperthreading—The ability to not only do multithreading, but to also split threads with processors and complete transactions even faster

- ▶ USB 2.0 and Bluetooth with Hotplug support—For quickly identifying and configuring devices when they are connected

- ▶ Improved IPv6 support—For the next generation of TCP/IP

- ▶ Up to 128 processors, 4 billion unique users, 65,535 user-level processes

- ▶ NUMA (Non-Uniform Memory Access) support—To more efficiently scale CPUs

- ▶ CKRM (Class-based Kernel Resource Management)—For providing services differentiated at the user or job level

- ▶ Flexible I/O scheduling

In addition to the 2.6 enhancements, SLES 9 offers its own features, including new YaST (Yet Another Setup Tool) modules, support for ZENworks, and some developer tools.

SLES 9 supports both the x86 and x86-64 (AMD-64) processor platforms, as well as Itanium processors, and IBM Power and S/390 architectures. Support is included for USB 2.0, FireWire, Advanced Configuration and Power Interface (ACPI), and InfiniBand. And just to be politically correct, SLES adheres to the Linux Standard Base (LSB), File System Hierarchy Standard (FHS), and TeX Directory Standard (TDS)—all of which means that the operating system is truly Linux-based.

Before you get bogged down in all the acronyms, features, and such, let me put it simply: SuSE Enterprise Linux Server is the best enterprise-level implementation of true Linux available today. The important features and acronyms will appear in chapters throughout the book as they apply.

Installing SLES

Course Objectives Covered

8. Update the SLES 9 Installation (3037)

10. Perform the SLES 9 Base Installation Step (3038)

11. Perform the SLES 9 Configuration Step (3038)

12. Troubleshoot the Installation Process (3038)

Before you begin any installation, you need to be certain your system meets the requirements for the operating system. The recommended requirements for installation are

▶ 512MB (256MB is the minimum it will install on)

▶ 4GB free hard disk space (at least 500MB is needed)

▶ Network interface

When you are certain your system meets the requirements, you are ready to begin the installation. Insert the first CD into the computer and reboot the system. On most computers, the system will boot from the CD and you are ready to begin the installation. If this does not happen, you may need to reconfigure the BIOS and change the boot drive order to check for media in the CD/DVD drive first.

The first menu to appear offers a number of choices:

▶ Boot the Hard Disk—This stops the installation and boots the operating system already on the hard disk. Because this is the safest choice, it is the default.

▶ Installation—This is the option to select to begin the normal installation.

▶ Installation–ACPI Disabled—Choose this option if you need the Advanced Configuration and Power Interface to not interfere with the installation process.

▶ Installation–Safe Settings—Choose this option if DMA mode is needed to get around normal installation. Use this choice if the installation keeps failing with one of the other selections.

▶ Rescue System—This allows you to boot the system from the CD in the event that the hard drive boot files are damaged.

▶ Memory Test—This checks RAM only.

At the bottom of the screen, a number of function keys are identified:

▶ F1—Help

▶ F2—Toggle through screen display settings

▶ F3—Toggle through installation location choices

▶ F4—Toggle through languages

▶ F5—Choose a debugging output level

▶ F6—Include a driver update CD in the installation

To perform a normal installation, choose Installation from the menu, and press Enter. You must then walk through the interfaces presented in YaST2, the installation and system administration program. Although there can be deviations, based on your exact configuration, the following are the major screens—in order—that you must walk through:

1. Choose a language—You can click Accept to move on or Abort to cancel the installation.

2. Choose the installation mode—You can choose to perform a new installation (the default), update an existing system, repair an installed system, boot an installed system, or abort. For a normal installation, choose New Installation.

3. At this point, the system will probe for devices and show you a list of what it has identified. It will identify the system, keyboard, mouse, and so on as well as show you the recommended installation settings based on the chosen mode. Recommendations and settings fall within these categories:

   ▶ System

   ▶ Mode

   ▶ Keyboard layout

   ▶ Mouse

   ▶ Partitioning

> ▶ Software

> ▶ Booting

> ▶ Time Zone

> ▶ Language

> ▶ Default Runlevel

4. Three command buttons are available: Change—to alter any of the settings, Abort—to cancel, and Accept—to continue on. Choose Accept, and then click Continue and a warning message appears stating that YaST2 has obtained all the information required to install SuSE Linux. The installation will be carried out according to the settings made in the previous dialogs. To commit the installation and choices made, click the "Yes, install" button, not "No."

5. The hard disk is then prepared/partitioned. This will take a few minutes and you may need to make other changes manually later if you are implementing RAID or LVM devices. At a minimum, two partitions are created: `root` and `swap`.

6. Packages are installed next, and you will need to insert various CDs as prompted. Your goal is usually to complete the installation as quickly as possible, so you can always go back and add any packages at a later point in time.

7. You are prompted to give a password for the root user (and enter it twice for verification). The password can consist of digits, spaces, letters, and the standard punctuation characters. It is recommended that it contain at least five characters and—at a minimum—the case is mixed between upper and lower. If you enter more than eight characters, you will be prompted to truncate or change it.

8. Network configuration occurs next and a scan is automatically done to detect network cards, DSL connections, ISDN adapters, and modems. A summary screen shows you the values found as well as the current settings for Proxy (default is disabled) and VNC Remote Administration (default is disabled). You can change any of these values, go back, abort, or put the network settings shown to you into effect by clicking Next.

9. After the network configuration is written/saved, the Internet connection is tested. This operation is purely optional and you can choose to skip the test if you like. A successful test, however, gives you the option to run the YaST Online Update (YOU) and check for the latest release notes and updates. If updates are available, you can choose to

download and install them, or skip the update (which can be done at any later time from within YaST2).

10. Service configuration comes next, allowing you to configure such items as Certificate Management and OpenLDAP Server.

11. The user authentication method must be chosen. Three choices are available:

   ▶ NIS—To use if you are using an NIS server

   ▶ LDAP—To use if you are using an LDAP server for user data

   ▶ Local (`/etc/passwd`)—The choice to pick if you are storing passwords in `/etc/passwd` and `/etc/shadow`

12. You can add new local users at this point. The same password rules for creating the root user apply to creating passwords for the local users as well.

13. `SuSEconfig` now starts and writes the system configuration. The amount of time this takes will vary greatly from system to system based on the parameters that you've entered.

14. Release notes are displayed covering the following areas:

   ▶ General—Information that everybody should read

   ▶ Update—Covers changes not appearing in the Admin Guide

   ▶ Installation—More information about the installation

   ▶ Updates and Features—Covers technical changes and enhancements

   ▶ Providing Feedback—Tells how to contact SuSE, and so on

15. Hardware configuration of the graphics card, printers, and sound cards follows, and then the installation is complete. You must click the command button labeled Finish and then you can log in to the system.

Upon successful completion of these steps, a login screen will appear prompting for a username and password. After you give those entries, a Welcome menu thanks you for installing SuSE Linux Enterprise Server 9 and provides a list of URLs relating to this and other Novell products.

If there are problems with the installation, you should trace down the first occurrence where trouble appeared and look for a solution to it before continuing on. The best tool to use for any problem within this category is common sense.

For example, if the system will not read the media, verify that the CD set you have is good by checking to see if another system can read it. If the installation hangs, verify that your system meets the minimum system requirements and that power-saving features are not affecting your ability to do the installation.

Remember that the first menu to appear offers a plethora of choices besides Installation. Choosing one of the other choices can help you continue with the installation and repair any system files.

Drivers and Interfaces

Course Objectives Covered

13. Understand the Differences Between Devices and Interfaces (3038)

14. Understand How Device Drivers Work (3038)

Two terms are often confused when discussing hardware: devices and interfaces. In Linux, a device is any piece of hardware that you can actually touch—it has a physical presence. An interface, on the other hand, is a software component that allows access to the device. Every device must have an interface, but there can be more than one interface for any given device.

Drivers—software modules loaded into the kernel—create interfaces and act as the go-between for interfaces and devices. There are two types of drivers: kernel modules and user space modules. Kernel modules are loaded and removed at runtime and allow for access to hardware elements; they reside beneath `/lib/modules/<kernel-version>/`. User space modules provide additional drivers that work in the user space. Between an application and a physical printer, for example, there would reside a user space module and a kernel module.

The Linux Desktop

Course Objectives Covered

4. Overview of the Linux Desktop (3036)

5. Using the KDE Desktop Environment (3036)

6. Using the GNOME Desktop Environment (3036)

Although many administrators are perfectly content to work at the command line, Linux does offer a number of excellent graphical interfaces to choose from based on the X Window System. It is important to note, however, that if you are configuring a server that will not have a user interacting directly with it at all times, you can avoid using any graphical interface at all and achieve some gain in stability and performance.

The K Development Environment (KDE) desktop is the default and there are several elements of it that you should be familiar with.

Working with KDE

If you've never worked with Linux before, but have experience working with the Windows environment, you'll find that you are quickly able to understand the KDE desktop and work effectively within it. Figure 2.1 shows the basic desktop.

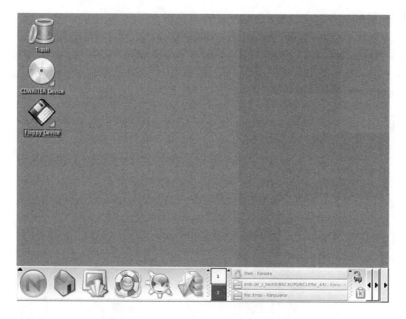

FIGURE 2.1
The basic KDE desktop.

Notice that icons appear on the desktop for entities that can be accessed. The three appearing in Figure 2.1 are the Trash (where deleted files are temporarily stored), the CDWRITER, and the Floppy. A green arrow at the bottom right of the CDWRITER icon indicates that it is mounted, and the lack of such an arrow beneath the icon for the floppy means that it is not yet mounted. Right-clicking on the icon for the device will bring up a context-sensitive menu, which will include such choices as Mount and Unmount.

In Figure 2.1, you will see a number of icons in a frame along the bottom of the screen—this area is known as the *kicker*. The green button with the Red N brings up a menu of all configured programs and functions and is known as the KDE menu. The blue house is used to bring up the KDE file manager, known as Konqueror. The monitor with the shell in front of it is used to open a terminal session (an interactive shell). The life preserver icon starts the SuSE HelpCenter. The globe with gear teeth starts the Konqueror Web browser. The icon of an envelope against an "E" brings up the email program, known as KMail.

To the right of these icons are two boxes—white and gray. They represent the virtual desktops. To the right of that is an area known as the taskbar where active tasks are listed. To the right of that is the System Tray where items such as the clock, loudspeaker, and so on can appear. The three arrows to the far right are used to scroll left, scroll right, and hide the panel (the entire lower area starting with the kicker).

KDE Menu

The KDE menu, shown in Figure 2.2, is divided into three sections. The first section lists the most frequently used applications, and the second section offers access to all applications. The third section lists the Actions that you can perform.

FIGURE 2.2
The KDE menu.

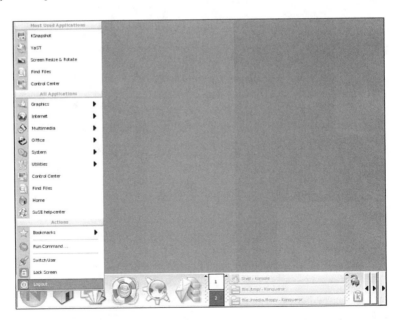

Konqueror

The Konqueror file manager, shown in Figure 2.3, automatically takes you to your own home directory and allows you graphical access to all entities. In the upper-right corner, there are four button choices. The question mark is used to access help. The underline is used to minimize the window. The square is used to restore the window to its regular size. The X button is used to close the window.

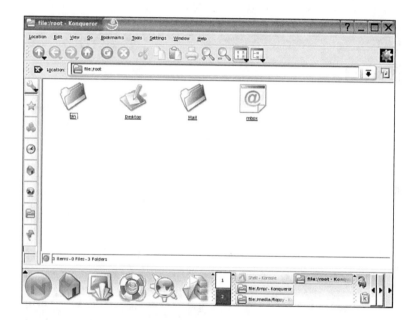

FIGURE 2.3
The Konqueror file manager.

A number of icons appear below the menu bar. Starting from the left, the up arrow is used to take you to the next higher level; for example, to /etc from /etc/cups. The left arrow moves you back to where you were previously. The right arrow moves you forward (after you've gone back). The house icon takes you to your home directory. The circle icon reloads, or refreshes the display. The X icon stops loading the current page. To the right of this are icons for cutting, copying, pasting, printing, and changing icon sizes and views.

A number of icons appear along the left frame. Starting from the top, the wrench icon allows you to configure the navigation area. The star shows your bookmarks. The cubes show your devices. The clock shows history. The house shows the home directory. The connected globe shows the network, including access to available Windows networks if SMB has been configured. The folders icon shows the root directory, and the flags show special KDE services.

Right-clicking on any item in the display area brings up a context-sensitive menu from which you can make choices such as copy, paste, and so on. Just clicking on the item will open it, or double-clicking on a folder will open it and show the entries beneath it.

Shell

Choosing to open a shell, by clicking on the third icon in the kicker, brings up an interactive shell, as shown in Figure 2.4.

FIGURE 2.4
You can interact with the command line by opening a shell.

The menu options along the top are: Session (open a new shell, new Linux console, print the screen, and so on), Edit (copy, paste, history, and so on), View (monitor for activity), Bookmark (add, edit), Settings (keyboard, fonts, size, and so on), and Help.

You can open as many shell sessions as you want, and the icon, just above the kicker, will automatically start a new shell session.

SuSE HelpCenter

The SuSE HelpCenter, shown in Figure 2.5, is the quickest way to access the SLES Admin Guide, as well as application manuals, documentation for developers, and online resources.

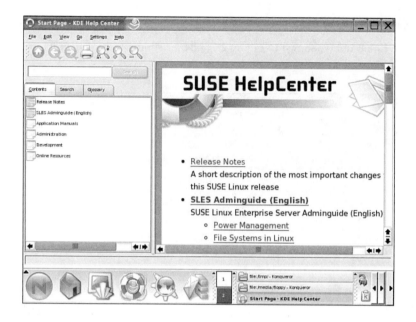

FIGURE 2.5
The SuSE
HelpCenter.

In the left frame, there are tabs allowing you to search for particular entities, for example, to access the glossary.

Web Browser

The Konqueror Web browser, shown in Figure 2.6, resembles the file manager and offers the same icons and menu items.

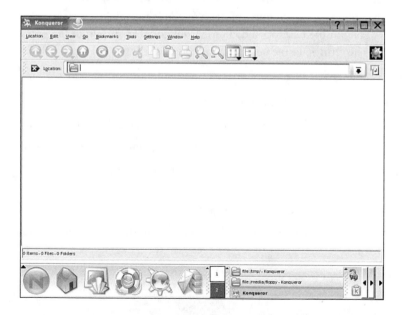

FIGURE 2.6
The Konqueror
Web browser.

KMail

The KMail utility, shown in Figure 2.7, offers a simple-to-use email interface.

FIGURE 2.7
The KMail utility.

Configuring the Desktop

You can access the configuration options for the KDE desktop in a number of different ways. The simplest of these methods is to right-click on an empty spot on the desktop and choose Configure Desktop from the pop-up menu. This brings up the configuration interface shown in Figure 2.8.

The configuration choices are divided into the following categories:

▶ Behavior—Icon settings and mouse actions.

▶ Multiple Desktops—Configure how many virtual desktops there are.

▶ Paths—Set the path for the desktop, trash, autostart, and documents.

▶ Background—Choose from a number of different pictures or select your own.

▶ Screen Saver—Configure and test screen saver settings.

▶ Size & Orientation—Set the screen size, refresh rate, and related variables.

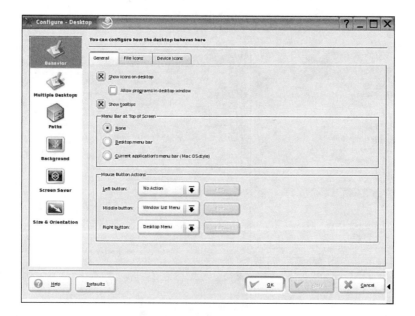

FIGURE 2.8
You can config-
ure the desktop
to your liking.

Working with Other Desktops

KDE is not the only desktop environment you have to choose from—it is just the one that comes up by default. When you log in—giving your user-name and password—a command button for Menu appears. Click on that command button, and choose Session Type. You will have a choice of ses-sion types to choose from, including Failsafe, admin, TWM (Tab Window Manager), FVWM (Feeble Virtual Windows Manager) and others.

In most implementations, GNOME is not one of the options available by default, unless you did a full install, or did a custom install and added it. The GNOME packages can be added at any time, and the easiest way to do so is through the YaST2 tool shown in Figure 2.9 and discussed in detail in Chapter 12, "Working with YaST."

After you've added this choice, it will appear along with the others to choose from as a Session Type when you log in. GNOME has all the features of KDE, and is expected to be the default user environment used by Novell Linux Desktop when it is released. Figure 2.10 shows the opening screen and Figure 2.11 shows the browser graphically depicting the drives.

FIGURE 2.9
You can add the
GNOME desktop
environment.

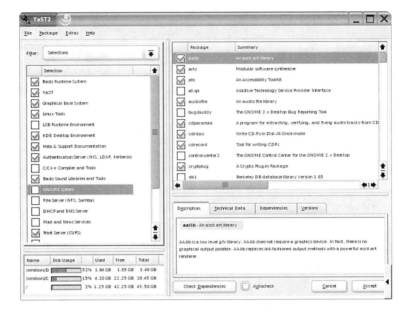

FIGURE 2.10
The default
GNOME desktop
environment.

A few things to note about the GNOME desktop are that the clock appears
in the upper-right corner, as opposed to the lower right in KDE, and the
menu options and hot buttons are along the top of the screen by default.

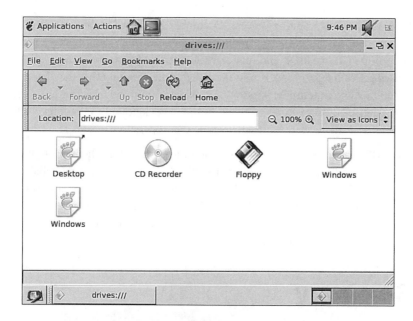

FIGURE 2.11
You can access drives through the browser.

The Applications menu holds the known applications, and the Actions menu allows you to choose such things as the screensaver and other utilities. The icon of a house takes you home, and the icon of a monitor opens a shell.

Working with Processes

Course Objective Covered

9. Manage Processes (3037)

Chapter 3, "Preliminary GNU and Unix Commands," goes into detail on processes and the utilities that allow you to interact with them. Before you get to Chapter 3, however, it is imperative that you understand what a process is. A *process* is any running task (in memory and on the CPU) within Linux. Programs and users can both start processes, and a process may be a short task that completes a simple operation and perishes, or it may be a daemon.

A daemon process is a system task that runs on its own and is not associated with any terminal. An example of this would be `init`—the process responsible for keeping everything else up and running.

Every process has a unique process ID number associated with it—its PID. The process may be started by another (its parent, which would have a parent process ID, or PPID), and may start other processes as well (child processes). Some processes run in the foreground, meaning that they need attention within a terminal window, and others run in the background. Many user processes can be switched from the background to the foreground, and the reverse, without affecting their operation.

The KDE System Guard, accessed by choosing System from the main KDE menu, followed by Monitor, and then KDE System Guard, has a tab labeled Process Table. By choosing this tab, you can see the processes that are running on the system, with their PID numbers and related information. If you click the Tree check box, the display will graphically depict the relationship of the processes to each other.

Summary

This chapter examined what Linux and SuSE Linux Enterprise Server 9 are. It walked through the installation of the operating system, and looked at the desktop and its features. The next chapter explores the command line and introduces you to the most useful tools in the Linux toolbox.

## CHAPTER 3

Preliminary GNU and Unix Commands

The NCLP practicum requires you to have a mastery of SuSE Linux Enterprise Server. Before you can have a mastery of any one specific implementation, however, you must first know and understand the basics of the operating system. This chapter does not focus on any specific testing objectives for the practicum, but provides you with the core set of skills that you must know in order to be able to work effectively with any Linux implementation.

This chapter covers the following course objectives:

1. Accessing the Command Line (3036)
2. Introduction to Command Shells (3036)
3. Understanding Command Syntax and Special Characters (3036)
4. Executing Commands at the Command Line (3036)
5. Common Command Line Tasks (3036)
6. Piping and Redirection (3036)
7. Changing Directories and Listing Directory Contents (3036)
8. Creating, Viewing, and Appending Files (3036)
9. Copying and Moving Files and Directories (3036)
10. Creating Directories (3036)
11. Deleting Files and Directories (3036)
12. Using **grep** to Search File Content (3036)
13. Understanding Regular Expressions (3036)
14. Introduction to Linux Text Editors (3036)
15. Using Command Line Editors to Edit (3036)

16. Using Desktop Editors to Edit Files in the Linux System (3036)

17. View Processes from the GUI and the Command Line Interface (3036)

18. Multiuser Processes and Multitasking in the Linux System (3036)

19. Monitor Processes (3038)

This chapter contains a great deal of content, and it is imperative that you understand and are comfortable with all of it before moving on. It cannot be stressed enough that the commands, utilities, and skills discussed in this chapter lay the foundation upon which all Linux administration is built.

Working at the Command Line

Course Objectives Covered

1. Accessing the Command Line (3036)

2. Introduction to Command Shells (3036)

3. Understanding Command Syntax and Special Characters (3036)

4. Executing Commands at the Command Line (3036)

5. Common Command Line Tasks (3036)

6. Piping and Redirection (3036)

To understand the command line and work there effectively, you must understand the processes that are taking place. Within Linux, the shell is the command interpreter. It takes commands that a user gives, processes them (or sends them to the appropriate utility/interacts with the kernel), and formats the finished results for the user. Thus, the shell is the mediator between the operating system and the user. Not only can it interpret commands, but it can also handle redirection (input and output), filename generation, some programming, variable substitution, piping, and a host of other services.

A number of different shells (interpreters) are available, and different vendors include different combinations of choices with their operating systems. The simplest of all is the Bourne shell (sh), which is one of the earliest ones created for the Unix platform and offers the smallest number of features. The Korn shell (ksh) was one of the first to expand upon, and deviate from, sh, and it includes a larger number of options. The Bourne Again shell (**bash**) took many of the features from Korn, and some new ones, and combined them with **sh**, while trying to reduce deviations. The Z shell (**zsh**) is the largest shell of all and added a whole new set of features to the Korn shell.

Not to be overlooked are shells created to make the environment more friendly to those familiar with the C programming language. The first of these was the C shell (**csh**), which added C-like features to the interpreter and deviated greatly from the Bourne shell. It has been expanded upon by Tom's C shell (**tcsh**) .

As a generalization, every vendor includes more than one shell for the user to choose from, but rarely do they include all the available shells. In many versions, there are three prevalent shells:

- ▶ bash
- ▶ tcsh
- ▶ zsh

Additionally, there are often two links within the operating system so that if a user attempts to use **sh**, they are really given **bash**, and if they attempt to use **csh**, they are really given **tcsh**.

All shells reside in the /bin directory and the default can be specified for the user in the user's /etc/passwd file entry.   **NOTE**

There are slight deviations in the way each shell carries out its tasks, but all perform a core set of functions. Throughout this section, we will look at the core functions for all shells and discuss differences as they apply.

Command-Line Interaction

When a command is entered, the shell must determine if the command is for it (internal) or not (external). If the command is an internal one, it does the processing and sends the output back without further interaction being needed. If the command cannot be found within the shell itself, it is assumed to be an external utility (such as **ls**, **cat**, **cal**, and so on). The command syntax for external commands is always assumed to be

```
{program name} {option(s)} {argument(s)}
```

Although it is always assumed that there are three components to the command, there need not be. The simplest command to give is simply the name of the utility, for example:

```
ls
```

This will return an output similar to

```
Desktop     sample      snapshot01.gif      snapshot02.gif
```

In this case, only the program name was given, and no options. This results in a listing of all files within the present directory being shown in the default format. An option can be specified to change the display to include/exclude information and/or change the format of the display. An example would be

```
ls -l
```

This changes the output to

```
total 34
drwx------      5     root     root     1024     Jul 19 16:34
➥Desktop
-rw-r--r--      1     root     root     155      Jul 19 16:48
➥sample
-rw-r--r--      1     root     root     12497    Jul 19 16:39
➥snapshot01.gif
-rw-r--r--      1     root     root     17257    Jul 19 16:50
➥snapshot02.gif
```

Here, the program name has been specified (`ls`), as well as an option to use with it (`-l`) to change the listing to the "long" format.

NOTE It is important to understand that whitespace must always be used to separate the parameters from one another. Whitespace can be either a space character or a tab character.

If the command were given as `ls-l`, an error message would be generated because there is no utility by the name of `ls-l`, and the interpreter would not be able to distinguish the program name from the option.

The options, as well as the arguments, are optional and never required. To complete the example, an argument can also be used with the command:

```
ls -l *.gif
```

This will result in the following display:

```
-rw-r--r--    1    root    root    12497    Jul 19 16:39
➥snapshot01.gif
-rw-r--r--    1    root    root    17257    Jul 19 16:50
➥snapshot02.gif
```

Alternatively, the argument can be used without the options, like this: **NOTE**

```
    ls *.gif
```

The number of arguments that can be given is not limited to one. Although
there may be limitations on the number of parameters an individual utility
will accept, typically you can string multiple requests together. For example,
instead of specifying

```
ls -l sa*
```

as one command and then following it with

```
ls -l *.gif
```

you can accomplish the same operation with

```
ls -l sa* *.gif
```

The result of the operation becomes

```
-rw-r--r--    1    root    root      155    Jul 19 16:48
➥sample
-rw-r--r--    1    root    root    12497    Jul 19 16:39
➥snapshot01.gif
-rw-r--r--    1    root    root    17257    Jul 19 16:50
➥snapshot02.gif
```

If the number of arguments you are giving becomes too long to be easily
readable on the command line, or if you simply want to break up the entry
a bit, you can use the backstroke character to signify that you are continuing
from one line to the next. For example

```
ls -l sa* \
*.gif
```

If you were giving hundreds of such arguments, you would use the backstroke following each entry to separate each. This would make entry easier
to view and the command would not execute until the Enter key is pressed
without being preceded by a backstroke. For example

```
ls -l sa* \
*.gif \
*.ead \
*.txt \
*.doc
```

Connecting Commands

In all the examples thus far, the Enter key is used to inform the shell that you have given a command that needs to be processed. You are not, however, limited to giving the shell only one command at a time.

Multiple commands, not connected to one another in any way, can be given on the same line as long as the semicolon (;) is used to connect them. For example, it is possible to see all the files in the current directory and the current date by giving the following two commands in succession:

```
ls
date
```

These are unrelated commands in that the output of the second has absolutely nothing to do with the output of the first. You can combine them on a single command line with a semicolon between the two and get the same result:

```
ls ; date
```

The semicolon is a special character signaling that multiple commands are on the same line. This character allows you to break the whitespace rule on both sides of it (**ls;date**) while giving you the same result.

If the commands *do* have something in common—the output of one is to become the input of the next—they are connected using a pipe (|). For example, if a list of files within a directory is too long to fit on one screen, you can view a screen at a time by using this command:

```
ls -l | more
```

Here the output of the **ls -l** command becomes the input of the **more** command. If the first part of the entire command line fails, the second part cannot possibly be executed.

Wildcards

Wildcards are characters used to signify other characters that the shell fills in. The two most common wildcard characters are the asterisk (*) and question mark (?). Although they are often confused, their meanings are different and can lead to completely different results.

The asterisk is used to signify any and all; anything and nothing; alpha and omega. For example

```
ls s*
```

will find all entries (files and directories) within the current directory starting with the letter "s" and having any number of characters following—including none. Possible results it could generate in the display include

```
s    sa    sam    samp    sampl    sample    samples
➡samples.gif
```

Note that it finds "s" alone, and "s" with any number of entries following it. In contrast, the question mark is a placeholder for one character, and only one character. Using the same file possibilities, the following command

```
ls s?
```

will only find entries (files and directories) in the current directory starting with the letter "s" and having only one character following. The resulting display generated is

```
sa
```

If you want to find only five-letter entries beginning with "s", the command to use would be

```
ls s????
```

To recap, the asterisk means all or none, and the question mark always means one. These two wildcards are not mutually exclusive, and can be used in combination with one another as the need arises. For example, to find only files with three-letter extensions, regardless of the filename, the command would be

```
ls *.???
```

To muddy the waters a bit, you can also use brackets ([ ]) to specify possible values. All the possible values must reside within the brackets and are used individually. The following example will find all entries that start with either "d" or "e" and have an unlimited number of characters following:

```
ls [de]*
```

To find only three-character entries that start with "d" or "e", the command would become

```
ls [de]??
```

The number of characters within the brackets can be virtually unlimited. Therefore, if you wanted to find all entries that start with a lowercase letter instead of a number (or other character), you could use "[abcdefghijklmnopqrstuvwxyz]". However, because this is a range, a much simpler way to signify it would be "[a-z]":

```
ls [a-z]*
```

The ranges need not be a complete set (though complete sets are easier to specify), and can jump around if needed. For example, if you only want to look for entries that fall within the range from "d" to "t", you could use either "[defghijklmnopqrst]" or "[d-t]". If the entry could be between the two values upper- and lowercase, you can either use "[DEFGHIJKLMNOPQRSTdefghijklmnopqrst]" or "[D-Td-t]".

Some more examples follow:

▶ All letters (upper- and lowercase): [A-z]

NOTE   **"[A-z]" is the same as saying "[A-Z]" and "[a-z]".**

▶ All numbers [0-9]

▶ All letters and numbers [A-z0-9]

▶ Not a number [!0-9]

▶ Not a letter [!A-z]

The Path Statement and Other Variables

When you enter a command at the command prompt and the shell cannot find it internally, it must look for a utility by that name externally. It does this by searching directories specified in the PATH variable, in the order they are listed, until it finds the first match. If no match is found after all listed directories have been searched, the result is an error message ("command not found").

There are several important things to know about the path:

1. You can view your path by using the `echo` command:

   ```
   echo $PATH
   ```

2. The path does not, by default, include the present directory. Thus you can create an executable file in your home directory, see it right before you (with `ls`), and when you type its name, you will be told that the command cannot be found. To circumvent this, you can give the full path to the file, add your home directory to your `PATH` variable, move the file to a directory in the path statement, or add the present directory variable (.) to the `PATH` variable.

3. Entries within the path are separated by colons (:).

4. The order of the `PATH` search should always include the most common directories where executables can be found first (the `bin` directories) and the user-specific directories (if any) at the end.

To add another directory to your path, you can redefine the entire statement, or simply append the new directory with the command

```
PATH=$PATH:{new directory}
```

Thus to add the directory `/home/edulaney` to the path, the command would be

```
PATH=$PATH:/home/edulaney
```

Or you can add a variable that signifies you always want the directory you are currently working in to be searched for the utility:

```
PATH=$PATH:./
```

For security reasons, it is always recommended that you not include the current directory in your path. If you must do so, however, it should be at the end of the PATH statement—as shown in the preceding example—not at the beginning.

For example, if your current PATH is equal to

```
/sbin:/usr/sbin:/usr/local/sbin:/root/bin:/usr/local/bin:/
usr/bin
```

then you want the new PATH to look like

```
/sbin:/usr/sbin:/usr/local/sbin:/root/bin:/usr/local/bin:/
usr/bin:./
```

NOTE

and not

```
./:/sbin:/usr/sbin:/usr/local/sbin:/root/bin:/usr/local/bin
:/usr/bin
```

because the directories are always searched in the order they appear in PATH.

Common Variables

Any variable that exists can display its values using the following syntax:

```
echo ${variable name}
```

Thus the command

```
echo $MAIL
```

will show the `mail` directory, $HOME the home directory, and so on. To see a complete list of the environmental variables that are defined, you can use two commands—env and set. Although the displays can differ slightly (environmental variables only versus local variables), for the most part the output of env is a subset of the output of set. Some of the variables that can display include the following:

▶ HOME—The directory you begin in, and where you end up when typing cd without any other parameters

▶ LINES—Number of lines within the display before pausing (more)

▶ LOGNAME—The username under which the current user is logged in

▶ PWD—The present working directory, or where you are now

▶ SHELL—Which interpreter you are using

▶ TERM—The type of terminal, or emulation, in use

▶ USER—This rarely differs from LOGNAME but can if the user is switching permission levels with commands such as su

NOTE   As a general rule, predefined system variables are always in uppercase.

You can change the value of variables as needed, or add your own to be referenced in programs or at the command prompt. For example, to create a new variable called TODAY, use the following syntax:

```
TODAY=Wednesday
```

You can now see the value of the variable by using the command

```
echo $TODAY
```

The result will be Wednesday. If you now use the command

```
set
```

the variable will appear there. However, if you use the following command, it will not:

```
env
```

The variable has been created locally, and can be referenced locally. In order for it to be accessible in subroutines and child processes, you must move it from local status into the environment, and this is accomplished via the export command:

```
export TODAY
```

This moves the variable to where it can be found in the environment, as well as locally, and accessed by subroutines and child processes. The variable, and its value, will be available for the duration of the session, and lost when you log out. To make the value permanent, you must add the entry to a profile.

To change the value of the variable, simply define its new value:

```
TODAY=Monday
```

Because it has already been exported, this need not be done again, and the new value will apply locally as well as in the environment. Should it be necessary to remove a variable, you can use the unset command.

Among those variables present and definable are those that present the prompt. The prompt is the visual message from the shell that tells you it is ready for input. The default prompts include

▶ $ as the last character for Bourne, BASH, and Korn shells

▶ % as the last character for C shell and Z shell

▶ > as the last character for tcsh

The primary prompt is either the variable PS1 or prompt, based on which shell you are using. In bash, a typical value for PS1 is

```
[\u@\h \W]\$
```

Dissected into its components, PS1 is equal to the following:

- ▶ The left bracket ([)
- ▶ The name of the current user
- ▶ The at symbol (@)
- ▶ The name of the current host
- ▶ A space
- ▶ The present working directory
- ▶ The right bracket (])
- ▶ The dollar sign ($)

An example of this prompt would be

```
[edulaney@server7 home]$
```

The backstroke (\) character is used to signify that a special value should be used. Different values that can be used for the prompt include those shown in Table 3.1.

TABLE 3.1 **Variables to Define the Prompt**

VALUE	RESULT
\d	Current date
\h	Name of host to first period
\n	New line
\s	Shell
\t	Time
\u	Username
\W	Current directory
\!	History number
\#	Command number
\$	Default prompt—$ for standard users, and # for root
\\	An actual backstroke (literal)
ABC	ABC (the value of that text, or any text given)

Looking at the variables on the system, you will find that more than PS1 exists. For example, earlier in this chapter, we discussed ending a line with a backstroke to signify that you are not finished entering input yet. If we look at the sequence of events, and include prompts, it would look like this:

```
[edulaney@server7 home]$ ls -l *.gif \
> *.fig \
> *.bmp
```

Note that the prompt changed from **PS1** to a greater-than sign (**>**). If it had stayed **PS1**, you would not know that it was still accepting input, so it changed from the primary prompt to a secondary prompt to signify the change in mode. The prompt represented (by default) by the greater-than sign is **PS2**. Its value can be changed from the default to any value you want, including all the special values given in the earlier table. Within most shells, there are three to four layers of prompts.

By now you've realized that the dollar sign (**$**) is used to signify a variable; when you have a variable named **EXAMPLE**, you view its contents by examining **$EXAMPLE**. Three other variables exist for a shell that can be useful in determining your environment.

▶ The first—**$$**—will show the process ID number of the shell now running:

```
echo $$
```

▶ The second—**$?**—will show the results of the last command that you ran in terms of whether it was successful (0) or not (1). For example, the **ls** utility accepts an option of **-F** that will differentiate between directories and files by putting a slash behind the name of directories. The **ls** utility does not have a **-z** option. Given this knowledge, the following sequence shows how **$?** can be utilized, and includes the prompts and output of each operation:

```
[edulaney@server7 home]$ ls -F
Desktop\     sample     snapshot01.gif     snapshot02.gif
[edulaney@server7 home]$ echo $?
0
[edulaney@server7 home]$ ls -z
ls: invalid option -- z
[edulaney@server7 home]$ echo $?
1
```

▶ The third variable—**$!**—will show the process ID number of the last child process started in the background. If no child processes have been started in the background, the result will be empty. For this discussion it is useful to know that placing an ampersand (**&**) at the end of the command will execute the command in the background. For example

```
[edulaney@server7 home]$ echo $!

[edulaney@server7 home]$ ls -F &
[edulaney@server7 home]$ echo $!
19321
[edulaney@server7 home]$
```

In the first instance, no job had been sent to the background, so the returned value was empty. A job was then sent to the background, and its process ID number could be found by echoing $!.

Quoting

One of the most difficult components of the shell to understand is often the use of quotes. There are a few rules to remember to make understanding the concept easier:

1. There are three types of quotes—double quotes ("), single quotes ('), and back quotes (`). Each has a different and distinct meaning. Double quotes are used to disable all characters except ', \, and $. Single quotes disable all characters except the back quote. The back quote substitutes the value for a command.

2. Quotes must always be used in even numbers. If you give an odd number, the shell believes that you have not finished with input yet and waits for more.

3. You can mix and match different types of quotes and embed them within one another.

Let's examine each rule in order. If you have a file named **sample of the worlds best cigars**, and you give this command:

```
cat sample of the worlds best cigars
```

The **cat** utility will first try to open a file named **sample**, then one named **of**, followed by four other files: **the**, **worlds**, **best**, **cigars**. The whitespace between the words is interpreted as delimiters between different files. In order to be able to see the file, the command must be changed to

```
cat "sample of the worlds best cigars"
```

The double quotes cancel the default meaning of the whitespace and allow the value between them to be interpreted as a single entry. The double quotes cancel the meaning of most special characters, but not all. For example, suppose there is a variable named **EXAMPLE** that is equal to 25:

```
echo $EXAMPLE
```

This will return "25". Likewise, the following will also return "25":

```
echo "$EXAMPLE"
```

And the following will return "$EXAMPLE":

```
echo '$EXAMPLE'
```

The single quotes go above and beyond the double quotes and also cancel out the meaning of the dollar sign.

Going in another direction

```
echo 'date'
```

will return "date". Substituting the single quotes for back quotes will have a different result:

```
echo `date`
```

will return the results of the **date** command. An alternative to the back quotes in the newer shells is to place the command within parentheses and treat it as a variable. Thus the date can be echoed as in the preceding example with the command:

```
echo $(date)
```

If you fail to use an even number of any quote set, **PS1** is replaced by **PS2**, and continues to be so until the total number of quotes used (each set) is an even number. This can be useful when you have a lengthy entry you want to break into lines during entry. The following example includes the prompts and also shows the use of one set of quotes (back quotes) within another (double quotes):

```
[edulaney@server7 home]$ EXAMPLE="Hi, the date
> and time now
> are `date`."
[edulaney@server7 home]$ echo $EXAMPLE
Hi, the date and time now are Thu Aug 10 11:12:37 EDT 2000
[edulaney@server7 home]$
```

In many instances, the quotes need to be mixed and matched. One of the biggest problems you will encounter, however, is that special characters make it difficult to display them as output. For example, assume the end result of an echo operation to be

```
Karen says "Hi"
```

If you use the command

```
echo Karen says "Hi"
```

the result will be

```
Karen says Hi
```

The shell interprets the quotation marks as meaning that the text within them should be taken as a single entry. The shell performs the operation given it, and loses the quotes in the process. To get around this, you must use the backslash (\) character to override the default meaning of the quotes:

```
echo Karen says \"Hi\"
```

Note that the backslash—literal—character must precede each incidence of the quotes, and is always only good for the character immediately following it.

Command History

The bash shell keeps a list of commands that you give it and allows you to reuse those commands from the list rather than needing to retype them each time. From the command line, you can use the up and down arrows to scroll through recent commands. You can also enter two bangs (!!) to rerun the very last command you gave.

Typing history shows all the commands that are stored, with an incrementing number on the left. Typing a single bang and one of those command numbers will rerun that command, as in !205.

NOTE Instead of seeing the entire history list, you can choose to see only the most recent entries by following the history command with the number of lines you want to see, like this:

```
history 5
history 10
```

Alternatively, you can type a bang followed by a set of characters and the shell will rerun the most recent command starting with those characters. For example

```
!ls
```

will rerun the most recent command that started with `ls`.

Important variables for history are

▶ `HISTFILE`—Points to the file holding the history of commands. By default, it is `.bash_history` in each user's home directory.

▶ `HISTSIZE`—The number of entries to keep each session.

▶ `HISTFILESIZE`—Identifies the number of command history entries to be carried over from one session to another (letting you run commands in this session that you ran in the previous one).

An internal alias for history, `fc`, also exists and can be used to recall and rerun commands as well.   **NOTE**

Command Aliasing

Although a plethora of commands and utilities are available within the operating system and shell, you can create aliases that make more sense to you, or that shorten the number of characters you have to type. For example, if you are familiar with working with the command line of Windows-based operating systems, you are accustomed to typing `dir` to see what files are there. A similar operation in Linux is possible with `ls -l`. It is possible to create an alias so that when you type `dir`, it is `ls -l` that runs using the following syntax:

```
alias dir="ls -l"
```

The syntax is always the alias followed by the actual command that will run when the alias is entered, separated by the equal sign (=). In rare instances, you can get away with not using the quotation marks around the aliased entry, but as a general rule, they should always be used.

For aliases to survive a session, they should be added to the `.bashrc` file within a user's home directory. If you do not put them within a file that is executed upon login (thus re-creating them), the created aliases are lost when you log out.   **NOTE**

Other Features and Notes

The Linux command line has a number of other features that should not be overlooked. Although they are not complicated enough to warrant a section of their own, it is useful to know of their existence:

- ▶ When typing a command, you can press the Tab key after entering a few characters and the shell will attempt to complete the name of the command you were typing.

- ▶ The command-line history can be edited to alter commands before running them again. The default editor in bash is emacs, and in zsh it is vi. Editors are discussed later in this chapter, in the section "Working with vi."

- ▶ When you press the Enter key, the shell first scans the command line and determines what elements it has been given by looking for white-space. It next replaces wildcards with any relevant filenames. Following that, it strips all quotes and substitutes variables. Lastly, it substitutes any embedded commands and then executes the entry.

- ▶ The test utility can be used in conjunction with $? to test almost anything. For example, to see if a file exists and is readable, use this combination:

```
test -r snapshot01.gif
echo $?
```

Complete syntax for all the test options can be found by typing man test.

- ▶ Two less-than signs (<<) are known simply as "here" and signify that processing is to wait until the string following them is given as a PS2 prompt on a line by itself. For example

```
cat << litter
```

will accept input at a PS2 prompt until the string "litter" is entered on a line by itself.

Processing Text

Course Objectives Covered

4. Executing Commands at the Command Line (3036)

5. Common Command Line Tasks (3036)

6. Piping and Redirection (3036)

8. Creating, Viewing, and Appending Files (3036)

The simplest text processing utility of all is `cat`, a derivative of the word *concatenate*. By default, it will display the entire contents of a file on the screen (standard output). However, a number of useful options can be used with it, including the following:

- ▶ `-b` to number lines
- ▶ `-E` to show a dollar sign (\$) at the end of each line (carriage return)
- ▶ `-T` to show all tabs as "^I"
- ▶ `-v` to show nonprinting characters except tabs and carriage returns
- ▶ `-A` to show the same as `-v` combined with `-E` and `-T`

To illustrate the uses of `cat`, assume that there is a four-line file named `example` with the following contents:

```
How much wood
could a woodchuck chuck
if a woodchuck
could chuck wood?
```

To view the contents of the file on the screen, exactly as they appear in the preceding example, the command is

```
cat example
```

To view the file with lines numbered, the command, and the output generated, will be

```
cat -b example
    1    How much wood
    2    could a woodchuck chuck
    3    if a woodchuck
    4    could chuck wood?
```

Note the inclusion of the tab characters that were not there before, but were added by the numbering process. They are not truly in the file, but only added to the display, as can be witnessed with the following command:

```
cat -Ab example
    1    How much wood$
    2    could a woodchuck chuck$
```

```
3     if a woodchuck$
4     could chuck wood?$
```

The only nonprintable characters within the file are the carriage returns at the end, which appear as dollar signs.

One of the most common uses of the **cat** utility is to quickly create a text file. From the command line, you can specify no file at all to display and redirect the output to a given filename. This then accepts keyboard input and places it in the new file until the end-of-file character is received (the key sequence is Ctrl+D, by default).

The following example includes a dollar sign ($) prompt to show this operation in process:

```
$ cat > example
Peter Piper picked a peck of pickled peppers
A peck of pickled peppers Peter Piper picked.
If Peter Piper picked a peck of pickled peppers,
Where's the peck of pickled peppers Peter Piper picked?
{press Ctrl+D}
$
```

The Ctrl+D sequence is pressed on a line by itself and signifies the end of the file. Viewing the contents of the directory (via the **ls** utility) will show that the file has now been created, and its contents can be viewed like this:

```
cat example
```

Note that the single redirection (>) creates a file named **example** if it did not exist before, and overwrites it if did. To add to an existing file, use the append character (>>).

NOTE

The Ctrl+D keyboard sequence is the typical default for specifying an end-of-file operation. Like almost everything in Linux, this can be changed, customized, and so on. To see the settings for your session, use this command:

```
stty -a
```

and look for "eof = ".

There is a utility of use in limited circumstances—**tac**—which will display the contents of files in reverse order (**tac** is **cat** in reverse order). Instead of displaying a file from line 1 to the end of the file, it shows the file from the end of the file to line 1, as illustrated in the following example:

```
$ tac example
Where's the peck of pickled peppers Peter Piper picked?
If Peter Piper picked a peck of pickled peppers,
A peck of pickled peppers Peter Piper picked.
Peter Piper picked a peck of pickled peppers
$
```

nl, head, and tail

Three simple commands can be used to view all or parts of files: `nl`, `head`, and `tail`. The first, `nl`, is used to number the lines, and is similar to `cat -b`. Both will number the lines of display, and by default, neither will number blank lines. There are certain options that `nl` can utilize to alter the display:

- ▶ `-i` allows you to change the increment (default is 1).
- ▶ `-v` allows you to change the starting number (default 1).
- ▶ `-n` changes the alignment of the display:
  - ▶ `-nln` aligns the display on the left.
  - ▶ `-nrn` aligns the display on the right.
  - ▶ `-nrz` uses leading zeros.
- ▶ `-s` uses a specified character between the line number and the text (default is a space).

The second utility to examine is `head`. As the name implies, this utility is used to look at the top portion of a file: by default, the first 10 lines. You can change the number of lines displayed by using a dash followed by the number of lines to display. The following examples assume there is a text file named `numbers` with 200 lines in it counting from "one" to "two hundred":

```
$ head numbers
one
two
three
four
five
six
```

```
seven
eight
nine
ten
$
$ head -3 numbers
one
two
three
$
$ head -50 numbers
one
two
three
{skipping for space purposes}
forty-eight
forty-nine
fifty
$
```

NOTE **When printing multiple files,** head **places a header before each listing identifying what file it is displaying. The** -q **option suppresses the headers.**

The `tail` command has several modes in which it can operate. By default, it is the opposite of **head**, and shows the end of file rather than the beginning. Once again, it defaults to the number 10 to display, but that can be changed by using the dash and a number:

```
$ tail numbers
one hundred ninety-one
one hundred ninety-two
one hundred ninety-three
one hundred ninety-four
one hundred ninety-five
one hundred ninety-six
one hundred ninety-seven
one hundred ninety-eight
one hundred ninety-nine
two hundred
$
$ tail -3 numbers
one hundred ninety-eight
one hundred ninety-nine
two hundred
```

```
$
$ tail -50 numbers
one hundred fifty-one
one hundred fifty-two
one hundred fifty-three
{skipping for space purposes}
one hundred ninety-eight
one hundred ninety-nine
two hundred
$
```

The `tail` utility goes beyond this functionality, however, by including a plus (+) option. This allows you to specify a starting point beyond which you will see the entire file. For example

```
$ tail +50 numbers
```

This will start with line 50 (skipping the first 49) and display all the rest of the file—151 lines in this case. Another useful option is -f, which allows you to *follow* a file. The command

```
$ tail -f numbers
```

will display the last 10 lines of the file, but then stay open—following the file—and display any new lines that are appended to the file. To break out of the endless monitoring loop, you must press the *interrupt* key sequence, which is Ctrl+C by default on most systems.

To find the interrupt key sequence for your session, use the command   **NOTE**

```
    stty -a
```

and look for "intr = ".

cut, paste, and join

The ability to separate columns that could constitute data fields from a file is provided by the `cut` utility. The default delimiter used is the tab, and the -f option is used to specify the desired field. For example, suppose there is a text file named **august** with three columns, looking like this:

```
one     two     three
four    five    six
seven   eight   nine
ten     eleven  twelve
```

Then the following command

```
cut -f2 august
```

will return

```
two
five
eight
eleven
```

However, the following example

```
cut -f1,3 august
```

will return the opposite:

```
one      three
four     six
seven    nine
ten      twelve
```

A number of options are available with this command; the two to be familiar with (besides -f) are -c and -d:

- ▶ -c allows you to specify characters instead of fields.

- ▶ -d allows you to specify a delimiter other than the tab.

To illustrate how to use the other options, the ls -l command will show: permissions, number of links, owner, group, size, date, and filename—all separated by whitespace, with two characters between the permissions and links. If you only want to see who is saving files in the directory, and are not interested in the other data, you can use

```
ls -l | cut -d" " -f5
```

This will ignore the permissions (first field), two sets of whitespace (second and third fields), number of links (fourth field), and display the owner (fifth field), ignoring everything following. Another way to look at this is that with ls -l the permissions always take up 10 characters, followed by whitespace of 3 characters, then the number of links, and whitespace that follows. The owner always begins with the 16th character and continues for the length of the name. The command

```
ls -l | cut -c16
```

will return the 16th character—the first letter of the owner's name. If an assumption is made that most users will use eight characters or less for their name, the command

```
ls -l | cut -c16-24
```

will return those entries in the name field.

The name of the file begins with the 55th character, but it can be impossible to determine how many characters after that to take because some filenames will be considerably longer than others. A solution to this is to begin with the 55th character, and not specify an ending character (meaning that the entire rest of the line is taken), as in this example:

```
ls -l | cut -c55-
```

Paste

Whereas the **cut** utility extracts fields from a file, they can be combined using either **paste** or **join**. The simplest of the two is **paste**—it has no great feature sets at all and merely takes one line from one source and combines it with another line from another source. For example, if the contents of **fileone** are

```
Indianapolis
Columbus
Peoria
Livingston
Scottsdale
```

And the contents of **filetwo** are

```
Indiana
Ohio
Illinois
Montana
Arizona
```

Then the following (including prompts) would be the display generated:

```
$ paste fileone filetwo
Indianapolis    Indiana
Columbus    Ohio
Peoria    Illinois
Livingston    Montana
Scottsdale    Arizona
$
```

If there were more lines in `fileone` than `filetwo`, the pasting would continue, but with blank entries following the tab. The tab character is always the default delimiter, but that can be changed to anything by using the `-d` option:

```
$ paste -d"," fileone filetwo
Indianapolis,Indiana
Columbus,Ohio
Peoria,Illinois
Livingston,Montana
Scottsdale,Arizona
$
```

You can also use the `-s` option to output all of `fileone` on a single line, followed by a carriage return and then `filetwo`:

```
$ paste -s fileone filetwo
Indianapolis    Columbus    Peoria    Livingston    Scottsdale
Indiana    Ohio    Illinois    Montana    Arizona
$
```

Join

You can think of the `join` utility as a greatly enhanced version of `paste`. It is critically important, however, to know that the utility can only work if the files being joined share a common field. For example, if `join` were used in the same example as `paste` was earlier, the result would be

```
$ join fileone filetwo
$
```

In other words, there is no display. `join` must find a common field between the files in question and, by default, expects that common field to be the first. For example, assume that `fileone` now contains these entries:

```
11111    Indianapolis
22222    Columbus
33333    Peoria
44444    Livingston
55555    Scottsdale
```

And the contents of `filetwo` are

```
11111    Indiana    500 race
22222    Ohio    Buckeye State
33333    Illinois    Wrigley Field
```

```
44444    Montana     Yellowstone Park
55555    Arizona     Grand Canyon
```

Then the following (including prompts) would be the display generated:

```
$ join fileone filetwo
11111    Indianapolis    Indiana    500 race
22222    Columbus     Ohio     Buckeye State
33333    Peoria     Illinois     Wrigley Field
44444    Livingston     Montanta     Yellowstone Park
55555    Scottsdale     Arizona     Grand Canyon
$
```

The commonality of the first field was identified and the matching entries
were combined. Whereas **paste** blindly took from each file to create the display, **join** will only combine lines that match and—of *critical importance*—it
must be an exact match with the corresponding line in the other file. This
point cannot be illustrated enough; for example, suppose **filetwo** had an
additional line in the middle:

```
11111    Indiana     500 race
22222    Ohio     Buckeye State
66666    Tennessee     Smokey Mountains
33333    Illinois     Wrigley Field
44444    Montana     Yellowstone Park
55555    Arizona     Grand Canyon
```

Then the following (including prompts) would be the display generated:

```
$ join fileone filetwo
11111    Indianapolis    Indiana    500 race
22222    Columbus     Ohio     Buckeye State
$
```

As soon as the files no longer match, no further operations can be carried
out. Each line is checked with the same—and only the same—line in the
opposite file for a match on the default field. If matches are found, they are
incorporated in the display; otherwise they are not. To illustrate one more
time—using the original **filetwo**:

```
$ tac filetwo > filethree
$ join fileone filethree
55555    Scottsdale     Arizona     Grand Canyon
$
```

Even though a match exists for every line in both files, only one match is found.

NOTE   **It is highly recommended that you overcome problems with `join` by first sorting each of the files to be used to get them in like order.**

You don't have to keep the defaults with `join` from looking at only the first fields for matches or from outputting all columns. The `-1` option lets you specify what field to use as the matching field in `fileone`, whereas the `-2` option lets you specify what field to use as the matching field in `filetwo`. For example, if the second field of `fileone` were to match with the third field of `filetwo`, the syntax would be

```
$ join -1 2 -2 3 fileone filethree
```

The `-o` option is used to specify output fields in the format `{file.field}`. Thus to only print the second field of `fileone` and the third field of `filetwo` on matching lines, the syntax would be

```
$ join -o 1.2 2.3 fileone filethree
Indianapolis     500
Columbus      Buckeye
Peoria     Wrigley
Livingston      Yellowstone
Scottsdale     Grand
$
```

Sort, Count, Format, and Translate

It is often necessary to not only display text, but to manipulate and modify it a bit before the output is shown, or simply gather information on it. Four utilities are examined in this section: `sort`, `wc`, `fmt`, and `tr`.

sort

The `sort` utility sorts the lines of a file in alphabetical order, and displays the output. The importance of alphabetical order, versus any other, cannot be overstated. For example, assume that the `fileone` file contains the following lines:

```
Indianapolis Indiana
Columbus
Peoria
Livingston
```

```
Scottsdale
1
2
3
4
5
6
7
8
9
10
11
12
```

When a sort is done on the file, the result becomes

```
$ sort fileone
1
10
11
12
2
3
4
5
6
7
8
9
Columbus
Indianapolis Indiana
Livingston
Peoria
Scottsdale
$
```

The cities are "correctly" sorted in alphabetical order. The numbers, however, are also in alphabetical order, which puts every number starting with "1" before every number starting with "2," and then every number starting with "3," and so on.

Thankfully, the **sort** utility includes some options to add a great deal of flexibility to the output. Among those options are the following:

▶ -d to sort in phone directory order (the same as that shown in the preceding example)

- ▶ -f to sort lowercase letters the same as uppercase

- ▶ -i to ignore any characters outside the ASCII range

- ▶ -n to sort in numerical order versus alphabetical

- ▶ -r to reverse the order of the output

Thus the display can be changed to

```
$ sort -n fileone
Columbus
Indianapolis Indiana
Livingston
Peoria
Scottsdale
1
2
3
4
5
6
7
8
9
10
11
12
$
```

> **NOTE** The sort **utility assumes all blank lines to be a part of the display and always places them at the beginning of the output. To prevent blank lines from being sorted, use the** -b **option.**

WC

The wc utility (named for "word count") displays information about the file in terms of three values: number of lines, words, and characters. The last entry in the output is the name of the file, thus the output would be

```
$ wc fileone
    17    18    86    fileone
$
```

You can choose to see only some of the output by using the following options:

▶ -c to show only the number of bytes/characters

▶ -l to see only the number of lines

▶ -w to see only the number of words

In all cases, the name of the file still appears, for example

```
$ wc -l fileone
    17      fileone
$
```

The only way to override the name appearing is by using the standard input redirection:

```
$ wc -l < fileone
    17
$
```

fmt

The `fmt` utility formats the text by creating output to a specific width. The default width is 75 characters, but a different value can be specified with the -w option. Short lines are combined to create longer ones unless the -s option is used, and spacing is justified unless -u is used. The -u option enforces uniformity and places one space between words and two spaces at the end of each sentence.

The following example shows how the `fileone` lines are combined to create a 75-character display:

```
$ fmt fileone
Indianapolis Indiana Columbus Peoria Livingston Scottsdale 1 2
3 4 5 6
7 8 9 10 11 12
$
```

To change the output to 60 characters, use this example:

```
$ fmt -w60 fileone
Indianapolis Indiana Columbus Peoria Livingston Scottsdale
1 2 3 4 5 6 7 8 9 10 11 12
$
```

The default for any option with fmt **is** -w, **thus** fmt -60 fileone **will give the same result as** fmt -w60 fileone.   **NOTE**

tr

The tr (translate) utility can convert one set of characters to another. Use the following example to change all lowercase characters to uppercase:

```
$ tr '[a-z]' '[A-Z]' < fileone
INDIANAPOLIS INDIANA
COLUMBUS
PEORIA
LIVINGSTON
SCOTTSDALE
$
```

NOTE It is extremely important to realize that the syntax of tr only accepts two character sets, not the name of the file. You must feed the name of the file into the utility by directing input (as in the example given), by piping to it (|), or using a similar operation.

Not only can you give character sets as string options, but you can also specify a number of unique values, including

- ► lower—All lowercase characters

- ► upper—All uppercase characters

- ► print—All printable characters

- ► punct—Punctuation characters

- ► space—All whitespace (blank can be used for horizontal whitespace only)

- ► alnum—Alpha characters and numbers

- ► digit—Numbers only

- ► cntrl—Control characters

- ► alpha—Letters only

- ► graph—Printable characters but not whitespace

For example, the output shown earlier can also be obtained like this:

```
$ tr '[:lower:]' '[:upper:]' < fileone
INDIANAPOLIS INDIANA
COLUMBUS
PEORIA
LIVINGSTON
SCOTTSDALE
$
```

Other Useful Utilities

A number of other useful text utilities are included with Linux. Some of these have limited usefulness and are intended only for a specific purpose, but are given because knowing of their existence and purpose can make your life with Linux considerably easier.

In alphabetical order, the additional utilities are as follows:

- ▶ expand—Allows you to expand tab characters into spaces. The default number of spaces per tab is 8, but this can be changed using the -t option. The opposite of this utility is unexpand.

- ▶ file—This utility will look at an entry's signature and report what type of file it is—ASCII text, GIF image, and so on. The definitions it returns (and thus the files it can correctly identify) are defined in a file called magic. This file typically resides in /usr/share/misc or /etc.

- ▶ more—Used to display only one screen of output at a time.

- ▶ od—Can perform an octal dump to show the contents of files other than ASCII text files. Used with the -x option, it does a hexadecimal dump, and with the -c option, it shows only recognizable ASCII characters.

- ▶ pr—Converts the file into a format suitable for printed pages— including a default header with date and time of last modification, file- name, and page numbers. The default header can be overwritten with the -h option, and the -l option allows you to specify the number of lines to include on each page—the default is 66. Default page width is 72 characters, but a different value can be specified with the -w option. The -d option can be used to double-space the output, and -m can be used to print numerous files in column format.

- ▶ split—Chops a single file into multiple files. The default is that a new file is created for every 1,000 lines of the original file. Using the -b option, you can avoid the thousand-line splitting and specify a number of bytes to be put into each output file, or use -l to specify a number of lines.

- ▶ uniq—This utility will examine entries in a file, comparing the current line with the one directly preceding it, to find lines that are unique.

Basic File Management

Course Objectives Covered

4. Executing Commands at the Command Line (3036)

5. Common Command Line Tasks (3036)

7. Changing Directories and Listing Directory Contents (3036)

In this section, you'll learn about a number of utilities used for managing files and directories. Some of these utilities—such as `cd` and `ls`—are of such importance that it was impossible to get this far in the book without using them in some of the examples. Here, we will expand upon them and explore their functions and uses in greater detail.

Working with cd and pwd

The `cd` command is used to change the directory you are working in. If you enter the command with no parameters, it will move you to whatever directory is defined by the HOME variable. If you specify any parameter with it, it is seen as denoting the directory you want to change to.

Some characters that can be of great use with `cd` are the single period (.) and double period (..). The former represents whatever directory you are currently in, whereas the latter represents the parent directory of the current one.

The `pwd` utility shows the present working directory—the one you are currently in. The same value that it returns is contained in the environmental variable PWD.

> **NOTE**
> Always remember that more than one item may have the same name in Linux. As a general rule, all uppercase entries represent variables, and all lowercase entries are files and utilities.

The following are some examples of how these two utilities can be used:

```
$ pwd
/usr/bin
$ echo $HOME
/usr/home/edulaney
$ cd
$ pwd
```

```
/usr/home/edulaney
$
```

This sequence showed the present working directory to be /usr/bin and the HOME variable to be equal to /usr/home/edulaney. Entering cd without any parameters changed to that directory.

```
$ pwd
/usr/home/edulaney
$ cd /
$ pwd
/
$ cd /usr/home/edulaney
$ pwd
/usr/home/edulaney
$ cd ..
$ pwd
/usr/home
$
```

In this sequence, the first change is to the root directory (/), then to /usr/home/edulaney. Using the shortcut for the parent of this directory, it was then possible to move back one directory.

Absolute and Relative Addressing

There are two methods of specifying paths to anything—files, directories, and so on: absolute and relative. When you give an absolute path, you take nothing into consideration, and you give a value that is always true. When you give a relative path, you take into account where you currently are, and you give a path relative to that.

To use an analogy, suppose two people live in the same city and state: Muncie, Indiana. The first person lives at 1909 Rosewood, and the second lives at 4104 Peachtree. If the first person wants to find/visit the second person, they can find out where they are via an absolute path known as their mailing address:

4104 Peachtree Lane
Muncie, IN 47304

This address says to

1. Find Indiana.

2. Within Indiana, find Muncie.

3. Within Muncie, find the section of the city falling within the 47304 zip code.

4. Within all earlier confines, find Peachtree Lane.

5. On Peachtree Lane, go to house number 4104.

> **NOTE** Absolute addresses will never change and will point to the entity regardless of where you are coming from.

The absolute address is the same whether the person coming to visit lives in Muncie or in Alaska. However, because the first person does live in Muncie as well, we can also tell them how to reach their destination using relative addressing:

1. Take Rosewood to Bethel and turn left.

2. Take Bethel to Jackson and turn right.

3. Take Jackson across the railroad tracks to the stop sign at Hawthorne.

4. Turn left on Hawthorne and go to the next stop, which is Peachtree.

5. Turn right on Peachtree Lane, and go to the first house on the right.

> **NOTE** Relative addresses will always change and are relative to where you are coming from.

Table 3.2 illustrates a few examples that can be used with the **cd** command.

TABLE 3.2 **Examples of Using the cd Command**

PRESENT WORKING DIRECTORY	NEW LOCATION	ABSOLUTE ADDRESS	RELATIVE ADDRESS
/usr/home/edulaney/ docs/proposals	/usr/home/ edulaney/docs	/usr/home/ edulaney/docs	..
/usr/home/edulaney/ docs/proposals	/usr/home/ edulaney	/usr/home/ edulaney	../..
/usr/home/edulaney/ docs/proposals	/usr/home/ edulaney/docs/ proposals/law_ order	/usr/home/ edulaney/docs/ proposals/law_ order	law_order
/usr/home/edulaney/ docs/proposals	/	/	../../ ../..

Working with ls

The ability to list files and directories is one of the most essential to any operating system, and the `ls` utility performs this function for Linux. When given by itself it lists the names of files and directories beneath the current directory in a column-style format. Entries are always—by default—given in alphabetical order and there is nothing to differentiate names of directories from names of files. An example would be

```
Desktop     emmett     filethree    junk2      questions
TestPro     errors     filetwo      mischief    sample
brio     example    Friday      myfile     sample of the world
dulaney     example2    garbage     numbers     simplesimon
eRRors     fileone    junk1     pull     snapshot01.gif
```

The listings are always in alphabetical order by default, with all uppercase entries coming before lowercase entries.   **■ NOTE**

There are a slew of options that can be used with this command, and one of the most useful is `-F`, which will indicate what type of entry is being displayed:

```
Desktop/     emmett     filethree    junk2      questions
TestPro     errors     filetwo      mischief*    sample
brio     example    Friday      myfile     sample of the world*
dulaney     example2    garbage     numbers     simplesimon
eRRors     fileone    junk1     pull     snapshot01.gif
```

Entries without any trailing characters added are standard files. Entries with a "/" on the end—such as Desktop—are directories. Those entries with a trailing asterisk (*) are executable. Symbolic links are signified by an at (@) symbol.

Another useful option is `-a`, which will show all files. By default, hidden files are not displayed by `ls`. A hidden file is any file that has a period (.) as its first character:

```
.      Desktop    emmett    filethree     junk2     questions
..      TestPro    errors    filetwo     mischief    sample
.bash_history    brio    example    Friday     myfile     sample
↪of the world
.bash_logout     dulaney     example2     garbage     numbers
↪simplesimon.fileone.swp     eRRors
fileone     junk1     pull     snapshot01.gif
```

> **NOTE** Periods can appear anywhere within a filename and appear as many times as you want. The only time they have any special significance is when they are the very first character of the name.

If you use -A in place of -a, it will leave off the first two entries ("." and ".."). Undoubtedly, however, the most useful option of all is -l, which will display a long list of the files. Entries look like this

```
drwx-------    5    root    root    1024    Aug 30 11:12
➥Desktop
-rw-r--r--     1    root    root    548     Aug 23 22:01
➥TestPro
-rw-r--r--     1    root    root    28      Aug 22 10:26    brio
```

There are essentially seven columns here, and they can be broken out as follows:

1. The permissions on the entry. Permissions are more fully discussed throughout subsequent chapters, but for now it is important to realize that the first character identifies what type of entry it is. A "-" indicates a file, whereas a "d" is a directory. Other possibilities for the first character are "c" for a character special file (such as a terminal), "b" for a block special device (such as a tape drive), "l" for a symbolic link, or "p" for a named pipe.

2. The number of links. If this is a directory, it will be equal to the number of entries beneath it. If it is a file, it is equal to the number of ways to reference it.

3. The name of the owner who created (or now owns) the entity.

4. The name of the group owning the file.

5. The size of the file.

6. The date of creation, or of modification into the current format.

7. The name.

Table 3.3 offers some of the other options for ls and their purpose.

TABLE 3.3   **Options for the ls Command**

OPTION PURPOSE

-c	List in order of time of last change/modification instead of alphabetical order

Table 3.3   Continued

OPTION PURPOSE

Option	Purpose
-d	List directories
-G	When used with -1, don't show the group
-i	Show the inode number (pointer) to each entry
-n	Show the owner and group by their numeric values instead of by name
-o	Same as -1G
-r	Reverse the order of the display
-R	Recursively show entries in subdirectories as well
-S	Sort
-u	Sort by last access time
-w	Specify screen width
-x	Show lines instead of columns
-X	Alphabetize by extension

Applying a touch

There are essentially three dates associated with a file or entry: creation, modification, and access. Using the **touch** utility, you can change the access and modification time associated with a file:

```
$
ls -l brio
-rw-r--r--    1    root    root    28    Aug 22 10:26    brio
$ touch brio
$ ls -l brio
-rw-r--r--    1    root    root    28    Aug 30 16:01    brio
$
```

There are a few options that can be used with the **touch** utility as well, as summarized in the following table:

OPTION PURPOSE

Option	Purpose
-a	Only change the access time
-m	Only change the modification time
-r	Use the time/date associated with a reference file to make the change instead of the current time/date

An example of the latter would be

```
$
ls -l tuesday wednesday
-rw-r--r--    1      root      root      85      Aug 22 10:26
➥tuesday
-rw-r--r--    1      root      root      85      Aug 29 13:08
➥wednesday
$ touch tuesday -r wednesday
ls -l tuesday wednesday
-rw-r--r--    1      root      root      85      Aug 29 13:08
➥tuesday
-rw-r--r--    1      root      root      85      Aug 29 13:08
➥wednesday
$
```

NOTE If you use the `touch` utility with the name of a file that does not exist, it will create the file with the current date and time and a size of zero.

Copying and Moving

Course Objectives Covered

4. Executing Commands at the Command Line (3036)

5. Common Command Line Tasks (3036)

9. Copying and Moving Files and Directories (3036)

10. Creating Directories (3036)

11. Deleting Files and Directories (3036)

System administration would be so much easier if nothing ever moved or changed. Unfortunately, it is very rare for anything to stay static any more, and changes take place at a nonstop pace. Linux offers two powerful utilities for copying and moving files: cp and mv, respectively, and a third utility—dd—that combines features of both.

cp

cp works with both files and directories and can move multiple entities at a time using wildcards. After the name of the utility, you must specify the source, followed by the target. The simplest use of all can be illustrated as follows:

```
$ ls -l fileone onefile
ls: onefile: No such file or directory
-rw-r--r--   1    root    root    85    Aug 22 10:26
↪fileone
$
$ cp fileone onefile
$ ls -l fileone onefile
-rw-r--r--   1    root    root    85    Aug 22 10:26
↪fileone
-rw-r--r--   1    edulaney    users    85    Aug 30 16:18
↪onefile
$
```

Notice that the original entry (source) remains unchanged, but now there is a second entry (target) as well. On the second entry, the contents are identical, but the date and time are those of the present (when **cp** was executed), not those of the source. Notice as well that the owner and group of the new file became that of the user executing the command. This is the same action that would take place if you were creating the target file completely from scratch.

To be able to copy a file—create a new entity equal in content to another—you need only read permission to the source.   **NOTE**

The -p option can be used to force as many of the old variables to remain the same. It preserves what it can in terms of attributes:

```
$ ls -l fileone nextfile
ls: nextfile: No such file or directory
-rw-r--r--   1    root    root    85    Aug 22 10:26
fileone
$
$ cp -p fileone nextfile
$ ls -l fileone nextfile
-rw-r--r--   1    root    root    85    Aug 22 10:26
↪fileone
-rw-r--r--   1    edulaney    users    85    Aug 22 10:26
↪nextfile
$
```

Notice that the date and time associated with the source were kept, but the owner and group still must change.

When you do a copy operation, the utility first checks to see if the source file exists. If it does, whatever file is specified as the target is created (with a size of zero), and the contents of the source are copied. The emphasis here is on the fact that the target is always created—regardless of whether it existed before or not. Here's an illustration:

```
$ ls -l fileone filetwo
-rw-r--r--    1    root    root    85    Aug 22 10:26
➥fileone
-rw-r--r--    1    root    root    16432    Aug 28 13:43
➥filetwo
$
$ cp fileone filetwo
$ ls -l fileone filetwo
-rw-r--r--    1    root    root    85    Aug 22 10:26
➥fileone
-rw-r--r--    1    edulaney    users    85    Aug 30 16:18
➥filetwo
$
```

The original contents of filetwo have been lost, except for any backup tape versions, as filetwo is *created* to be a copy of fileone. There is a -i (as in inquire) option, which can be used to always ask if you really want to erase the contents of the target file if it already exists:

```
$ ls -l fileone filetwo
-rw-r--r--    1    root    root    85    Aug 22 10:26
➥fileone
-rw-r--r--    1    root    root    16432    Aug 28 13:43
➥filetwo
$
$ cp -i fileone filetwo
cp: overwrite 'filetwo'?
```

At the prompt, you can enter "y" to perform the operation, or anything else to stop it.

You can copy a number of files from one directory to another so long as the last item on the command line is a valid directory path into which the files will be copied:

```
$ ls -l /usr/home/sdulaney
-rw-r--r--    1    root    root    85    Aug 22 10:26    exit
$
$ cd /usr/home/examples
$ ls -l s* q*
-rw-r--r--    1    root    root    585    Aug 23 12:16
```

```
➥questions
-rw-r--r--    1     root     root     1985     Aug 24 15:17
➥samples
-rw-r--r--    1     root     root     8501     Aug 25 18:30
➥snapshot01.gif
$ cp s* q* /usr/home/sdulaney
$ cd ../sdulaney
$ ls -l
-rw-r--r--    1     root     root     85       Aug 22 10:26     exit
-rw-r--r--    1     root     root     585      Aug 31 22:50
➥questions
-rw-r--r--    1     root     root     1985     Aug 31 22:50
➥samples
-rw-r--r--    1     root     root     8501     Aug 31 22:50
➥snapshot01.gif
$
```

To move an entire directory from one location to another, use the `-r` or `-R` option to recursively move the directory as well as any subdirectories and files beneath it. Other options that can be used include `-f` to force a copy without any prompting (the opposite, so to speak, of `-i`); `-u` to copy only when the source file is more recent (updated) than the target; and `-v` for verbose mode (show all operations, rather than perform them silently).

Lastly, the `-P` option will reproduce the entire path to a file in another location—creating directories and subdirectories as needed to do so.

mv

The **move** utility (`mv`) can be used for several operations. At the risk of being overly simplistic, this includes the ability to

1. Rename a file

2. Rename a directory

3. Move a file from one directory to another

4. Move a subdirectory from one directory to another

5. Move an entity to another partition or media

The simplest operation is to rename a file in its current directory:

```
$ ls -l file*
-rw-r--r--    1     root     root     85       Aug 22 10:26
➥fileone
-rw-r--r--    1     root     root     16432    Aug 28 13:43
```

```
➥filetwo
$
$ mv fileone filethree
$ ls -l file*
-rw-r--r--    1    root    root    85      Aug 22 10:26
➥filethree
-rw-r--r--    1    root    root    16432    Aug 28 13:43
➥filetwo
$
```

The dates, permissions, and everything else associated with `fileone` stay with `filethree`. This is because when a file is moved within the same directory (or even on the same partition), all that changes is the information about the name—no physical operation takes place; only the descriptor is changed. The move has become a simple rename operation.

NOTE As simplistic as it may sound, always remember that when you copy a file, you leave the original intact and create something that did not exist before—thus a new set of attributes is created for the new entity. When you move a file, however, the default action is a rename—you are changing only the name of the original entity and not creating anything new.

One way to put it in perspective is that if you copy a file that is 9MB in size, it will take longer than if you copy a file that is 9 bytes in size. With move being used as a rename, it will take the same amount of time to do the operation regardless of the size of the file.

As with the copy operation, if you attempt to move a file to a name that already exists, the contents of the target are lost. Here's an illustration:

```
$ ls -l file*
-rw-r--r--    1    root    root    85      Aug 22 10:26
➥fileone
-rw-r--r--    1    root    root    16432    Aug 28 13:43
➥filetwo
$ mv fileone filetwo
$ ls -l file*
-rw-r--r--    1    root    root    85      Aug 22 10:26
➥filetwo
$
```

The `-i` option (as in inquiry or interactive) can be used to prompt before overwriting, and the opposite of it is `-f` (for force), which is the default operation. The `-u` option will only do the move if the source file is newer, and `-v` turns on verbose mode. The `-b` option makes a backup of the target file, if it exists, with a tilde as the last character—essentially performing a pseudo-copy operation:

```
$ ls -l help*
-rw-r--r--    1    root    root    85    Aug 22 10:26
➥helpfile
$ mv -b helpfile helpfiletwo
$ ls -l help*
-rw-r--r--    1    root    root    85    Aug 22 10:26
➥helpfiletwo
$
$ ls -l file*
-rw-r--r--    1    root    root    85    Aug 22 10:26
➥fileone
-rw-r--r--    1    root    root    16432    Aug 28 13:43
➥filetwo
$ mv -b fileone filetwo
$ ls -l file*
-rw-r--r--    1    root    root    85    Aug 22 10:26
➥filetwo
-rw-r--r--    1    root    root    16432    Aug 28 13:43
➥filetwo~
$
```

In the first instance, there was not an existing file with the target name present, so the -b option was ignored. In the second instance, a file by the name of the target was in existence, so the original target file is renamed with a tilde (~) as the last character.

The -b option can also be used with cp to perform the same action during a copy as it does with mv.   **NOTE**

dd

The device-to-device (dd) utility is used to copy a file from one device to another. It goes beyond that in functionality, however, for it can convert a file during the copy process from one format to another. It can convert from EBCDIC to ASCII (and reverse), change uppercase to lowercase (and reverse as well), and work with bytes, blocks, or keywords.

The most common use for dd is copying files to and from removable media, and you must use arguments that can include

▶ **bs**—block file size

▶ **if**—input file

▶ **of**—output file

Removing Files and Directories

When files are no longer needed, they can be removed from the system with the **rm** (remove) command. Be careful using this command, for Linux offers no undelete command or function like those found in other operating systems.

```
$ ls -l file*
-rw-r--r--    1    root    root    85      Aug 22 10:26
➥fileone
-rw-r--r--    1    root    root    16432   Aug 28 13:43
➥filetwo
$ rm fileone
$ ls -l file*
-rw-r--r--    1    root    root    16432   Aug 28 13:43
➥filetwo
$
```

When used with the **-i** option, a prompt appears before each file to be deleted. Pressing Y deletes the file, and pressing any other character skips the file.

```
$ ls -l t*
-rw-r--r--    1    root    root    85      Aug 22 10:26
➥today
-rw-r--r--    1    root    root    16432   Aug 28 13:43
➥tuesday
$ rm -i t*
rm: remove 'today'?
```

The **-f** option forces deletion, and **-v** puts the utility in verbose mode. The **-r** or **-R** option recursively deletes directories (including subdirectories and files beneath). In order to delete a file, you have to have write permissions within the directory where it resides.

NOTE Write permission is only required on the directory from which you are deleting the file—not on the file itself.

A safer utility, **rmdir**, can be used to delete directories that have nothing beneath them. It will only delete empty directories and cannot be used for

directories that have files or subdirectories beneath them. The only option
that can be used with `rmdir` is `-p` to remove parent directories (if empty).

```
$ ls -R kdulaney
kdulaney:
docs

kdulaney/docs:
attempt
$
$ rmdir kdulaney
rmdir: kdulaney: Directory not empty
$
```

Because there is a file (`attempt`) within `kdulaney/docs`, and a subdirectory
(`docs`) beneath `kdulaney`, the directory `kdulaney` cannot be deleted with
the `rmdir` utility. There are three possible ways to accomplish the task:

1. Use the `rm -r` command.

2. Delete `attempt` with `rm`, and then delete `docs` with `rmdir`, and—
   finally—delete `kdulaney` with `rmdir`.

3. Delete `attempt` with `rm`, and then delete `kdulaney/docs` with
   `rmdir -p`.

**Because `rmdir` can only delete empty directories, it is naturally a safer utility to
use than `rm` for cleaning a system.**   **NOTE**

Making Directories

Now that you've learned how to copy, move, and delete directories, the only
order of business left is to make a directory, which you can do by using the
`mkdir` command. Used without options, it creates a child directory (subdirectory) in the current directory. There are two options that work with it as
well:

▶ `-m`—To specify permissions other than the default for the new directory (covered in a later chapter)

▶ `-p`—To create a parent and child in one command

Here are some examples of the utility:

```
$ pwd
/usr/home
```

```
$ mkdir edulaney
$
```

This created the subdirectory **edulaney** beneath
`/usr/home`(`/usr/home/edulaney`).

```
$ pwd
/usr/home
$ mkdir kdulaney/docs
mkdir: cannot make directory 'kdulaney/docs': No such file or
➥directory
$
$ mkdir -p kdulaney/docs
$ cd kdulaney
$ cd docs
$
```

In the first attempt, the utility fails as you cannot create multiple directories
by default. If you use the **-p** option, however, the multiple directories are
created.

Standard Output and Input

Course Objectives Covered

4. Executing Commands at the Command Line (3036)

5. Common Command Line Tasks (3036)

6. Piping and Redirection (3036)

Standard output is where displays usually go—to your screen. When you
give the following command

```
ls -F
```

a listing of the subdirectories and files beneath the current directory is displayed on your screen. The default location for standard output, therefore, is
to your screen. If you do not want the results displayed on your screen,
however, you can redirect them to another location, such as a file.
Redirection of standard output is possible through the use of the greater-
than sign (>). For example, to send the results to a file, the command
would be

```
ls -F > myfile
```

The first order of business the shell undertakes when given this command is that it creates a file named `myfile` with a size of zero. It then allows the `ls` utility to run and places the output within the newly created file rather than on your screen. It is important to note the order of operations. Suppose you give a nonexistent command, such as this one:

```
ls -z > myfile
```

The file named `myfile` is still created with a size of zero that then stays at zero. The error appears on your screen, but this is after the file was created. This is also important because if you attempt to add more information to the file, the file will be overwritten first. To add more information, you must append to the file using two greater-than signs (>>):

```
ls -l >> myfile
```

This adds the new information to the end of the existing file and keeps the original contents intact. In some situations, you want a command to run but don't care at all about what the results are. For example, I might want a database to compile and need to run a utility for this to happen. I don't care about the messages generated—I just want the utility to run. When this is the case, you can send the results to nowhere by specifying /dev/null:

```
ls -F > /dev/null
```

The results are sent to this device, which is also known as the *trashcan*, never to be saved or displayed.

Standard input is typically the keyboard, or interpreted to be among the arguments given on the command line. You can, however, specify redirection of standard input using the less-than sign (<). Rarely is there ever a need for this, but it is available. For example

```
cat myfile
```

will give the same results as

```
cat < myfile
```

In the world of Linux, numerical values exist for these items as well. Standard input (abbreviated **stdin**) is 0, and standard output (abbreviated **stdout**) is 1. These numbers can be used with the redirection, but this is rarely done. An example would be

```
ls -F 1> myfile
```

NOTE There can be *no space* between 1 and the > sign. If there is, the meaning is changed.

This example states that standard output is to be redirected to the file named `myfile`. The numbers are important for one reason only—because a third possibility exists as well. Standard error (abbreviated `stderr`) has a value of 2. For an example of standard error, think of the `ls -z` command you saw earlier. Even though the output was being sent to a file, the command was a nonexistent one and the error message appeared on the screen. The error could be sent to the file with the following command:

```
ls -z 2> myfile
```

The problem is that now the error will be sent there, but the output (in the absence of an error) will appear on the screen. To send both output and errors to the same file, the command becomes

```
ls -z > myfile 2>&1
```

This states that the output is to go to a file named `myfile` and further that standard error (2) is to go to the same location as standard output (1). Another alternative is to send errors to one location and output to another, like this:

```
ls -z > myfile 2>errors
```

Let's look at the order of operations here: The shell first creates two files (`myfile` and `errors`) with zero sizes (whether or not they existed before). If the command is successful, the output goes to `myfile`. If the command is unsuccessful, the errors go to `errors`. If these were truly log files, the only other modification might be to append versus zero each time the operation is run:

```
ls -z >> myfile 2>>errors
```

tee for Two

There is a miscellaneous utility that really stands alone and does not fit well with any section: `tee`. This utility, as the name implies, sends output in two directions. The default for most processes is to write their output to the screen. Using redirection (>), you can divert the output to a file, but what if you want to do both?

The `tee` utility allows output to go to the screen *and* to a file as well. The utility must always be followed by the name of the file which you want `output` to write to, for example

```
$ ps -f | tee example
UID          PID  PPID  C STIME TTY          TIME CMD
root       19605 19603  0 Aug10 pts/0     00:00:34 bash
root       30089 19605  0 Aug20 pts/0     00:00:00 vi fileone
root       30425 19605  0 Aug20 pts/0     00:00:00 paste -d
➥fileone filetwo?
root       32040 19605  0 Aug22 pts/0     00:00:00 cat
root        1183 19605  0 Aug23 pts/0     00:00:00 awk -F:
➥questions
root       30778 19605  0 14:25 pts/0     00:00:00 ps -f
$
$ cat example
UID          PID  PPID  C STIME TTY          TIME CMD
root       19605 19603  0 Aug10 pts/0     00:00:34 bash
root       30089 19605  0 Aug20 pts/0     00:00:00 vi fileone
root       30425 19605  0 Aug20 pts/0     00:00:00 paste -d
➥fileone filetwo?
root       32040 19605  0 Aug22 pts/0     00:00:00 cat
root        1183 19605  0 Aug23 pts/0     00:00:00 awk -F:
➥questions
root       30778 19605  0 14:25 pts/0     00:00:00 ps -f
$
```

As illustrated, the output appears on the screen, and is written to the file as well. This can be an extremely useful utility whenever a file is needed and you also want to view the output.

xargs

Another powerful utility to know is `xargs`. To understand the power of this utility, consider the `find` utility, which is limited in the results it can return to values within the filesystem structure. The only real text within the structure is the name of the entity and not the data itself (the pointer points to that). To illustrate, suppose the user `edulaney` put out a memo several months back on acceptable use of the company refrigerator in the break room. Since then, user `edulaney` has quit the company and several new employees (who would benefit from knowing this policy) have joined. You want to find the file and reprint it.

About the closest you can get to accomplishing this with `find` (and its results) would be

```
$ find / -user edulaney -type f -exec grep -i refrigerator {}
➥\;
stored in the refrigerator overnight will be thrown out
$
```

The **type f** option must be used or else errors will occur every time **grep** tries to search a directory. In this case, the line from the file is found, but there is no way of knowing what file it is contained in—rendering the result pretty much useless.

Enter the **xargs** utility: Analogous to a pipe, it feeds output from one command directly into another. Arguments coming into it are passed through with no changes, and turned into input into the next command. Thus, the command can be modified to

```
$ find / -user edulaney -type f | xargs grep -i refrigerator
/home/edulaney/fileone:stored in the refrigerator overnight
will be thrown out
$
```

The desired file is indicated, and can now be found and printed for the new employees.

Food for thought: If **xargs** works like a pipe, why wouldn't the following command suffice?

```
$ find / -user edulaney -type f | grep -i refrigerator
```

Answer: Because the **grep** operation would take place on the names of the files, not the content of the files. The **xargs** utility pipes the entire name (thus the contents) into the next command in succession (**grep**, in this case), not just the resulting filename.

Working with Processes

Course Objectives Covered

   5. Common Command Line Tasks (3036)

  17. View Processes from the GUI and the Command Line Interface (3036)

  18. Multiuser Processes and Multitasking in the Linux System (3036)

  19. Monitor Processes (3038)

In this section, you'll learn about utilities used to manage a process and see how processes are utilized for all transactions. In the previous sections, many utilities and commands were discussed—each time one of them is issued, a process is started to carry out the request, as you will see in greater detail.

What Is a Process

Crucial to understanding this section is knowing that a process is *any* instance, command, or utility in execution. When you issue the command `ls`, as was discussed earlier, a process is started to run the utility and return the results.

Even the shell with which you are interacting is running as a process. When you give a command to be carried out, the shell will look to see if it can do so without any outside help. (Assume the command was really just an empty line: No other utilities are needed to return another prompt.) If your shell cannot perform the command, it will call another process to perform the action. The other process called is a child to your shell, which has become a parent to the new process.

When the child has completed performing its task, it returns its results to the parent, and then goes away. Because Linux is a multitasking operating system, there can be more than one child for any given parent. If the child cannot perform all of the tasks on its own (think of compiling an annual report), the child may need to call one or more additional processes. When it does this, it becomes the parent to those child processes.

Barring any restrictions coded into it, every process has the ability to be a parent or child.   **NOTE**

On a system, at any given time, there will be processes that you are running, there may be processes that others are running, and there will be processes that the system itself is running. The latter are often *daemons*—services that are running without interaction to provide functionality to the operating system. Examples of services daemons can perform include printing, running scheduled jobs, sending mail, monitoring run state, and so forth.

Working with ps

The **ps** command is key to any interaction with processes and is used to show process status. When run by itself (no options), **ps** will show the processes that you currently have running, with the last line always being itself (it is a running process as well). For example

```
$ ps
PID     TTY     TIME      CMD
19605   pts/0   00:00:34  bash
30089   pts/0   00:00:00  vi
30425   pts/0   00:00:00  paste
32040   pts/0   00:00:00  cat
 1183   pts/0   00:00:00  awk
30679   pts/0   00:00:00  ps
$
```

The first column is the process ID number—this is a unique number assigned to every process that executes. When the system is booted, the numbers begin incrementing until they reach a defined limit, then begin again through the numbering, using only the numbers that are free.

The second column indicates the terminal with which the user responsible for the process is associated. Because the list is only of processes for the user issuing the command, all terminal listings should be the same.

The third column indicates the amount of processor time that the process is utilizing. In most cases, processes can run quickly, sit idle, and so on, and utilize very little time. A very high time reading can indicate a process that is dragging down the performance of the system.

The fourth column is the name of the process (command) itself. In the first line, there is the user's shell—which must be there, or there would not be a user here at all: The user's shell is known as the session leader. The last line is the command that just executed. Those entries in between are other processes that the user is running.

The **ps** utility has a number of options to make it more flexible. The **-a** option removes obvious choices. For example, you know that you have to have a shell running or you would not be interacting with the system, so it isn't really as important to see that as others. Using the **-a** option, the display changes just slightly:

```
$ ps -a
PID     TTY     TIME      CMD
30089   pts/0   00:00:00  vi
```

```
30425   pts/0    00:00:00    paste
32040   pts/0    00:00:00    cat
 1183   pts/0    00:00:00    awk
30685   pts/0    00:00:00    ps
$
```

ps -a **will show all processes associated with the current** tty *except* **the session leader. Also note that the PID associated with** ps **increments with every running, as each requires a new process. It does not increment by one, in this case, for several other processes ran (probably in the background) between the first and second running of** ps.

Using either the -A or the -e option (all or everything), it is possible to see every process running and not just those linked to the current **tty**:

```
$ ps -e
  PID TTY          TIME CMD
    1 ?        00:00:04 init
    2 ?        00:00:00 migration/0
    3 ?        00:00:00 ksoftirqd/0
    4 ?        00:00:00 migration/1
    5 ?        00:00:00 ksoftirqd/1
    6 ?        00:00:00 events/0
    7 ?        00:00:00 events/1
    8 ?        00:00:00 kacpid
    9 ?        00:00:00 kblockd/0
   10 ?        00:00:00 kblockd/1
   11 ?        00:00:00 kirqd
   14 ?        00:00:00 khelper
   15 ?        00:00:00 pdflush
   16 ?        00:00:07 pdflush
   18 ?        00:00:00 aio/0
   17 ?        00:00:00 kswapd0
   19 ?        00:00:00 aio/1
  175 ?        00:00:00 kseriod
  437 ?        00:00:00 scsi_eh_0
  439 ?        00:00:00 scsi_eh_1
  479 ?        00:00:00 reiserfs/0
  480 ?        00:00:00 reiserfs/1
  659 ?        00:00:00 kcopyd
 1463 ?        00:00:00 khubd
 1739 ?        00:00:02 dhcpcd
 1924 ?        00:00:00 syslogd
 1930 ?        00:00:00 klogd
```

```
1979 ?        00:00:00 portmap
1980 ?        00:00:10 resmgrd
2042 ?        00:00:00 slpd
2152 ?        00:00:01 cupsd
2305 ?        00:00:33 powersaved
2402 ?        00:00:00 sshd
2495 ?        00:00:00 hwscand
2531 ?        00:00:00 slapd
3023 ?        00:00:00 master
3159 ?        00:00:00 cron
3164 ?        00:00:07 nscd
3334 ?        00:00:00 kdm
3385 tty1     00:00:00 mingetty
3386 tty2     00:00:00 mingetty
3387 tty3     00:00:00 mingetty
3388 tty4     00:00:00 mingetty
3389 tty5     00:00:00 mingetty
3390 tty6     00:00:00 mingetty
3531 ?        00:00:00 gpg-agent
7235 ?        00:00:00 qmgr
6751 ?        00:00:00 gpg-agent
6898 ?        00:00:22 X
6899 ?        00:00:00 kdm
6930 ?        00:00:00 kde
6965 ?        00:00:00 gpg-agent
6989 ?        00:00:00 kdeinit
6992 ?        00:00:00 kdeinit
6994 ?        00:00:00 kdeinit
6997 ?        00:00:00 kdeinit
7005 ?        00:00:00 artsd
7015 ?        00:00:00 kdeinit
7016 ?        00:00:00 kwrapper
7018 ?        00:00:00 kdeinit
7019 ?        00:00:03 kdeinit
7021 ?        00:00:00 kdeinit
7023 ?        00:00:00 kdeinit
7025 ?        00:00:02 kdeinit
7027 ?        00:00:03 kdeinit
7032 ?        00:00:00 kdeinit
7036 ?        00:00:00 kpowersave
7037 ?        00:00:01 suseplugger
7039 ?        00:00:00 susewatcher
7043 ?        00:00:00 kdeinit
7049 ?        00:00:00 krandrtray
7053 ?        00:00:01 kdeinit
```

```
 7054 pts/1    00:00:00 bash
 7116 ?        00:00:00 kdeinit
 8886 ?        00:00:04 kdeinit
13641 ?        00:00:00 pickup
13737 pts/1    00:00:00 ps
$
```

There are several things to notice in the display shown. In no particular order, they are as follows:

▶ Processes started when the system came up have the lowest number PIDs (notice items 1 through 19). As a general rule, these are mission-critical processes, and if they were not there, some or all of the system would be unusable.

▶ Not all processes are tied to a terminal. If a question mark (**?**) is present, it indicates that the process is running on the system without terminal interaction and/or without a terminal being default standard output.

▶ For every terminal without a user, there is a **getty**, or **mingetty**, running. This process sits and waits for a user to attempt to log on. Even though no user is using **tty1** through **tty6**, it is easy to see that six other terminals can be used.

Other options that can be used to determine what information to display are

▶ **l** to display a long listing (think of **ls -l**)
▶ **u** to show username and related stats
▶ **f** to show a full listing (everything possible)

The latter is often used, and favored by administrators, for the additional columns it adds to the display:

```
$ ps -f
UID        PID  PPID  C STIME TTY          TIME CMD
root       7054  7053  0 Oct12 pts/1    00:00:00 /bin/bash
root      13745  7054  0 09:45 pts/1    00:00:00 ps -f
$
```

There are four new columns that were not there before. The first column identifies the user ID associated with the process. The third column is the Parent Process ID—showing which process this one reports back to. The fourth column identifies whether scheduling is involved, and the fifth column is the time at which the process started.

Notice that when using f, the CMD now lists the entire command and not just the first portion, as was done with the other displays.

These options can be combined with one another, and the most common combination is ef, which displays all processes in a full format:

```
$ ps -ef
UID         PID   PPID  C STIME TTY         TIME CMD
root          1      0  0 Sep28 ?       00:00:04 init [5]
root          2      1  0 Sep28 ?       00:00:00 [migration/0]
root          3      1  0 Sep28 ?       00:00:00 [ksoftirqd/0]
root          4      1  0 Sep28 ?       00:00:00 [migration/1]
root          5      1  0 Sep28 ?       00:00:00 [ksoftirqd/1]
root          6      1  0 Sep28 ?       00:00:00 [events/0]
root          7      1  0 Sep28 ?       00:00:00 [events/1]
root          8      6  0 Sep28 ?       00:00:00 [kacpid]
root          9      6  0 Sep28 ?       00:00:00 [kblockd/0]
root         10      6  0 Sep28 ?       00:00:00 [kblockd/1]
root         11      1  0 Sep28 ?       00:00:00 [kirqd]
root         14      6  0 Sep28 ?       00:00:00 [khelper]
root         15      7  0 Sep28 ?       00:00:00 [pdflush]
root         16      6  0 Sep28 ?       00:00:07 [pdflush]
root         18      7  0 Sep28 ?       00:00:00 [aio/0]
root         17      1  0 Sep28 ?       00:00:00 [kswapd0]
root         19      6  0 Sep28 ?       00:00:00 [aio/1]
root        175      1  0 Sep28 ?       00:00:00 [kseriod]
root        437      1  0 Sep28 ?       00:00:00 [scsi_eh_0]
root        439      1  0 Sep28 ?       00:00:00 [scsi_eh_1]
root        479      6  0 Sep28 ?       00:00:00 [reiserfs/0]
root        480      7  0 Sep28 ?       00:00:00 [reiserfs/1]
root        659      6  0 Sep28 ?       00:00:00 [kcopyd]
root       1463      1  0 Sep28 ?       00:00:00 [khubd]
root       1930      1  0 Sep28 ?       00:00:00 /sbin/klogd
➥-c 1 -2 -x
bin        1979      1  0 Sep28 ?       00:00:00 /sbin/portmap
root       1980      1  0 Sep28 ?       00:00:10 /sbin/resmgrd
daemon     2042      1  0 Sep28 ?       00:00:00 /usr/sbin/slpd
lp         2152      1  0 Sep28 ?       00:00:01
➥/usr/sbin/cupsd
root       2495      1  0 Sep28 ?       00:00:00 [hwscand]
root       3023      1  0 Sep28 ?       00:00:00
➥/usr/lib/postfix/master
```

```
root        3159      1   0 Sep28 ?          00:00:00
➥/usr/sbin/cron
root        3164      1   0 Sep28 ?          00:00:07
➥/usr/sbin/nscd
root        3334      1   0 Sep28 ?          00:00:00
➥/opt/kde3/bin/kdm
root        3385      1   0 Sep28 tty1       00:00:00 /sbin/mingetty
➥--noclear tty1
root        3386      1   0 Sep28 tty2       00:00:00 /sbin/mingetty
➥tty2
root        3387      1   0 Sep28 tty3       00:00:00 /sbin/mingetty
➥tty3
root        3388      1   0 Sep28 tty4       00:00:00 /sbin/mingetty
➥tty4
root        3389      1   0 Sep28 tty5       00:00:00 /sbin/mingetty
➥tty5
root        3390      1   0 Sep28 tty6       00:00:00 /sbin/mingetty
➥tty6
postfix     7235   3023   0 Sep28 ?          00:00:00 qmgr -l -t
➥fifo -u
root        6899   3334   0 Oct12 ?          00:00:00 -:0
root        6930   6899   0 Oct12 ?          00:00:00 /bin/sh
➥/usr/X11R6/bin/kde
root        6989      1   0 Oct12 ?          00:00:00 kdeinit:
➥Running...
root        6992      1   0 Oct12 ?          00:00:00 kdeinit:
➥dcopserver --nosid
root        6994   6989   0 Oct12 ?          00:00:00 kdeinit:
➥klauncher
root        6997      1   0 Oct12 ?          00:00:01 kdeinit: kded
root        7015      1   0 Oct12 ?          00:00:00 kdeinit:
➥knotify
root        7016   6930   0 Oct12 ?          00:00:00 kwrapper
➥ksmserver
root        7018      1   0 Oct12 ?          00:00:00 kdeinit:
➥ksmserver
root        7019   6989   0 Oct12 ?          00:00:03 kdeinit: kwin
➥-session 117f0000020001096402165000000063920000_1097649388_
➥170101
root        7021      1   0 Oct12 ?          00:00:00 kdeinit:
➥kwrited
root        7023      1   0 Oct12 ?          00:00:00 kdeinit:
➥khotkeys
root        7025      1   0 Oct12 ?          00:00:02 kdeinit:
➥kdesktop
root        7027      1   0 Oct12 ?          00:00:03 kdeinit:
➥kicker
```

```
root       7032      1   0 Oct12 ?        00:00:00 kdeinit:
➥klipper
root       7036      1   0 Oct12 ?        00:00:00 kpowersave
root       7043      1   0 Oct12 ?        00:00:00 kdeinit:
➥kio_uiserver
root       7049      1   0 Oct12 ?        00:00:00 krandrtray -
➥session 117f0000020001096403627000000063920018_1097649388_
➥152381
root       7053   6989   0 Oct12 ?        00:00:01 kdeinit:
➥konsole
root       7054   7053   0 Oct12 pts/1    00:00:00 /bin/bash
root       8886   6989   0 Oct13 ?        00:00:05 kdeinit:
➥konqueror --silent
postfix   13641   3023   0 08:24 ?        00:00:00 pickup -l -t
➥fifo -u
root      13747   7054   0 09:45 pts/1    00:00:00 ps -ef
$
```

Working with pstree and top

Two commands that are closely related to **ps** offer slightly different views of
the processes. The first of these is **pstree**, which will graphically depict the
relationship between the processes as shown in Figure 3.1.

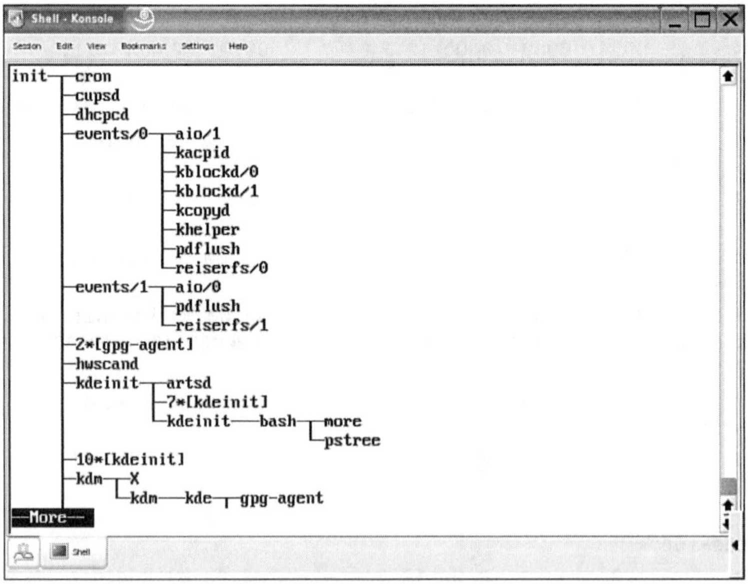

FIGURE 3.1
The pstree
utility graphically
shows the rela-
tionship between
processes.

This graphically depicts the children beneath the main processes, and shows
where each process fits in—what process is the parent of it, and so on.

The second utility related to **ps** is **top**. Not only does it show the current processes, but it stays active and continually updates the display. Additionally, the top of the screen depicts information about how many days the system has been up, the number of users, memory and swap statistics, and so on.

When **top** is running, you can press any of the following keys to interact with it:

- ▶ h—Help
- ▶ q—Quit
- ▶ s—Set the delay between updates (default is five seconds)
- ▶ spacebar—Update now rather than waiting for renewal interval
- ▶ u—Display a single user only

The columns show the standard PID/CMD information, as well as the amount of memory and the number of CPU processes being utilized.

Ending a Process

Processes can be started in a plethora of ways. They are started automatically by the system as daemons, and started by the user in attempting to get a job done. Some processes start other processes, and the list goes on.

Under normal circumstances, a child process acts on behalf of, and reports to, a parent. When the child is no longer needed, it goes away on its own accord. There are situations, however, where processes become runaways— they are no longer needed, yet they continue to run and consume processes.

A parent process cannot (or should not) cease as long as there are child processes associated with it. Given that, a child process that fails to cease could keep a number of unneeded processes on a system. To illustrate, assume that a user's shell calls another process (A), which cannot do everything needed, and thus it calls another (B), and it in turn starts another (C).

Under normal conditions, when Process C finishes, it will report back to Process B and go away. Process B will massage the data, report back to Process A, and go away. Process A will do whatever it needs to with the data, and then return it to the user's shell and go away.

For a non-normal condition, assume that Process C has a glitch and does not end after reporting back to Process B. It continues to run: This prevents Process B from ending because it still has a child associated with it. We can assume that Process B returns its values to Process A, and it then returns its values to the user's shell. Process A, like Process B, cannot end because it still has a child associated with it. Because there is a glitch in Process C, three processes that are no longer needed continue to run.

Yet another possibility for the glitch (and it would depend on how applications are written) is that Process B could go ahead and end without Process C going away. Process A could do its task, and go away as well. What happens in this instance is that only Process C remains a problem, but now it has nonexistent parents above it, and has no idea who it reports to—it becomes a true runaway.

To solve problems with erratic processes, there is the `kill` command. This utility works with the following syntax:

```
kill {option} PID
```

Thus to get rid of the `cat` process, the sequence would be

```
$ ps -f
UID          PID  PPID  C STIME TTY          TIME CMD
root       19605 19603  0 Aug10 pts/0     00:00:34 bash
root       30089 19605  0 Aug20 pts/0     00:00:00 vi fileone
root       30425 19605  0 Aug20 pts/0     00:00:00 paste -d
➥fileone filetwo?
root       32040 19605  0 Aug22 pts/0     00:00:00 cat
root        1183 19605  0 Aug23 pts/0     00:00:00 awk -F:
➥questions
root       30900 19605  0 14:25 pts/0     00:00:00 ps -f
$
$ kill 32040
$
```

This "politely" asks the process to terminate. It is polite because there are 32 different ways to kill a process (*signals* to send), and this is the safest method of doing so. In a great many instances, the process will simply ignore the request and continue on. When that happens, you can use one of the other 32 ways by specifying the number to use. Among the possibilities are

- ▶ -1 On hangup/disconnect
- ▶ -2 Using an interrupt (Ctrl+C) sequence
- ▶ -3 Upon quit
- ▶ -9 Without regard—immediately
- ▶ -15 (the default)

NOTE

To see a list of signals on your system, use the command `kill -1`**. The first 32 signals are standard, but many times a list of up to 64 is shown. Those signals between 33 and 64 are not standard and are intended for real-time application use.**

To illustrate, assume the `cat` process will not go away politely; the sequence of operations then becomes

```
$ ps -f
UID         PID   PPID  C STIME TTY         TIME CMD
root      19605  19603  0 Aug10 pts/0    00:00:34 bash
root      30089  19605  0 Aug20 pts/0    00:00:00 vi fileone
root      30425  19605  0 Aug20 pts/0    00:00:00 paste -d
➥fileone filetwo?
root      32040  19605  0 Aug22 pts/0    00:00:00 cat
root       1183  19605  0 Aug23 pts/0    00:00:00 awk -F:
➥questions
root      30996  19605  0 14:25 pts/0    00:00:00 ps -f
$
$ kill 32040
$ ps -f
UID         PID   PPID  C STIME TTY         TIME CMD
root      19605  19603  0 Aug10 pts/0    00:00:34 bash
root      30089  19605  0 Aug20 pts/0    00:00:00 vi fileone
root      30425  19605  0 Aug20 pts/0    00:00:00 paste -d
➥fileone filetwo?
root      32040  19605  0 Aug22 pts/0    00:00:00 cat
root       1183  19605  0 Aug23 pts/0    00:00:00 awk -F:
➥questions
root      30998  19605  0 14:25 pts/0    00:00:00 ps -f
$
$ kill -9 32040
[3]- Killed
$ ps -f
UID         PID   PPID  C STIME TTY         TIME CMD
root      19605  19603  0 Aug10 pts/0    00:00:34 bash
root      30089  19605  0 Aug20 pts/0    00:00:00 vi fileone
root      30425  19605  0 Aug20 pts/0    00:00:00 paste -d
➥fileone filetwo?
root       1183  19605  0 Aug23 pts/0    00:00:00 awk -F:
➥questions
root      31000  19605  0 14:25 pts/0    00:00:00 ps -f
$
```

It is highly recommended that signal 15 (terminate) always be attempted before signal 9 (kill) is used. It is also highly recommended that you make certain there are no child processes beneath a process before killing it. If child processes exist, they should be removed first before proceeding further.

Just when you thought it couldn't get any more bloody, another command—killall—can be used to get rid of a process by name, versus PID. killall also has the ability (with the -w option) to wait for processes to die, and to require confirmation (with the -i option) before killing.

Background and Foreground

When a process is started, the default is for it to run in the foreground. In the foreground, it becomes the only job the user can work on and interaction is based upon completion of the job. For example, when a user runs ls -l, the display appears on his or her terminal, and he or she is unable to issue another command until ls has finished.

To run a process in the background, simply add an ampersand (&) to the end—this allows you to run more than one command at the same time. For example, the sleep command simply allows the process to wait a given number of seconds before anything else happens and it can be used by itself as a means of illustration:

```
$ sleep 90 &
[5] 31168
$
```

The number that appears in the brackets is equal to the number of jobs you currently have running in the background. The number following it (31168 in this case) is the process ID (PID) number of this job.

> **NOTE** The PID of the last job placed in the background can also be referenced as $!.

Placing the job in the background allows the user to continue working and starting other processes. If you *must* wait for a process to finish before starting another, the wait command, used with the PID of the process, can cease processing until the specified process finishes. For example

```
$ sleep 120 &
[5] 31175
```

```
$
$ wait 31175
```

The prompt does not return as long as 31175 remains a valid PID.

jobs

To see the jobs that you have running in the background, use the command
jobs:

```
$ jobs
[1]   Stopped              vi fileone  (wd: ~)
[2]-  Stopped              paste -d' fileone filetwo ' (wd: ~)
[4]+  Stopped              awk -F: questions (wd: ~)
[5]   Done              sleep 120
$
```

Jobs that were terminated (#3) do not appear, and jobs that have finished
(#5) will only show up one time (the next time jobs is run, #5 will not
appear). If the job is the most recent job that can run, or is running, a plus
sign (+) will follow the job number brackets. The next most recent job is
indicated by a minus sign (-). The wd information references the working
directory.

The -l option will add the PID numbers to the display, and the -p option
can be used to show only the PID numbers of the processes. The -n option
can be used to show only jobs that have been suspended.

fg

A job that is running in the background can be moved to the foreground
through the use of the fg command. The syntax for fg allows reference to a
job using a percent sign (%) and the job number. For example, the following
sequence starts a two-minute sleep sequence in the background, and then
moves it into the foreground:

```
$ sleep 120 &
[5] 31206
$
$ fg %5
sleep 120
```

Notice that the command being executed is echoed to the screen as it is
brought to the foreground. Where %5 was used, you can also reference the
two most recent jobs by %+ and %-, respectively. If you don't know the job
number (and can't remember to use the jobs command), you can refer to a

job by a portion of its name when using it after the percent sign and question mark (%?). For example

```
$ fg %?v
vi fileone
```

bg

The opposite of the foreground (**fg**) command is the background (**bg**) command. This allows you to take a job running in the foreground and move it to the background. Before you can do so, however, you must suspend the job (in order to get the prompt back).

Suspending a job is accomplished by pressing the keyboard sequence equal to the **susp** signal—Ctrl+Z, by default. When suspended, the job will stop and not start again until moved into the foreground or background. For example

```
$ sleep 180
{Ctrl+Z pressed}
[5]+    Stopped           sleep 180
$
```

Issuing the **bg** command will now move the job into the background and change the status to Running.

Changing Priorities

Course Objectives Covered

   4. Executing Commands at the Command Line (3036)

   5. Common Command Line Tasks (3036)

   18. Multiuser Processes and Multitasking in the Linux System (3036)

When a process starts, it does so at a default priority of zero. This puts it on an even keel with all other processes competing for attention from the CPU and other resources. The priorities for the processes can be changed through the use of two utilities, **nice** and **renice**.

nice

Processes can be started at different priorities using the **nice** utility. There are 40 different levels that **nice** can be used with (half negative and half positive), including

▶ 19 (lowest priority)

▶ 0 (default priority)

▶ -20 (highest priority)

A user can use only the negative numbers, meaning that the user can only lower a process and not raise it. You can also specify an increment (default is 10), with the **-n** option, that **nice** will use to change the priority over time. The root user (superuser) has the ability to give a negative increment, whereas all other users cannot.

Negative values are confined to use only by the superuser.   **NOTE**

If only the **nice** command is given, it will show the scheduling priority used by default.

renice

The **nice** utility can only be used when starting a process, and cannot be used with a process already running. That is where the **renice** utility comes into play. The utility uses the same priorities available to **nice** and is followed by one of three options:

▶ -p for PIDs

▶ -g for a process group

▶ -u for a group associated with a user

Working with grep and sed

Course Objectives Covered

4. Executing Commands at the Command Line (3036)

5. Common Command Line Tasks (3036)

8. Creating, Viewing, and Appending Files (3036)

12. Using `grep` to Search File Content (3036)

13. Understanding Regular Expressions (3036)

14. Introduction to Linux Text Editors (3036)

15. Using Command Line Editors to Edit (3036)

In this section, you'll learn about two important utilities used for working with files and output. The `grep` family of utilities is used to find values, and the `sed` utility can change the value of strings. Many of the utilities discussed previously will be used in the examples in this section.

The grep Family

The utility with the funny name (something common in Linux) is really an acronym for the function that it performs: "Globally look for Regular Expressions and then Print the results." In layman's terms, it is one of the most advanced search utilities you can use. In order to be proficient with it, however, you must understand what a regular expression is and how to use it in searching for matches to a query.

There are a number of rules for regular expressions, and these eight constitute the most important:

1. Any non-special character will be equal to itself.

2. Any special character will be equal to itself if preceded by a backslash (\).

3. The beginning of the line can be signified by an up caret (^), and the end of the line by a dollar sign ($).

4. A range can be expressed within brackets ([]).

5. An up caret (^) as the first character of a bracket will find values not matching entries within the brackets.

6. A period (.) can signify any single character.

7. An asterisk (*) stands for anything and everything.

8. Quotation marks are not always needed around search strings, but can be needed, and should be used as a general rule.

Table 3.4 offers some examples and elaboration on each of the preceding rules.

Using Regular Expressions

TABLE 3.4

RULE	CHARACTERS	SEARCH RESULT
1	c (any character without a special purpose)	Matches "c" anywhere within the line
1	apple	Matches "apple" anywhere within the line
2	$	Every line that has a carriage return (every line)
2	\$	Every line that contains a dollar sign
3	^c	Every line that begins with the character "c"
3	c$	Every line that ends with the character "c"
4	[apple]	Every line that has an "a", "p", "l", or "e" (because the brackets are interpreted as a range, the second occurrence of the "p" is completely ignored)
4	[a-z]	Any lowercase letter
4	[:lower:]	Any lowercase letter. Other special values that can be used include [:alnum;], [:alpha:], [:digit:], [:upper:]
5	[^a-z]	Everything but lowercase letters
5	[^0-9]	Anything but digits
6	c.	Two-letter words beginning with "c"
6	c..$	Three-letter words at the end of the line that begin with "c"
7	c*	Any word beginning with "c" (and including just "c")
8	"c*"	Any word beginning with "c" (and including just "c")
8	"c apple"	The letter "c" followed by a space and the word "apple"

To illustrate some of these operations using **grep**, assume there is a small file named **garbage** with the following contents:

```
I heard about the cats last night
and particularly the one cat that
ran away with all the catnip
```

If you want to find all occurrences of the word cat, the syntax becomes

```
$ grep "cat" garbage
I heard about the cats last night
and particularly the one cat that
ran away with all the catnip
$
```

In this instance, the three-letter sequence "cat" appears in every line. Not only is there "cat" in the second line, but also "cats" in the first, and "catnip" in the second—all matching the character sequence specified. If you are interested in "cat" but not "cats", the syntax becomes

```
$ grep "cat[^s]" garbage
and particularly the one cat that
ran away with all the catnip
$
```

This specifically removes a four-letter sequence of "cats" while finding all other three-letter sequences of "cat". If we truly were only interested in "cat" and no deviations thereof, there are a couple of other possibilities to explore. The first method would be to include a space at the end of the word and within the quotation mark:

```
$ grep "cat " garbage
and particularly the one cat that
$
```

This finds four-letter combinations equal to that given—meaning that nothing must follow. The only problem (and it is a big one) that if the word given is the last entry in a line of a large file, it would not necessarily be followed by a space, and thus not be returned in the display. Another possibility is to eliminate "s" and "n" from the return display:

```
$ grep "cat[^sn]" garbage
and particularly the one cat that
$
```

This accomplishes the task, but would not catch other words where the fourth character differed from an "s" or "n". To eliminate all fourth characters, it is better to use

```
$ grep "cat[^A-z]" garbage
I heard about the cats last night
```

```
and particularly the one cat that
ran away with all the catnip
$
```

This removes both the upper- and lowercase character sets.

Options for grep

The default action for **grep** is to find matches within lines to strings specified and print them. This can be useful for pulling out key data from a large display, for example, to find what port user **karen** is on:

NOTE

The who **command, used in the following example, merely shows who is logged on to the system.**

```
$ who | grep "karen"
karen     pts/2     Aug 21 13:42
$
```

From all the output of the **who** command, only those having the string "karen" are displayed. As useful as this is, there are times when the actual output is not as important as other items surrounding it. For example, if you don't care where **karen** is logged on, but want to know how many concurrent sessions she has, you can use the -c option:

```
$ who | grep -c "karen"
1
$
```

NOTE

You can also modify it to use a logical "or" (||) to tell you if the user has not come in yet if the operation fails:

```
    who | grep "karen" || echo "She has not come in yet"
```

The -c option is used to *count* the number of lines that would be displayed, but the display itself is suppressed. The -c option is basically performing the same task as this:

```
$ who | grep "karen" | wc -l
1
$
```

But the **-c** option is much quicker and more efficient by shaving an additional operation from the process. Other options that can be used with **grep** include the following:

- ▶ **-f** uses a file to find the strings to search for.

- ▶ **-H** includes in the display a default header of the filename from which the match is coming (if applicable) that appears at the beginning of each line, whereas **-h** prevents the header from appearing (the default).

- ▶ **-i** to ignore case. If this option did not exist, you would conceivably have to search a text file for "karen", "Karen", "KAREN", and all deviations thereof to find all matches.

- ▶ **-L** prints filenames that do not contain matches, whereas **-l** prints filenames that do contain matches.

- ▶ **-n** to show line numbers in the display. This differs from numbering the lines (which **nl** can do) because the numbers that appear denote the numbering of the lines in the existing file, not the output.

- ▶ **-q** quiets all output and is usually just used for testing return conditions.

- ▶ **-s** prevents any errors that occur from displaying error messages. This is useful if you do not want errors stating that you have inadequate permissions to view something when scanning all directories for a match.

- ▶ **-v** serves as the "not" option. It produces the opposite display of what not using it would. For example **who | grep -v karen** will show all users who are not **karen**.

- ▶ **-w** forces the found display to match the whole word. This provides the best solution to the earlier discussion of finding "cat" but no derivatives thereof.

- ▶ **-x** forces the found display to match the whole line.

The options can be mixed and matched, as desired, as long as one parameter does not cancel another. For example, it is possible to search for whole words and include header information by using either **-wH** or **-Hw**. You cannot, however, say that you want to see line numbers, and only see a final count (**-nc**) as the two options cancel each other out.

Some examples of how these options can be used follow. For the first, assume that we want to get a long list (**ls -l**) of the subdirectories beneath the current directory, and have no interest in actual filenames. Within the output of `ls -l`, the first field shows the permissions of the entry. If the entry is a file, the first character is "-", and if it is a directory, it is "d". Thus the command would be

```
ls -l | grep "^d"
```

If you want to know how many words are in the spelling dictionary, you can find out in a number of ways, including

```
wc -l /usr/share/dict/words
```

or

```
grep -c "." /usr/share/dict/words
```

Both of these generate a number based on the number of lines within the file. Suppose, however, you want to find out only how many words there are that start with the letter "c" (upper- or lowercase):

```
grep -ic "^c" /usr/share/dict/words
```

Or you want to find words that are in the last half of the alphabet:

```
grep -ic "^[n-z]" /usr/share/dict/words
```

The preceding example could also be expressed as   **NOTE**

```
grep -ci "^[^a-m]" /usr/share/dict/words
```

or

```
grep -vci "^[a-m]" /usr/share/dict/words
```

Suppose you have a number of different strings you want to find, not just one. You can search for them individually, requiring a number of operations, or you can place the search criteria in a text file, and input it into **grep** using the **-f** option. The following example assumes that the file **wishlist** already exists:

```
$ cat wishlist
dog
cat
fish
$
$ grep -if wishlist /usr/share/dict/words
```

Approximately 450 lines are displayed as all matches of all combinations of the three words are displayed. You can also continue one line to another to input multiple search sequences by using an uneven number of quotation marks to put the shell into input mode (**PS2** prompt):

```
$ grep -ic "dog
> cat
> fish" /usr/share/dict/words
457
$
```

fgrep

The first attempt to greatly enhance **grep** was **fgrep**—as in either "file grep" or "fast grep." This utility was created under the days of Unix and prior to Linux. It enhanced **grep** by adding the ability to search for more than one item at a time (something that **grep** has since gained with the **-f** option). The tradeoff for gaining the ability to search for multiple items was an inability to use regular expressions—never mind what the acronym stood for.

Adding the additional functionality to **grep**, and facing the inability to use regular expressions here, **fgrep** still exists but is rarely used in place of **grep**. In fact, one of the options added to **grep** is **-F**, which forces it to interpret the string as a simple string and work the same way **fgrep** would (the default action is **-G** for basic regular expressions).

NOTE   For most practical purposes, grep -F **is identical to** fgrep.

egrep

The second attempt to enhance **grep** was **egrep**—as in "extended grep." This utility combined the features of **grep** with those of **fgrep**—keeping the use of regular expressions. You can specify multiple values that you want to look for within a file (**-f**), on separate lines (using uneven numbers of quotation marks), or by separating with the pipe symbol (|). For example

```
$ cat names
Jan May
Bob Mays
Shannon Harris
Richard Harriss
William Harrisson
Jim Buck
$
```

```
$ egrep "Jim|Jan" names
Jan May
Jim Buck
$
```

It also added two new variables:

- ▶ ? to mean zero or one
- ▶ + to mean one or more

Assume you can't recall how Jan spells her last name—is it May or Mays? Not knowing if there really is an "s" on the end, you can ask for zero or one occurrences of this character:

```
$ egrep "Mays?" names
Jan May
Bob Mays
$
```

Even though there was no "s", Jan's entry was found—as were those that contained the character in question. With the plus sign (+), you know that at least one iteration of the character exists, but are not certain if there are more. For example, does Shannon spell her last name with one "s" or two?

```
$ egrep "Harris+" names
Shannon Harris
Richard Harriss
William Harrisson
$
```

To look for values of greater length than one character, you can enclose text within parentheses "( )". For example, if you want to find Harriss and Harrisson (not Harris), the "on" becomes an entity with zero or more occurrences:

```
$ egrep "Harriss(on)?" names
Richard Harriss
William Harrisson
$
```

Since the creation of egrep—again in the days of Unix—most of the features have been worked into the version of grep included with Linux. Using the -E option with grep, you can get most of the functionality of egrep.

NOTE **For most practical purposes,** grep -E **is identical to** egrep.

sed

The name **sed** is an acronym for "stream editor," and it is as accurate a description as any possible. The utility accepts input (text) to flow through it like a river or stream. It edits that text and makes changes to it based on the parameters it has been given. The syntax for **sed** is

```
sed {options} {commands} filename
```

The number of options is very limited, but the commands are more numerous. These are the accepted options:

- ▶ -e to specify a command to execute
- ▶ -f to specify a file in which to find commands to execute
- ▶ -n to run in quiet mode

As mentioned, the commands are plentiful and the best way to understand them is to examine a few examples. One of the simplest commands to give it, or any editor, is to substitute one string for another. This is accomplished with the **s** (for substitute) command, followed by a slash, the string to find, a slash, the string to replace the first value with, and another slash. The entire entry should be placed within single quotes:

```
's/old value/new value/'
```

Thus an example would be

```
$ echo I think the new neighbors are getting a new air pump |
➥sed 's/air/heat/'
```

And the output displayed becomes

```
I think the new neighbors are getting a new heat pump
```

The string "air" was replaced by the string "heat". Text substitution is one of the simplest features of **sed**, and also what it is used for most of the time, for it is here that its power and features truly excel.

It is important to recognize that sed **is not an interactive editor. When you give it the commands to execute, it does so without further action on the user's part.**   **NOTE**

By default, **sed** works by scanning each line in successive order. If it does not find a match after searching the entire line, it moves to the next. If it finds a match for the search text within the line, it makes the change and immediately moves on to examine the next line. This can provide some unexpected results. For example, suppose you want to change the word "new" to "old":

```
$ echo I think the new neighbors are getting a new air pump |
➥sed 's/new/old/'
```

The output becomes

```
I think the old neighbors are getting a new air pump
```

The second occurrence of the search phrase is not changed because **sed** finished with the line after finding the first match. If you want all occurrences within the line to be changed, you must make the search *global* by using a "g" at the end of the command:

```
$ echo I think the new neighbors are getting a new air pump |
➥sed 's/new/old/g'
```

The output becomes

```
I think the old neighbors are getting an old air pump
```

The global parameter makes **sed** continue to search the remainder of the line, after finding a match, until the end of the line is reached. This handles multiple occurrences of the same phrase, but you must go in a different direction if you want to change more than one value.

This can be accomplished on the command line with the -e option used to flag every command. For example

```
$ echo this line is shorter | sed -e 's/line/phrase/' -e
➥'s/short/long/'
```

The output becomes

```
this phrase is longer
```

The second method is to place all the substitution criteria in a file and then summon the file with the -f option. The following example assumes the file wishlist2 already exists:

```
$ cat wishlist2
s/line/phrase/
s/short/long/
$
$ echo this line is shorter | sed -f wishlist2
this phrase is longer
$
```

Both produce the same results, but using a file to hold your commands makes it exponentially easier to change criteria if you need to, keep track of the operations you are performing, and rerun the commands again at a later time.

NOTE **It is important to understand that when there are multiple operations, sed completes all of the first one first before starting the second. It completes all of the second—for the entire file, line, and so on—before starting the third, and so on.**

Technically (but this is not recommended), you could also complete the same operation by using semicolons after each substitution, or going into input mode through an uneven number of single quotes:

```
$ echo this line is shorter | sed 's/line/phrase/;
➥s/short/long/'
```

or

```
$ echo this line is shorter | sed '
> s/line/phrase/
> s/short/long/'
```

Restricting Lines

If you have a large file, you may not want to edit the entire file, but only selected lines. As with everything, there are a number of ways you can go about addressing this issue. The first method would be to specify a search clause and only make substitutions when the search phrase is found. The search phrase must precede the operation and be enclosed within slashes:

```
/search phrase/ {operation}
```

For example, assume you have the following file named **tuesday**:

```
one     1
two     1
three    1
three    1
two     1
one     1
```

You want the end result displayed to be

```
one     1
two     2
three    3
three    3
two     2
one     1
```

In this case, the search should be for the word *two*. If it is found, any 1s should be converted to 2. Likewise, there should be a search for the word *three* with any 1s following converted to 3:

```
$ cat wishlist3
/two/  s/1/2/
/three/  s/1/3/
$
$ sed  -f wishlist3 tuesday
one 1
two 2
three 3
three 3
two 2
one 1
$
```

By design, sed changes only the values displayed, not the values in the original file. To keep the results of the change, you must redirect output to a file, like this   NOTE

```
    sed  -f wishlist3 tuesday > wednesday
```

Sometimes the actions specified should take place not on the basis of a search, but purely on the basis of the line number. For example, you may only want to change the first line of a file, the first 10 lines, or any other combination. When that is the case, you can specify a range of lines using this syntax:

```
First line,last line
```

To change all non-"one"s to that value in the first five lines, use this example:

```
$ cat wishlist4
1,5 s/two/one/
1,5 s/three/one
$
$ sed -f wishlist4 tuesday
one 1
one 1
one 1
one 1
one 1
one 1
$
```

Printing

The default operation for **sed** is simply to print. If you gave no parameters at all, an entire file would be displayed without any editing truly occurring. The one caveat to this is that **sed** must always have an option or command. If you simply gave the name of a file following **sed** and nothing more, it would misinterpret it as a command.

You can give a number of lines for it to display, however, followed with the **q** command (for quit), and see the contents of any file. For example

```
sed 75000q /usr/share/dict/words
```

will display all of the **words** file because the number of lines within the file is far less than 75,000. If you only want to see the first 60, you can use

```
sed 60q /usr/share/dict/words
```

The antithesis, or opposite, of the default action is the **-n** option. This prevents lines from displaying that normally would. For example

```
sed -n 75000q /usr/share/dict/words
```

will display nothing. Although it may seem foolish for a tool designed to display data to have an option that prevents displaying data, it can actually be a marvelous thing. To put it into perspective, though, you must know that the **p** command exists and is used to force a print (the default action).

In an earlier example, the file **tuesday** had numbers changed to match their alpha counterpart. Some of the lines in the file were already correct, and did not need to be changed. If the lines aren't being changed, do you really need to see their output—or are you only interested in the lines being changed? If the latter is the case, the following will display only those entries:

```
$ cat wishlist5
/two/ s/1/2/p
/three/ s/1/3/p
$
$ sed -nf wishlist5 tuesday
two 2
three 3
three 3
two 2
$
```

To print only lines 200 to 300 of a file (no actual editing taking place), the command becomes

```
sed -n '200,300p' /usr/share/dict/words
```

Deleting

The **d** command is used to specify deletion. As with all **sed** operations, the line is deleted from the display only, and not from the original file. The syntax is always

```
{the specification} d
```

Use this example to delete all lines that have the string "three":

```
$ sed '/three/ d' tuesday
one 1
two 1
two 1
one 1
$
```

To delete lines 1 through 3, try this:

```
$ sed '1,3 d' tuesday
three 1
two 1
one 1
$
```

> **NOTE** In all cases, the d command forces the deletion of the entire line. You cannot use this command to delete a portion of a line or a word. If you want to delete a word, substitute the word for nothing:

```
sed 's/word//'
```

Appending Text

Strings can be appended to a display using the **a** command. Append always places the string at the end of the specification—after the other lines. For example, to place a string equal to "The End" as the last line of the display, the command would be

```
$ sed '$a\
The End\' tuesday
one 1
two 1
three 1
three 1
two 1
one 1
The End
$
```

The dollar sign ($) is used to specify the end of the file, while the backslashes (\) are used to add a carriage return. If the dollar sign is left out of the command, the text is appended after every line:

```
$ sed 'a\
The End\' tuesday
one 1
The End
two 1
The End
three 1
The End
three 1
The End
two 1
The End
one 1
The End
$
```

If you want the string appended following a certain line number, add the line number to the command:

```
$ sed '3a\
Not The End\' tuesday
one 1
two 1
three 1
Not The End
three 1
two 1
one 1
$
```

In place of the append, you can use the insert (i) command to place strings before the given line versus after:

```
$ sed '3i\
Not The End\' tuesday
one 1
two 1
Not The End
three 1
three 1
two 1
one 1
$
```

Other Commands

There are a few other commands that can be used with **sed** to add additional functionality. The following list shows some of these commands:

▶ **b** can be used to branch execution to another part of the file specifying what commands to carry out.

▶ **c** is used to change one line to another. Whereas "s" will substitute one string for another, "c" changes the entire line:

```
$ sed '/three/ c\
four 4' tuesday
one 1
two 1
four 4
four 4
two 1
one 1
$
```

▶ r can be used to read an additional file and append text from a second file into the display of the first.

▶ w is used to write to a file. Instead of using the redirection (> `filename`), you can use w `filename`:

```
$ cat wishlist6
/two/ s/two/one/
/three/ s/three/one/
w friday
$
sed -f wishlist6 tuesday
one 1
one 1
one 1
one 1
one 1
one 1
$
$ cat friday
one 1
one 1
one 1
one 1
one 1
one 1
$
```

▶ y is used to translate one character space into another.

A Word to the Wise

When working with **sed** and performing more than one change, substitution, or deletion operation, you must be *very* careful about the order that you specify operations to take place in. Using the example of the **tuesday** file used earlier, assume that the numbering is off. You want to change all *ones* to *two*, all *twos* to *three*, and all *threes* to *four*. Here's one way to approach it, with the results it generates:

```
$ cat wishlist7
s/one/two/
s/two/three/
s/three/four/
$
$ sed -f wishlist7 tuesday
four 1
```

```
four 1
four 1
four 1
four 1
four 1
$
```

The results are neither what was expected, or what was wanted. Because **sed** goes through the entire file and does the first operation, it would have first changed the file to

```
two  1
two  1
three 1
three 1
two  1
two  1
```

After that, **sed** will go through the file again, to perform the second operation. This causes the file to change to

```
three 1
three 1
three 1
three 1
three 1
three 1
```

When it comes time for the third iteration through the file, every line is now the same and will be changed—completely defeating the purpose. This is one of the reasons that **sed**'s changing the display only and not the original file is a blessing.

In order to solve the problem, you need only realize what is transpiring, and arrange the order of operations to prevent this from happening:

```
$ cat wishlist8
s/three/four/
s/two/three/
s/one/two/
$
$ sed -f wishlist8 tuesday
two  1
three 1
four 1
four 1
```

```
three 1
one 1
$
```

Other Useful Utilities

A number of other useful text utilities are included with Linux. Some of these have limited usefulness and are intended only for a specific purpose, but knowing of their existence and purpose can make your life with Linux considerably easier.

In alphabetical order, the additional utilities are as follows:

▶ awk—Often used in conjunction with sed, awk is a utility/language/tool with an enormous amount of flexibility for manipulating text. The GNU implementation of the utility is called gawk (as in GNU awk) but is truly the same.

▶ cmp—Compares two files and reports if they are the same, or where the first difference occurs in terms of line number and character.

▶ comm—Looks at two files and reports what they have in common.

▶ diff—Allows you to see the differences between two files.

▶ diff3—Similar to diff, but works with more than two files.

▶ perl—A programming language useful for working with text.

▶ regexp—A utility that can compare a regular expression against a string to see if there is a match. If there is a match, a value of 1 is returned and if there is no match, a value of 0 is returned.

Working with vi

Course Objectives Covered

8. Creating, Viewing, and Appending Files (3036)

14. Introduction to Linux Text Editors (3036)

15. Using Command Line Editors to Edit (3036)

16. Using Desktop Editors to Edit Files in the Linux System (3036)

When vi came into being, it was a revolutionary application. This was in the early days of Unix, and the editors that came with the operating system were incredibly crude and difficult to manage. Many times, you could not see the line you were working on (as with **ed**); instead, you would specify the line, specify the change, and then ask to see the line printed to tell if your change was correct.

The **vi** editor (pronounced "v—eye") was created by a graduate student named Bill Joy (later to become famous as one of the founders of Sun Microsystems). He created an editor that was *visual*—hence the "v"—and *interactive*—hence the "i". With this editor, you can see the lines in the file, and see the changes being made *as you make them.*

By today's standards, **vi** is now considered to be crude—who wants to work with such an application when such entities as WordPerfect and Microsoft Word exist? The answer is that you *must* know the basics of this editor because it is a powerful administrators' tool. The following points are among its benefits:

- ▶ Every version of Linux ships with this editor—you can be assured that it will reside on whatever machine you use.

- ▶ It has very low overhead. When a system is damaged and configuration files must be modified before it can be brought up, you are often prevented from starting large applications. This minimal overhead is possible because **vi** does not have the buttons and scrollbars common in GUI (graphical user interface) applications.

- ▶ Though considered a "screen" editor, **vi** also incorporates features from "line"-type and "command"-style editors.

The learning curve can be steep when first starting with **vi**. Lacking are the function keys and other niceties. In their place are mnemonics ("u", for example, stands for undo, and "o" for open a line, and so on).

Starting vi

You start **vi** by typing **vi** on the command line along with the name of a file to create (if it does not already exist) or edit (if it does already exist). If the file you want to work on is in a directory other than your present working directory, you can supply the full path to the file as well.

The following example starts **vi** in the current directory to create a file named **first**:

```
$ vi first
```

Because the file does not already exist, this brings up a blank screen with tildes (~) used to signify that you are working in the file that is currently empty. There is one tilde for each blank line on the screen. The information at the bottom of the screen gives the filename and the fact that it is a "New File."

If the file does exist, the lines of the file are shown (and any blanks within the screen are indicated by tildes). The bottom of the screen now reports the name of the file and the number of lines and characters.

Regardless of whether the file is new or existing, vi always starts automatically in command mode. This means it is waiting for you to tell it to do something. You cannot just start typing away or begin making changes— you must first tell it what to do.

Navigation

The easiest commands involve navigation. Table 3.5 lists the navigation keys that can be used in vi.

TABLE 3.5   vi **Navigation Keys**

KEY	RESULT
-	Move to the first character of the previous line
$	Move to the last position of the current line
(	Move backward one sentence
)	Move forward one sentence
{	Move to the beginning of the previous paragraph
}	Move to the beginning of the next paragraph
^	Move to the first character of the current line (ignoring spaces)
+	Move to the first character of the next line
0	Move to the beginning of the current line
b	Move backward to the beginning of the previous word
B	Move backward to the beginning of the previous word, ignoring symbols and punctuation
e	Move to the end of the next word
E	Move to the end of the next word, ignoring symbols and punctuation
ENTER\ RETURN	Move to the beginning of the next line

Table 3.5 Continued

KEY	RESULT
h	Move left one space
j	Move down one line
k	Move up one line
l	Move right one space
w	Move to the beginning of the next word
W	Move to the beginning of the next word, ignoring symbols and punctuation
G	Move to the last line of the file
xG	"Goto" line number x

The last entry of the table signifies that a line number can be used in conjunction with "G" to move to that line: For example, **5G** will move the cursor from wherever it happens to be in the file to line 5. The ability to use numbers with commands is a constant throughout all of **vi**—if you precede a command by a number, it is interpreted as meaning you want to do something a number of times equal to that number. For example, the command **10h** will move the cursor 10 spaces to the left.

The arrow keys can also be used for navigation, but only if they are mapped correctly on the terminal. In order for them to function properly, the right arrow must send the same key sequence as pressing l would, the left arrow must send the same key sequence as pressing h would, and so on.

Changing Text

When you reach a word to be changed, there are an almost endless number of ways to make the change. In the earlier table, the letter "w" was used to signify a word when discussing navigation. Using similar mnemonics, it can be combined with "c" for change and thus the command becomes **cw**.

This tells the editor that you intend to change the word, so it removes the current word from view, and places the editor in "insert" mode. You now enter a new word, and then press Esc to exit out of insert mode and enter command mode once again.

Whenever you want to exit insert mode, regardless of the method used to place you into it, you always press Esc to return to command mode.

NOTE

There are a number of combinations that the **change** command can be used in conjunction with. Table 3.6 offers a synopsis of the possibilities.

TABLE 3.6	vi **Change Text Combinations**
KEY SEQUENCE	**RESULT**
c$	Change from here to the end of the line
c)	Change from here to the end of the sentence
c^	Change from here to the beginning of the line
c}	Change the remainder of the paragraph
3cw	Change the next three words
r	Replace an individual character
R	Go to "Replace" mode—overwriting exiting text with new text

Notice that so many of the choices in Table 3.6 begin with the current cursor position and making changes from that point to the beginning or end of the line. If you need to change an entire line, regardless of where the cursor resides within the line, you can use the command **cc**. In a similar vein, the command **C** is the same as **c$**; selecting all text from the current cursor position to the end of the line.

Saving Files

After a change has been made, and you are finished with the editor, it is time to save the file. Just like everything in **vi**, there are numerous ways to accomplish this. Most of the ways require entering command mode, and this is accomplished by pressing the colon key (:) and typing another command.

> **NOTE** As a matter of history, the use of the colon to precede a command is a carryover from an earlier editor: **ex**.

You can save the file, under its current name, by typing

:w

This saves (writes) the file, but leaves you in the editor. To exit the editor, you then enter

```
:q
```

You are then returned to the Linux command-line prompt, having quit the editor. This sequence is useful if you want to write your changes out several times prior to quitting, as you can always enter `:w` and continue with edits.

If you want to write and quit at the same time, however, you can combine the operation into a single command:

```
:wq
```

This will write the file and quit the editor. A shortcut to this operation (which makes no mnemonic sense whatsoever) is to enter **ZZ**, which will also write and quit.

If you want to save the file by a different name (for purposes such as keeping the original intact), you can use the `:w` syntax and follow it by the new name. It is worth pointing out at this point that if you make *any* changes to a file, the default operation of **vi** is to not let you exit the editor until you save the changes. If you try to leave by using `:q`, you will be notified that changes have been made with an error message:

```
No write since last change (use ! to override)
```

The error message spells out what must be done to get around the default. If you made changes that you do not want to save—having clobbered too much text to undo, changed your mind, and so on—you can exit the file and leave it in the state of the last save operation with this command:

```
:q!
```

Saving a Portion of a File

Not only can you save the entire file, but **vi** allows you to save only part of a file by specifying the line numbers you want to write. By now you've probably figured out that every line can be referenced by a number, and this operation requires using this syntax:

```
:first_line, last_linew FileName
```

Pay special attention to the "w" attached to the last line number. This must be there to identify the operation as a write request. Two wildcards can be used for either line number specification:

▶ $ to signify the last line in the file

▶ . to signify the current line

Some examples of commands to save only a portion of the file are shown in Table 3.7.

TABLE 3.7	Examples of Saving Portions of a File
KEY SEQUENCE	**RESULT**
`:.,12w newfile`	Saves lines from where the cursor currently is to line 12 in a file named `newfile`
`:2, 5w newfile`	Saves lines 2 to 5 in a file named `newfile`
`:12, $w newfile`	Saves lines from 12 to the end of the file in a file named `newfile`

Inserting and Deleting

Changing existing text is simple enough if there is already text there. Inserting, however, allows you to add to the text already there, and is the mode you want to go into when starting a new file. When working within a line, you can choose to insert or append, as well as open a new line above or below the current one. Table 3.8 lists the possibilities.

TABLE 3.8	Keys to Enter Input Mode
KEY SEQUENCE	**RESULT**
a	Inserts text after cursor (append)
A	Inserts text at the end of the current line
i	Inserts text before cursor
o	Opens a new line below the cursor
O	Opens a new line above the cursor
s	Removes the current letter and places you in insert mode— this is known as the "substitute" command
S	Substitute mode for the whole line

Regardless of the method by which you enter insert mode, the means by which you leave this mode is by pressing Esc.

Deleting text is accomplished by pressing x to delete a single character. It can also be preceded by a number to indicate how many characters to delete. For example:

`16x`

will delete the next 16 characters. To delete the character before the cursor, substitute the X command in place of x.

If you want to delete something other than characters, you can use the **d** (delete) command with a sequence indicating what you want to delete. Table 3.9 lists the possibilities.

Key Sequences for Deletion **TABLE 3.9**

KEY SEQUENCE	RESULT
d$	Deletes from here to the end of the line
d)	Deletes the remainder of the sentence
d}	Deletes the remainder of the paragraph
d0	Deletes from here to the beginning of the line
db	Deletes the previous word
dl	Deletes a letter
7dl	Deletes seven letters
dw	Deletes a word
7dw	Deletes four words—dw will not only delete the word, but also deletes the space after the word. To delete only to the end of a word, use de instead.

Navigating Screens

All of the discussion thus far has been about changing text that appears on the screen. The vi editor shows 23 lines within a screen. If your file exceeds 23 lines, as a great many will, you have a number of screens that you can work with. For an analogy, think of viewing screens one at a time when using more or less commands.

Table 3.10 shows the methods of navigating between multiple screens.

TABLE 3.10	Key Sequences for Moving Between Screens

KEY SEQUENCE	RESULT
Ctrl+F	Move forward one screen
Ctrl+B	Move backward one screen
Ctrl+D	Move forward one-half screen
Ctrl+U	Move backward one-half screen
Ctrl+E	Scroll the screen up one line
Ctrl+Y	Scroll the screen down one line
H	Move to the top line of the screen
L	Move to the last line of the screen
M	Move to the middle line of the screen

NOTE   You can use numbers before each of these operations as well. 7H moves the cursor seven lines below the top line on the screen, and 7L moves the cursor seven lines above the last line on the screen.

Searching for Text

Another method of moving through the file besides using navigational keys is to perform a search. You can search the file for string values, and the screen containing the first occurrence of that string will become your current view of the file.

Searches are initiated by pressing the slash key (/) and entering the string value to search for. As you enter the search text sequence, the editor will move through the file looking for a match.

When you have entered the search string, press Enter to signify that you are done. All searches automatically begin at the top of the document. To move the cursor to the next instance, use the n command (for next). To move backward through the file, use the N command.

Two characters can be used with the search to specify where the located text must reside:

▶ ^ to signify that the text must be at the start of the line

▶ $ to signify that the text must be at the end of the line

For example, to find the string "is" only if these two characters are the last two characters on the line, the search syntax would be

`/is$`

You can also use many of the wildcard options present in **grep** and similar utilities:

- ▶ \ to ignore the following character's special value

- ▶ [] to find multiple values

- ▶ \< to find matches at the beginning of a word

If you need to find values and change them, you can do so using the substitute command (**s**), with syntax that resembles **sed**:

`:first_line, last_line s/old string/new string/`

For example, to change all occurrences of "speed" to "pace" in lines between the first and thousandth, the command is

`:1,1000 s/speed/pace/`

Copying Text

Text can be copied into the buffer to be reused from one part of the file to another or moved. As simplistic as it sounds, when you copy text, you leave the original where it is and make a duplicate elsewhere. However, when you move text, you take it from one location in the file and place it in another. Whether you are copying or moving, the **p** command is always the counterpart of the operation; standing for print/put/place, it completes the operation.

Unfortunately, the "c" mnemonic had already been used for change when **vi** was being created and there weren't a whole lot of other good choices left. Given that, Bill Joy chose to use **y** for **yank**. Table 3.11 shows a series of key sequences that can be used for copying text.

Key Sequences for Copying Text	**TABLE 3.11**

KEY SEQUENCE	RESULT
y$	Yanks from here to the end of the line
y)	Yanks the remainder of the sentence
y}	Yanks the remainder of the paragraph

Table 3.11   Continued

KEY SEQUENCE	RESULT
y0	Yanks from here to the beginning of the line
yb	Yanks the previous word or part of a word
yl	Yanks a single letter
7yl	Yanks the next seven letters
yw	Yanks a single word
7yw	Yanks the next seven words
yy	Yanks an entire line
7yy	Yanks seven lines
Y	The same as y$

To do a copy operation, you move to the desired location in the file where the text should go, and then use the **p** command. To do a move operation, delete the text after yanking it, and then move to the desired location and use the **p** command to place the file where you want it.

Other Operations

If there is one single **vi** command you should commit to memory, it is **u**—the undo command. This command will undo the previous action, and only the previous action. It has a counterpart—**U**—which will do all previous actions to the current line. It is important to note, however, that **U** will only buffer changes for one line (the current one); this prevents you from making changes to four lines and then moving to the first and undoing them.

> **NOTE** If you mess up four lines and cannot put back in the first line what was changed, your only salvation is to exit the file without saving.

So many of the operations discussed in this section revolve around line numbers—you can move to a particular line by specifying its number, you can save only specific lines, and so on—that it is often helpful to have the lines numbered as you view them. Turning on line numbering in **vi** is accomplished by first going to command mode with a colon (:)(sometimes called colon mode; this will move the cursor to the bottom of the screen), and then entering the command **set number** followed by Enter. This will turn on line numbering.

The numbers appear only within the editor, just as if you were viewing them with the `nl` command, and are not saved out with the file. Incidentally, `set number` can be abbreviated as `set nu`. If you only want to see the number of the line you are currently on, you can press Ctrl+G, and the line number (as well as the total number of lines within the file) will appear at the bottom of the screen.

If you need to run an external command while in the editor, you can do so by using the syntax

`:!{command}`

For example, to see a list of files in the current directory while working in `vi`, the command would be

`:!ls -l`

This will show the listing, then prompt you to press Return (Enter) to go back to the file you are working within.

If you need to copy the contents of another file into this one, you can do so by using the syntax

`:r {filename}`

For example, to bring the contents of a file named `first` into this file, the command is

`:r first`

This inserts the text from the other file directly into the location in this file where the cursor resides.

Lab Exercise 3-1: Starting and Stopping a Service

In this exercise, you will start a service, and then kill it.

Complete the following steps:

1. To start the **yes** service and have it output to a file in the background, type the following:

   ```
   yes >/dev /null &
   ```

   This starts the service and directs it to the file **/dev/null**. The "&" tells the system to put the process in the background. This also returns the PID (process ID number).

2. To verify that the service is running, type the following:

   ```
   ps ax
   ```

   This returns a list of the services running. Near the bottom of the list, you see the PID, and under the command column, you see **yes**.

3. At the prompt, type the following:

   ```
   kill -9 [PID #]
   ```

4. Verify that the process has been killed by typing the following:

   ```
   ps ax
   ```

5. Look for the PID in the list. If it is not there, it worked!

Summary

This chapter covered a great deal of material as it examined what you need to know to understand the basics of GNU and Unix commands. All the following chapters assume that you understand the tools and utilities discussed here and will build upon them. The next chapter looks at the Linux filesystem.

Metacharacter Summary

Table 3.12 lists the metacharacters that appeared in this chapter, and their purpose.

Metacharacters Used in GNU and Unix Commands   **TABLE 3.12**

METACHARACTER	PURPOSE
' '	Cancel the special meaning of anything but the backquote
" "	Cancel the special meaning of most characters
$	Treat the next string as a variable
$( )	Allow a command to be treated as a variable
*	Any number of characters
;	Separate dissimilar commands
?	Any single character
[ ]	Any of the enclosed characters
\	Treat the next character literally
` `	Execute the enclosed command
|	Allow one command's output to be the next command's input
<	Input redirection
<<	"Here"
>	Output redirection
>>	Output append

Command Summary

Table 3.13 lists the commands that were discussed in this chapter.

TABLE 3.13	GNU and Unix Commands

UTILITY	DEFAULT PURPOSE
&	Start a process in the background
bg	Move a job to the background
cat	Display the contents of a file
cd	Change from the current directory to another
cp	Copy a file or directory
cut	Extract a field from each line of a file
dd	Copy files between media
egrep	Originally combined features of grep and fgrep with new possibilities; can now be emulated with grep -E
fg	Move a job to the foreground
fgrep	Originally offered features not found in grep, but can now be emulated with grep -F
find	Locate a file based on given criteria
fmt	Allows you to format the output to fit the desired display
grep	Displays lines that contain the given string
head	Display the beginning lines of a file
jobs	Display a list of jobs running in the background
join	Combine columns from two files into a single display
kill	End a process
killall	End several processes
ls	List files and directories on the system
mkdir	Make directories
mv	Rename/move a file or directory
nice	Start a process at a priority other than the default
nl	Number the lines of a file
paste	Put the contents of two files in a single display
ps	Show the running processes
pstree	Graphically depict the relationship between processes

Table 3.13   Continued

UTILITY	DEFAULT PURPOSE
pwd	Display the current directory—always in absolute format
renice	Change the priority of a running process
rm	Remove files and directories
rmdir	Remove empty directories
sed	Allows text to be changed before being displayed
sort	Sorts the lines of the file
stty	Show the settings for the terminal
tac	Display the contents of a file in reverse order
tail	Display the last lines of a file
tee	Send output to default and to a file
top	Show and monitor system information and processes
touch	Change the times associated with a file
tr	Translate one set of characters into another
wait	Suspend further processing until another process completes
wc	Count the number of words, lines, and characters/bytes within a file
xargs	Pass the output of one command into another

CHAPTER 4

Working with Files

This chapter focuses on working with files and the Linux filesystem. This chapter covers the following course objectives:

1. Managing File Permissions and Ownership (3036)
2. Describe Basic Linux User Security Features (3037)
3. Secure Files and Directories with Permissions (3037)
4. Implement and Monitor Enterprise Security Policies (3037)
5. Set Up and Configure Disk Quotas (3037)
6. Use ACLS for Advanced Access Control (3038)

Working with File Permissions and Ownership

Course Objectives Covered

1. Managing File Permissions and Ownership (3036)
2. Describe Basic Linux User Security Features (3037)
3. Secure Files and Directories with Permissions (3037)
4. Implement and Monitor Enterprise Security Policies (3037)

Permissions determine who can and cannot access files and directories, as well as what type of access the permission holders have. The first 10 characters of an `ls -l` listing of any entity resemble the following:

```
-rwxrwxrwx
```

The first character identifies the type of entity: "-" for a standard file, "d" for directory, "b" for a block device (such as a tape drive), "c" for a character device, "l" for a link, or "p" for a pipe. The remaining nine characters can be broken into three groups, as shown in Figure 4.1.

FIGURE 4.1
Permissions
divide into three
sections.

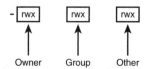

When a user attempts to access a file, the first check is to determine if the user is the owner of the file. If so, the first set of permissions apply. If the user is not the owner, a check is completed to see if the user is a member of the group owning the file. If he or she is a member of the group, the second set of permissions applies. If he or she is not the owner of the file, and not a member of the owning group, the third set of permissions applies.

Standard Permissions

The available permissions that can be assigned to an entity—either owner, group, or other—are

▶ r—To read a file. This is the only permission needed to copy a file as well. When applied to a directory, it grants the ability to read (see) the files within the directory.

▶ w—To write a file. Writing allows you to change the contents, modify, and overwrite files. When this permission is applied to a directory, you can delete and move files within the directory (even if you don't specifically have write permission to an individual file).

▶ x—To execute the file if it contains scripts or can otherwise be run by the system. On a directory, it allows you to change to a specific directory. When applied in conjunction with read on a directory, it allows you to search the directory.

▶ -(dash)—Indicates the absence of a permission. For example, r-x would indicate that the user can read and execute, but cannot write.

Thus, to summarize the 10 fields in the permissions, they are

1. What type of entity (file, directory, and so on)

2. Whether the owner can read

3. Whether the owner can write

4. Whether the owner can execute

5. Whether the group can read

6. Whether the group can write

7. Whether the group can execute

8. Whether others (not group or owner) can read

9. Whether others can write

10. Whether others can execute

Numerical values can be associated with these permissions as well:

PERMISSION	NUMERICAL VALUE
r	4
w	2
x	1
-	0

The numerical values make it possible to add a set of permissions and make them easier to understand. For example, if a file has permissions for the user of "rwx", the numerical value becomes $4(r)+2(w)+1(x)=7$. The full set of permissions for the file can be computed as shown in Figure 4.2.

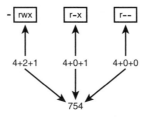

FIGURE 4.2
Numerical values for the file's permissions.

Table 4.1 extrapolates on the numerical conversion and outlines some of the 100+ possible values for a file's permissions.

Examples of Permission Values for Files   **TABLE 4.1**

NUMERICAL VALUE	PERMISSIONS
1	--------x
2	-------w-

Table 4.1   Continued

NUMERICAL VALUE	PERMISSIONS
3	- - - - - - -wx
4	- - - - - -r- -
5	- - - - - -r-x
6	- - - - - -rw-
7	- - - - - -rwx
10	- - - - -x- - -
11	- - - - -x- -x
22	- - - -w- -w-
33	- - - -wx-wx
55	- - -r-xr-x
77	- - -rwxrwx
100	- -x- - - - -
101	- -x- - - - -x
111	- -x- -x- -x
222	-w- -w- -w-
311	-wx- -x- -x
322	-wx-w- -w-
400	r- - - - - - -
444	r- -r- -r- -
511	r-x- -x- -x
544	r-xr- -r- -
644	rw-r- -r- -
666	rw-rw-rw-
755	rwxr-xr-x
777	rwxrwxrwx

The default permissions for all newly created files are 666 (rw-rw-rw-), and for directories 777 (rwxrwxrwx). This number is altered, however, by the presence of a variable known as umask. The umask variable is equal to a number that is subtracted from the default permissions to arrive at the permissions that apply per user.

To see the value of umask, simply enter the command at a prompt:

```
$ umask
022
$
```

With a **umask** value of 022, the permissions assigned to new files now becomes 644 (rw-r--r--), and for directories 755 (rwxr-xr-x), as shown in Figure 4.3.

```
Files:                    Directories:
666 -rw-rw-rw-            777 drwxrwxrwx
-022 -----w--w-          -022 -----w--w-
===========              ===========
644 -rw-r--r--            755 drwxr-xr-x
```

FIGURE 4.3
Computing default permissions on newly created entities after subtracting the value of umask.

You can change the value of **umask** by specifying a different value on the command line (**umask 15**, for example), and this value will be used for the session. The variable is defined in the login information, and will revert to its normal value at the beginning of each session.

Changing Values

To change permissions on a file or directory, you can use the **chmod** utility. The arguments the utility will accept can be either numeric or symbolic. For example, to change the permissions of a file to allow all to read and write to it, you could write this:

```
$ ls -l turbo
-rw-r--r-- 1  root    root              14  Sep 6 22:42
➥turbo
$ chmod 666 turbo
$ ls -l turbo
-rw-rw-rw- 1  root    root              14  Sep 6 22:42
➥turbo
$
```

In symbolic format, "u" signifies user, "g" is group, and "o" is other. You can choose to add to existing permissions:

```
$ ls -l turbo
-rw-r--r-- 1  root    root              14  Sep 6 22:42
➥turbo
$ chmod go+w turbo
$ ls -l turbo
```

```
-rw-rw-rw-  1  root    root              14  Sep 6 22:42
➥turbo
$
```

Or you can specify exact permissions:

```
$ ls -l turbo
-rw-r--r--  1  root    root              14  Sep 6 22:42
➥turbo
$ chmod ugo=rw turbo
$ ls -l turbo
-rw-rw-rw-  1  root    root              14  Sep 6 22:42
➥turbo
$
```

The plus sign (+) is used to add to the existing permissions, whereas the minus sign (-) removes from existing permissions. The equal sign (=) ignores existing permissions and sets the value to whatever is specified. A -c option causes chmod to echo the names of files that are changed, whereas -f cancels the display of any error messages.

In conjunction with chmod, the chown utility can be used to change the owner of the entity. The syntax is

```
chown {new user} {entity}
```

Thus, to change the owner of a file, the sequence would be

```
$ ls -l turbo
-rw-rw-rw-  1  root    root              14  Sep 6 22:42
➥turbo
$ chown edulaney turbo
$ ls -l turbo
-rw-rw-rw-  1  edulaney    root          14  Sep 6 22:42
➥turbo
$
```

NOTE

Changing the owner does not change permissions or any other values, just as changing permissions did not change the owner, and so on. Only the root user can change the file's ownership.

If you are changing a directory and want to recursively change all the entities beneath it, you can use the -R option.

A cousin of the other two utilities, chgrp, can be used to change the group associated with the entity. Once again, the -R option is available to recursively change all the files and subdirectories beneath a directory as well. The root user can make any group changes she wants, as long as she is the owner of the file, and belongs to the group she is making the changes to.

If you are the root user and changing both the owner and group at the same time, you can use chown and separate the two values by a colon:

```
$ ls -l turbo
-rw-rw-rw-  1  edulaney    root              14  Sep 6 22:42
➥turbo
$ chown kristen:business turbo
$ ls -l turbo
-rw-rw-rw-  1  kristen     business          14  Sep 6
➥22:42  turbo
$
```

The command will fail if either the owner or the group are not in existence. You can also use chown to change only the group by using only the second part of the argument:

```
$ ls -l turbo
-rw-rw-rw-  1  kristen     business          14  Sep 6
➥22:42  turbo
$ chown :users turbo
$ ls -l turbo
-rw-rw-rw-  1  kristen     users             14  Sep 6
➥22:42  turbo
$
```

Access Control Lists

Course Objective Covered

6. Use ACLS for Advanced Access Control (3038)

The permissions that are used throughout the operating system to secure files and directories can be thought of as Access Control Lists (ACLs) for they define what can be done with each entity. Using the getfacl utility to Get File ACL information, you see the exact same information, but it is displayed slightly differently:

```
$ getfacl turbo
# file: turbo
# owner: kristen
# group: users
user::rw-
```

```
group:rw-
other::rw-
$
```

This utility can be used for files and directories and allows the use of wild-cards and regular expressions.

Working in conjunction with `getfacl` is `setfacl`, which is used to Set File ACL information, and is thus a substitute for `chmod`. Figure 4.4 shows the many options available with this utility.

FIGURE 4.4
The `setfacl` utility offers numerous options.

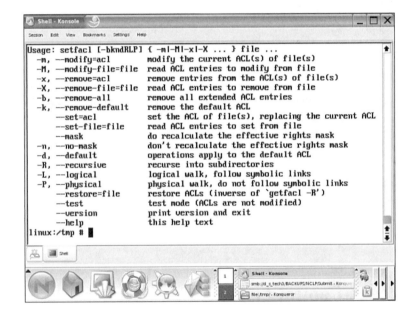

The following example sets the permissions on the turbo file equal to those on a file named `slowmotion`:

```
$ getfacl slowmotion
# file: slowmotion
# owner: kristen
# group: users
user::rw-
group:r--
other::r--

$ getfacl slowmotion | setfacl -set-file=- turbo
$ getfacl turbo
# file: turbo
# owner: kristen
```

```
# group: users
user::rw-
group:r--
other::r--

$
```

The benefit of **setfacl** over **chmod** is that it does offer a number of options—like that shown in the example—which are available only in it.

Special Permissions

Three special permissions are used in rare circumstances. Read, write, and execute are always used (or their absence expressed), but sometimes you need to do a bit more with a file or directory. The three special permissions are

- ▶ Set User ID (SUID)
- ▶ Set Group ID (SGID)
- ▶ Sticky bit

These permissions are discussed in the following sections.

SUID

The Set User ID permission is used when you have an executable file that a normal user would not be able to run, but must. For example, only the root user should be able to do function **xyz** (start backups, do restores, log in to other devices, and so on) because of the security ramifications, but what if you need the users to run a shell script to perform this action because you don't have time to do it personally?

You can create the shell script as root, and set the SUID permission such that whoever runs the script will become root only within the framework of that script. Before and after the script, they are themselves, but the script runs as root.

The numerical permission of SUID is 4000, and is added to the value of other permissions. When applied, it changes the "x" that would appear in the execute field for the owner's permission set to an "s":

```
$ ls -l turbo2
-rwxrwxrwx  1  root    root           542  Sep 9 20:02
➡turbo2
$ chmod 4777 turbo2
```

```
$ ls -l turbo2
-rwsrwxrwx  1  root   root              542  Sep 9 20:02
➥turbo2
$
```

Remember: The value of using this permission is that the process runs as the owner of the person who created it (root in this case) and not as the person executing it. To do the same operation in symbolic format, the command would be

```
chmod u+s turbo2
```

SGID

Similar in nature to SUID, the Set Group ID permission is used when you need the person executing the file to be a member of the group owning the file (and not the owner). This changes the "x" in the group permission to an "s", and the numerical value is 2000:

```
$ ls -l turbo2
-rwxrwxrwx  1  root   root              542  Sep 9 20:02
➥turbo2
$ chmod 2777 turbo2
$ ls -l turbo2
-rwxrwsrwx  1  root   root              542  Sep 9 20:02
➥turbo2
$
```

To use the symbolic syntax, the command would be

```
chmod g+s turbo2
```

Sticky Bit

The last permission does not work as the other special permissions do. With a numeric value of 1000, its operations differ when applied to a directory versus a file. When applied to a directory, it prevents users from deleting files from folders that grant them the write permission *unless* they are the owner of the file. By default, any user who has write permission to a directory can delete files within that directory even if the user doesn't have write permission to that file.

When the sticky bit permission is applied to a file, the file becomes "sticky" (hence the name). The first time the file is run or accessed, and loaded into memory, it stays loaded into memory or swap space so that it can run faster than if it had to be read from the drive.

If the file is not executable, the last permission bit ("x" for the other category) becomes "T". If the file is an executable file or a directory, the last bit becomes a "t". Figure 4.5 illustrates the difference.

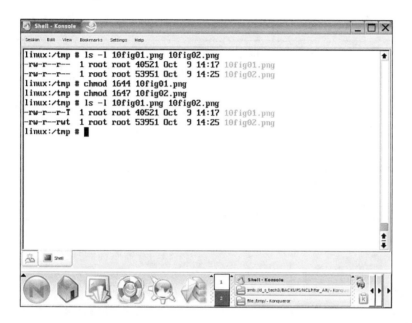

FIGURE 4.5
The sticky bit can be a lowercase or uppercase t, based on executable status.

Working with Links

The purpose of a link is to allow one file to be referenced by more than one name. There are any number of reasons why you would want or need to do this, for example:

1. For historic purposes—Assume you want to combine all the vendor information into a single file. In the past, marketing has always had a file where they kept similar information and called it `vendor`, while accounting kept their information in a file called `contacts`, and admin called theirs `references`. When you create the single file, you can make it available by all three names so that all parties can find it as they formerly did.

2. To make the nonlocal look local—Assume there is a template that all users are to use when making system modification requests. This file can exist in the root user's home directory (`/root`), and a link created within each user's home directory (`/home/user`) to make it appear as if it exists within their directory.

The utility to create links is `ln`. When you create a link, you are merely creating another pointer to an already existing entity; because this is the case, only one inode is used, not two. Because there is only one copy, you are also saving disk space.

> **NOTE** When you link to a file to give others access, you must make certain they have appropriate permissions to access the file, or you are defeating your purpose.

Two types of links can be created: hard and symbolic. Both are examined in the following sections.

Hard Links

The simplest of the two link types is the hard link. It is created by default with `ln`, and its use can be illustrated as follows:

```
$ ls -l
drwx------  5    root root         1024 Sep 22 23:57
➥Desktop
-rw-r--r--  1    root root           81 Sep 23 00:25
➥friday
-rw-r--r--  1    root root           81 Sep 23 00:38
➥monday
-rw-r--r--  1    root root          152 Sep 23 00:26
➥tuesday
-rw-r--r--  1    root root           38 Sep 23 00:26
➥wednesday
$
$ ln monday thursday
$ ls -l
drwx------  5    root root         1024 Sep 22 23:57
➥Desktop
-rw-r--r--  1    root root           81 Sep 23 00:25
➥friday
-rw-r--r--  2    root root           81 Sep 23 00:38
➥monday
-rw-r--r--  2    root root           81 Sep 23 00:38
➥thursday
-rw-r--r--  1    root root          152 Sep 23 00:26
➥tuesday
-rw-r--r--  1    root root           38 Sep 23 00:26
➥wednesday
$
```

Notice that the attributes related to the time of the new entry (thursday) remained the same as those associated with monday and did not assume the current time—as would be done with a copy operation. This is because there is only one set of data, even though there are now two ways of referencing it. The second column from the left indicates the link count for files: the number of ways this same set of data can be referenced. The link count has incremented from one to two.

Another way to verify that it is the same data is to view the inodes. Every entity must have its own inode, as was discussed earlier. If, however, you have only one set of data and multiple ways of accessing it, all the access methods (names) will share the same inode:

```
$ ls -i
18471 Desktop        18538 monday        18536 tuesday
18535 friday         18538 thursday      18537 wednesday
$
```

As you add links to the data, the link count will increment, and as you remove links, the link count will decrement. The data that the links point to will remain on the system as long as anything at all points to it. For example, the file thursday was linked to monday. If monday is now deleted, thursday will still remain, but the link count will decrement to one: Linux does not care which file was created first. It's only when the link count drops to zero that the data will no longer exist on the system.

To put it into perspective, every time you create a file from scratch, you are creating a link to the data (with a link count of one). When you remove the link (delete the file), the count becomes zero and the data goes away.

When the contents of the files are viewed, there is no indication that they are links of each other.

To prove the link exists, however, any modification made to either file is made to both because they both reference the same data. This can be readily illustrated:

```
$ ls -l
drwx------ 5     root root         1024 Sep 22 23:57
➥Desktop
-rw-r--r-- 1     root root           81 Sep 23 00:25
➥friday
-rw-r--r-- 2     root root           81 Sep 23 00:38
➥monday
-rw-r--r-- 2     root root           81 Sep 23 00:38
➥thursday
```

```
-rw-r--r-- 1     root root              152 Sep 23 00:26
➥tuesday
-rw-r--r-- 1     root root               38 Sep 23 00:26
➥wednesday
$
$ cat >> monday
Ingredients include carbonated water, high fructose corn syrup
and/or sugar, citric acid, and natural flavoring.
{press Ctrl+D}
$
$ ls -l
drwx------ 5     root root             1024 Sep 22 23:57
➥Desktop
-rw-r--r-- 1     root root               81 Sep 23 00:25
➥friday
-rw-r--r-- 2     root root              194 Sep 24 15:09
➥monday
-rw-r--r-- 2     root root              194 Sep 24 15:09
➥thursday
-rw-r--r-- 1     root root              152 Sep 23 00:26
➥tuesday
-rw-r--r-- 1     root root               38 Sep 23 00:26
➥wednesday
$
```

The same effect of a change to one entity being made to both would apply to permissions, owner, group, and so on. Hard links cannot be across filesystems, and must always be local. Users can create links to files, but not to directories; however, the root user can also create links to directories with the -F or -d options.

Symbolic Links

To make a symbolic link, you must use the -s option with ln. A symbolic link is what one might equate with "shortcuts" in the Windows operating systems: small files that point to another file. The primary purpose for a symbolic link is to get around the shortcomings of hard links. As such, they allow users to link to directories, and allow links to cross filesystems.

To illustrate how a symbolic link is created, consider the following example:

```
$ ls -l
drwx------ 5     root root             1024 Sep 22 23:57
➥Desktop
-rw-r--r-- 1     root root               81 Sep 23 00:25
➥friday
```

```
-rw-r--r-- 2    root root              194 Sep 24 15:09
➥monday
-rw-r--r-- 2    root root              194 Sep 24 15:09
➥thursday
-rw-r--r-- 1    root root              152 Sep 23 00:26
➥tuesday
-rw-r--r-- 1    root root               38 Sep 23 00:26
➥wednesday
$
$ ln -s friday saturday
$ ls -l
drwx------ 5    root root             1024 Sep 22 23:57
➥Desktop
-rw-r--r-- 1    root root               81 Sep 23 00:25
➥friday
-rw-r--r-- 2    root root              194 Sep 24 15:09
➥monday
lrwxrwxrwx 1 root root                  6 Sep 24 15:49
➥saturday -> friday
-rw-r--r-- 2    root root              194 Sep 24 15:09
➥thursday
-rw-r--r-- 1    root root              152 Sep 23 00:26
➥tuesday
-rw-r--r-- 1    root root               38 Sep 23 00:26
➥wednesday
$
```

There are several items to note about this transaction:

1. The link count on friday did not change.

2. The new file will always have the first column equal to "lrwxrwxrwx" to indicate that it is a link.

3. The date and time on the new file are not equal to the old file, but instead are the current date and time—this is because a new file has been created (with its own inode).

4. To the right of the file name is a graphical indication of the file really being referenced.

5. The new file has a size associated with it, but the size is equal to the pointer only.

The last point is worth dwelling on for a moment. The file friday has a size of 81, and saturday has a size of 6. This is completely transparent to the user as any operation done on saturday is sent to friday instead. To illustrate

```
$ cat friday
this is the way that one and one
will equal two
and two and two
will equal four
$
$ cat saturday
this is the way that one and one
will equal two
and two and two
will equal four
$
$ wc friday
     4     18     81 friday
$ wc saturday
     4     18     81 saturday
$
```

In other words, saturday is just a symbolic (name) representation of friday. Whatever action you attempt to do is sent to the first file through the pointer held in the second. This can lead to unexpected results: Because the file is a pointer, it can be pointing to something that no longer exists, or is currently unavailable (remember, they can span filesystems). Consider the following sequence of events where the file being pointed to is removed:

```
$ rm friday
$ ls -l
drwx------ 5     root root          1024 Sep 22 23:57
➥Desktop
-rw-r--r-- 2     root root           194 Sep 24 15:09
➥monday
lrwxrwxrwx 1 root root                 6 Sep 24 15:49
➥saturday -> friday
-rw-r--r-- 2     root root           194 Sep 24 15:09
➥thursday
-rw-r--r-- 1     root root           152 Sep 23 00:26
➥tuesday
-rw-r--r-- 1     root root            38 Sep 23 00:26
➥Wednesday
$ wc saturday
wc: saturday: No such file or directory
$
```

This can lead to frustration and aggravation on the part of users, for the error messages will tell them that saturday does not exist, whereas every listing of the directory will show that it does. As an administrator, it is imperative for you to understand that the file does exist, but it is a pointer to a file that no longer does.

When you view symbolic links in most graphical utilities, their names are italicized and a small box holding an arrow is added to the bottom left of the icon.

A large number of the system files are links to other items. For example, the /dev directory holds a plethora of symbolic links to devices that can be accessed via different names and in different locations.

Finding System Files

With all the files on the system, and all the different directories and subdirectories that exist, finding something you are looking for can sometimes be a daunting task. Thankfully, there are a number of utilities in Linux that can help ease this burden. In this section, we will look at a few of the unique utilities and examine how you can use them to help find what you are looking for.

The utilities to be examined, in order, are

- ▶ locate
- ▶ updatedb
- ▶ which
- ▶ find

The locate utility looks through a database file (instead of the actual directory tree) to find files that match a name given. The database is named locatedb and is usually found in a subdirectory beneath the /var directory (common locations include /var/state or /var/lib).

The locatedb database is updated through the use of the updatedb command. By default, updatedb runs on a regular basis (usually once a day), but it can be run manually as well. The advantage to using locate (and thus locatedb) is that it is much faster to search a database for an entry than the entire filesystem. The downside is that files created after the last time updatedb was run cannot be found using the locate utility.

By default, updatedb runs through the filesystem and updates the locatedb database with entries anywhere it finds them. You can, however, create an optional file named updatedb.conf in the /etc directory. If the updatedb.conf file exists, only directories listed in it will be used to create the database.

An example of the use of the locate command would be

```
$ locate grep
/opt/kde/share/apps/kmail/pics/kmmsgreplied.xpm
/usr/bin/egrep
/usr/bin/fgrep
/usr/bin/grep
/usr/bin/zgrep
/usr/bin/zipgrep
/usr/doc/dosemu-0.98.5/bugreports.txt
/usr/doc/grep-2.2
/usr/doc/grep-2.2/ABOUT-NLS
/usr/doc/grep-2.2/AUTHORS
/usr/doc/grep-2.2/INSTALL
/usr/doc/grep-2.2/NEWS
/usr/doc/grep-2.2/README
/usr/doc/grep-2.2/THANKS
/usr/doc/grep-2.2/TODO
/usr/lib/python1.5/grep.pyc
/usr/lib/python1.5/grep.pyo
/usr/lib/xemacs-20.4/lisp/efs/dired-grep.elc
/usr/lib/xemacs-20.4/lisp/packages/igrep.elc
/usr/man/de/man1/egrep.1.gz
/usr/man/de/man1/grep.1.gz
/usr/man/man1/egrep.1.gz
/usr/man/man1/fgrep.1.gz
/usr/man/man1/grep.1.gz
/usr/man/man1/zgrep.1.gz
/usr/man/man1/zipgrep.1.gz
/usr/share/locale/de/LC_MESSAGES/grep.mo
/usr/share/locale/es/LC_MESSAGES/grep.mo
/usr/share/locale/fr/LC_MESSAGES/grep.mo
/usr/share/locale/ko/LC_MESSAGES/grep.mo
/usr/share/locale/nl/LC_MESSAGES/grep.mo
/usr/share/locale/no/LC_MESSAGES/grep.mo
/usr/share/locale/pl/LC_MESSAGES/grep.mo
/usr/share/locale/ru/LC_MESSAGES/grep.mo
/usr/share/locale/sl/LC_MESSAGES/grep.mo
/usr/share/locale/sv/LC_MESSAGES/grep.mo
/usr/share/vim/bugreport.vim
$
```

The `which` command is similar to the `locate` command. Instead of looking through a database, however, `which` looks through the directories listed in your path statement. When it finds a match in a directory for a name you give, it stops immediately and reports what it found. How is this useful? Suppose there are 14 versions of `grep` on your system; `which` will tell you the first one it finds via the path search, and thus the one that is executed when you use the command.

The following simple example illustrates this:

```
$ which grep
/usr/bin/grep
$
```

If you had to think of an analogy for the `find` utility, it would be to the Swiss army knife in the real world, or to `grep` on steroids in the operating-system world. This tool is capable of looking at all entries in the filesystem and displaying results that meet criteria given. In many ways it is the vast possibilities of the "criteria" you can specify that allow this tool to be so powerful. The syntax is simply

```
find [starting point] [criteria]
```

The default starting point is the present working directory, but can be specified to be anything. Whatever starting point is used, the search will recursively move from there to all of its subdirectories.

The criteria can be any of the options shown in Table 4.2.

Parameters for `find`   **TABLE 4.2**

OPTION	PURPOSE
`-atime` *days*	Tests true if the file was accessed within the number of days specified
`-ctime` *days*	Tests true if the file was changed within the number of days specified
`-exec` *command*	Executes a command. You must specify that the command is for a group "{}" and continuing on "\;"
`-group` *name*	Tests true if the file belongs to the specified group
`-inum` *number*	Tests true if the file has that inode number
`-links` *number*	Tests true if the number of links is equal to the specified number

Table 4.2   Continued

OPTION	PURPOSE
-mount	Only looks on the local filesystem
-mtime *days*	Tests true only if the file was modified within the number of days specified
-name *file*	True only if matching the name given
-perm *permission*	True if matching the given permissions
-print	Prints the names of matching files
-size *number*	True if matching the number of blocks or characters
-type *type*	True if matching the specified type (d=directory, f=file, b=block file, c=character file)
-user *name*	True only if owned by the named user

For example, to find all files on the system, beginning with the root directory, that are named **grep**, you would use these specifications:

```
$ find / -name "grep"
/usr/bin/grep
$
```

Notice that the -**print** option did not need to be specified: This is the default action. Notice also, that unlike **locate**, it found an exact match and not just entries that had the four letters somewhere in the name. If you want to find matches that are portions of words, you need to use the asterisk (*) wildcard (**find / -name "*grep*"**).

When you find the match, you can perform an action on it, such as obtaining a long listing:

```
$ find / -name "grep" -exec ls -l {} \;
-rwxr-xr-x 1 root     root       70652  Aug 11 1999
➥/usr/bin/grep
$
```

NOTE

Be very careful with the -exec option, as you can specify anything following it— including move, remove, and so on. The option -ok can be used in place of -exec to force a prompt before every action is taken.

To find which files have been accessed, use the -**atime** option. If the number following is preceded by a plus sign (+), it returns entries in which the access day was more than the number given. If the number following is preceded by a minus sign (-), it returns entries in which the access day was less than the number given. For example, to find files beneath the current directory that have not been accessed for 10 days or more, specify **+10**:

```
$ find . -atime +10
```

To find files that have been accessed within the last two days, specify **-2**:

```
$ find . -atime -2
```

To find only directories beneath the current directory, specify **d**:

```
$ find . -type d
```

To find all files associated with user edulaney, use the following sequence:

```
$ find / -user edulaney
/home/edulaney
/home/edulaney/.bash_logout
/home/edulaney/.bashrc
/home/edulaney/.cshrc
/home/edulaney/.inputrc
/home/edulaney/.login
/home/edulaney/.logout
/home/edulaney/.profile
/home/edulaney/.tcshrc
/home/edulaney/.seyon
/home/edulaney/.seyon/phonelist
/home/edulaney/.seyon/protocols
/home/edulaney/.seyon/script.CIS
/home/edulaney/.seyon/script.PCBoard
/home/edulaney/.seyon/script.QWK
/home/edulaney/.seyon/script.unix
/home/edulaney/.seyon/startup
/home/edulaney/fileone
/home/edulaney/filethree
/home/edulaney/filetwo
/home/edulaney/.bash_history
$
```

Notice that the result includes directories and files that are visible and hidden.

Working with Quotas

Course Objective Covered

5. Set Up and Configure Disk Quotas (3037)

Quotas are used to limit the amount of space available to a user or group. By default, Linux does not impose any quotas, and thus each user is limited in the amount of hard disk space he or she can consume only by the amount of space available on the system.

When quotas are used, they must be applied per each partition, and this offers flexibility in that the level applied to one partition can differ from that applied to another. Each quota also operates independently of any other. For example, quotas can be applied on a partition limiting kristin to 7MB, evan to 5MB, and spencer to 3MB. This gives the three of them a combined total of 15MB of storage space. If, however, they all belong to the sales group, and it is limited to 10MB, one or more of the users will not be able to store files after the 10MB limit is reached even though they have room left within their individual quota.

To turn quotas on, you must edit the `/etc/fstab` file. A current entry within the file would read

```
/dev/hda3 /home ext2 defaults  1   2
```

The first field is the filesystem, and the second is the mount point. The third field is the filesystem type, and the fourth is options for the filesystem. The fifth field identifies the order in which the filesystem would be used by a dump, and the sixth field is the order in which `fsck` would use it.

It is the fourth field where a modification must be made to use quotas, and this is accomplished by changing the line to read:

```
/dev/hda3 /home ext2 defaults,usrquota  1   2
```

In some cases, it may be necessary for the kernel to be recompiled to support quotas, but this is not always the case. After the file has been edited, go to the root of the partition where the quota is to be. As the root user, create a file called either **quota.user** or **quota.group**. The permissions on the file must be equal to read and write by the root user only, and this is accomplished with the **chmod** command. Thus, the sequence following the edit is

```
$ touch quota.user
$ chmod 600 quota.user
```

> **NOTE**
>
> The touch **command used in the following example was discussed in Chapter 3,** "Preliminary GNU and Unix Commands."

You must then reboot, and the utilities that can be used are

- quotaon—To enable the use of the quotas. The -a option can be used to enable for every filesystem having usrquota in /etc/fstab; otherwise, you must specify the filesystem.

- quotaoff—To disable the use of the quotas.

- edquota—To edit and change the quota limits. The -u option allows you to specify a user, or -g is used for a group. The -t option can be used for a "soft limit."

- repquota—To generate a report of disk usage and the specified quota (created with edquota). Options with this tool include -a to check all filesystems in /etc/fstab; -g to see the report for groups; -u to see the report for users (default); and -v to show numbers even if they are zero. Any user can run this utility to see their own numbers, but root will see the report for all users.

- quota—Similar to repquota, it shows the quotas in existence. Any user can see their own, and root can see all.

- quotacheck—Only available to root, it scans the system and creates report files with the current usage.

- quotastats—Shows the amount of used space for each individual user and group.

> **NOTE**
>
> Not all the utilities are available in all implementations of Linux.

By default, when a user or group reaches the quota limit, he or she is no longer allowed to save any further entries. If you set a "soft limit," it means the user can exceed the limit, but only for a short period of time (defined as a grace period; the default is seven days).

Summary

This chapter focused on the topics you need to work with files and the filesystem. The next chapter looks at basic Linux system administration.

Command Summary

Table 4.3 lists the commands that were discussed in this chapter.

TABLE 4.3	Utilities in This Chapter
UTILITY	**DEFAULT PURPOSE**
chgrp	Change an entity's group association
chmod	Change an entity's permissions
edquota	Create quotas for users or groups
getfacl	Shows the Access Control List for a file
locate	Find a file from the locatedb database
quotaoff	Turn off user/group quotas
quotaon	Turn on user/group quotas
repquota, quota, quotacheck, and quotastats	View quota usage
setfacl	Set/modify the Access Control List for a file
SGID	Set the group ID when running a file
Sticky bit	Change the operation of files and directories
SUID	Set the user ID when running a file
umask	A numerical variable subtracted from the default permissions when creating new files and directories
updatedb	Update the locatedb database
which	Find a file from the path statement

## CHAPTER 5

Basic Linux Administration

This chapter focuses on the basics of Linux administration. This chapter covers the following course objectives:

1. Managing User Accounts (3036)
2. Archiving Files with `tar` (3036)
3. Compressing and Uncompressing Files with `gzip` and `bzip2` (3036)
4. Describe Basic Linux User Security Features (3037)
5. Manage Linux Users and Groups (3037)
6. Manage and Secure the Linux User Environment (3037)
7. Configure User Authentication with PAM (3037)
8. Backup and Restore the File System (3037)
9. Use System Logging Services (3037)
10. Configure SuSE Linux Enterprise Server Time (3037)
11. Understand the Linux User Authentication (3038)
12. Develop a Backup Strategy (3038)
13. Backup Files with `tar` (3038)
14. Work with Magnetic Tapes (3038)
15. Copy Data with `dd` (3038)
16. Mirror Directories with `rsync` (3038)
17. Monitor the Operating System (3038)

It is important for you to know the topics in this chapter in order to function as an administrator. The subject matter discussed in this chapter easily falls into the daily journal of the average Linux system administrator.

Creating and Managing Users

Course Objectives Covered

1. Managing User Accounts (3036)

4. Describe Basic Linux User Security Features (3037)

5. Manage Linux Users and Groups (3037)

6. Manage and Secure the Linux User Environment (3037)

11. Understand the Linux User Authentication (3038)

During the installation of the operating system, at least one user (root/ superuser) is added to the system. This is the most powerful user on the system, and literally able to do almost anything. After the installation, it is often necessary to add additional users and modify variables associated with existing ones. Both tasks will be examined further in this section.

To understand what is involved, however, it is important to know the files the operating system uses to deal with users. The first file of importance is the /etc/passwd file. Fields are delimited by colons, and a sample would resemble the following:

```
root:x:0:0:root:/root:/bin/bash
bin:x:1:1:bin:/bin:
daemon:x:2:2:daemon:/sbin:
adm:x:3:4:adm:/var/adm:
lp:x:4:7:lp:/var/spool/lpd:
sync:x:5:0:sync:/sbin:/bin/sync
shutdown:x:6:11:shutdown:/sbin:/sbin/shutdown
halt:x:7:0:halt:/sbin:/sbin/halt
mail:x:8:12:mail:/var/spool/mail:
news:x:9:13:news:/var/spool/news:
uucp:x:10:14:uucp:/var/spool/uucp:
operator:x:11:0:operator:/root:
games:x:12:100:games:/usr/games:
gopher:x:13:30:gopher:/usr/lib/gopher-data:
ftp:x:14:50:FTP User:/home/ftp:
man:x:15:15:Manuals Owner:/:
majordom:x:16:16:Majordomo:/:/bin/false
postgres:x:17:17:Postgres User:/home/postgres:/bin/bash
mysql:x:18:18:MySQL User:/var/lib/mysql:/bin/false
nobody:x:65534:65534:Nobody:/:/bin/false
edulaney:x:1000:100:emmett:/home/edulaney:/bin/bash
kdulaney:x:1001:100:karen:/home/kdulaney:/bin/tcsh
sdulaney:x:1002:100:spencer:/home/sdulaney:/bin/zsh
```

The seven fields can be broken down as follows:

- ▶ The login name of the user—This must be unique per system, but is free text and can be edited and modified with any editor at any time. Among the entries shown in the example, `bin` is the owner of executables, `daemon` is used for system services, and `adm` owns the log files. Other entries are users (such as `edulaney`) or individual services (such as `ftp`).

- ▶ The password—This can be an encrypted entry held within this field, or an "x". In the case of the latter, the single character merely indicates that the values are stored elsewhere—in the `/etc/shadow` file.

Placing the passwords in the `shadow` **file adds additional security. Everyone can read the** `passwd` **file, but only the root user can read the** `shadow` **file.**   ██ **NOTE** ██

- ▶ The numerical userid (UID)—This is an incremental number unique for every user and is how the operating system truly references the user (remember that the login name is changeable text). The root user is always number 0, and maintenance/service accounts use small numbers (typically up to 99). Regular user accounts typically start at 1000 (this is for SLES, but will differ with other Linux vendors) and increment from there. For security reasons, you can rename root to any other text value, but the number 0 is always the identifier.

- ▶ The numerical groupid (GID)—This identifies the default group associated with the user. The **root** group is always 0, and lower numbers are used for system groups. Regular users are assigned groups at a beginning number listed in the `/etc/login.defs` file.

- ▶ Free text used for descriptive purposes—One of the main utilities that looks at this field is `finger`, which simply returns information about a user to anyone querying.

- ▶ The home directory of the user—This is where the users start when they log in, and where files are held to define their environmental variables.

- ▶ The shell to use for the user—If no data is in this field, the default shell is used.

The /etc/shadow file is used to hold the password and information about the aging parameters. Here's an example:

```
root:awYeiEwzMpfo6:11144:0::7:7::
bin:*:10547:0::7:7::
daemon:*:10547:0::7:7::
adm:*:10547:0::7:7::
lp:*:10547:0::7:7::
sync:*:10547:0::7:7::
shutdown:*:10547:0::7:7::
halt:*:10547:0::7:7::
mail:*:10547:0::7:7::
news:*:10547:0::7:7::
uucp:*:10547:0::7:7::
operator:*:10547:0::7:7::
games:*:10547:0::7:7::
gopher:*:10547:0::7:7::
ftp:*:10547:0::7:7::
man:*:10547:0::7:7::
majordom:*:10547:0::7:7::
postgres:*:10547:0::7:7::
mysql:*:10547:0::7:7::
nobody:*:10547:0::7:7::
edulaney:aw0VvUAsWpigo:11144:0::7:7::
kdulaney:awzIG94wrzGqY:11144:0::7:7::
sdulaney:awf7Zbxwu.NmQ:11144:0::7:7::
```

The eight fields are

▸ The login name of the user, which is the only field that must match with the /etc/passwd file.

▸ An encrypted hash of the password. If no password has been defined on system accounts, an asterisk (*) is often used. If no password is defined on newly created accounts, an exclamation mark (!) often appears. Under no conditions can this field be left blank for a functioning user.

▸ The day the password was last changed, expressed in the number of days that have passed since 1/1/1970. An entry of 12711, for example, would mean 12,711 days had passed and it is now October 19, 2004.

▸ Minimum password age expressed in how many days a user must wait between being allowed to make password changes. A value of 0 means the users can make changes as often as they like.

▶ Maximum password age expressed in how many days a user is allowed to keep this password. A value of 90 would mean the password must be changed every 90 days, whereas 99999 (the default) essentially means that no change is required.

▶ The number of days before the password expires when a warning starts appearing to change the password. This is usually 7.

▶ The number of days after the password expires to wait before disabling the account. This field is often blank.

▶ The expiration date for the password, again in days since 1/1/1970. This field is often blank.

Creating User Accounts

New users can be created manually, or by using utilities. To do so manually, simply append an entry to the /etc/passwd file (it is strongly recommended that you make a backup copy of the file before changing). You can leave the password field blank, and then assign a password using the passwd utility. If you simply leave it blank, it is a valid account without a password:

```
$ cat >> /etc/passwd
evan::504:100:EvanD:/home/evan:/bin/bash
{press Ctrl+D}
$
$ passwd evan
New user password: {enter password}
Retype new user password: {enter password again}
passwd: all authentication tokens updated successfully
$
$ tail -1 /etc/passwd
evan:petKv.fLWG/Ig:504:100:EvanD:/home/evan:/bin/bash
$
```

Any user can use the passwd utility to change his or her password. Only the root user, however, can use it to change the password of another user. ▰ NOTE ▰

Notice that this method places the encrypted password in the /etc/passwd file itself, and does not utilize the /etc/shadow file. Provided the home directory exists, and the user is the owner of it, the user can now be an authenticated user.

A utility provided with Linux (most vendors also have their own utilities as well) to simplify this process is **useradd**. You must use options with the utility, and a key one is **-D** to display default settings. Here's an example:

NOTE The useradd **utility is intended for use by** su **or** root. **Typical users will get an error message when they attempt to use it.**

```
$ useradd -D
GROUP=100
HOME=/home
INACTIVE=-1
EXPIRE=
SHELL=/bin/bash
SKEL=/etc/skel
GROUPS=dialout,uucp.video,audio
$
```

These are the defaults that will be used when a new user is created with this utility. The defaults come from the text file /etc/login.defs. Therefore, the following sequence is possible:

```
$ useradd kerby
$ tail -1 /etc/passwd
kerby:x:1002:100::/home/kerby:/bin/bash
$ tail -1 /etc/shadow
kerby:!:12711:0:99999:7:::
$
$ passwd kerby
New user password: {enter password}
Retype new user password: {enter password again}
passwd: all authentication tokens updated successfully
$ tail -1 /etc/shadow
kerby:M3cMnQDwHjRD6:12711:0:99999:7:::
$
```

Note that the /etc/shadow file is used, and the values used to create the entries in the two files come directly from the defaults, which are shown in Table 5.1.

Defaults for /etc/shadow

TABLE 5.1

DEFAULT	FILE RESULT
GROUP	Becomes the fourth field of passwd
HOME	Becomes the sixth field of passwd, with the %s variable becoming the name given on the command line (which becomes the first field of both passwd and shadow)
SHELL	Becomes the seventh field of passwd
PASS variables	Entered into appropriate fields of shadow

The SKEL variable was not utilized in this example. By default, useradd will make the entries in the passwd and shadow files, but will not create the home directory for the user. If you use the -m option, useradd will also create the home directory for the user and copy files from the SKEL location (a skeleton, or template of files that you want copied for every new user) into the new directory. In typical SLES 9 implementations, /etc/skel holds the following files:

- .bash_history
- .bashrc
- .dvipsrc
- .emacs
- .exrc
- .fonts
- .kermrc
- .muttrc
- .profile
- .urlview
- .xcoralrc
- .xemacs
- .xim.template
- .xinitrc.template
- .xtalkrc
- Documents
- bin
- public_html

All the hidden files are used for processing (setting up variables, environment, and so on) with the various shells.

There are a number of options that can be used with **useradd** to override default settings, and they include the following:

- ▶ -c to specify the free text (fifth field of **passwd**) associated with the user. Most Linux implementations default to an empty entry here or a variation of their name.

- ▶ -d to specify a home directory different than /home/{username}.

- ▶ -e to change expiration date (format: mm/dd/yyyy).

- ▶ -f for the variable defining how many days after expiration the account becomes disabled. The default of -1 prevents it from being disabled even after expiration.

- ▶ -g to specify a different GID.

- ▶ -r for a system directory.

- ▶ -s to choose a different shell.

- ▶ -u to specify a UID: By default, the next available number is used. If you try to use a number that is already in use, the utility fails and identifies which user already has that number.

Switching Between passwd and shadow

In the manual example for creating a new user, the encrypted password appears in the /etc/passwd file and not the /etc/shadow file. If you want to do manual additions, and still use /etc/shadow, the pwconv utility can be irreplaceable. This utility reads the entire **passwd** file and converts new entries into shadow file entries.

The opposite of pwconv is pwunconv, which takes entries from the **shadow** file and places them in the appropriate format in the **passwd** file. As a final step, pwunconv removes the **shadow** file completely.

The su Utility

The entries in the **passwd** file represent valid accounts that can log in. Any user can sit at the system and give the correct username and password combination to log in as that user. Any user already logged in can also use the su utility to change identity to another user if they know the other user's password. This creates a subshell, if you will, where one user becomes another, and can revert to his own identity by typing exit.

Although there are dozens of harmful reasons why a user might want to become another, there are also very legitimate reasons as well. If **su** is given without a user name following it, it tries to make the user the superuser (root), needing the password for that account. Therefore, as an administrator, it is possible for you to log in as a typical user without root permissions and begin your day. The lack of root permissions can be a blessing as it can keep you from deleting entries you unintentionally typed, and so on. When a user comes up with a problem, you can use **su** to become root—with all rights and privileges as if you had logged in as such—fix the user's problem, and then exit back to your regular account again.

Managing User Accounts

After an account has been created, you can manage and modify it manually or through the use of utilities. For example, if a user named Karen Dulaney gets married, and her name changes to Karen Brooks, you can edit the **passwd** and **shadow** files and change the first field of each from **kdulaney** to **kbrooks**. Because the same UID is in place, all files and such associated with her continue to remain so. The home directory can be renamed, and the change made in **passwd** as well (it is always recommended that home directory and username match for administrative purposes).

As another example, if Karen gets promoted to administration, it may be necessary to remove her from the **users** group and place her in the **root** group. This can also be accomplished by manually editing the **/etc/passwd** file and changing the GID field. Similar examples can be given, endlessly, for each field within the files.

The **usermod** **utility should be used by** su **or the** root **user. Typical users will get an error message when they attempt to use it.** **NOTE**

Just as **useradd** is intended to simplify the addition of users to the system— and avoid manual entries—**usermod** is meant to simplify changing existing values. Options/flags must be used with the utility, and these are the possibilities:

- ▶ -c to replace the descriptive text with a new value.
- ▶ -d to alter the home directory.
- ▶ -e to change the password expiration date.
- ▶ -f to set the inactive parameter.

▶ -G to change secondary group membership. More than one group can be given as long as commas separate entries.

▶ -g to change the GID.

▶ -l to change the login name.

▶ -m (must be used with -d) to make the new home directory.

▶ -p to change the password.

▶ -s for a different shell.

▶ -u to change the UID.

Aside from the text description, most of the values require the user to not be logged in while the change is made. Here's an example of a change:

```
$ grep krist /etc/passwd
kristin:petKv.fLWG/Ig:506:100:kristin:/home/kristin:/bin/bash
$ usermod -l kristen kristin
$ grep krist /etc/passwd
kristen:petKv.fLWG/Ig:506:100:kristin:/home/kristin:/bin/bash
$ ls -l /home
drwxr-xr-x 4 evan    users 1024 Jul 6 11:16 evan
drwxr-xr-x 4 kristin users 1024 Aug 8 10:29 kristin
drwxr-xr-x 4 spencer users 1024 Jul 6 11:16 spencer
$ usermod -d /home/kristen -m kristen
$ ls -l /home
drwxr-xr-x 4 evan    users 1024 Jul 6 11:16 evan
drwxr-xr-x 4 kristin users 1024 Aug 8 10:29 kristin
drwxr-xr-x 4 spencer users 1024 Jul 6 11:16 spencer
$ grep krist /etc/passwd
kristen:petKv.fLWG/Ig:506:100:kristin:/home/kristen:/bin/bash
$
```

The usermod utility has the -p option to allow for the changing of passwords, but that can be accomplished more commonly with the passwd utility discussed earlier. The standalone utility is safer in that it requires you to enter the value twice, and thus helps prevent entering a value that is off by one character from what you were thinking (preventing you from logging in).

If there are a large number of passwords that need to be changed (think system break-in), you can do a batch change with the chpasswd utility. To use it, create a text file with one entry per line. Each line consists of the username and new password, separated by a colon. For example

```
$ cat > changes
kristen:spea23ker
evan:pho78ne
kdulaney:fla98sh
{Ctrl+D}
$
$ chpasswd < changes
$
```

The passwords are in clear text, and for that reason, you will want to remove the batch file from your system as soon as possible. An alternative is to use encrypted passwords and use the -e option with chpasswd.

It is a good idea to encourage users to use good passwords. Good passwords consist of at least six characters, which are a mix of letters, characters, and numbers and would not be easily guessed.

NOTE

Removing Users

When a user account is no longer needed, there are a number of ways you can deal with the situation. The first question you have to address is why the account is no longer needed. When you know that, you can formulate a plan for dealing with it. Table 5.2 offers some scenarios and methods of proceeding.

Solutions for Unneeded User Accounts

TABLE 5.2

PERCEIVED REASON FOR NOT NEEDING ACCOUNT	PROPOSED SOLUTION
User has been temporarily transferred to Siberia	If it is a temporary situation, you do not want to delete the account—doing so will remove all references that may be needed later. To temporarily disable the account, edit the /etc/passwd file and place a pound sign (#) at the beginning of the line. This will make the entire line a comment and disable the account.
User's password has been jeopardized by a hacker	Change the password to another value to keep the other party out. For further security, rename the login name and home directory.

Table 5.2   Continued

PERCEIVED REASON FOR NOT NEEDING ACCOUNT	PROPOSED SOLUTION
User has left the organization	Remove the account from /etc/passwd and /etc/shadow and delete the home directory.

The `userdel` utility can also be used to remove the user. This utility removes the user from system files (`passwd` and `shadow`), but you must still remove any files associated with them.

Working with Groups

Course Objectives Covered

4. Describe Basic Linux User Security Features (3037)

5. Manage Linux Users and Groups (3037)

6. Manage and Secure the Linux User Environment (3037)

Just as it is important to know the parameters behind user variables to understand how to work with them, you must also understand group constructs. The primary file holding group information is /etc/group, a sample of which would be

```
root::0:
wheel::10:
bin::1:bin,daemon
daemon::2:bin,daemon
sys::3:bin,adm
adm::4:adm,daemon
tty::5:
disk::6:
lp::7:daemon,lp
mem::8:
kmem::9:
operator::11:
mail::12:mail
news::13:news
uucp::14:uucp
man::15:
majordom::16:
```

```
database::17:
mysql::18:
games::20:
gopher::30:
dip::40:
utmp::45:
ftp::50:
nobody::65534:
users::100:
```

There are four fields to each entry in the file. The first field is the text name (maximum of eight characters) associated with the group (used for `ls -l` listings and the like). The third field is the numerical GID that must be unique on the system. The second field—blank in all cases by default—holds a password that can be required for use. The fourth field can be used to list the members of the group.

Creating a New Group

To create a new group, you can manually edit the `/etc/group` file and append an entry to it. If you do so, you must be certain to use a unique text name and GID number. The **groupadd** utility can also be used to simplify the operation:

```
$ groupadd -g 101 sales
$ tail -1 /etc/group
sales:!:101:
$
```

The **-g** option is used to specify the GID number to use. If the number is not unique, the utility will fail. As a general rule, GIDs 0—99 are reserved for system groups:

```
$ groupadd -g 101 marketing
groupadd: GID 101 is not unique.
$
```

Similarly, if you attempt to reuse a group name, the utility fails:

```
$ groupadd -g 102 sales
groupadd: Group `sales' already exists.
$
```

There are only a few other options available with **groupadd** besides **-g**. Chief among them, the **-o** option can be used to create a non-unique group (allowing the same **gid** to be used). The **-p** option allows you to specify a password, and **-r** creates a system group.

To further define your group, you can resort to manual editing, or use the **gpasswd** utility. When issued with only the name of a group, it prompts for a password to associate with the group:

```
$ gpasswd sales
Changing the password for group sales
New Password: {enter value}
Re-enter new password: {enter value again}
$ tail -1 /etc/group
sales:QJHexo2Pbk7TU:101:
$
```

If you tire of the password, or find it unwieldy, you can use the -r option to remove it.

```
$ gpasswd -r sales
$ tail -1 /etc/group
sales::101:
$
```

The exclamation point appears in the second field as a placeholder to identify that other users can join, and so on. You cannot add or delete more than one user at a time with **gpasswd**.

Picking a Group

When a user is a member of more than one group, his or her default group is the one defined by the fourth field of the **/etc/passwd** file. The **id** utility will show information about the user, including all the groups the user is a member of:

```
$ id
uid=501(edulaney) gid=100(users) groups=100(users),101(sales)
$
```

To change groups, utilize the **newgrp** utility and the name of the other group you want to make your default. Non-group members trying to become a part of the group have to give a password, whereas group members do not:

```
$ id
uid=501(edulaney) gid=100(users) groups=100(users),101(sales)
$ newgrp sales
$ id
```

```
uid=501(edulaney) gid=101(sales) groups=100(users),101(sales)
$ newgrp marketing
Password: {enter value}
$ id
uid=501(edulaney) gid=102(marketing) groups=100(users),
➥101(sales),102(marketing)
$
```

Modifying Groups

After groups have been created, you can modify their entries by manually editing the files, using **gpasswd**, or the **groupmod** utility. This tool allows you to change values (name and GID) associated with the group. The parameters that can be used with **groupmod** include

- ▶ -g to specify a new GID
- ▶ -n to change the name of the group to a new text value
- ▶ -o to allow a duplicate group ID number to be used
- ▶ -p to specify a password
- ▶ -A to add a user to the group
- ▶ -R to remove a user from the group

For example

```
$ tail -1 /etc/group
sales:x:101:edulaney,kristen,kerby,martha
$ groupmod -g 105 sales
$ tail -1 /etc/group
sales:x:105:edulaney,kristen,kerby,martha
$
$ groupmod -n business sales
$ tail -1 /etc/group
business:x:105:edulaney,kristen,kerby,martha
$
```

When groups are no longer needed, they can be deleted by manually removing the lines from the files, or by using the **groupdel** command. The utility cannot be used if any user has the group as his default group, and it only removes the entry from **/etc/group**.

Working with PAM

Course Objectives Covered

4. Describe Basic Linux User Security Features (3037)
7. Configure User Authentication with PAM (3037)

To increase security, Pluggable Authentication Modules (PAM) can act as intermediaries between users and applications. When users are authorized in PAM, they are free to access the applications that are available to them. The beauty of this arrangement is that you can change any one element in the process, and not affect anything else. For example, suppose you are requiring users to enter a password to authenticate themselves, and then giving them access to 10 applications. You can change the authentication method from a password to a fingerprint scan, and then allow them the access to the applications without having to reconfigure anything but the authentication method.

Global files are located beneath `/etc/security`. Individual configuration files for PAM modules are located beneath `/etc/pam.d`, as shown in Figure 5.1.

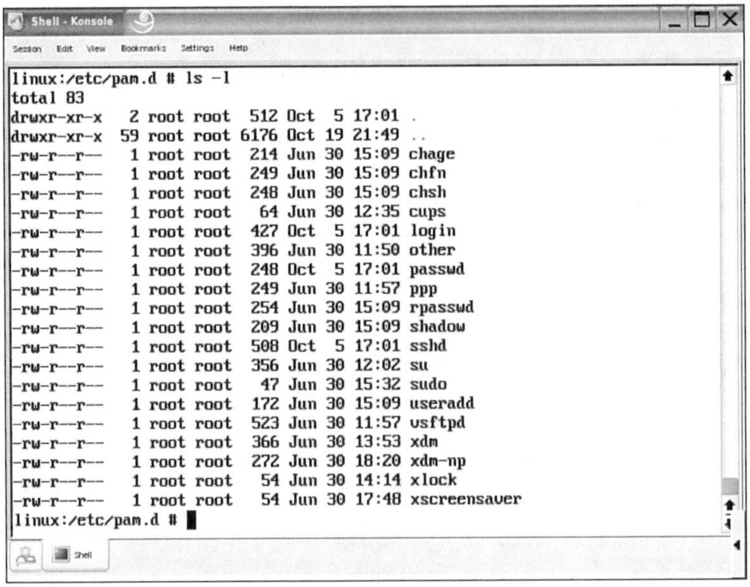
Shell - Konsole
Session Edit View Bookmarks Settings Help
linux:/etc/pam.d # ls -l
total 83
drwxr-xr-x 2 root root 512 Oct 5 17:01 .
drwxr-xr-x 59 root root 6176 Oct 19 21:49 ..
-rw-r--r-- 1 root root 214 Jun 30 15:09 chage
-rw-r--r-- 1 root root 249 Jun 30 15:09 chfn
-rw-r--r-- 1 root root 248 Jun 30 15:09 chsh
-rw-r--r-- 1 root root   64 Jun 30 12:35 cups
-rw-r--r-- 1 root root 427 Oct 5 17:01 login
-rw-r--r-- 1 root root 396 Jun 30 11:50 other
-rw-r--r-- 1 root root 248 Oct 5 17:01 passwd
-rw-r--r-- 1 root root 249 Jun 30 11:57 ppp
-rw-r--r-- 1 root root 254 Jun 30 15:09 rpasswd
-rw-r--r-- 1 root root 209 Jun 30 15:09 shadow
-rw-r--r-- 1 root root 508 Oct 5 17:01 sshd
-rw-r--r-- 1 root root 356 Jun 30 12:02 su
-rw-r--r-- 1 root root   47 Jun 30 15:32 sudo
-rw-r--r-- 1 root root 172 Jun 30 15:09 useradd
-rw-r--r-- 1 root root 523 Jun 30 11:57 vsftpd
-rw-r--r-- 1 root root 366 Jun 30 13:53 xdm
-rw-r--r-- 1 root root 272 Jun 30 18:20 xdm-np
-rw-r--r-- 1 root root   54 Jun 30 14:14 xlock
-rw-r--r-- 1 root root   54 Jun 30 17:48 xscreensaver
linux:/etc/pam.d #
Shell

FIGURE 5.1
Configuration files exist for each program that uses PAM modules.

Notice that the names that appear here have the same name as the utility
with which they are associated. When a user uses one of these applications,
a check is made in this directory for an associated configuration file. If
found, it is read and acted upon.

Some of the configuration files are only a single line, whereas some are more
lengthy. Figure 5.2 shows the contents of the **su** configuration file.

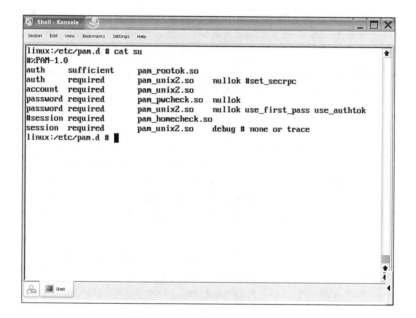

FIGURE 5.2
The configuration
file for su.

There are four fields to each line in the file. The first field identifies the
module type, and the second is the control flag. The third field lists the
modules to use, and the fourth field (which is optional) lists any arguments
that are needed.

There are four possible values for the module type:

▶ account—This identifies a need to see if the user has permission to
use the service he wants to.

▶ auth—This identifies a need to check the user's authenticity. This is
most often accomplished with a password.

▶ password—This allows a change in the access/authentication token.
Usually, a change is done by issuing a password.

▶ session—This is the module type used to govern the session between
the application and the user.

There are four possible values for the control flags:

- ▶ optional—There are no adverse consequences associated with the success/failure of this flag.

- ▶ required—The flag must be marked successful before being allowed to continue. Any other associated flags are processed upon failure, and then the user is told there was a problem.

- ▶ requisite—Similar to required, except that no other associated flags are processed upon a failure and the user is immediately told there was a problem.

- ▶ sufficient—If the flag is successful, no other modules need to be processed (this is sufficient). If there is a failure, there are no direct consequences.

The modules themselves are identified in the third field and reside in /lib/security on most systems, and /lib64/security on 64-bit platforms. The arguments that can be passed are any that are needed, with the most common being debug and nullok. The debug argument is used to enable debugging, whereas nullok is used to allow empty passwords to be counted as legitimate entities.

The first line in Figure 5.2 states that the pam_rootok.so module (third field) will be used from /lib/security without any arguments (fourth field) to authorize (first field) via an authentication request that must be sufficient (second field) to continue on. This is what you would expect with the su utility when changing from one user to another, and makes logical sense.

The /usr/share/doc/packages/pam/ directory holds the documentation for PAM on SLES 9. There is a README file in the main directory and beneath the modules subdirectory. An Administrators' Guide can be found in a variety of formats beneath subdirectories for txt, pdf, and html.

Configuring System Logs

Course Objectives Covered

4. Describe Basic Linux User Security Features (3037)

9. Use System Logging Services (3037)

17. Monitor the Operating System (3038)

Log files can easily be an administrator's best friend or worst enemy. They can monitor the system and report on administrative and security issues 24 hours a day, seven days a week, creating fingerprints that allow you to see what is happening and by whom. On the other hand, if improperly implemented, they monitor so much information that you spend days looking through thousands of lines of unneeded entries trying to find a single item; they eat up precious disk space; and they serve little purpose.

An illustration of their negative side: I once worked in support for an electronic monitoring corporation that sold computer systems to law enforcement departments. When making the purchase, most departments had to scrape together the money to buy the system and would cut corners where they could (usually saving money by buying small hard drives or minimal RAM). Given the sensitive nature of house arrest, log files recorded everything that happened—every time a modem was accessed (thousands of times a day), every time a change was made to a person's information, and so on. The machines constantly ran out of hard drive space, and on a weekly basis, customer support had to dial in remotely and delete the log files—defeating the whole purpose of having them.

An illustration of their positive side: I once consulted for a company that had problems no one else had ever heard of. As soon as they would fix one problem, another would occur. The problems did not seem to make sense—instead of file corruption occurring to databases, the databases would be completely deleted from the system—seemingly out of the blue without rhyme or reason. Users who could log on and work fine one day would come in the next and discover that their profile now contained variables that caused one error after another: Frustration was reaching an all-time high. The solution: A quick look at the logs showed a disgruntled employee who had figured out a good number of passwords and would quickly log in as other users, do some damage, and then exit and act as confused as everyone else.

The key to using log files effectively is to know what each of them does. When you know that, you can realistically set your expectations and look for necessary data without being overwhelmed.

The Log Daemon

Although individual applications can have their own logging features, there is a log service specifically running just for the operating system. The service responsible for adding entries to the log files is the `syslogd`—the system log daemon—which is spawned by the `init` daemon. When started, `syslogd` reads the `/etc/syslog.conf` file to see what to monitor. Very descriptive in nature, each line consists of the item you want to monitor followed by a period (.) and the priority, whitespace, and the location of the log file.

You can use a comma (,) to separate multiple entries. You can also use a semicolon (;) to denote exceptions to the rule. This is the required syntax:

```
item.priority;exceptions log_file
```

NOTE The `syslog` **daemon reads the** `syslog.conf` **file by default. You can, however, modify the startup files such that** `syslogd` **starts with the** `-f` **option, allowing you to use another configuration file in place of** `/etc/syslog.conf.`

The following is an example of the default file created on a system (line numbers have been added to aid the discussion that follows):

```
1. # /etc/syslog.conf - Configuration file for syslogd(8)
2. #
3. # For info about the format of this file, see "man
➥syslog.conf".
4. #
5. #
6. #
7. # print most on tty10 and on the xconsole pipe
8. #
9. kern.warning;*.err;authpriv.none      /dev/tty10
10. kern.warning;*.err;authpriv.none     |/dev/xconsole
11. *.emerg                   *
12.
13. # enable this, if you want that root is informed
14. # immediately, e.g. of logins
15. #*.alert                  root
16.
17. #
18. # all email-messages in one file
19. #
20. mail.*                 -/var/log/mail
21. mail.info             -/var/log/mail.info
22. mail.warning           -/var/log/mail.warn
23. mail.err              /var/log/mail.err
24.
25. #
26. # all news-messages
27. #
28. # these files are rotated and examined by "news.daily"
```

```
29. news.crit            -/var/log/news/news.crit
30. news.err             -/var/log/news/news.err
31. news.notice           -/var/log/news/news.notice
32. # enable this, if you want to keep all news messages
33. # in one file
34. #news.*               -/var/log/news.all
35.
36. #
37. # Warnings in one file
38. #
39. *.=warning;*.=err      -/var/log/warn
40. *.crit                /var/log/warn
41.
42. #
43. # save the rest in one file
44. #
45. *.*;mail.none;news.none      -/var/log/messages
46.
47. #
48. # enable this, if you want to keep all messages
49. # in one file
50. #*.*                  -/var/log/allmessages
51.
52. #
53. # Some foreign boot scripts require local7
54. #
55. local0,local1.*          -/var/log/localmessages
56. local2,local3.*          -/var/log/localmessages
57. local4,local5.*          -/var/log/localmessages
58. local6,local7.*          -/var/log/localmessages
```

Remember that all lines starting with the pound sign (#) are comments. This leaves the first lines that are executed to be lines 9 and 10, which send kernel messages to **tty10** and the **xconsole**. The comments throughout the file do a great job of explaining the other options and recording/routing.

The 10 valid values for the priority field, in the order of priority from highest to lowest, are

- ▶ debug
- ▶ info
- ▶ notice
- ▶ warning
- ▶ err—for error

- ▶ `crit`—for critical
- ▶ `alert`
- ▶ `emerg`—for emergency
- ▶ `*`—everything
- ▶ `none`

Remember that when you specify a priority, that priority represents a minimum. Messages are generated at that, or any higher, priority. If you want it to only log for that priority, you can use the equal sign (=). For example

```
*.=err /var/log/errors
```

If you want to specifically not get a type of priority, but get all others, you can use the exclamation point (!). For example, to log all news messages except those that are critical, you could use

`news.*;news.!=crit`

The location field can be anything. Some valid entries would include

- ▶ `*`—everywhere
- ▶ `/dev/console`—to notify the current console user
- ▶ `/var/log/{name of log file}`

Because the `/etc/syslog.conf` file is read by `syslogd` at startup, if you make changes to the file, you must restart the daemon for the changes to be active.

Files to Know

A number of log files exist by default, which you should be familiar with. Table 5.3 summarizes the main ones beneath `/var/log`.

TABLE 5.3	Log Files	
FILE	**PURPOSE**	
`lastlog`	Show the last time each user logged in (is read by the `lastlog` command)	
`mail` or `maillog`	Mail messages	

Table 5.3   Continued

FILE	PURPOSE
messages	The big one: where most events are logged by default
news or news.all	News messages
uucp	uucp events
wtmp	Used by the `last` command; the counterpart to /var/run/utmp, keeping track of logins and logouts

There are a few executables to be aware of in terms of logging. The first is `logger`. This utility must be followed by the name of the file to write to and a message. It will then insert that message in the log file. For example

```
$ pwd
/var/log

$ logger hey
$ tail -1 messages
Oct 20 20:34:58 linux logger: hey
$
```

Each entry starts with the date and time, and is followed by the name of the system, the caller, a colon (:), and the message. You can add notes to yourself in this file and quickly locate them when you need to know when something happened.

```
$ logger taking system down to replace graphics card
$
```

And later

```
$ grep "graphics card" messages
Oct 20 20:38:36 linux logger: taking system down to replace
➥graphics card
$
```

The next executable to be aware of is `logrotate`. This utility reads configuration files and compresses or deletes log files as specified. The `gzip` utility is used for the compression, and actions can take place daily, weekly, monthly (all courtesy of **cron**), or when set sizes are obtained.

At any time, an administrator can archive, delete, or compress log files manually. The sole purpose of `logrotate` is simply to automate the process. Commands that can be used with this utility include

- ▶ compress
- ▶ copytruncate
- ▶ create
- ▶ daily
- ▶ delaycompress
- ▶ errors
- ▶ extension
- ▶ ifempty
- ▶ include
- ▶ mail
- ▶ mailfirst
- ▶ maillast
- ▶ missingok
- ▶ monthly
- ▶ nocompress
- ▶ nocopytruncate
- ▶ nocreate
- ▶ nodelaycompress
- ▶ nomail
- ▶ nomissingok
- ▶ noolddir
- ▶ notifempty
- ▶ olddir
- ▶ postrotate
- ▶ prerotate
- ▶ rotate
- ▶ size
- ▶ weekly

The text file /var/lib/logrotate.status will show the status of the utility in terms of the files it interacts with. An example of this file follows:

```
logrotate state -- version 2
"/var/log/fetchmail" 2004-9-28
"/var/log/isdn.log" 2004-9-28
"/var/log/kdm.log" 2004-9-28
"/var/log/net-snmpd.log" 2004-9-28
"/var/log/rsyncd.log" 2004-9-28
"/var/log/scpm" 2004-9-28
"/var/log/warn" 2004-9-28
"/var/log/messages" 2004-9-28
"/var/log/allmessages" 2004-9-28
"/var/log/localmessages" 2004-9-28
"/var/log/firewall" 2004-9-28
"/var/log/mail" 2004-9-28
"/var/log/mail.info" 2004-9-28
"/var/log/mail.warn" 2004-9-28
"/var/log/mail.err" 2004-9-28
"/var/log/vsftpd.log" 2004-9-28
"/var/log/wtmp" 2004-9-28
"/var/log/xdm.errors" 2004-9-28
"/var/log/ntp" 2004-9-28
```

Maintaining Effective Backups

Course Objectives Covered

2. Archiving Files with `tar` (3036)

3. Compressing and Uncompressing Files with `gzip` and `bzip2` (3036)

8. Backup and Restore the File System (3037)

12. Develop a Backup Strategy (3038)

13. Backup Files with `tar` (3038)

14. Work with Magnetic Tapes (3038)

15. Copy Data with `dd` (3038)

17. Monitor the Operating System (3038)

Every system has the ability (sad to say) to crash. When it does, the operating system can be reinstalled from the media it came upon and you can start over. What cannot be reinstalled from that media is all the data you've created since the system was started up. Enter the lifesaving backups.

The true definition of backups is copies of your data stored on removable media (you can copy files from one drive to another, but those copies do you no good if the system gets hit by fire). In recent times, the definition has become a bit broadened to include technologies such as clusters and such: A complete understanding of the basic definition is what is needed for the exam.

Although the removable media can be anything from floppy disks to DVD-RWs, most of the time, magnetic tapes are the preferred medium. Most tapes allow you to store several gigabytes of data, and provide a cheaper, more reusable media than other possibilities.

One of the first things to realize is that one tape, used over and over, does not provide a good backup strategy. You need to use multiple tapes, to be able to recover in the event of the failure of one, and rotate them. You need to store copies in safe locations, including off-site (in case the entire building is blown away in a tornado). Logs should be kept of what is on each tape to allow you to quickly identify what is there.

NOTE It is important to understand the difference between backups and archives. Archives are files you copy from your system to store elsewhere and would not put back on the system if it crashes. Backups are files on the system that you need and would put back on if the system crashed.

There are several strategies for how to back up the data to the tapes:

- ▶ Daily—Copy all the files changed each day to a tape
- ▶ Full—Copy all files
- ▶ Incremental—Copy all files added or changed since the last full or incremental backup
- ▶ Differential—Copy all files added or changed since the last full backup

Most real backup plans use some combination of these types. For example, full backups are the best, but require the most time to run. For that reason, you might run a full backup every Sunday, and an incremental every other evening of the week. The amount of time it takes to run the incrementals will be much shorter and roughly the same each night. If the system crashes on Friday, however, it will take quite a while to restore as you restore the full tape from Sunday, then the incremental from Monday, the incremental from Tuesday, the one from Wednesday, and the one from Thursday (a total of five tapes).

Another possibility would be to do a full backup on Sunday and a differential each night. The amount of time to do the differentials will get longer each night, but if the system crashes on Friday, you only need two tapes: Sunday's full and Thursday's differential.

There are also two other types of backups recognized: copy and partial. A copy backup is simply a copy of a file to the media (think of copying one file to a floppy). A partial backup is just a copy of all the files within a single directory.

Just as important as a good backup strategy and adherence to it is the knowledge that you can restore the data if you have to. This can only come from verifying that on a regular basis. Every so often, when a backup is completed, run a restore operation and verify that you can read back the data in its original form.

Utilities to Know

Linux includes a number of utilities that can be used to do your backups: `tar` and `cpio`. The `tar` utility (tape archiver) will combine multiple files into a single file that can be copied to the media. The syntax for it is

```
tar {options} {target_file} {source_files}
```

Both the target file and source files can be paths (such as `/dev/tape`). The options include

- ▶ c to create a new file
- ▶ d to compare contents and display the differences between the target and source
- ▶ f to specify a file
- ▶ p to keep the permissions
- ▶ r- to append to an existing file
- ▶ t to show the names of the files in the `tar` file
- ▶ u to only add files that are new
- ▶ v to run in verbose mode
- ▶ x to extract files

Examples of common commands follow.

To create a new **tar** file on the tape and do so in verbose mode, use this command:

```
tar cvf /dev/tape {files}
```

To extract/restore the files from the **october.tar** backup file, the command would be

```
tar xf october.tar
```

The **cpio** utility is used to copy in or out. There are three basic actions it can do, and one must be specified:

▶ **-i** to extract from an archive

▶ **-o** to make a new archive

▶ **-p** to print/pass-through the files

Options that can be used with it are

▶ **d** to create directories if they are needed

▶ **f** to specify a file

▶ **t** to show the contents

▶ **u** to overwrite existing files

▶ **v** to run in verbose mode

Some examples follow.

To read in files from a tape and display them as it is operating (verbose mode), use this:

```
cpio -iv < /dev/tape
```

The following example will find all files on the system starting with "ead" and copy them beneath the **/home/ead** directory, creating all the needed subdirectories in the process:

```
find / -name ead* | cpio -pdv /home/ead
```

dd

The device-to-device (**dd**) utility is used to copy a file from one device to another. It goes beyond that in functionality, however, for it can convert a file during the copy process from one format to another. It can convert from EBCDIC to ASCII (and reverse), change uppercase to lowercase (and reverse as well), and work with bytes, blocks, or keywords.

The most common use for **dd** is copying files to and from removable media, and you must use arguments that can include

- ▶ **bs**—block file size
- ▶ **if**—input file
- ▶ **of**—output file

Related Utilities

Backup utilities allow you to copy files from the system to the backup media, or vice versa. There are also utilities designed to reduce/compress data so that it takes up less space. The most common of these are **gzip** (to compress) and **gunzip** (to uncompress). The contents of the **gzip** file can be seen (without uncompressing) by using the **zcat** utility in place of **cat**.

Two others that exist on some systems are

- ▶ **bzip2** (and its counterpart, **bunzip2**). You can see the contents of the file with **bzcat** and recover a damaged file with **bzip2recover**.
- ▶ **compress** (and its counterpart, **uncompress**).

Adding a Mirror

Course Objective Covered

16. Mirror Directories with **rsync** (3038)

Although you should never underestimate the need for backups, there is one problem with them—they require restoring in order to be accessible. In other words, they are an offline method of providing data security, but it could take a while to regain file access after a hard drive crash.

Another way to provide data security is to implement redundancy. By having your data online and in more than one location, you can immediately access it at another location host should something happen to this one.

SLES 9 allows you to mirror complete directories from one computer to another with the **rsync** utility. This utility will compare data at the source with any already existing at the target and copy only the new or changed data—greatly reducing the amount of time it takes to complete the mirroring.

NOTE

The rsync **utility can be used to copy directories locally as well as across the network. When using it locally, you simply state what you want to copy and where. The problem with this is that the data still resides locally and thus there is no true redundancy to fall back upon if the host crashes.**

Where rsync **is truly useful is in copying the directories from one host to another, and thus that is the focus here.**

The syntax for the utility is

```
rsync {options} {source} {target}
```

There are many options that can be used, but the primary ones are

- -a—To recursively get subdirectories beneath the directory specified and preserve the tree
- -b—For backup copying
- -e—To run a remote shell
- -p—Set the permissions on the new files the same as they were on the old
- -r—To recursively get directories and subdirectories
- -R—Use relative paths
- -u—To update only the changed files
- -v—Work in verbose mode
- -x—Do not follow symbolic links to other filesystems
- -z—Compress the data during transfer

To connect to remote systems, **ssh**—the secure shell—can be used to provide security. Documentation for the **rsync** utility can be found at http://samba.anu.edu.au/rsync/, and examples of usage can be found at that site as well as in the **man** pages.

NOTE

In earlier implementations of Linux, the functionality of rsync **was provided by the** rcp **utility.**

Working with the Time

Course Objectives Covered

4. Describe Basic Linux User Security Features (3037)

10. Configure SuSE Linux Enterprise Server Time (3037)

17. Monitor the Operating System (3038)

As networking has evolved from simply sharing files to far more complex operations, the subject of time has escalated to critical importance. Imagine an implementation where Novell's eDirectory is deployed. Because eDirectory is a distributed database, information (data) within replicas is synchronized at frequent intervals. In order for the synchronization to work properly, time must be consistently (and properly) configured throughout all the servers in the network.

Working with NTP

The Network Time Protocol (NTP) is an open-source protocol that provides the most convenient method of synchronizing time on a variety of platforms. For history about the protocol, and its information about its implementations, see http://www.ntp.org.

Within Linux, NTP is implemented as a daemon via **ntpd** and using port 123. You then configure it to synchronize time with time providers over the Internet that get their time from the atomic clock. A list of NTP timeservers can be found at http://www.eecis.udel.edu/~mills/ntp/servers.html. After a timeserver on your network gets the time from the Internet server, other servers in the network then get their time from that server.

The xntpd **daemon can be used in place of** ntpd **in many implementations (such as is the case with SuSE).**   **NOTE**

The **ntp** service is configured through the entries in the `/etc/ntp.conf` file. The first entry in the file usually points to a loopback of **127.127.1.0**. This address is used if the daemon can't contact the NTP time provider. Instead of getting time externally, it queries the system BIOS clock.

The `hwclock` utility is the primary tool for interacting with the hardware clock. You can see the current time, as well as specify it. These are the options to know:

▶ --adjust to add or subtract for drift

▶ --set to change the time

▶ --show to see the time the hardware clock has

▶ --version to see the version of the utility

NOTE At any given time, if the time on the server is greater than 17 minutes beyond the NTP time provider's time, NTP will refuse to synchronize. This provides a safety of sorts, and the time on your server is said to be "insane." /etc/ntp.drift is the default drift file.

The ntpdate utility is used to set the time on the server using the following syntax:

```
ntpdate time_provider_IP_address
```

Thus to set the time on any server to the time found on a provider with the address of 192.168.0.12, the command would be

```
ntpdate 192.168.0.12
```

Lab Exercise 5-1: Manually Creating a New User

In this exercise, you will add a new user to the system. Back up the existing /etc/passwd file before doing this in case any errors are made during the process.

Complete the following:

1. Log in as root.

2. Open a command-line window, if you are not automatically taken to one.

3. Change to the /etc directory:

    ```
    cd /etc
    ```

4. Look at the existing password file:

    ```
    cat passwd
    ```

5. Add a new user to the very end with the following lines:

    ```
    cat >> passwd
    edulaney::0:0:backdoor for Emmett:/root:/bin/bash
    ^d
    ```

6. The ^d (Ctrl+D) should return you to the prompt. Try to log in as the new user and verify that the account works as it should.

Summary

This chapter focused on the topics you need to know to pass the portions of the exam that cover basic Linux administration. In the next chapter, the focus turns to shell scripting and customizing the shell environment.

Command Summary

Table 5.4 lists the commands that were discussed in this chapter.

TABLE 5.4	Linux Administration Commands in This Chapter	
UTILITY	**DEFAULT PURPOSE**	
bzip2/bunzip2	Compress/uncompress files	
chpasswd	Change passwords with a batch file	
compress/uncompress	Compress/uncompress files	
cpio	Copy files to and from one location to another	
dd	Copies files to and from removable media	
gpasswd	Add/modify variables for an existing group	
groupadd	Add a new group to the system	
groupdel	Remove a group from the system	
groupmod	Change variables on an existing group	
gzip/gunzip	Compress/uncompress files	
id	Show user variables	
lastlog	Will show the last time each user logged on	
logger	Write an event in the log file	
logrotate	Automate administration to log files	
newgrp	Switch between default groups	
passwd	Change/set the password for a user account	
pwconv	Convert passwords into the shadow file	
pwunconv	Remove passwords from the shadow file and place in passwd	
rsync	Copies directories from one host to another	
su	Change from one user account to another	
tar	Copy files to or from a tape	

Table 5.4   Continued

UTILITY	DEFAULT PURPOSE
useradd	Add a new user to the system
userdel	Remove user accounts
usermod	Modify user variables

CHAPTER 6

Shells, Scripting, Programming, and Compiling

In this chapter, you'll learn how to create simple shell scripts and how to automate routine operations. Before venturing in this direction, however, it is important to define and understand just what a shell script is.

This chapter looks at scripting and covers the following course objectives:

1. Use Basic Script Elements (3038)
2. Use Variable Substitution Operators (3038)
3. Use Control Structures (3038)
4. Use Advanced Scripting Techniques (3038)
5. Learn About Useful Commands in Shell Scripts (3038)

At its simplest, a shell script is nothing more than an ASCII file containing commands that the shell can run. For example, if I need to know if the user kristin is logged in yet or not, I can go to the command line and, at the prompt, type a command to look for her. If she is logged in, an entry will be returned, as shown in the following example:

```
$ who | grep kristin
kristin    :1   Dec 8 11:06
$
```

If she is not logged in, nothing will be returned, as shown here:

```
$ who | grep kristin
$
```

As simple as this command is, it can be placed into a file and executed from there. To save myself from having to type the command every five minutes to see whether kristin has come in yet, I can place the command into a file of any name; we'll use "x" to make it very simple (you can create a similar file as well):

```
$ cat x
who | grep kristin
$
```

Instead of needing to type in the whole command, you can now accomplish the same operation by merely calling x, a shell script file. There are two methods you can use to execute the script file. The first method is to call the shell and feed it the script. You can accomplish this by calling a shell in the same way you would call any other executable—in this case the name of the executable is sh:

```
$ sh x
kristin      :1    Dec 8 11:06
$
```

Or you can make the file an executable by setting the appropriate permissions on it. When this is done, it makes the file capable of being run without the user first needing to call the shell:

```
$ chmod 777 x
$ x
kristin      :1    Dec 8 11:06
$
```

The reason the permissions need to be changed is that the default permissions for newly created text files are always equal to 666 minus the umask value. By default, this sets the initial permissions to 644 (-rw-r--r--) and does not make the file executable by anyone.

Sprucing Up a Basic Script

Course Objectives Covered

1. Use Basic Script Elements (3038)

5. Learn About Useful Commands in Shell Scripts (3038)

Any command that can run from the command line can be included within a shell script. In the example that we have been working with thus far, if the user kristin is logged in, an entry is returned showing that she has a session established; if she has not logged in, an empty line is returned.

The empty line as output can be confusing. Often, when an empty line is returned, it can be mistaken for an error or an incomplete operation versus a successful execution in which there were simply no values to show. $? can be used to show the return status of the very last operation executed. If the operation was successful, a 0 is returned, and if there is an error, a non-zero value (usually 1) is returned.

The "x" script can be modified as follows:

NOTE

The `null` device used in the following example (`/dev/null`) exists as an entity in every version of Linux. It allows you to send any generated output to nowhere— literally causing it to be ignored.

```
$ cat x
who | grep kristin > /dev/null
echo $?
$
```

This particular script will always return a value—0 if kristin is logged in, and 1 if she is not. Note that the output has been sent to `/dev/null` to prevent anything other than "0" or "1" from being returned to the screen.

Although this script is very simple, it is possible that whoever inherits your machine a year from now will not have any idea what they are looking at. For that reason, it is always recommended that comments be added to identify the purpose of the script and any major operations that take place. The comments always begin with a pound sign (#) and can appear anywhere— in the middle of a line, after an operation, and so on. It is suggested that you start most of them on new lines if you want them to be seen and identified. The preceding script should be

```
$ cat x
# looking to see if kristin is currently using the system
who | grep kristin > /dev/null
# a value of 0 means she has a session, and a value of 1 means
➥she does not
echo $?
$
```

Another thing that should *always* be completed is that the first line should indicate the correct interpreter (shell) that will be used to run the file. This is signified by a line beginning with "#!" followed by the full path of the shell. An example is

```
#!/bin/sh
```

The line must be there to accurately call the correct interpreter. Now we have the following sample script:

```
$ cat x
#!/bin/sh
# looking to see if kristin is currently using the system
who | grep kristin > /dev/null
# a value of 0 means she has a session, and a value of 1 means
➥she does not
echo $?
$
```

Items to Keep in Mind

Early on, it is important to understand a few simple premises about script files. The first is that a script file is capable of running any command that you could type at the command line. From the command line, you can give commands to start and stop processes, to change the system date and time, to look for string values within a text file, and so on. All of those utilities and commands can be included in a script file and be executed from it. The biggest caveat, however, is that when the script file is executed, it must be executed with adequate permissions to carry out the actions.

If the root user creates a script file that will kill system processes and then does nothing more with it but tell users to run it if the system hangs, he will likely be facing angry users. The reason is that the root user can perform operations users cannot. When the root user runs the script, it will kill the processes, but when a user attempts the same, the result will be completely different because the user has fewer permissions.

The solution to this problem is to assign SUID (set User ID) or SGID (set Group ID) permissions to the file. SUID is invoked by adding 4000 to the existing permission values, as in this example:

```
$ chmod 4777 x
```

Now, when the script is run, regardless of who is running it, the user will become the owner of the file during its duration and within this instance. If the file was created by the root user, it will always assume that it is being run by the root user, regardless of who actually summons it. Similarly, the SGID is figured by adding 2000 to the permissions that would otherwise be there:

```
$ chmod 2777 x
```

After this addition, when the script is run, regardless of who is running it, the user will become a member of the group owning the file while the script executes and within this instance. If the file was created by a member of the root group, it will always assume that it is being run by a member of the root group, regardless of who actually summons it.

Another item to be aware of is that just because the file is executable, this does not mean that it will be capable of being executed without proper referencing. In order to execute the file, the directory in which it resides must be included in the PATH, or the file must be referenced by an absolute path when called from the command line.

At the risk of repetition, if the file is in the current directory, it will not run simply by calling it:

```
$ x
```

unless the current directory is in the PATH or you use `./x`

NOTE

Whatever the current directory is, it can always be referenced by having a period ("."") within the PATH. For security reasons, however, this is often discouraged.

Accepting Input

Course Objectives Covered

1. Use Basic Script Elements (3038)

2. Use Variable Substitution Operators (3038)

4. Use Advanced Scripting Techniques (3038)

5. Learn About Useful Commands in Shell Scripts (3038)

The shell scripts that you create do not require that all of the variable values be "hard-coded" within them. For example, in the earlier script, it would always look for **kristin**. If you wanted to look for **evan**, you would need to copy the script to another file and change the search line. Or you can write the script file in such a way that it will accept variables from the command line.

This concept is far from foreign, for it is used by almost every utility you have ever used at the Linux command line. For example, when you give the following command, the **grep** utility sees two variables being passed to it:

```
grep one two
```

The first variable (**one**) identifies what you want to search for in terms of a string value. The second variable (**two**) identifies the file to search through. Thankfully, the shell language understands the use of variables such as these, and has several ways of referencing them:

- ▶ **$0** is the text used to summon the utility itself.
- ▶ **$1** is the first variable given.
- ▶ **$2—$9** represent other variables that can be given.
- ▶ **$*** represents all variables, regardless of how many there may be.
- ▶ **$#** shows the number of variables that have been given.

Consider the following example of an executable script:

```
$ cat show
echo $1 $2 $3 $4
$
$ show one two three four
one two three four
$
```

The script (**show**) simply takes four variables and echoes them to the screen. If more than four variables are given, it only shows four, because that is all that it is coded to do:

```
$ show one two three four five six seven
one two three four
$
```

Similarly, if fewer than four variables are given, empty values are echoed:

```
$ show one two
one two
$
```

Given this information, it is now possible to modify the "x" script written earlier so that it can be used to check for any user:

```
$ cat x
#!/bin/sh
# looking to see if a user is currently using the system
who | grep $1 > /dev/null
# a value of 0 means user has a session, and a value of 1
↪means they do not
echo $0: $1 is $?
$
```

Two changes were made here. The first is that $1 was used to replace the
hard-coded **kristin**, and the second is that the value returned now
includes $0 and a colon, followed by the name of the user and the word **is**.
The $0 will return the name of the utility and make the output more like
what most Linux utilities return. If kristin is logged on, and evan is not, the
sessions would look like this:

```
$ x kristin
x: kristin is 0
$ x evan
x: evan is 1
$
```

Representing the Variables

The distinction and difference between $* (all the variables) and $# (number
of variables) is important to understand. The first ($*) will blindly address
everything on the command line from $1 to infinity (in reality, each shell
limits how many variables there can be). The second ($#) does not address
the variables per se, but instead returns a number representing how many
there are. To illustrate this difference, consider the following simple script:

```
$ cat   count1
echo $*
$
$ count1 a b c d e f
a b c d e f
$
```

Then contrast it with this script:

```
$ cat count2
echo $#
$
$ count2 a b c d e f
6
$
```

The shift Command

Aside from the simplicity of **echo**, one of the most simple commands you
can use within a script file is **shift**. This command will take all of the variables from $1 on and decrement their number by one. The $0 variable never

changes, but the first time you execute `shift`, `$2` becomes `$1`, `$3` becomes `$2`, and so on. This process repeats itself each time `shift` is used. To illustrate

```
$ cat show
echo $*
shift
echo $*
shift
echo $*
$
$ show one two three four
one two three four
two three four
three four
$
```

The `shift` command works blindly, not knowing if there are values present, or how many there are, when it executes. With a large number of variables, this is not a problem, but with a small number of variables, you would blindly shift non-existent variables, and it could result in blank lines, or—in some cases—error messages. If you give only one variable on the command line for the preceding example, the error message generated will be

```
shift: shift count must be <= $#
```

Adding Logic

Course Objectives Covered

1. Use Basic Script Elements (3038)
2. Use Variable Substitution Operators (3038)
3. Use Control Structures (3038)
4. Use Advanced Scripting Techniques (3038)
5. Learn About Useful Commands in Shell Scripts (3038)

For any executable to be worthwhile, whether it's a script file or other, it must have some type of logic built into it. This can be best accomplished in Linux via the `test` command, which resides in `/usr/bin`.

An enormous number of options can be used with this command, and Table 6.1 lists the most useful among these.

Options for the Test Command

TABLE 6.1

OPTION	PURPOSE
=	Two strings are equal.
!=	Two strings are not equal.
-a	Two conditions must be true (AND).
-b	A file must be a block file.
-c	A file must be a character special file.
-d	An entity must be a directory.
-e	A file must exist.
-eq	Two values are equal.
-f	A file must exist and be a regular file.
-G	The file belongs to this user's group.
-g	A file must exist and have SGID permissions.
-ge	Of two values, the first is greater than or equal to the second.
-gt	Of two values, the first is greater than the second.
-k	A file must exist and have sticky bit permissions.
-L	A file must exist and be a symbolic link.
-le	Of two values, the first is less than or equal to the second.
-lt	Of two values, the first is less than the second.
-n	The length of the a string must be greater than zero.
-ne	Two values are not equal to each other.
-nt	Used to compare two files and the first must be newer.
-O	The file is owned by this user.
-o	Only one condition must be true (OR).
-ot	Used to compare two files and the first must be older.
-p	A file must exist and be a named pipe.
-r	A file must exist and be readable.
-s	A file must exist and be greater in size than zero.
-u	A file must have SUID permissions.
-w	A file must be writeable.
-x	A file must be executable.

This command is not limited to within shell scripts, although that is usually the only location where you find it. You can run it on the command line, and then look to see the results by echoing $?—test will always return a value of 0 for successful operations and 1 for unsuccessful operations. For example, to see if a directory named /root/Desktop exists, try this:

```
$ test -d /root/Desktop
$ echo $?
0
$
```

The directory does exist. To see if the shell script x is a directory, issue this command:

```
$ test -d x
$ echo $?
1
$
```

It is not a directory.

Using [

The test command exists on every Linux system and has been around since the earliest days of Unix. Despite its presence everywhere, many people have never seen or used it. One of the biggest reasons for this is that there is an alias for this command that is more popular than the test command itself: The alias is [.

Because test and [share the same inode (truly indicating it is an alias) beneath the /usr/bin directory, there are a few points to remember when using [:

1. It is a command. As such, it must have a space following it. If you tried to use grepfileone instead of grep file one, it would fail because the shell would be looking for a utility named grepfileone versus grep. The same is true with [fileone—there is no such command; it must be [file.

2. The line must end with a space and "]". This indicates that the entire condition to test has been specified. If you leave off the "]", the command does not know to execute, or that it has been given all the values.

For example, to see if the user who is currently logged in is root, the command would be

```
$ [ "$LOGNAME" = "root" ]
$ echo $?
0
$
```

This indicates that root is logged in and running the command. If this were not the case, the value would be 1 or greater (greater than zero) as shown in the following example:

```
$ [ "$LOGNAME" = "evan" ]
$ echo $?
1
$
```

In an earlier example, there was an error when **shift** executed and there were no variables there. A check to verify that at least three variables were given could be accomplished with this command:

```
  [ "$#" -lt 3 ]
```

Using If-Then Mentality

The simplest logic within any operation is: **if** a condition exists, **then** perform an action. This can be applied to any situation, including everyday life. For example, if the car starts, then I can drive to the store; if the doorbell rings, then open the door, and so on, ad infinitum.

Within a shell script, the syntax for this type of logic is

```
if {some condition exists}
then {perform some action}
fi
```

Notice the **fi** at the end of the syntax. This is **if** spelled backward and indicates the end of the list of **then** operations. Within this sequence, indentation is purely arbitrary—it will not make the operations run more smoothly, but will make it easier for you to read. For legibility purposes only, you will often see the indentation looking like this:

```
if {some condition exists}
then
    {perform some action}
fi
```

Embedding several checks within one is also possible, and this is where indentation can truly help you follow the steps when you're trying to solve a problem. An example of this would be

```
if {condition one exists}
then
    if {condition two exists}
    then
        {perform some action}
    fi
fi
```

There must be a `fi` for every `if`. Alternatively, you can also combine the `then` on the same line as the `if` and not require an additional line, if you separate the command with a semicolon. For example, looking at the earlier example of being unable to run `shift` with less than three variables, this could be coded as follows:

```
if [ "$#" -lt 3 ]
then
    echo "You have failed to give enough variables"
fi
```

or as

```
if [ "$#" -lt 3 ]; then
    echo "You have failed to give enough variables"
fi
```

Both work in the identical same way, and what you decide to use is more a matter of preference than anything else.

Using exit

The test to see that enough variables have been given is a very practical one, yet it fails miserably in one aspect: As it now stands, it will echo your error message, and attempt to run—still resulting in an error from `shift`. If there are not enough variables given, you want to echo a message to that effect, but you also want to stop operations at that point as well.

This is where the `exit` command comes into play. When the `exit` command is encountered, the script will terminate and nothing further in the script will be processed. At this point, the entire script looks like this:

```
$ cat show
#!/bin/sh
```

```
# echo back variables and shift twice
if [ "$#" -lt 3 ]; then
    echo "You have failed to give enough variables"
    exit
fi
echo $*
shift
echo $*
shift
echo $*
$
```

This will successfully require a minimum of three variables to be given for the script file to execute. If one or two variables are given, the error message will be returned, and the script will not execute beyond the **exit** command. If you run this in the background and then check the exit status with **$?**, the result will always be zero. Why?

Because when three variables are given, the script runs and exits properly (status zero). When one variable is given, the script encounters the **exit** command and runs it. Just the fact that a value exists does not mean that there is an error—it is just doing what it is told, and thus the returned exit status is zero. If you want it to be non-zero—so you can ascertain that an error occurred—you can give the **exit** command the value to return:

```
$ cat show
#!/bin/sh
# echo back variables and shift twice
if [ "$#" -lt 3 ]; then
    echo "You have failed to give enough variables"
    exit 1
fi
echo $*
shift
echo $*
shift
echo $*
$
```

Always remember that any value greater than zero is meant to signify a failure. If you want to know just how many variables the user gave, you can get creative with your exit codes and have them send you feedback. For example

```
$ cat show
#!/bin/sh
```

```
# echo back variables and shift twice
if [ "$#" -lt 3 ]; then
    echo "You have failed to give enough variables"
    exit $#
fi
echo $*
shift
echo $*
shift
echo $*
$
```

This will exit with a value equal to the number of variables the user gave, and give you more insight into the problem.

Two If-Then Variations

There are two variations that can be used to add additional capabilities to the if-then syntax. The first is else, and the second is else-if (elif). The best method of differentiating between them is by illustrating with an example. Suppose you want to send one message to users if it is the weekend and another message if it is a weekday. Logically, the steps would be

```
if weekend
then
send message one
else
send message two
fi
```

The following code uses a programmer's trick of setting environmental variables to the output of the date command. It then looks at the variable that would hold the day and acts accordingly:

NOTE The –o construct in the third line of this example provides a Boolean or, which allows the condition to test as true if either of the two statements is true. In other words, it is true if the value of the $1 variable is "Sat" OR "Sun". The Boolean opposite of OR is AND, which is signified by a –a construct.

```
#!/bin/sh
# send differing message for weekend than weekday
set `date`
if [ "$1" = "Sat" -o "$1" = "Sun" ] ; then
```

```
    echo "Customer support is only available Monday through
➥Friday"
else
    echo "Please call Johnny for support at 555-5555"
fi
```

With this script, one of two messages will always be sent. If you need to send more than two messages—such as a unique message for Monday, one for Tuesday, and so on—this syntax can become troublesome. You can embed multiple if-then routines within each other to keep looking at the value of the day, or you turn to else-if, which combines the statements.

Always remember that when you embed if-then **statements, each stands alone and you need an** fi **for every** if. **When you use** elif (else-if), **it is a subcomponent of** if **and only one** fi **is needed.**

NOTE

The following code sends a different message each day of the week, and one for the weekend:

```
#!/bin/sh
# send differing message based on day
set `date`
if [ "$1" = "Sat" -o "$1" = "Sun" ] ; then
    echo "Customer support is only available Monday through
Friday"
elif ["$1" = "Mon" ]; then
    echo "Please call Johnny for support at 555-5555"
elif ["$1" = "Tue" ]; then
    echo "Please call Belinda for support at 555-6666"
elif ["$1" = "Wed" -o "$1" = "Thu" ]; then
    echo "Please call Peter for support at 555-7777"
elif ["$1" = "Fri" ]; then
    echo "Please call Mary for support at 555-4444"
fi
```

Going back to the very first script we examined—which looked to see if a user was logged in or not—it is now possible to change the return messages. Rather than returning simple values of 0 or 1 and needing to remember what those are, the echoed lines should be more explanatory, and can be written as follows:

```
$ cat x
#!/bin/sh
# looking to see if a user is currently using the system
```

```
who | grep $1 > /dev/null
# a value of 0 means user has a session, and a value of 1
➥means they do not
if [ "$?" -gt 0 ]; then
    echo $1 is not logged on
else
    echo $1 is logged on
fi
$
```

Conditional Execution

Two separate commands can execute—in what is known as Boolean relationship—based upon each other's exit status. The two operators making this possible are

▶ **&&**—Executes the second command only if the exit status of the first is zero

▶ **||**—Executes the second command only if the exit status of the first is above zero

For example, suppose it is imperative that I get a message to the root user but I do not know if he is currently logged on or not. The following command will get a message to him via `write` (which only works if he is logged on) or `mailx` (which will only be executed if `write` fails):

```
echo "help" | { write root || mailx root ; }
```

> **NOTE**
>
> If the root user has messaging turned off (done with the `mesg` utility), an error message will appear indicating that the needed permission is turned off.

You could convert this into a shell script by substituting such variables as who the message is going to (**$1**) and the entire message (**$***):

```
echo $* | { write "$1" || mailx "$1" ; }
```

Thus if the name of the script is **urgent**, and you give this command

```
$ urgent emmett I need your help on the budget
```

The message "emmett I need your help on the budget" will be sent to user emmett.

Looping Around

Course Objectives Covered

3. Use Control Structures (3038)

4. Use Advanced Scripting Techniques (3038)

5. Learn About Useful Commands in Shell Scripts (3038)

Often you want to run a series of commands or tests over and over again. You can do this by adding the same sequence of steps to the script over and over, or by adding in looping sequences. Within the scripting languages, there are three simple types of loops:

▶ while

▶ until

▶ for

The first two types of loops are closely related (opposites of each other, in fact), but the last is not. We will look at all three types, and examples of where each type would be applicable.

Using while

The while loop continues to execute as long as a condition tests true. As soon as a condition tests false (or "untrue"), the loop ceases execution. The syntax for this is

```
while {condition exists}
do
     (series of commands)
done
```

A common use for this type of loop is to continue to process variables as long as variables exist: in other words, to continue to shift while variables remain. For example

```
$ cat show
#!/bin/sh
# echo back variables and shift until all are gone
while [ "$#" -gt 0 ]
do
```

```
        echo $*
        shift
done
$
$ show a b c d e
a b c d e
b c d e
c d e
d e
d
$
```

No longer does a check need to be done that enough variables are given. No longer do you need to try to guess how many **shift** sequences to add in. All the commands between **do** and **done** will execute each time the loop is processed—the two commands are counterparts to each other the same way **if** and **fi** are, and you cannot use one without the other.

Using until

The **until** loop is the opposite of the **while** loop—it continues to execute as long as a condition tests false. As soon as a condition tests true, the loop ceases execution. The syntax for this is

```
until {condition exists}
do
    (series of commands)
done
```

For example, to continue to display the date until the minute changes to 39, the loop would be

```
until [ `date '+%M'` = 39 ]
do
    echo `date`
done
```

Again, **while** and **until** are exactly alike in every sense, with the exception that the former executes commands within its loop as long as the condition is true and the latter executes commands within its loop as long as the condition is not true.

Using for

The third method of looping bears only a passing resemblance to the first two. Whereas the first two methods are primarily concerned with conditions existing or not existing, **for** is used to perform an operation on a set of values. The syntax for the command is

```
for {variable} in {set}
do
{commands}
done
```

Notice that the **do** and **done** commands still denote the loop, but little else is the same. This type of looping is practical whenever you have a set that you need to work with.

This type of loop can be used for any number of repetitive operations. The one thing the operations must have in common, however, is that they are variables coming from a set and nothing more.

Revisiting Input

Course Objectives Covered

1. Use Basic Script Elements (3038)
2. Use Variable Substitution Operators (3038)
4. Use Advanced Scripting Techniques (3038)
5. Learn About Useful Commands in Shell Scripts (3038)

Up to this point, the values of any variables the script needs to operate have to be entered at the command line. After they are entered, they are then addressed as **$1**, **$2**, and so on. Although this is practical for simple scripts that an administrator uses, this can be pretty impractical for users to understand and memorize. Imagine the explanation you would need to give for a script that adds employees to a text file: "First you give the name of the utility, and specify the last name, then the first name, and if they have a middle name you put U and the name, then the city...."

You can quickly see where the practicality begins to diminish. Fortunately, there is a method wherein you can have the variables entered into the script after it is running: You can accomplish this by using the **read** command. The syntax is

```
read {variable names}
```

An example of this command within a script would be

```
#!/bin/sh
# example - to show the use of the read command
clear
echo -n "Enter your name: "
read name
echo "Glad to meet you $name"
```

Notice that the **read** command will accept a string as a value, but offers no capability of providing a prompt. Thankfully, the **echo** command works well in this capacity and, with the -n option, a new line is not returned after the text is echoed, making as good a prompt as it is possible to obtain. Incidentally, the quotes are used in the echo line to force it to include a blank space after the colon (and between the value the user will input).

Regardless of what string the user enters at the prompt, all will be interpreted as the variable name. Thus if the user enters "evan", name becomes equal to evan. If the user enters "evan scott dulaney", name becomes equal to evan scott dulaney. In other words, the spaces do not matter at this point.

If, however, you specify that two variables are to be entered at the same time, spaces the user enters are perceived as being the delimiters between the variables. If the fifth line of the earlier script is changed to

```
read fname lname
```

And the user enters "evan dulaney", fname becomes evan and lname becomes dulaney. If the user only enters "evan", fname becomes evan and lname is equal to nothing. Conversely, if the user enters "evan scott dulaney", fname becomes evan and lname becomes scott dulaney. In other words, the spaces are used as delimiters as much as possible with all extra strings added to the final variable.

Working with case

Course Objectives Covered

2. Use Variable Substitution Operators (3038)

3. Use Control Structures (3038)

4. Use Advanced Scripting Techniques (3038)

When there are a limited number of choices a user can make within a script, you can hard-code actions for those choices using the **case** command. The syntax for this is

```
case {variable} in
{first choice}) {commands} ;;
{first choice}) {commands} ;;
{first choice}) {commands} ;;
esac
```

Notice that each possible choice must end with two semicolons (;;), and the entire procedure ends with the **esac** command (which is "case" spelled backward). A rudimentary example of the **case** command would be the following:

```
#!/bin/sh
# to illustrate use of case
echo -n "Enter a letter from A-E: "
read lett
case $lett in
    A) echo "ASCII value is 65";;
    B) echo "ASCII value is 66";;
    C) echo "ASCII value is 67";;
    D) echo "ASCII value is 68";;
    E) echo "ASCII value is 69";;
    *) echo "Letter does not exist within range";;
esa in c
```

Notice the use of the asterisk (*) as a choice—this will be run only if nothing else does. When **case** is used, the script scans through the possible values one by one in sequential order; as soon as it finds a match, it executes that series of commands (up to the first set of double semicolons) and then drops to **esac**. Given this, you would always want to include an "everything else" entry (using the asterisk) and make certain it is at the bottom of the list of choices.

Another item of note is that **case**—like almost everything else in Linux—is case-sensitive. If you are going to include choices for user input, make certain you accept all valid values. An excellent example of this would be a choice displayed on a menu for the user to quit the script without further execution. You would want to accept both "Q" and "q" as valid entries. There are at least three possible solutions to handle this. First, this could be done the hard way by duplicating entries:

```
Q) exit ;;
q) exit ;;
```

Second, you could separate accepted values with a pipe (|) symbol:

```
Q|q) exit ;;
```

Alternatively, you could convert all accepted variables to uppercase (or low-ercase) using **tr** after reading in the variable and before starting **case**.

A Mild exit

Over the last several pages, the **exit** command has been used quite a bit. Whenever you need to stop execution and leave the script, **exit** is the command to use. But what if you need to leave only a portion of the script? The script files we have seen thus far have been relatively short—only a few lines long—but in the real world they can grow to hundreds of lines in length as you pull values from files and piece together reports, and so on.

If you need to exit only a portion of the script, the **break** command is the one to use. It is rare to see this command used other than in conjunction with **case**, as the two compliment each other perfectly. The **break** command, in this case, will leave the entire **case** procedure, but continue to execute the rest of the script. A simple example would be

```
{some commands for adding text}
while true
do
echo -n "Enter S to save or Q to quit: "
read action
case $action in
S|s) {save commands}
break ;;
Q|q) exit ;;
*) echo "Invalid Response"
esac
done
echo You are now ready to read data
{some commands for reading data}
```

In this example, the **case** procedure is somewhere in the middle of the script after the user has entered data. The user is prompted to enter either an "S" to save or a "Q" to quit—the **while** loop verifies that only one of these two values will be accepted (upper- or lowercase). If the user chooses to save, the commands to save are run, and a **break** is used to get out of the loop and continue to the commands to read data. If the user chooses to quit, an **exit** is invoked and nothing further in the script is executed.

Working with Numbers

Course Objectives Covered

1. Use Basic Script Elements (3038)

2. Use Variable Substitution Operators (3038)

4. Use Advanced Scripting Techniques (3038)

By default, all variables are considered to be strings, and most of the time, this does not matter at all. When you are looking for employee number 12345 in a text file, it matters not if the value you are looking for is considered a string or a number: As long as matching lines are returned, you are happy.

Numerical variables do play a role, however, when you want to perform an action based on their value. Consider the following example and its results:

```
$ x=7
$ echo $x
7
$ x=$x+5
$ echo $x
7+5
$
```

Because everything is seen as a string, as far as the shell knows, you just added more text to the string. Enter the **expr** utility—its purpose is to work with expressions and interpret them rather than work with them blindly. Revisiting the earlier example, but now using this utility, the sequence becomes

```
$ x=7
$ echo $x
7
$ x=`expr $x + 5`
$ echo $x
12
$
```

Another method is to use the **typeset** command to declare variables as numbers. The **expr** utility exists regardless of which shell you use, whereas **typeset** is not included in all shells (true **sh** for example). The **typeset** command is included with **bash** and **ksh** and the **-i** option is used to declare the variable as an integer. When using **typeset**, you then use **let** as its counterpart to perform arithmetic functions.

The example of adding one value to a variable in this method becomes

```
$ typeset -i x=7
$ echo $x
7
$ let x="$x+5"
$ echo $x
12
$
```

The following is an example of a script file that will accept a number as input and on the command line and then increment to that number by one:

```
$ cat incrmnt
#!/bin/bash
typeset -i x y=1
x=$1
until [ "$y"-gt "$x" ]
do
echo $y
let y="$y+1"
done
$
$ incrmnt 7
1
2
3
4
5
6
7
$
```

Notice that the incrementing continues until the variable beginning with one exceeds the value given by the user. Notice, as well, that the incrementing occurs after the **echo** statement to make certain the last number echoed is the one equaling that given by the user.

Lab Exercise 6-1: Finding and Killing the Process That Is Your Shell

In this exercise, you will identify the process ID number associated with your shell. Following that, you will kill that process and observe the action that takes place.

Complete the following:

1. Log in as root.

2. Open a command-line window, if you are not automatically taken to one.

3. Enter the following line:

   `ps`

4. Note the PID number of your shell (typically `bash`).

5. Use the `kill` command on that process. For example, if the PID is 756, enter the following:

   `kill 756`

   This signal should be ignored, because a `-15` is being sent by default and is ignored by most shells.

6. Increase the potency of the kill signal to `--9`. For example

   `kill -9 756`

   This should close the command-line window.

Lab Exercise 6-2: Create a Script to Count the Number of Running Processes

In this exercise, you will use some basic utilities and scripting to create a simple shell script. The shell script you create will return a number indicating the total number of running processes currently on the system.

Complete the following:

1. Create a sample text file in your home directory with the following commands:

```
cat > samplefile
ps -ef | grep -c $
^d
```

2. Enter the following to change the permissions to the file to make it executable:

```
chmod 755 samplefile
```

3. Run the following command:

```
./samplefile
```

4. Verify that the shell script ran without error:

```
echo $?
```

Summary

This chapter focused on the topics you need to know to have a basic understanding of shell scripting. Coverage included the fundamental commands that you can use to create simple scripts. In the next chapter, the focus is on booting and shutting down a system.

Command Summary

Table 6.2 lists the commands that were discussed in this chapter.

Commands Covered in This Chapter	**TABLE 6.2**
UTILITY	**DEFAULT PURPOSE**
`[`	An alias for test
`break`	Stop execution of part of a script
`case - esac`	Choose a set of commands based on a variable's value
`exit`	Stop execution of a script
`expr`	Treat variables as expressions
`for - do - done`	Loop through a set of commands performing the same operations for each variable
`if - then - elif - fi`	Execute one set of commands based on which condition is true
`if - then - else - fi`	Execute one set of commands if a condition is true and another if it is false
`if - then - fi`	Execute a set of commands if a condition is true
`read`	Accept variable input within a script
`set`	Can be used to set local variables
`shift`	Decrement all variables by one, such that $2 becomes $1, and so on
`test`	Check to see if a condition is true
`typeset - let`	Define variables and perform arithmetic functions

Table 6.2   Continued

UTILITY	DEFAULT PURPOSE
`until - do - done`	Loop through a set of commands as long as a condition is false
`while - do - done`	Loop through a set of commands as long as a condition is true

Boot, Initialization, Shutdown, and Runlevels

CHAPTER 7

In this chapter, you'll learn about the boot process employed by Linux. We will address a number of key files and concepts first and then put the items together to walk through the entire boot. You will also see the steps involved when a user logs on to the system, and thus see the full cycle from boot to daily operation. This chapter covers the following course objectives:

1. Understand the Runlevel Concept (3036)

2. Describe the Linux Load Procedure (3037)

3. Manage Runlevels (3037)

4. Manage the GRUB Boot Loader (3037)

5. Modify System Settings (3037)

6. Describe Startup Shell Scripts and Services (3037)

7. Troubleshoot the Boot Process of a SLES 9 System (3038)

8. Configure and Install the GRUB Boot Loader (3038)

9. Understand How Device Drivers Are Loaded (3038)

10. Understand the `sysfs` File System (3038)

11. Understand How the SLES 9 Hotplug System Works (3038)

12. Understand the `hwup` Command (3038)

Understanding Runlevels

Course Objectives Covered

1. Understand the Runlevel Concept (3036)

3. Manage Runlevels (3037)

Before diving into the topic of booting the system, it is important to understand the concept of runlevels. In many operating systems, there are only two runlevels—functioning and turned off (halted). In Linux, however, there are seven different levels of functionality at which the operating system can run. These levels are shown in Table 7.1.

TABLE 7.1 **Runlevels in Linux**

RUNLEVEL	DESCRIPTION
0	The system is down.
1	Only one user is allowed in.
2	Multiple users are allowed in, but without NFS.
3	Multiple users and NFS.
4	Differs per implementation.
5	The X environment.
6	Shutdown and reboot.

The following paragraphs elaborate on each of the states a bit.

At level 0, the system is in a shutdown state requiring a manual reboot. This can be called a halt, or powerdown, as well as a shutdown. When changing to this level, files are synchronized with the disk and the system is left in a state where it is safe to power it off.

Level 1 puts the system in single-user mode, and is also known as administrative mode. This allows only one user (traditionally the root user) to access the system and prevents anyone else from getting in. Often, it restricts the login to only one terminal as well: the one defined as the console. This is the level to use when rebuilding the kernel and doing similar tasks.

Level 2 is multiple-user mode—allowing more than one user to log in at a time. This is the level where background processes (daemons) start up and additional filesystems (root is always mounted), if present, are mounted. NFS is not running.

Level 3, also known as network mode, is exactly the same as level 2 only with networking or NFS enabled.

Level 4 is left to each vendor to define what they want to define it as, if anything.

Level 5 is also known as a hardware state. Here, the command prompt is available, and users are allowed to log in and out of the X environment.

Level 6 represents a shutdown and automatic reboot: the same result as changing to runlevel 0 and then rebooting the machine. It can be called a "warm boot" because power is never removed from the components, whereas runlevel 0 represents a "cold boot" because power must be turned off and then restored.

> **NOTE**
>
> An easy way to summarize the runlevels is that 2, 3, and 5 are operational states of the computer—it is up and running and users are allowed to conduct business. All other runlevels involve some sort of maintenance or shutdown operation preventing users from processing, with the exception of 4, which differs across implementations.

Typing the command `runlevel` at a prompt will show two values: the previous runlevel and the current runlevel. For example

```
$ runlevel
N 5
$
```

In this case, the current runlevel is 5, and the "N" means that there was no previous level (None). These values are derived by examining the `/var/run/utmp` log file, which keeps track of all changes. If this file is corrupt, or the values cannot be found within it, the only value returned is "unknown."

Changing Runlevels

Course Objectives Covered

1. Understand the Runlevel Concept (3036)

2. Describe the Linux Load Procedure (3037)

3. Manage Runlevels (3037)

5. Modify System Settings (3037)

6. Describe Startup Shell Scripts and Services (3037)

7. Troubleshoot the Boot Process of a SLES 9 System (3038)

9. Understand How Device Drivers Are Loaded (3038)

Two commands can be used to change the runlevel at which the machine is currently operating: `shutdown` and `init`. In reality, the `shutdown` command is nothing more than an interface to `init`, offering a few more friendly features.

The `init` utility resides in the `/sbin` directory and must be followed by a number (0–6) or the letters "S" or "s". The numbers identify which runlevel to change to, and the "S" and "s" signify single-user mode ("S" allows only root, whereas "s" does not care which single user). To change to runlevel 2, the command would be

```
init 2
```

> **NOTE**
>
> The `telinit` **utility works the same as** `init`, **and can be used in place of it. It is just a link to** `init`.

The `shutdown` utility offers a few more options. It informs all users currently logged in that the system is changing state and allows a time (delay) to be specified before the change takes place. Options that work with the utility are

- ▶ `-F` to force `fsck` to run after the reboot (the default)
- ▶ `-f` to prevent `fsck` from running after the reboot, thus creating a fast reboot
- ▶ `-h` to halt after shutdown (level 0)
- ▶ `-k` to send out a warning to all users but not really change state
- ▶ `-r` to reboot after shutdown (level 6)
- ▶ `-t` to specify the number of seconds before the change begins

If no parameters are specified, the default runlevel shutdown attempts to go to is level 0. An example of using the utility would be

```
$ shutdown -h -t3 now
```

This forces a change to runlevel 0 (`-h`) three seconds (`-t`) from the current time (now). Notice that a time must always be specified. If any other text followed the time, it would be interpreted as the warning message to send out to users.

You can also notify users by using the `write` **command to send a message to individual users or** `wall` **to write to all users and tell them of the upcoming shutdown.**

Finally, if you want to stop a shutdown after you have summoned it, but before it has begun, you can call **shutdown** once more with the -c (cancel) option.

By default, only the root user can run `shutdown`. **You can create a file in the** /etc **directory named** shutdown.allow **to list other users you want to be able to run the command.**

Three minor utilities also exist as links to the **shutdown** utility:

- ▶ `halt` (which implements `shutdown -h`)
- ▶ `reboot` (which implements `shutdown -r`)
- ▶ `poweroff` (the same as `halt`)

Regardless of which command you use to shut the system down, you must use one of them to properly halt processes and close files. If you do not properly shut the system down, there is an excellent chance of corruption occurring within the filesystem.

The inittab File

Course Objectives Covered

1. Understand the Runlevel Concept (3036)
2. Describe the Linux Load Procedure (3037)
3. Manage Runlevels (3037)
5. Modify System Settings (3037)
6. Describe Startup Shell Scripts and Services (3037)
7. Troubleshoot the Boot Process of a SLES 9 System (3038)
9. Understand How Device Drivers Are Loaded (3038)

The main file for determining what takes place at different runlevels is the /etc/inittab (initialization table) file. This text file is colon-delimited and divided into four fields. The first field is a short ID, and the second identifies the runlevel at which the action is to take place (blank means all). The third field is the action to take place, and the last field is the command to execute.

The following file is a representative of what every inittab file looks like:

```
#
# /etc/inittab
#
# Copyright (c) 1996-2002 SuSE Linux AG, Nuernberg, Germany.
# All rights reserved.
#
# Author: Florian La Roche, 1996
# Please send feedback to http://www.suse.de/feedback
#
# This is the main configuration file of /sbin/init, which
# is executed by the kernel on startup. It describes what
# scripts are used for the different run-levels.
#
# All scripts for runlevel changes are in /etc/init.d/.
#
# This file may be modified by SuSEconfig unless CHECK_INITTAB
# in /etc/sysconfig/suseconfig is set to "no"
#

# The default runlevel is defined here
id:5:initdefault:

# First script to be executed, if not booting in emergency (-b)
mode
si::bootwait:/etc/init.d/boot

# /etc/init.d/rc takes care of runlevel handling
#
# runlevel 0  is  System halt   (Do not use this for
➥initdefault!)
# runlevel 1  is  Single user mode
# runlevel 2  is  Local multiuser without remote network (e.g.
➥NFS)
# runlevel 3  is  Full multiuser with network
# runlevel 4  is  Not used
# runlevel 5  is  Full multiuser with network and xdm
# runlevel 6  is  System reboot (Do not use this for
➥initdefault!)
```

```
#
l0:0:wait:/etc/init.d/rc 0
l1:1:wait:/etc/init.d/rc 1
l2:2:wait:/etc/init.d/rc 2
l3:3:wait:/etc/init.d/rc 3
#l4:4:wait:/etc/init.d/rc 4
l5:5:wait:/etc/init.d/rc 5
l6:6:wait:/etc/init.d/rc 6

# what to do in single-user mode
ls:S:wait:/etc/init.d/rc S
~~:S:respawn:/sbin/sulogin

# what to do when CTRL-ALT-DEL is pressed
ca::ctrlaltdel:/sbin/shutdown -r -t 4 now

# special keyboard request (Alt-UpArrow)
# look into the kbd-0.90 docs for this
kb::kbrequest:/bin/echo "Keyboard Request -- edit /etc/inittab
➡to let this work."

# what to do when power fails/returns
pf::powerwait:/etc/init.d/powerfail start
pn::powerfailnow:/etc/init.d/powerfail now
#pn::powerfail:/etc/init.d/powerfail now
po::powerokwait:/etc/init.d/powerfail stop

# for ARGO UPS
➡sh:12345:powerfail:/sbin/shutdown -h now THE POWER IS FAILING

# getty-programs for the normal runlevels
# <id>:<runlevels>:<action>:<process>
# The "id" field  MUST be the same as the last
# characters of the device (after "tty").
1:2345:respawn:/sbin/mingetty --noclear tty1
2:2345:respawn:/sbin/mingetty tty2
3:2345:respawn:/sbin/mingetty tty3
4:2345:respawn:/sbin/mingetty tty4
5:2345:respawn:/sbin/mingetty tty5
6:2345:respawn:/sbin/mingetty tty6
#
#S0:12345:respawn:/sbin/agetty -L 9600 ttyS0 vt102

#
#  Note: Do not use tty7 in runlevel 3, this virtual line
```

```
#  is occupied by the programm xdm.
#

#  This is for the package xdmsc, after installing and
#  and configuration you should remove the comment character
#  from the following line:
#7:3:respawn:+/etc/init.d/rx tty7


# modem getty.
# mo:235:respawn:/usr/sbin/mgetty -s 38400 modem

# fax getty (hylafax)
# mo:35:respawn:/usr/lib/fax/faxgetty /dev/modem

# vbox (voice box) getty
# I6:35:respawn:/usr/sbin/vboxgetty -d /dev/ttyI6
# I7:35:respawn:/usr/sbin/vboxgetty -d /dev/ttyI7

# end of /etc/inittab
```

The line `id:5:initdefault:` is of great importance, as it identifies the default runlevel the system will initially attempt to go to after each boot. The lines beneath that identify that at each runlevel, the shell script `rc` (beneath `/etc/rc.d`) that is to run—using a different variable for each level. This script looks for scripts within subdirectories of `/etc/rc.d` based on the runlevel: or for example, there are `/etc/rc.d/rc0.d`, `/etc/rc.d/rc1.d`, and so on. Within those subdirectories are script files that start with either an "S" or a "K". Scripts that start with "K" identify processes/daemons that must be killed when changing to this runlevel, and scripts starting with "S" identify processes/daemons that must be started when changing to this runlevel.

The line `ca::ctrlaltdel:/sbin/shutdown -r -t 4 now` defines what happens when Ctrl+Alt+Del is pressed. If the terminals get killed off, they are started up again thanks to the action of **respawn**. Other actions that can be specified are

- ▶ boot—To run at boot time
- ▶ bootwait—To run at boot time and prevent other processes until finished
- ▶ kbrequest—Send a request for keyboard action/inaction
- ▶ off—Don't run the command

- ▶ once—Only run the command once

- ▶ ondemand—Same as `respawn`

- ▶ powerfail—Run in the event of a `powerfailure` signal

- ▶ powerokwait—Wait until the power is okay before continuing

- ▶ sysinit—Run before any users can log on

- ▶ wait—Allow completion before continuing on

It is the `init` daemon that is responsible for carrying out changes that need to be taken in relation to runlevels. This daemon is summoned by the `init` utility (remember, the `init` utility is also called by `telinit` and `shutdown`).

The `init` daemon is one of the first services to come alive upon a boot and it reads and executes entries in the `/etc/inittab` file. After completion, the `init` daemon stays active and respawns any processes that are supposed to run but die off, as well as interacting with the log files (`utmp` and `wtmp` from beneath `/var` or `/etc`).

NOTE

`/var/run` **and** `/etc` **log files hold valuable information. A discussion of them appears later in this chapter.**

If you modify the `/etc/inittab` file, the changes you make will not be active until the system reboots, or you run this command:

```
init q
```

Enter LILO

Course Objectives Covered

2. Describe the Linux Load Procedure (3037)

5. Modify System Settings (3037)

7. Troubleshoot the Boot Process of a SLES 9 System (3038)

9. Understand How Device Drivers Are Loaded (3038)

All of the details given thus far in this chapter (runlevels, `inittab`, and so on) are the same for Unix and Linux. Linux differs from Unix, however, in that it also has the Linux Loader (LILO). It allows Linux to coexist on your machine with other operating systems: Up to 16 images can be swapped back and forth to designate what operating system will be loaded on the next boot.

By default, LILO boots the default operating system each time, but you can enter the name of another operating system at the "BOOT:" prompt, or force the prompt to appear by pressing Shift, Ctrl, or Alt during the boot sequence. Entering a question mark (or pressing Tab) will show the available operating systems as defined in the /etc/lilo.conf file: This is a text file that can range from simple to complex based on the number of OSes you have. An example of the file with only one operating system (Linux) would be (numbering has again been added to facilitate discussion):

```
1.   #
2.   # /etc/lilo.conf - generated by Lizard
3.   #

4.   # target

5.   boot = /dev/hda1
6.   install = /boot/boot.b

7.   # options

8.   prompt
9.   delay = 50
10.  timeout = 50
11.  message = /boot/message

12.  default = linux

13.  image = /boot/vmlinuz-pc97-2.2.10-modular
14.  label  = linux
15.  root   = /dev/hda1
16.  vga    = 274
17.  read-only
18.  append = "debug=2 noapic nosmp"
```

Line 5 identifies the partition to boot from, and line 6 specifies the boot sector file. Lines 8 through 12 identify the default as linux, and the prompt and timeout both have values of 50 deciseconds: You must press Shift or another key within this time period or LILO begins loading the default. Line 13 specifies the name of the kernel, line 14 identifies its label, and line 15 names the root partition. The remaining lines identify the type of filesystem and such.

Changes can be made to the file and are active when you run /sbin/lilo.

Different options that can be used with the lilo command are

- ▶ -b to specify the boot device
- ▶ -C to use a different configuration file
- ▶ -D to use a kernel with a specified name
- ▶ -d to specify how long the wait should be in deciseconds
- ▶ -I to be prompted for the kernel path
- ▶ -i to specify the file boot sector
- ▶ -m to specify the name of the map file to use
- ▶ -q to list the names of the kernels (which are held in the /boot/map file)
- ▶ -R to set as a default for the next reboot
- ▶ -S to overwrite the existing file
- ▶ -s to tell LILO where to store the old boot sector
- ▶ -t to test
- ▶ -u to uninstall LILO
- ▶ -v to change to verbose mode

Enter GRUB

Course Objectives Covered

2. Describe the Linux Load Procedure (3037)

4. Manage the GRUB Boot Loader (3037)

5. Modify System Settings (3037)

7. Troubleshoot the Boot Process of a SLES 9 System (3038)

8. Configure and Install the GRUB Boot Loader (3038)

9. Understand How Device Drivers Are Loaded (3038)

To use an analogy, the Linux Loader (LILO) can be thought of as a first-generation utility. It is still in use, and common in Debian and some other implementations, but is being surpassed in many installations by GRUB.

GRUB is a multiboot loader that was originally created by Erich Stefan Boleyn and is now maintained by GNU. The name is an acronym for GRand Unified Bootloader, and the simplest way to get information on it is to use the `info grub` command.

GRUB, by default, installs in the `/boot/grub` directory and the file `menu.1st` contains the boot information. The following is an example of this file, with line numbers added:

```
1.   # Modified by YaST2. Last modification on Thu Jul 29
➥16:07:47 2004

2.   color white/blue black/light-gray
3.   default 0
4.   timeout 8
5.   gfxmenu (hd0,1)/boot/message

6.   ###Don't change this comment - YaST2 identifier: Original
➥name: linux###
7.   title Linux
8.   kernel (hd0,1)/boot/vmlinuz root=/dev/hda2 splash=silent
➥desktop hdc=ide-scsi hdclun=0 showopts
9.   initrd (hd0,1)/boot/initrd

10.  ###Don't change this comment - YaST2 identifier: Original
➥name: floppy###
11.  title Floppy
12.  root (fd0)
13.  chainloader +1

14.  ###Don't change this comment - YaST2 identifier: Original
➥name: failsafe###
15.  title Failsafe
16.  kernel (hd0,1)/boot/vmlinuz root=/dev/hda2 showopts
➥ide=nodma apm=off acpi=off vga=normal nosmp noapic maxcpus=0 3
17.  initrd (hd0,1)/boot/initrd
```

Notice that devices are referred to using the `(hd0,1)` syntax. The name of the device can always be broken into the four fields that each character stands for:

1. The type of drive: **h** for IDE, or **s** for SCSI

2. The type of device: **d** for disk

3. The number of the disk expressed in numeric format

4. The number of the partition

There must always be a minimum of two partitions: the filesystem itself (often referred to as root) and a swap partition. The swap partition is the memory and some hard drive space. The swap partition is always a minimum of the amount of RAM installed on the machine, but can be more. The ability to use a swap partition greater than the amount of installed RAM is known as using virtual memory.

Related Boot Files and Utilities

Course Objectives Covered

   2. Describe the Linux Load Procedure (3037)

   7. Troubleshoot the Boot Process of a SLES 9 System (3038)

 10. Understand the `sysfs` File System (3038)

 11. Understand How the SLES 9 Hotplug System Works (3038)

 12. Understand the `hwup` Command (3038)

There are a few other files and utilities to be aware of before walking through a boot. The first of these is the **dmesg** utility. This utility enables you to display bootup messages generated from LILO (in `/var/log/messages`). By default, when you type in **dmesg**, the messages are displayed on your screen. If there is a problem, however, and you want to save the messages for troubleshooting purposes, you can use this command:

```
dmesg > {filename}
```

The listing that is returned is rather lengthy, but it is important to check as it can be an invaluable aid in troubleshooting.

As you look at the file on your system, notice the order of operations as the system comes up. Notice, as well, how the first line identifies the kernel version and vendor.

Other files to be aware of are

   ▶ `/var/log/messages`

   ▶ `/etc/conf.modules`

   ▶ `/etc/modules.conf`

   ▶ `utmp`

   ▶ `wtmp`

The first file, messages, is written to by cron and other processes, and can be useful in troubleshooting problems. It is some of the contents of this file that are displayed by the dmesg command. The second and third files are one and the same, but differ based on vendor (on some systems, conf. modules is used, and on others, modules.conf is used). The purpose of this file is to hold information used by the kernel to identify the machine. The file is a C++ source file and usually not accessed by administrators unless corruption has occurred.

The utmp and wtmp files have been mentioned previously. They are log files that act as counterparts of each other and exist in either /etc or elsewhere. If elsewhere, utmp is beneath /var/run and wtmp is beneath /var/log. By default, when the system comes up, entries are written to utmp, and when the system goes down, entries are written to wtmp.

The last command can be used to look at the most recent entries in wtmp—showing users and system state changes:

```
$ last
root     pts/0                         Mon Oct  9 14:58
➥still logged in
root     :0                            Mon Oct  9 14:21
➥still logged in
reboot   system boot  2.2.10           Mon Oct  9 14:15
➥(03:01)
root     pts/1                         Mon Oct  9 11:35 -
➥down    (02:15)
root     pts/0                         Mon Oct  9 11:35 -
➥down    (02:15)
root     :0                            Mon Oct  9 11:34 -
➥down    (02:16)
reboot   system boot  2.2.10           Mon Oct  9 11:33
➥(02:16)
root     pts/0                         Tue Oct  3 11:18 -
➥crash (6+00:15)
root     :0                            Mon Oct  2 16:31 -
➥11:28 (6+18:56)
reboot   system boot  2.2.10           Mon Oct  2 16:23
➥(6+21:26)
root     :0                            Mon Sep 25 16:32 -
➥17:20   (00:48)
reboot   system boot  2.2.10           Mon Sep 25 16:29
➥(00:51)
root     :0                            Mon Sep 25 16:18 -
➥16:25   (00:06)
reboot   system boot  2.2.10           Mon Sep 25 16:06
➥(00:18)

wtmp begins Mon Sep 25 16:06:45 2000
```

Sysfs is a virtual filesystem mounted under `/sys` that is virtually generated by the kernel upon boot and holds the information about the devices and interfaces on the Linux system. By changing into the `/sys/bus` and `sys/devices` directories, you can find files that identify the entities connected with the system.

In order for a device to be usable, it must have a driver. If the device is hotpluggable (USB, Firewire, and so on), the Hotplug feature will kick in when the kernel has triggered an event indicating that something has happened (a USB drive has been plugged in, and so on).

Upon occurrence/notification of the event, the script file `/sbin/hotplug` runs to add the device. Hotplug can call the `hwup` script (also in `/sbin/hotplug`) to look for the appropriate configuration file for the device beneath `/etc/sysconfig/hardware`. If it is a network device, instead of a system device, `ifup` is called instead of `hwup`.

Hotplug agents can be found beneath `/etc/hotplug` and the file named blacklist holds entries for modules that should never be loaded for one reason or another.

Booting from Start to Finish

Course Objectives Covered

2. Describe the Linux Load Procedure (3037)

7. Troubleshoot the Boot Process of a SLES 9 System (3038)

Now that you've looked at different elements of the boot, it is now possible to put it all together and run through the steps of a boot from start to finish:

1. When any machine is started, it first does a Power On Self Test (POST) to verify that internal parts and processes are working. This occurs regardless of any operating system.

2. The boot loader for the operating system begins. With Linux, that is LILO. By default, it waits 50 deciseconds (5 seconds) for you to press a key and identify another operating system you want to boot. If no key is pressed, the default of Linux is loaded.

3. The kernel is loaded from the hard drive, or floppy drive, or other specified location into memory. By default, it is located within the `/boot` directory and exists in compressed state; as it loads into memory, it uncompresses.

4. The kernel is booted and messages are written to /var/log/messages.

5. Modules, default and other, from /etc/modules.conf or /etc/conf.modules are loaded.

6. The kernel passes control over to the init daemon, which begins reading the /etc/inittab file. Because of this, the init daemon will always have a process ID of 1 and be the parent of many other daemons.

7. Normally, a check of the filesystem (fsck) is carried out and the local filesystem is mounted. Other operations can include mounting remote filesystems, cleaning up temporary files, and so on.

8. The system begins changing to the runlevel specified by the initdefault parameter. In so doing, it runs scripts beneath the /etc/rc.d directory and usually starts other processes/daemons such as a print server, cron, sendmail, and so on.

9. The terminals become active for login (getty has initiated), and the boot process is finished.

Enter the User

Course Objectives Covered

2. Describe the Linux Load Procedure (3037)

7. Troubleshoot the Boot Process of a SLES 9 System (3038)

After the system is up, the user(s) can now use it. The init daemon has started a getty process for each terminal telling it to listen for a connection. If you run ps -ef, you will see a getty process running on each terminal that can log in that does not currently have a user using it. The program responsible for printing the login prompt is the command getty (get a tty). getty prompts for the user's login name.

This login name has been assigned by the system administrator. Most often, the login name is the user's initials, first name, last name, or some combination derived from the initials or names. The username is considered a *known* entity; anyone wanting to send a message to or interact with the user will do so using this name, and it will also appear in directory listings as the owner of files and directories.

After the user has entered his or her login name, getty spawns, or starts, the /bin/login utility. The login utility prompts the user to enter his or her password. The user enters the password (which does not print on the screen for security reasons). If the user enters the password incorrectly, the system responds with a generic message stating that the login is incorrect.

The `login` command accepts the password entered by the user and encrypts it using the same mechanism used by the `passwd` command to put the password in the `/etc/passwd` file. If the encrypted values match, the password is correct. Otherwise, the password entered by the user is incorrect. The `login` command cannot decrypt the password after it has been encrypted. When the password is entered properly, the next phases of the system files (`utmp`/`wtmp`) are updated.

The `/etc/profile` shell script is run to set up variables for all users, and then the user is moved to his home directory and his login shell (as specified in the `/etc/passwd` file) is invoked. If there are customization files within the home directory (such as `.profile` for BASH or `.login` for C shell), they are executed next; the user's initial environment is configured, and the shell starts executing.

Summary

This chapter focused on the topics you need to know to pass questions related to the booting and initialization of the Linux operating system. We also examined the different runlevels and how to change from one to another. In the next chapter, the focus turns to filesystems and becomes SuSE-specific.

Command Summary

Table 7.2 lists the commands that were discussed in this chapter.

Commands for Booting and Initialization	TABLE 7.2
UTILITY	**DEFAULT PURPOSE**
dmesg	Print out the bootup messages
grub	Linux boot loader
halt, shutdown, reboot	Interfaces to shutdown
init	Change the runlevel

Table 7.2   Continued

UTILITY	DEFAULT PURPOSE
last	View the most recent entries in the wtmp file
lilo	Configure the Linux Loader
runlevel	Show the current runlevel of the system
shutdown	An interface to init with more options
telinit	Same as init

CHAPTER 8

Working with Filesystems

This chapter focuses on Linux filesystems and how to interact with them. This chapter looks at and covers the following course objectives:

1. Understanding the File System Hierarchy (3036)
2. Identify File Types in the Linux Systems (3036)
3. Select a Linux File System (3037)
4. Configure Linux File System Partitions (3037)
5. Configure a File System with Logical Volume Management (3037)
6. Configure and Manage a Linux File System (3037)
7. Monitor the File System (3038)

In this chapter, you'll also learn about the utilities used to work with disks and filesystems.

Laying Out the Filesystem

Course Objective Covered

1. Understanding the File System Hierarchy (3036)

The Standard Disk Layout

During the installation of Linux, a number of directories are created to hold system files. Under any normal installation, regardless of the vendor, the file structure depicted in Figure 8.1 will be created.

FIGURE 8.1
The standard
directory layout
in Linux.

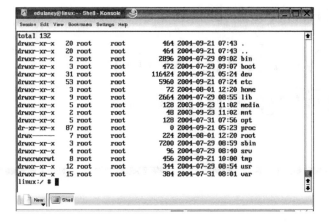

The /sys directory does not appear in Figure 8.1. This is a virtual entity created by the addition of devices to the system and was discussed in Chapter 7, "Boot, Initialization, Shutdown, and Runlevels."

Together, these directories adhere to the Filesystem Hierarchy Standard (FHS). Each of these directories is discussed in the following sections.

More information about the Filesystem Hierarchy Standard can be found at http://www.pathname.com/fhs/.

The / Directory

Everything begins at the root directory (/). This is the beginning directory of which everything else becomes a subdirectory, or subcomponent beneath the root directory. When specifying locations and using absolute addressing, you always start with the root directory; it is impossible to go back any further.

The single and double period that appear at the top of the listing in Figure 8.1 are shortcuts that appear in each directory. The single period (.) is a shortcut for the directory you are currently in, and the double period (..) is a shortcut for the parent directory of this directory. In the case of /, there is no parent directory for it, but the shortcut appears in the listing anyway.

The bin Directory

The `bin` directory holds the binaries (executables) that are essential to using the Linux operating system. A large number of the utilities discussed thus far are located here, including

- ► cat
- ► cp
- ► date
- ► dd
- ► gzip
- ► ls
- ► mkdir
- ► mv
- ► ps
- ► rm
- ► sed
- ► vi

As a rule of thumb, the executable/binary files located in this directory are available to all users. Binary files that are not critical to the operation of the system or needed by all users are commonly placed in **/usr/bin** instead of here.

The boot Directory

The `boot` directory houses the files needed to boot the system, minus configuration files, as well as the kernel. In some implementations, the kernel is stored in the / directory (a holdover from the days of Unix), but in most newer versions, **/boot** is used. This directory contains all the files needed to boot (including the kernel) *except* the configuration files.

The dev Directory

The `dev` directory holds the device definitions. When you drag a file to a graphical icon of the floppy drive on the desktop, it is possible because a definition for the floppy drive is held in the **/dev** directory. There is a definition file associated with every device, whether it is a terminal, drive, driver, and so on. The following listing shows a few of the files beneath the directory (some of the names have been changed to make the entries more decipherable):

brw-rw-rw-	1	root	root	2,	4	Aug 10	1999	floppy
brw-r-----	1	root	operator	3,	1	Aug 10	1999	hard
➥drive1								
crw-rw----	1	root	lp	6,	0	Aug 10	1999	lp0
crw-rw----	1	root	lp	6,	1	Aug 10	1999	lp1
crw-rw----	1	root	lp	6,	2	Aug 10	1999	lp2
brw-rw-r--	1	root	disk	23,	0	Aug 10	1999	cd
crw-r-----	1	root	kmem	1,	1	Aug 10	1999	mem
crw-rw-rw-	1	root	root	1,	3	Aug 10	1999	null
crw-rw-rw-	1	root	root	10,	1	Sep 13	10:29	mouse
brw-------	1	root	root	1,	0	Aug 10	1999	ram0
brw-------	1	root	root	1,	1	Aug 10	1999	ram1
brw-------	1	root	root	1,	2	Aug 10	1999	ram2
brw-------	1	root	root	1,	3	Aug 10	1999	ram3
brw-------	1	root	root	31,	0	Aug 10	1999	rom0
brw-------	1	root	root	31,	1	Aug 10	1999	rom1
br--------	1	root	root	31,	8	Aug 10	1999	rrom0
br--------	1	root	root	31,	9	Aug 10	1999	rrom1
brw-rw-r--	1	root	disk	15,	0	Aug 10	1999	sonycd
crw--w--w-	1	root	root	4,	0	Aug 10	1999	tty0
crw-rw----	1	root	tty	4,	1	Jul 6	15:27	tty1
crw-rw----	1	root	tty	4,	10	Aug 10	1999	tty10
crw-rw----	1	root	tty	4,	11	Aug 10	1999	tty11
crw-rw----	1	root	tty	4,	12	Jul 6	15:27	tty12
crw-rw----	1	root	tty	4,	13	Aug 10	1999	tty13
crw-rw----	1	root	tty	4,	14	Aug 10	1999	tty14
crw-rw----	1	root	tty	4,	15	Aug 10	1999	tty15

Note first that the files do not resemble listings you've examined previously. The first character of the permissions is either "b" or "c" to indicate how data is read—by block or by character. Typically devices that require constant interaction such as the mouse, terminal (tty), and such are character-based. Devices that do not require interaction after a process is started, such as floppy drives, memory (RAM and ROM), CD drives, and such are block-based.

The second item of note is that the size of the files is not expressed in bytes, but in pairs of numbers separated by a comma. The creation of such special files is beyond the scope of either of the current NCLP exams, but you should know that the mknod utility must be used to create device files, and you should know that the following types of files exist in Linux:

▶ Normal files—Those that contain data used by users or applications.

▶ Directories—Containers that hold files or other directories.

▶ Device files—One file exists for each physical device.

▶ Links—Pointers to other files.

▶ Sockets—Files used to exchange data between two running processes.

▶ Pipes (also known as FIFOs for First In, First Out)—Like sockets, they are used to exchange data, but the data is queued and can only flow one way.

As the listing illustrated, just some of the entries you will find beneath here are for the floppy drive, printer, and terminals.

The etc Directory

In everyday language, "etc." is used to mean "and so on." In the Linux world, however, the etc directory is used to hold configuration files and samples that are specific to this machine. For example, ABC Corporation and DEF Corporation can both install the same version of Linux on Intel-based machines at their sites. When they do, both will have **root** directories, both will have /**bin** directories with matching sets of utilities in them, and so on.

One major difference between the two machines will be the values that can be found in the /etc directory. The users who log on at ABC are not the same as those who can log on at DEF; thus, user accounts are stored in /etc. The groups are not the same at the two organizations; again, those related files will be stored here. Other files include

▶ motd—The Message of the Day file for displaying text when logging on

▶ X11—A folder holding X Windows values

▶ HOSTNAME—The name of the machine

▶ hosts—A file that maps host names to IP addresses for other machines available through a network

▶ SuSE-release—The version number of the server

▶ inittab—The configuration file for startup and the runlevels (the init process)

▶ profile—The login script for the shell

In a nutshell, the /etc directory holds system configuration files specific to a machine and some sample configuration files.

The home Directory

This directory will hold subdirectories that are the home directories for users. For example, user edulaney, when entering the command `cd`, will be placed in `/home/edulaney` providing that that variable (the default) is used when setting up the account.

Each user's `home` directory is used to provide him or her with a location where he or she can store files, as well as where individual configuration files can be found and accessed. Some services, such as `ftp` and `http`, will also create directories beneath `home`.

Files that are used to configure the environment for the user, such as `.profile`, `.bashrc`, and `.bash_history`, are stored in the `home` directories.

NOTE For security reasons, there is not a `/home/root` directory. The home directory for the root user is `/root`.

The lib Directory

Shared library files needed by binaries (such as those in the `/bin` directory) are located in the `/lib` directory and subdirectories beneath it. Generally, the libraries consist of executables written in the C language.

The media Directory

The `media` directory is used for mounting removable media. Two subdirectories are created here by default—`cdrom` and `floppy`. Other devices—such as `dvd`, `dvdrecorder`, or `cdrecorder`, as shown in Figure 8.2—may appear as well if they are installed.

The mnt Directory

The `mnt` directory is used to hold external filesystems that are mounted. The entities that appear in this directory are never on this filesystem, but rather external resources that can be linked to and accessed from here. The external resources can be other filesystems, or devices.

The devices will appear as directories with common names. The `tmp` subdirectory here is intended to hold temporary files, but the use of `/tmp` is preferred. External filesystems are loaded—and thus appear beneath this directory—with the `mount` command, and removed with the `umount` command.

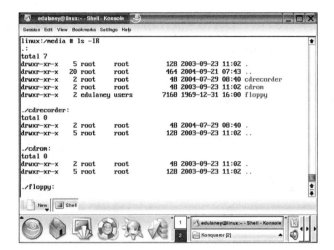

FIGURE 8.2
The /media
directory holds a
subdirectory for
each removable
device.

The opt Directory

The **opt** directory is used to hold optional (add-in) application software. Not all applications install themselves here, but when they do, they create a subdirectory for their variables using the application name. For example, if an application were named **DEF**, the directory it should create would be

/opt/DEF

There is no requirement that third-party applications *must* write their values here, but it is traditional from the days of Unix. Some common subdirectories to find here include

- ▶ **kde**—For the K Desktop Environment variables
- ▶ **mozilla**—For the browser
- ▶ **netscape**—For the browser
- ▶ **novell**—For NNLS files

The proc Directory

The **proc** directory is the virtual filesystem. It is dynamically generated and updated and holds information about processes, the kernel, and related system information.

Processes are depicted as folders, each having permissions and variables associated with it. Other system information is most commonly depicted as files, as shown in the following listing:

```
$ ps
  PID TTY          TIME CMD
15193 pts/0    00:00:00 bash
15220 pts/0    00:00:00 sleep
15222 pts/0    00:00:00 sleep
15236 pts/0    00:00:00 ps
$ ls -l
dr-xr-xr-x  3 root     root            0 Sep 20 08:34 15193
dr-xr-xr-x  3 root     root            0 Sep 20 08:34 15220
dr-xr-xr-x  3 root     root            0 Sep 20 08:34 15222
dr-xr-xr-x  4 root     root            0 Sep 20 08:34 bus
-r--r--r--  1 root     root            0 Sep 20 08:34
➥cmdline
-r--r--r--  1 root     root            0 Sep 20 08:34
➥cpuinfo
-r--r--r--  1 root     root            0 Sep 20 08:34
➥devices
-r--r--r--  1 root     root            0 Sep 20 08:34 dma
-r--r--r--  1 root     root            0 Sep 20 08:34 fb
-r--r--r--  1 root     root            0 Sep 20 08:34
➥filesystems
dr-xr-xr-x  2 root     root            0 Sep 20 08:34 fs
dr-xr-xr-x  4 root     root            0 Sep 20 08:34 ide
-r--r--r--  1 root     root            0 Sep 20 08:34
➥interrupts
-r--r--r--  1 root     root            0 Sep 20 08:34
➥ioports
-r--------  1 root     root     67112960 Sep 20 08:34 kcore
-r--------  1 root     root            0 Sep 20 08:16 kmsg
-r--r--r--  1 root     root            0 Sep 20 08:34 ksyms
-r--r--r--  1 root     root            0 Sep 20 08:34
➥loadavg
-r--r--r--  1 root     root            0 Sep 20 08:34 locks
-r--r--r--  1 root     root            0 Sep 20 08:34 mdstat
-r--r--r--  1 root     root            0 Sep 20 08:34
➥meminfo
-r--r--r--  1 root     root            0 Sep 20 08:34 misc
-r--r--r--  1 root     root            0 Sep 20 08:34
➥modules
-r--r--r--  1 root     root            0 Sep 20 08:34 mounts
dr-xr-xr-x  4 root     root            0 Sep 20 08:34 net
dr-xr-xr-x  3 root     root            0 Sep 20 08:34
➥parport
-r--r--r--  1 root     root            0 Sep 20 08:34
➥partitions
-r--r--r--  1 root     root            0 Sep 20 08:34 pci
-r--r--r--  1 root     root            0 Sep 20 08:34 rtc
```

```
dr-xr-xr-x    2 root      root              0 Sep 20 08:34 scsi
lrwxrwxrwx    1 root      root             64 Sep 20 08:34 self -
➥> 15252
-r--r--r--    1 root      root              0 Sep 20 08:34
➥slabinfo
-r--r--r--    1 root      root              0 Sep 20 08:34 sound
-r--r--r--    1 root      root              0 Sep 20 08:34 stat
-r--r--r--    1 root      root              0 Sep 20 08:34 swaps
dr-xr-xr-x   10 root      root              0 Sep 20 08:34 sys
dr-xr-xr-x    4 root      root              0 Sep 20 08:34 tty
-r--r--r--    1 root      root              0 Sep 20 08:34 uptime
-r--r--r--    1 root      root              0 Sep 20 08:34
➥version
$
```

The `init` process will always have a PID number of 1. Because of this, you can get a quick glance at what is the current state of the system by looking at `/proc/1` with the command

```
$ ls -l /proc/1
```

The root Directory

The `root` directory is the home directory for the root user. For security purposes, it is beneath the `/` directory rather than being a subdirectory of `/home`. For true security, it is further recommended that you move this directory to another location and rename it to a less obvious (and inviting) name.

The sbin Directory

The `/bin` directory holds standard executables that most users utilize; the `/sbin` directory holds binary executables for system administration. Many of these utilities are used for booting the system and once resided beneath the `/etc` directory. The following list shows some of the files located beneath this directory:

- ▶ dump
- ▶ fdisk
- ▶ fsck
- ▶ halt
- ▶ ifconfig
- ▶ init
- ▶ mkfs

- ▶ poweroff

- ▶ reboot

- ▶ SuSEconfig

- ▶ shutdown

- ▶ YAST2

NOTE   SuSEconfig **utilizes files found in** /etc/sysconfig/.

The srv Directory

The /srv directory holds the files for the services that are available on the server—each in a separate subdirectory. Figure 8.3 shows an example of this directory with the www (for Apache) and ftp services.

FIGURE 8.3
The /srv directory holds a subdirectory for each service on the server.

The tmp Directory

As the name implies, the tmp directory is used to hold temporary files. Nothing that is to be kept other than for a short time should be placed here as many systems clean (delete) all entries in this directory on either shutdown or startup.

Examples of files that exist beneath /tmp are shadow copies of files opened for editing, any application's temporary files (stored between operations), and so on.

The usr Directory

Originally an acronym for "user-specific resources," `usr` is now an enormous directory with a large number of subdirectories. Subdirectories beginning with X are used to define the X Windows environment. The `bin` subdirectory, as has been the case each time the same name has been encountered, contains user binary (executable) files. The files placed here include

- cut

- diff

- file

- grep

- killall

- nl

- passwd

- wc

As a general rule, necessary utilities for all users are stored in /bin, whereas ones that are helpful to have (but not critical) are stored in /usr/bin. Those for the system administrative tasks are stored in /sbin.

Not all the subdirectories beneath /usr are necessary and they will differ slightly based upon the type of installation chosen.   NOTE

The `include` directory holds C program header files, whereas `lib` offers more libraries for the C-based programs. The `local` directory is a temporary holding facility used during installation and the subdirectories beneath it should be empty.

The `sbin` directory (yet again) holds system-specific binaries. Most of the utilities found in this subdirectory are related to managing the system from the standpoint of adding users, and groups as well as working with networking. These are noncritical utilities in that the system could function without them, and an administrator could manage without them as well; it would be more difficult, but certainly possible.

The `share` directory holds information specific to the machine for certain utilities, and holds the `man` directories for manual pages. Lastly, the `src` directory contains the operating-system source code.

The var Directory

The name var is derived from the word *variable*, and the data contained beneath this directory is fluctuating in nature. There are typically a number of subdirectories here used to hold dynamic files, such as spools, logs, and so on.

The main directories to know among these variables are

- ▶ lock—Holds locked files
- ▶ log—Used for log files such as those created by login and logout (wtmp), who is currently using the system (utmp), and those for mail, the spooler, and so on
- ▶ run—Files needed for the runlevel
- ▶ spool—Spooled data waiting for processing (such as printing)

Other Directories

Other directories can be created and exist beneath the / directory. Those listed in the preceding sections are always present, and the two that follow may be present:

- ▶ install—As the name implies, it holds information about the installation, such as scripts, errors, and so on.
- ▶ lost+found—On a perfect system, this directory should be empty. When corruption occurs, however, the results are placed in this directory.

The Hard Disk Layout

Partitioning your hard disk divides a single disk into many logical sections or drives. The partition itself is a set of contiguous sectors on the disk that are treated as an independent disk. The partition table is the index on the disk that describes how the sections of the disk relate to the actual partitions.

There is a long-standing argument about the need for multiple partitions. Most DOS and Windows users are used to having their entire hard disk, regardless of the size, represented as one disk. Although this may seem convenient for some users, it is not desirable in the Unix or Linux world.

By using multiple partitions, you can encapsulate your data and limit filesystem corruption to a single filesystem. This limits the potential data loss. You can also increase disk efficiency. Depending on the purpose of your system, you can format different filesystems with different block sizes. If you have lots of smaller files, you want smaller blocks.

Multiple partitions are also useful to limit data growth. This ensures that users who require extra disk space do not crash the system by consuming all available root filesystem space.

There are some constraints that must be considered when planning your disk layout:

▶ To prevent data loss and corruption, partitions must not overlap.

▶ To maximize usage of the disk, there should be no gaps between partitions.

▶ You do not have to fully partition your disk.

▶ Partitions cannot be moved, resized, or copied without the use of special software.

When working with the disk drives, you must remember the naming convention used. All devices in a Linux system are represented as device files. These files are named with specific conventions to make it easier to identify the associated device.

IDE hard disks are identified with the name /dev/hd followed by the letter "a", "b", "c", or "d". The letter identifies the drive as the first disk on the first IDE controller (a), or the second disk on the second IDE controller (d).

SCSI disks are identified in a similar manner, except the device name is /dev/sd followed by a letter. These names, /dev/sda, refer to the entire disk.

After the drive has been partitioned, a number is added to the device name. Primary partitions are numbered 1–4, and extended or logical partitions are numbered 5 and higher.

The partition table was originally written in the disk boot sector, and as this was a predefined size, there was a limit to four partition table entries. These are now referred to as primary partitions. One primary partition may be subdivided into logical partitions. The partition used to hold the logical partitions is called an extended partition. Linux imposes its own limits on the number of partitions on a drive.

Partitions must be labeled to identify the format of the data that will be subsequently written on them. This is important for mounting the partition or performing filesystem repairs. Each filesystem has a code associated with it, and is used by **fdisk** to specify the filesystem type.

Some of the valid filesystem types are listed in Table 8.1.

> **NOTE** You can obtain a current list of the filesystems available by using the **fdisk** utility, and choosing m, then l. This is discussed further in the "Working with Hard Disks" section later in this chapter.

TABLE 8.1 Valid Filesystem Types

CODE	FILESYSTEM TYPE
5	Extended
6	FAT16
7	HPFS
8	AIX
85	Linux Extended
86	NTFS
1b	Windows 95 FAT32

At the very least, your Linux system will require the following:

- A boot partition
- A swap partition

You can also have any other primary or extended partitions as desired. It is recommended that you use a primary partition for the boot partition. This eases recovery in case of problems later, as only a small amount of data is lost.

While running, Linux will swap pages of memory out to disk when the contents have not been used for some time. This is much slower than adding more physical memory. If you find your system is swapping a lot, it is time to add more memory.

As discussed earlier, if necessary you can fit everything, including your swap file, in a single partition. However, this does not limit how the filesystem is managed and the growth of the data within the filesystem. For example, if your user mailboxes are on the root filesystem and it fills up, the system will effectively hang.

Despite the ability to run everything in one partition, this is not good prac-
tice. The filesystems listed in Table 8.2 are good candidates to be placed in
their own partition.

Filesystems Needing Partitions

FILESYSTEM NAME	PRIMARY/ EXTENDED	DESCRIPTION
/boot	Primary	This is where your kernel images are located. If you are using LILO or plan to support other operating systems, it is best that this partition be the first on the disk.
/root	Primary	This is your root filesystem.
/usr	Extended	Most application data is stored here, including system binaries, documentation, and the kernel sources.
/home	Extended	This is where home directories for the users on the system are located. Depending on the number of users you have and the amount of disk space required, you may need multiple home directory partitions.
/var	Extended	This is a spool partition, containing files for log and error messages, Usenet news, mailboxes, and so on.
/tmp	Extended	This is a temporary storage place for files that are being processed. Compilers and many applications create many files in this area. Often these files are short-lived, but they can sometimes be very large.

Working with Hard Disks

Course Objectives Covered

1. Understanding the File System Hierarchy (3036)
2. Identify File Types in the Linux Systems (3036)

3. Select a Linux File System (3037)

4. Configure Linux File System Partitions (3037)

In order to use a hard disk with Linux (and every operating system), at least one partition must exist on the disk. A partition is a portion of the disk (some or all) that has been properly formatted for storing data. Although there must be a minimum of one primary partition on the hard drive, there can be up to a total of four if a DOS-style partition table is used (the default), and each partition must be formatted before use. A partition must be a primary partition in order for the operating system to be able to boot from it.

If you want, a primary partition (only one) can be further subdivided into extended partitions (known as logical drives). Again using DOS-style partitions, up to four logical drives can be created from a primary partition, but none of them are bootable by the operating system.

NOTE **The maximum number of partitions you can have if all are primary is four. The maximum number of partitions you can have if mixing and matching primary and extended is three primary partitions and four logical drives (for a grand total of seven).**

In actuality, the theoretical limit on SCSI disks is 15 partitions, and on IDE is 63. The limitations mentioned previously are enforced with the DOS-style partition table used as a default.

All partitions must be referenced in the /dev directory, and the first partition on the first disk is either

- ▶ hda1—For IDE
- ▶ sda1—For SCSI

The name of the device can always be broken into the four fields that each character stands for:

1. The type of drive: h for IDE, or s for SCSI.

2. The type of device: d for disk.

3. The number of the disk expressed in alphabetic format: a for the first, b for the second, and so on.

4. The number of the partition. Numbers 1–4 are set aside for use on primary partitions, whether or not you have that many, and the logical drives start numbering with 5.

There must always be a minimum of two partitions: the filesystem itself (often referred to as root), and a swap partition. The swap partition consists of the memory and some hard drive space. The swap partition is always a minimum of the amount of RAM installed on the machine, but can be more (16MB is the minimum recommendation for hard drive space). For example, if you have 64MB installed on a machine and the swap partition needs 128MB, it can use a 64MB swap partition to read and write from as processing is done. The ability to use a swap partition greater than the amount of installed RAM is known as using virtual memory.

If you run out of room in the partition (or have not configured such), a swap file will always be created for the same purpose, but the use of the partition is preferred.

Linux can work with either swap files or swap partitions, but partitions provide more system efficiency.

██NOTE██

One other note about hard drives: Linux prefers the number of cylinders on a drive to be 1024 or less. If the number is larger, there can be complications with software that runs at boot time, or booting/partitioning with other operating systems.

Creating Partitions

The primary tool to use in creating disk partitions is `fdisk`. The `fdisk` utility will divide the disk into partitions and write the partition table in sector 0 (known as the superblock). When run without parameters, `fdisk` brings up a menu of choices with which you can interact. You can avoid the menu, however, and run `fdisk` with these options:

▶ `-l` to just list the partition tables

▶ `-v` to print the version of `fdisk` only

If neither of these options are used, `fdisk` first checks to see if the number of cylinders on the default device (`hda1`) is greater than 1024 and warns you of such if true. It then prompts for a command. You can start `fdisk` with a device other than the default by specifying that on the command line. For example, to start it with the third IDE drive, use this command:

```
$ fdisk /dev/hdc
```

After the utility has started, entering "m" provides for help in the form of a menu:

```
a    toggle a bootable flag
b    edit bsd disklabel
c    toggle the dos compatibility flag
d    delete a partition
l    list known partition types
m    print this menu
n    add a new partition
o    crate a new empty DOS partition table
p    print the partition table
q    quit without saving changes
s    create a new empty Sun disklabel
t    change a partition's system id
u    change display/entry units
v    verify the partition table
w    write table to disk and exit
x    extra functionality (experts only)
```

The following examples illustrate what can be done with this utility, moving from simple actions to more complex. First, to see the partition table, give the **p** command (this gives you the same result as you would have gotten by using the command **fdisk -1**). The result looks like this:

```
Disk /dev/hda: 20.4 GB, 20416757760 bytes
255 heads, 63 sectors/track, 2482 cylinders
Units = cylinders of 16065 * 512 = 8225280 bytes
```

Device Boot	Start	End	Blocks	Id	System
/dev/hda1	1	50	401593+	82	Linux swap
/dev/hda2 *	51	2482	19535040	83	Linux

The information here shows that there are two partitions (1–2) on a single IDE disk (**hda**). The second partition is bootable, and the first partition is the swap partition.

To modify the system, you would first enter the **d** command to delete the partition. A prompt asks which partition number (1–4), and you would give the appropriate number and it would be gone.

To create a new partition, enter the **n** command. The prompt changes to

```
e     extended
p     primary partition (1-4)
```

If you have already created other partitions, the prompts may not appear. For example, if you already have an extended partition, you will not be able to create another because it already exists. If you enter **p** for primary, you are next prompted for the number (1–4) to create; if you give a number that's already used, it will fail as you must first delete the partition before re-adding it.

To change a third partition to a swap file, if one existed, the sequence would be

```
Command (m for help): t
Partition number (1-4): 3
Hex code (type L to list codes): 82
Changed system type of partition 3 to 82 (Linux swap)
```

To change an existing swap file to a Linux partition, run the procedure shown in the preceding snippet for it, and make the change to 83. Typing L at the hex code prompt will show all the possible filesystem types (as will just pressing "l" at the main **fdisk** menu). Refer to Table 8.1 earlier in the chapter for a list of the types.

Creating Filesystems

After all changes have been made, you can quit **fdisk**, and then format any partitions you need to. If you write the changes, an alert will appear indicating that the partition table has been altered, and the disks will be synchronized. You should reboot your system to ensure that the table is properly updated.

You can make dozens of changes with fdisk **and lose them all if you use "q" to quit the tool. If you want to save the changes you've made, you must write them with "w".**   **NOTE**

Formatting of the partitions is accomplished with the **mkfs** (as in Make Filesystem) utility or **mkreiserfs**. You must use options with this utility to indicate the type of filesystem to make (**-t**), the device, size, and any options you want. For example, to format the newly created fourth partition for DOS, the command would be

```
$ mkfs -t msdos /dev/hda4 3040632
```

Be extremely careful when using `fdisk` and `mkfs`, as both have the ability to render a system inoperable if incorrect parameters are used.

> **NOTE** The `mkfs` **utility can be used to format floppy disks as well as hard drives, but the utility** `fdformat` **is much simpler to use for the former.**

As stated previously, you can choose from a number of different filesystems that are supported in Linux. Regardless of the number, they fall into three broad categories—traditional, journaling, and virtual. Traditional filesystems include ext2, vfat, and so on. Journaling filesystems include ReiserFS (the SuSE default) and ext3. Virtual filesystems, also known as Virtual Filesystem Switch (VFS), are actually hybrids that exist between the processes and the other filesystems (traditional or journaling).

Maintaining Filesystem Integrity

Course Objective Covered

7. Monitor the File System (3038)

After the filesystem has been created, you can gather information about it and perform troubleshooting using three tools: `df`, `du`, and `fsck`. The first two display information only, and do not allow you to make any changes, and the latter can be a lifesaver in bringing a down system back up and operational once more.

The `df` utility shows the amount of free disk across filesystems. A number of options/parameters can be used with the utility as well:

- ▶ `-a`—All (include those that have 0 block)
- ▶ `-h`—Display in "human-readable" form
- ▶ `-l`—Local filesystems only
- ▶ `-m`—List in MBs
- ▶ `-t`—Only show those filesystems of a particular type
- ▶ `-T`—Show the filesystem type

For example, the default output, and results with specified options, look
like this:

```
$ df
Filesystem              1k-blocks        Used Available Use%
➥Mounted on
/dev/hda1               1980969        573405    1305178  31% /
/dev/hda3               5871498          5212    5562198   0% /home
$
$ df -T
Filesystem      Type    1k-blocks        Used Available Use%
➥Mounted on
/dev/hda1       ext2    1980969        573408    1305175  31% /
/dev/hda3       ext2    5871498          5212    5562198   0% /home
$
$ df -h
Filesystem              Size   Used Avail Use% Mounted on
/dev/hda1               1.9G   560M  1.2G  31% /
/dev/hda3               5.6G   5.1M  5.3G   0% /home
$
$ df -a
Filesystem              1k-blocks        Used Available Use%
➥Mounted on
/dev/hda1               1980969        573406    1305177  31% /
/dev/hda3               5871498          5212    5562198   0% /home
devpts                         0           0          0   -
➥/dev/pts
/proc                          0           0          0   -
➥/proc
noname:(pid12019)              0           0          0   -
➥/auto
$
$ df -am
Filesystem              1M-blocks        Used Available Use%
➥Mounted on
/dev/hda1                   1934         560       1275  31% /
/dev/hda3                   5734           5       5432   0%
➥/home
devpts                         0           0          0   -
➥/dev/pts
/proc                          0           0          0   -
➥/proc
noname:(pid12019)              0           0          0   -
➥/auto
$
```

The "ext2" listed for filesystem type stands for Second Extended Filesystem, and is the default used by many versions of Linux. ReiserFS is the default created during the installation of SuSE 9.0 and above.

Whereas the df utility deals with partitions, the du utility shows disk usage by files and directories. From df, you can see that 560MB of hda1 is used, but you have no way of knowing by what. The du utility is the next step, showing how much space each item is using beginning at whatever starting location you specify. For example, starting in the /root directory (the home directory of the root user), the utility will show the amount of space used by the subdirectories:

```
14      ./.seyon
2       ./Desktop/Autostart
2       ./Desktop/Trash
8       ./Desktop/Templates
20      ./Desktop
22      ./.kde/share/config
1       ./.kde/share/apps/kfm/tmp
1       ./.kde/share/apps/kfm/bookmarks
8       ./.kde/share/apps/kfm
6       ./.kde/share/apps/kdewizard/Work/Windows
7       ./.kde/share/apps/kdewizard/Work
1       ./.kde/share/apps/kdewizard/Themes
9       ./.kde/share/apps/kdewizard
1       ./.kde/share/apps/kpanel/applnk
1       ./.kde/share/apps/kpanel/pics
3       ./.kde/share/apps/kpanel
3       ./.kde/share/apps/kdisknav
5       ./.kde/share/apps/kwm/pics
6       ./.kde/share/apps/kwm
1       ./.kde/share/apps/kdisplay/pics
2       ./.kde/share/apps/kdisplay
2       ./.kde/share/apps/kdehelp
34      ./.kde/share/apps
1       ./.kde/share/icons/mini
2       ./.kde/share/icons
2       ./.kde/share/applnk
1       ./.kde/share/mimelnk
1       ./.kde/share/sounds
63      ./.kde/share
64      ./.kde
119     .
```

If the -a option is used, files are listed and not just directories. Other options that work with the du utility are

- ▶ -b—To display the list in bytes
- ▶ -c—To show a grand total
- ▶ -h—"Human readable" output
- ▶ -k—To display the list in KBs
- ▶ -l—To show the number of links
- ▶ -m—To display the list in MBs
- ▶ -s—To only show totals
- ▶ -x—To only show directories on this (not different) filesystems

The grand utility in this category is fsck, the filesystem check utility. Not only will it check the filesystem, but if errors are encountered, it can be used to correct them. The utility utilizes entries in the /etc/fstab file to tell it which filesystems to check during startup if configured to run automatically. The -A option also tells the utility to use this file.

NOTE

The /etc/fstab **file is always read by** fsck **and related utilities but never written to. As an administrator, you need to update the file—placing each filesystem on its own line—when you want to make modifications to the operation of system utilities.**

The following is an example of this file:

```
/dev/hda2              /                        reiserfs
➥defaults               1 1
/dev/hda1              swap                     swap          pri=42
➥0 0
devpts                /dev/pts                 devpts
➥mode=0620,gid=5        0 0
proc                  /proc                    proc
➥defaults               0 0
usbdevfs              /proc/bus/usb            usbdevfs      noauto
➥0 0
/dev/cdrecorder       /media/cdrecorder        auto          ro,
➥noauto,user,exec       0 0
/dev/cdrom            /media/cdrom             auto          ro,
➥noauto,user,exec       0 0
/dev/fd0             /media/floppy            auto
➥noauto,user,sync        0 0
```

When you run `fsck`, it shells out to the appropriate interface based upon the filesystem in use. For example, with a Linux filesystem (EXT2), a common series of events would be as follows:

```
$ fsck -A
Parrelizing fsck version 1.14 (9-Jan-1999)
E2fsck 1.14, 9-Jan-1999 for EXT2 FS 0.5b, 95/08/09
/dev/hda1 is mounted.

WARNING!!! Running e2fsck on a mounted filesystem may cause
SEVERE filesystem damage.

Do you really want to continue (y/n)? y
Pass 1: Checking inodes, blocks, and sizes
Pass 2: Checking directory structure
Pass 3: Checking directory connectivity
Pass 4: Checking reference counts
Pass 5: Checking group summary information
/dev/hda3: 927/1521664 files (0.3% non-contigous),
➥215482/6081768 blocks
$
```

Running `fsck-A` in SuSE generates the dialog shown in Figure 8.4.

FIGURE 8.4
You must enter
"Yes" to run the
utility in SuSE.

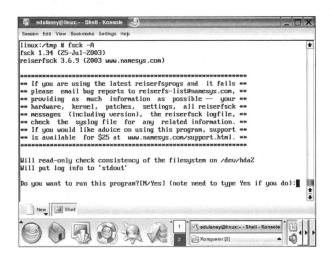

Most of the other passes are self-explanatory, but the first requires some further detail. Blocks and sizes are understandable, but inodes need some definition. An inode is a table entry that stores information about every file on the system. It is within the inode that information about the file is stored—in much the same way that a phone book holds information about people in a city.

Every item that appears in a directory listing has an inode associated with it. The inode holds the following types of information:

1. A unique inode number
2. The type of entry that it is (file, directory, pipe, and so on)
3. Permissions on the file in numerical format
4. The physical size of the file
5. The number of links to the entry
6. The owner of the file
7. The group owning the file
8. Times of creation, modification, and access
9. A pointer to the actual location of the data on the disk

The inode numbers begin with 1 and increment from there, causing files copied during installation to have small numbers, and recently created files to have much larger numbers. When files and directories are deleted, their associated inode number is marked as usable once more.

When corruption occurs, files are dumped to the /**lost+found** directory, using their inode number as names. To see the inode numbers associated with files, you can use the -**i** option with **ls**:

```
$ ls -l
drwx------ 5       root root                1024 Sep 22 23:57 Desktop
-rw-r--r-- 1       root root                  81 Sep 23 00:25 monday
-rw-r--r-- 1       root root                 152 Sep 23 00:26 tuesday
-rw-r--r-- 1       root root                  38 Sep 23 00:26
➥wednesday
$
$ ls -li
18471 drwx------ 5      root root                1024 Sep 22 23:57
➥Desktop
18535 -rw-r--r-- 1      root root                  81 Sep 23 00:25
➥monday
18536 -rw-r--r-- 1      root root                 152 Sep 23 00:26
➥tuesday
```

```
18537 -rw-r--r-- 1      root root              38 Sep 23 00:26
➥wednesday
$
```

If a file is moved, it maintains the same inode. If a file is copied, the original file maintains the same inode, but the new entry must have a new inode associated with it:

```
$ mv monday friday
$ ls -li
18471 drwx------ 5      root root            1024 Sep 22 23:57
➥Desktop
18535 -rw-r--r-- 1      root root              81 Sep 23 00:25
➥friday
18536 -rw-r--r-- 1      root root             152 Sep 23 00:26
➥tuesday
18537 -rw-r--r-- 1      root root              38 Sep 23 00:26
➥wednesday
$ cp friday monday
$ ls -li
18471 drwx------ 5      root root            1024 Sep 22 23:57
➥Desktop
18535 -rw-r--r-- 1      root root              81 Sep 23 00:25
➥friday
18538 -rw-r--r-- 1      root root              81 Sep 23 00:38
➥monday
18536 -rw-r--r-- 1      root root             152 Sep 23 00:26
➥tuesday
18537 -rw-r--r-- 1      root root              38 Sep 23 00:26
➥wednesday
$
```

Mounting and Unmounting

There will always be a local filesystem, for it is upon that filesystem that Linux is installed. If the filesystem is large enough to hold everything you interact with, that is all you need. In most cases, however, the local filesystem is not sufficient to hold everything you need. When that is the case, you can mount other filesystems to make them accessible in your environment.

The **mount** command is used without parameters to show what filesystems are currently available. A sample of the output would be

```
/dev/hda1 on / type ext2 (rw)
/dev/hda3 on /home type ext2 (rw)
```

```
devpts on /dev/pts type devpts (rw, gid=5,mode=620)
/proc on /proc type proc (rw)
noname: (pid11973) on /auto type nfs (rw)
```

This reads from the dynamic file /etc/mtab and relays the device, the mount point, the type of filesystem, and the permissions (rw is read/write). In addition to read/write, filesystems can be mounted as read only (ro), not allowing users (nouser), only able to run binaries (exec) or not (noexec), not running certain files (nosuid), or controllable by all users (user), and interpret special devices on the filesystem (dev).

The entries listed in the preceding output, and that are there by default, appear in the /etc/fstab file—mentioned earlier in regard to the fsck utility. If there are additional filesystems you want to always mount, you should add their entries to this file. The command mount -a will read the fstab file and mount/remount all entries found within.

If you do not want filesystems always mounted, you can dynamically load other filesystems using the device name with the mount utility.

For example, to mount the CD drive, the command is

```
$ mount /mnt/cdrom
```

On some Linux flavors, and on some hardware, you may have to use variations of **NOTE**

```
    mount /media/cdrom
```

or

```
    mount -t iso9660 /dev/cdrom   /media/cdrom
```

The same is true for mounting a DVD drive.

And the entry added to mount looks like this:

```
/dev/hdc on /mnt/cdrom type iso9660 (ro,noexec,nosuid,nodev)
```

The /mnt directory holds readily accessible definitions for external devices such as the CD-ROM drive and floppy drives. Options that can be used with the mount command are

▶ -a to read through the /etc/fstab file and mount all entries.

▶ -f to see if a filesystem can be mounted (but not mount it). An error message returned means that it cannot be found, and no error message means that it was found in /etc/fstab or /etc/mtab.

▶ -n prevents the /etc/mtab file from being dynamically updated when a filesystem is added.

▶ -r mounts the filesystem as read-only.

▶ -t allows you to specify the type of the filesystem being mounted.

▶ -w mounts the filesystem as read/write (the default).

The opposite of mounting a filesystem when it is needed is unmounting it when it no longer is needed. This is accomplished with the **umount** utility. To unload the CD drive when no longer needed, the command would be

```
$ umount /mnt/cdrom
```

Options that can be used with the **umount** utility are

▶ -a—Unload every entry in /etc/mtab.

▶ -n—Unload but not update /etc/mtab.

▶ -r—If the unload fails, remount it as read-only.

▶ -t—Unload all entries of a specific file type.

Hard Disks and YaST

SuSE allows you to use the YaST (Yet Another Setup Tool) utility to interact with disks and perform creation and partitioning tasks graphically. Figure 8.5 shows the System submenu and the choices it presents.

FIGURE 8.5
The System sub-menu offers the disk-related choices in YaST.

Choose Partitioner, and the warning shown in Figure 8.6 appears. Heed this warning carefully for it fully means what it says—you can do irreversible damage if you are not careful.

FIGURE 8.6
Know what you are doing before changing partition information.

After you choose Yes, the partition table shown in Figure 8.7 appears.

FIGURE 8.7
The Partitioner shows the devices installed.

Most of the choices are self-explanatory—you can create, edit, delete, resize, and so on. Of particular note is the LVM choice—Logical Volume Management. Logical volumes offer great benefit over traditional volumes. They can be managed with sensible names like DATA (instead of sda1), and you can combine multiple hard disks/partitions into what appears to be a single entity (a volume group). After this group is created, you can increase it by adding more hard disks as needed (up to 256 logical volumes).

To use LVM, at least one partition must be configured as type 83, or the error shown in Figure 8.8 will appear.

FIGURE 8.8
A minimum of one partition of type 83 must be present.

You can create partitions of this type and then use LVM. Alternatively, you can also choose LVM from the System submenu of YaST (instead of choosing Partitioner) and proceed from there, as shown in Figure 8.9.

FIGURE 8.9
LVM requires you to create a volume group.

After making any changes, you must always choose to apply them before exiting in order to save your changes.

Summary

This chapter focused on the topics you need to know about the Filesystem Hierarchy Standard (FHS) and the standard layout of the Linux filesystem.

Command Summary

Table 8.3 lists the commands that were discussed in this chapter.

Commands for Managing Filesystems **TABLE 8.3**

UTILITY	DEFAULT PURPOSE
df	See the amount of disk free space
du	See disk usage statistics
fdisk	Used to partition the disk and work with the partition table
fsck	Used to check the filesystem status
mkfs	Create a filesystem
mkreiserfs	Create a Reiser filesystem
mount	Mount a filesystem
umount	Unmount a filesystem

CHAPTER 9

Managing Printing

This chapter focuses on printing. It examines the topic from the exam perspective, as well as the real-world perspective, and includes legacy information you may need to know if your environment includes a number of older versions of Linux.

This chapter covers the following course objectives:

1. Installing a Printer in the Linux System (3036)
2. Configure and Manage Network Printing Services (3037)

At the risk of oversimplifying, you can set up and configure a small network in one afternoon, and then spend the rest of the week trying to configure the printers to work properly. This situation is not as bad as it was a few years ago, thanks to standardization in printer technology and improvements in operating-system features, but it is still far more frustrating than it should be.

Compared with a number of other operating systems, Linux is far more straightforward and configurable in terms of printer setup than some. The best way to understand the printing operations within Linux is simply to jump in and start with the simplest of operations and then deviate from there. In order to accomplish this, we start with the basic model and move up from there.

Printing a File

Let's start the discussion by looking at the legacy method of printing and move up from there. Traditionally, the daemon running within the Linux operating system for the sole purpose of providing printing services is `lpd`—the line printer daemon. This daemon has been around, and is virtually unchanged in operation, since the early days of Unix. The first utility written to allow jobs to be submitted to the daemon was `lp`. This utility still exists and is included in many versions of Linux, but is generally overlooked in favor of `lpr`, which is a newer utility with more logical options.

NOTE **This discussion focuses on LPRng. CUPS, an alternative to LPRng, is discussed later in this chapter.**

Figure 9.1 shows the process running in SuSE.

A user can choose to print a file in one of two ways:

▶ From within a graphical interface

▶ From the command line

FIGURE 9.1
The `lp` service is running.

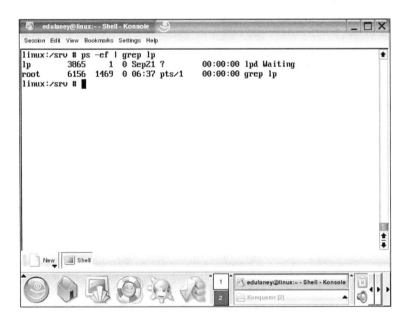

The simplest syntax to use to from the command line is

```
lpr {filename}
```

So if you wanted to print a file named Saturday, the command would be

```
lpr Saturday
```

When this command is issued, a number of other processes kick in, as shown in Figure 9.2. In this case, the printer does not exist, and the print job will spool to nothing, allowing us to examine what is taking place.

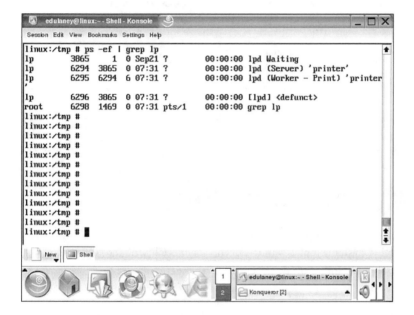

FIGURE 9.2
When a file is submitted for printing, a number of processes are started.

After the print job is sent to the appropriate queue for a printer, the daemon removes the job from the printer and produces the finished output. As long as the file exists, entries for it remain in the spooler beneath /var/spool/lpd as shown in Figure 9.3.

Once properly configured and functioning, the printing service in Linux runs very smoothly.

FIGURE 9.3

The spooler holds
files for the print
job.

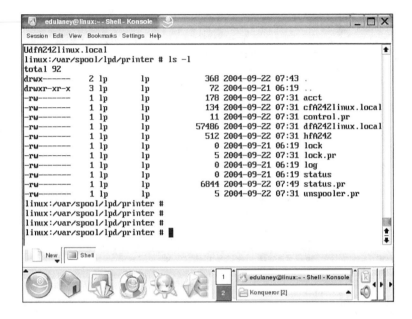

```
UdfA242linux.local
linux:/var/spool/lpd/printer # ls -l
total 92
drwx------   2 lp        lp            368 2004-09-22 07:43 .
drwxr-xr-x   3 lp        lp             72 2004-09-21 06:19 ..
-rw-------   1 lp        lp            178 2004-09-22 07:31 acct
-rw-------   1 lp        lp            134 2004-09-22 07:31 cfA242linux.local
-rw-------   1 lp        lp             11 2004-09-22 07:31 control.pr
-rw-------   1 lp        lp          57486 2004-09-22 07:31 dfA242linux.local
-rw-------   1 lp        lp            512 2004-09-22 07:31 hfA242
-rw-------   1 lp        lp              0 2004-09-21 06:19 lock
-rw-------   1 lp        lp              5 2004-09-22 07:31 lock.pr
-rw-------   1 lp        lp              0 2004-09-21 06:19 log
-rw-------   1 lp        lp              0 2004-09-21 06:19 status
-rw-------   1 lp        lp           6844 2004-09-22 07:49 status.pr
-rw-------   1 lp        lp              5 2004-09-22 07:31 unspooler.pr
linux:/var/spool/lpd/printer #
linux:/var/spool/lpd/printer #
linux:/var/spool/lpd/printer #
linux:/var/spool/lpd/printer #
```

Moving Up to CUPS

In newer Linux implementations, including SuSE, CUPS (Common Unix
Printing System) replaces much of the functionality of `lpr`/`lpd`. From an
operations standpoint, however, there is great similarity:

1. The user submits the print job.

2. The file is spooled—in this case beneath `/var/spool/cups/`.

3. The `cupsd` daemon formats the data in the spool and sends it to the
   printer.

4. When the job is done printing, the daemon removes the files from the
   queue.

The `/etc/cups/cupsd.conf` file (or `/etc/cups/cupsd.y2` sample file) contains an enormous amount of narrative and comments that fully explain
how to configure `cups`. Although space does not allow printing the file in its
entirety here, it is *highly* recommended that you carefully walk through the
file on your system and make certain you understand the options available.

The `/etc/init.d/cups stop` command is used to stop the service, and the
`/etc/init.d/cups start` command is used to manually start it (once configured, it should start automatically at boot using the startup script
`/etc/init.d/cups`).

Formatting a File

When discussing printing options, one utility to be aware of that is valuable for formatting is `pr`. The primary purpose of this utility (`/usr/bin/pr`) is always to convert the contents of a text file before sending the output to a printer.

The output includes a default header with date and time of last modification, filename, and page numbers. The default header can be overwritten with the `-h` option, and the `-l` option allows you to specify the number of lines to include on each page—with the default being 66. Default page width is 72 characters, but a different value can be specified with the `-w` option. The `-d` option can be used to double-space the output, and `-m` can be used to print numerous files in column format.

Installing a Printer

Course Objectives Covered

1. Installing a Printer in the Linux System (3036)

2. Configure and Manage Network Printing Services (3037)

NOTE

Before installing any printer, you should verify that it is supported in Linux by checking the printer database at http://www.linuxprinting.org/ and the SuSE Linux Enterprise Server printer database at http://hardwaredb.suse.de/.

As with almost everything in Linux, there are a number of different ways to install a printer. The easiest printer to install is one connected locally, via YaST. After connecting the printer, start YaST (you may be prompted for the root password), and then choose Hardware, Printer. A scan of the current environment will occur, as shown in Figure 9.4.

The printer should be autodetected, as shown in Figure 9.5.

FIGURE 9.4
YaST simplifies printer configuration and installation.

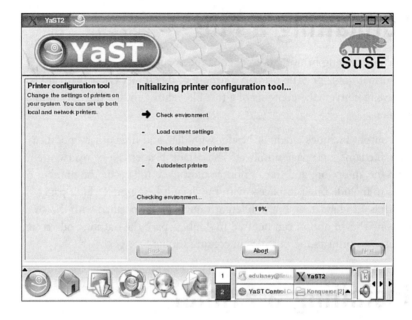

FIGURE 9.5
Autodetection recognizes most printers.

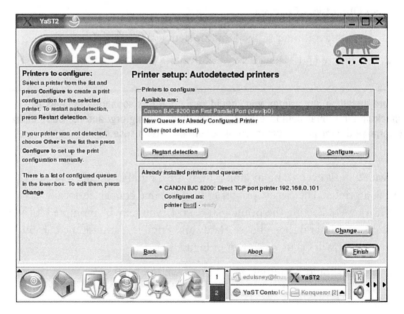

By choosing the Configure button, you can change any of the settings that were automatically created for the printer. The first dialog box that appears is shown in Figure 9.6, and the Edit Configuration screen is in Figure 9.7.

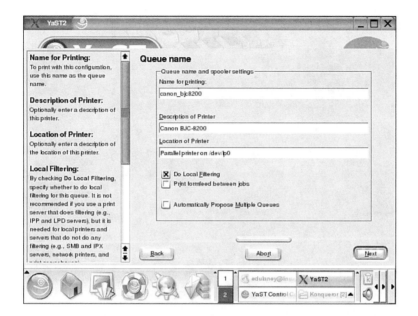

FIGURE 9.6
You can change the settings that were automatically configured.

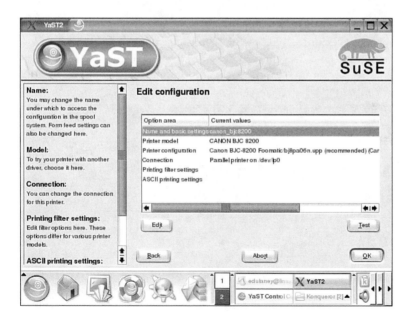

FIGURE 9.7
It is possible to edit any of the configuration settings within YaST.

When you click the Test button shown in Figure 9.7, it submits a print job using the `lpr` command. You can choose to print a graphics file or text file.

You can also choose to install the printer using the Add Printer Wizard in KDE, as shown in Figure 9.8.

FIGURE 9.8
The Add Printer
Wizard can also
be used to add a
printer.

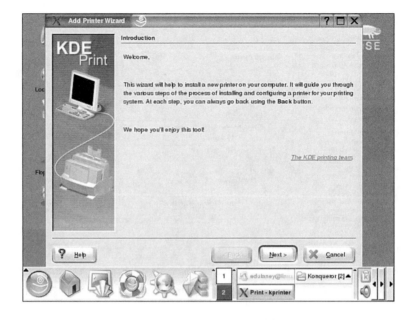

An alternative method for configuration is to use kprinter. This is accessed
by pressing (N) for the KDE menu, then choosing Utilities, Printing,
Printing Manager. This utility, shown in Figure 9.9, allows you to interact
with all aspects of the printing function, including manage jobs.

FIGURE 9.9
The Printing
Manager provides
an interface to
all printing
functions.

Regardless of the method used to add the printer, a number of things happen when it successfully joins the system:

- ▶ A print queue is added to `/etc/cups/printers.conf`.
- ▶ A `ppd` file for the printer is placed in `/etc/cups/ppd` for settings.
- ▶ The print queue is added to `/etc/printcap`.

A network printer can be set up just as easily, and will support SMB (Standard Message Block—for printing from Windows-based clients), IPP (Internet Printing Protocol), and the LPD protocol previously discussed. Most of these options are available to you when choosing the printer type, as illustrated by Figure 9.10.

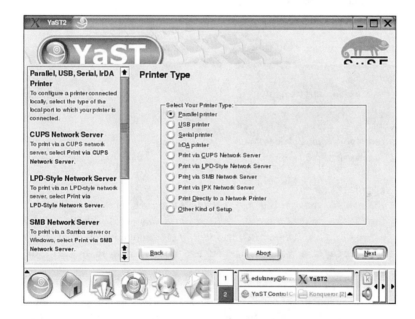

FIGURE 9.10
You can choose CUPS printers as a type.

Basic Configuration Files

There are a few files needed for the print service to work. Chief among these are `printcap`, `lpd.perms`, and `lpd.conf`. The `/etc/printcap` file is a database defining what each known printer is capable of. A default version of this file after adding the printer with LPRng is shown in the following listing:

```
# /etc/printcap: printer capability database. See printcap(5).
# You can use the filter entries df, tf, cf, gf etc. for
```

```
# your own filters. See the printcap(5) manual page for further
# details.
#
# Default Postscript printer on "print-serv"
#lp|ps|postscript:\
#          :client:lp=postscript@print-serv
#lp|ps|postscript:\
#          :server:oh=print-serv:\
#          :sd=/var/spool/lpd/ps:\
#          :lp=/dev/lp1:\
#          :sh:mx#0
## The Super Quick Guide to LPRng Printcaps
##   Patrick Powell <papowell@lprng.com>
##       Thu Nov 15 13:31:08 PST 2001
# VERSION=3.8.21
#
# LPD print queue configuration - Default options
#    The printcap entry below sets defaults.  Add default
options
#    or other entries here
#
#.common:
#    :sd=/var/spool/lpd/%P
#    :sh:mx=0:mc=0
#
#    [Translation:
#    .common - the period (.) causes LPRng to treat this as a
#    'information only entry.  This idea was stolen^H^H^H^H^H^H
#    borrowed from the Unix 'hidden' file convention, i.e. file
#    names starting with a period are not displayed by 'ls' or
#    matched by '*'
#    :sd=/var/spool/lpd/%P
#    Spool queue directory for temporary storage of print jobs.
#    The %P will be expanded with the print queue name.  Each
#    print queue MUST have a different spool queue directory,
#    and by using %P this is guaranteed.
#    :sh  - suppress banners or header pages
#    :mx=0 - maximum job size in K bytes (0 is unlimited)
#    :mc=0 - maximum number of copies (0 is unlimited)
#    ]
#
```

```
# LPD print queue definitions: Define print queues
#
# Printer on Parallel Port (i.e. - /dev/lpt0)
#lp:lp=DEVICE:tc=.common
#     Example:
#       lp:tc=.common:lp=/dev/lpt0
#       [Translation:
#        lp - name of the print queue
#        :tc=.common - include the options in the .common
#          printcap entry the 'tc' options will be put at the
#          START of the printcap entry
#        :lp=/dev/lpt0  - open and write the print job to
#          /dev/lpt0
#       ]
#
# Printer on Serial Port (i.e. - /dev/tty00)
#         Use the :stty to set the speed, bits, and parity using
#         'stty(1)' options.  Note: almost all printers use 8
#         bits, no parity.
#lp:tc=.common:lp=DEVICE:stty=STTY OPTIONS
#     Example:
#       lp:tc=.common:lp=/dev/tty0:stty=19200 raw crtscts
#       [Translation:  lp, :tc, :lp as for A) above.
#        :stty= options used to configure serial port
#       ]
#
# Printer on Network Print Server (i.e. - HP JetDirect)
#     connecting via a TCP/IP socket. IPADDR is IP address or
#     Fully Qualified Domain Name of the print server, PORT is
#     the TCP/IP port.
#
#     HP JetDirect uses port 9100 by default.
#
#     Warning: check the Network Print Server documentation for
#     correct port number.  Most non-HP Network Print Servers
#     and non-HP printers do not use port 9100.
#
#lp:tc=.common:lp=IPADDR%PORT
#     Example:
#       lp:tc=.common:lp=10.0.0.2%9100
#       [Translation:  lp, :tc, as for A) above.
```

```
#        lp=10.0.0.2%9100 - open a connection to 10.0.0.2, port
9100
#        and write the print job to this port.
#     ]
#
# D) printer on Network Print Server (i.e. - HP JetDirect or
#     LPD server) connecting via the LPD print protocol.  QUEUE
#     is the name of the print queue and IPADDR is the IP
#     address or Fully Qualified Domain Name of the print
#     server.
#
#     Warning: check the Network Print Server documentation for
#     correct QUEUE name.  The 'lp' queue is used on the HP
#     JetDirect as the default print queue.  If there are
#     multiple printer ports on the device then the QUEUE name
#     is used to select the port.
#
#     Warning: Using this protocol with JetDirect units will
#     almost always cause a 'banner page' to be generated by
#     the JetDirect unit. Check the HP documentation on how to
#     disable this most annoying feature. Usually you simply
#     telnet to the JetDirect and then use the simple
#     configuration menu presented when you first make
#     connection.
#
#lp:tc=.common:lp=QUEUE@IPADDR
#
#     Example:
#     lp:tc=.common:lp=lp@10.0.0.2
#       [Translation:  lp, :tc, as for A) above.
#       lp=lp@10.0.0.2 - open a connection to 10.0.0.2, port
#       515, and use the RFC1179 (LPD) protocol to transfer the
#       job to the QUEUE print queue.
#     ]
#
# Step 4:   Format Conversion (Filter) Required?
#
#     You may discover that your printer does not support
#     PostScript or requires a special initialization to be
#     done.  This is handled by a filter program.  The 'ifhp'
```

```
#     filter program is supplied with LPRng and supports a very
#     wide number of printers.  If you need to have a filter,
#     then add the following lines to the printcap
#     entry:
#
#     :filter=PATH_TO_IFHP_FILTER
#     :ifhp=IFHP_OPTIONS
#
#     Note: the LPRng :filter= option replaces the legacy BSD
#     lpd options :if, :vf, ... options that specify filters for
#     'f' format, 'v' format, and so forth (yes, yes, :if is
#     for 'f' format, don't ask). The :filter option specifies a
#     default filter for all job formats. Most modern filters
#     such as IFHP,  Magikfilter, and RedHat print filters are
#     smart enough to determine the job format and perform the
#     appropriate conversions.
#
#     Examples:
#
#     lp:tc=.common:lp=/dev/lpt0
#       :filter=/usr/libexec/filters/ifhp
#       :ifhp=model=hp4simx
#
#     lp:tc=.common:lp=10.0.0.2%9100
#       :filter=/usr/libexec/filters/ifhp
#       :ifhp=model=hp4simx
#
#     lp:tc=.common:lp=lp@10.0.0.2
#       :filter=/usr/libexec/filters/ifhp
#       :ifhp=model=hp4simx
#
#   IFHP Options:
#     For almost all simple configurations you will only need
#     to supply the model of printer that you have attached.
#     See the /etc/ifhp.conf file for a complete listing of
#     supported models. The default model is for an HP
#     Laserjet 4 SiMx,  which supports PostScript,  PCL,  and
#     PJL.
#
```

```
#    Warning:
#      IF:
#        Your model of printer normally provides status and
#        error reporting over a TCP/IP link
#      AND:
#        You are using lp=IPADDR%PORT to connect to the
#        printer
#      THEN:
#        The IFHP filter will normally expect to have status
#        information returned by the printer to tell it that
#        the printer is in working condition.  This will have
#        a small but significant overhead on job throughput,
#        but you will also get error information.
#
#      HOWEVER:
#        If the printer SHOULD return status but CANNOT due to
#        either the printer hardware configuration or it is on
#        a unidirectional and not bidirectional parallel
#        printer port,  then you must use :model=...,status@
#        to tell the IFHP filter not to expect status
#        information.
#
#      Example:
#        lp:tc=.common:lp=10.0.0.2%9100
#          :filter=/usr/libexec/filters/ifhp
#          :ifhp=model=hp4simx,status@
#
# Step 5: Queue creation and LPD restart
#    Run the following commands to create your spool queues and
#    then tell the LPD server that it should use them:
#      su
#      checkpc -f
#      lpc reread
printer:\
    :cm=lpdfilter drv=upp method=auto color=yes:\
    :lp=192.168.0.101%9100:\
    :sd=/var/spool/lpd/printer:\
    :lf=/var/spool/lpd/printer/log:\
    :af=/var/spool/lpd/printer/acct:\
    :if=/usr/lib/lpdfilter/bin/if:\
    :ar:lpd_bounce:lpr_bounce:force_localhost@:\
    :tr=:cl:lk:sh:
```

```
canon_bjc8200:\
    :cm=lpdfilter drv=upp method=auto color=yes:\
    :lp=/dev/lp0:\
    :sd=/var/spool/lpd/canon_bjc8200:\
    :lf=/var/spool/lpd/canon_bjc8200/log:\
    :af=/var/spool/lpd/canon_bjc8200/acct:\
    :if=/usr/lib/lpdfilter/bin/if:\
    :la@:\
    :tr=:cl:lk:sh:
```

Notice the warnings that appear within this file. You should know what is in this file and how to edit/change it for purposes of passing the exam (any text editor will do).

In a nutshell, printcap's **purpose is to identify the printer and queue. It also holds some definitions. Within this file, you would also list the path to a remote printer if the user is printing across a network.**   **NOTE**

When CUPS is used, this file is much simpler:

```
# This is a dummy printcap file that is automatically generated
by the
# CUPS software for old applications that rely on it.
```

The /etc/lpd.perms file, as the name implies, holds the permissions for the printing service and its options. The values held here determine the operation of many utilities as well as basic spooling and printing operations. The documentation included in the file is some of the best ever written, and for that reason, the default version of the file follows (some of the comment lines have been shortened due to space constraints):

```
################################################################
# LPRng - An Extended Print Spooler System
#
# Copyright 1988-2001 Patrick Powell, San Diego, CA
#       papowell@lprng.com
# See LICENSE for conditions of use.
#
################################################################
# MODULE: TESTSUPPORT/lpd.perms.proto
# PURPOSE: prototype printer permissions file
# $Id: lpd.perms.in,v 1.49 2003/04/15 23:37:41 papowell Exp $
```

```
###############################################################
# Printer permissions data base
## #
##                       LPRng - An Enhanced Printer Spooler
##                          lpd.perms file
##                       Patrick Powell papowell@lprng.com
##
## VERSION=3.8.25
##
## Access control to the LPRng facilities is controlled by
## entries in a set of lpd.perms files.  The common location
## for these files are: /etc/lpd.perms,  /usr/etc/lpd.perms,
## and /var/spool/lpd/lpd.perms.
## The locations of these files are set by the perms_path entry
## in the lpd.conf file or by compile time defaults in the
## src/common/defaults.c file.
##
## Each time the lpd server is given a user request or carries
## out an operation,  it searches to the perms files to
## determine if the action is ACCEPT or REJECT.  The first
## ACCEPT or REJECT found terminates the search.
## If none is found,  then the last DEFAULT action is used.
##
## Permissions are checked by the use of 'keys' and matches.
## For each of the following LPR activities,  the following
## keys have a value.
##
## Key          Match Connect Job    Job    LPQ  LPRM  LPC
##                            Spool  Print
## SERVICE      S     'X'     'R'    'P'    'Q'  'M'   'C'
## USER         S     -       JUSR   JUSR   JUSR JUSR  JUSR
## HOST         S     RH      JH     JH     JH   JH    JH
## GROUP        S     -       JUSR   JUSR   JUSR JUSR  JUSR
## IP           IP    RIP     JIP    JIP    RIP  JIP   JIP
## PORT         N     PORT    PORT   PORT   PORT PORT  PORT
## UNIXSOCKET   V     SK      SK     SK     SK   SK    SK
## REMOTEUSER   S     -       JUSR   JUSR   JUSR CUSR  CUSR
## REMOTEHOST   S     RH      RH     JH     RH   RH    RH
## REMOTEGROUP  S     -       JUSR   JUSR   JUSR CUSR  CUSR
## CONTROLLINE  S     -       CL     CL     CL   CL    CL
## PRINTER      S     -       PR     PR     PR   PR    PR
```

```
## FORWARD        V      -       SA      -       -       SA      SA
## SAMEHOST       V      -       SA      -       SA      SA      SA
## SAMEUSER       V      -       -       -       SU      SU      SU
## SERVER         V      -       SV      -       SV      SV      SV
## LPC            S      -       -       -       -       -       LPC
## AUTH           V      -       AU      AU      AU      AU      AU
## AUTHTYPE       S      -       AU      AU      AU      AU      AU
## AUTHUSER       S      -       AU      AU      AU      AU      AU
## AUTHFROM       S      -       AU      AU      AU      AU      AU
## AUTHSAMEUSER   S      -       AU      AU      AU      AU      AU
##    REMOTEIP is an alias for REMOTEHOST
##    REMOTEPORT is an alias for PORT
##    IP is an alias for HOST

##
## KEY:
##    JH = HOST      IP address/DNS name of host in control file
##    RH = REMOTEHOST     connecting host IP address/DNS Name
##    JUSR = USER           user in control file
##    CUSR = REMOTEUSER  user making control operation request
##    JIP= IP        IP address/DNS name of host in control file
##    RIP= REMOTEIP      IP address/DNS name of requesting host
##    PORT=              connecting host origination port
##    SK=         true (match) if connection from a unix socket
##    CONTROLLINE= pattern match of control line in control file
##
##    SA= IP of source of request == IP of host in control file
##    SU= user name making request == user in control file
##    SV= IP of source of request = IP of server host or server
##        Localhost
##    LPC= lpc command globmatched against values
##    AU= Authorization check on transfer
##        AUTH will be true (match) if authenticated request
##        AUTHTYPE will match authentication type of request to
##            pattern
##        AUTHUSER will match client authentication id to
##            pattern
##        AUTHFROM will match request originator authentication
##            id to pattern
##        AUTHSAMEUSER will match requestor authentication id
##            to authentication id in job
##
```

```
## Match: S = globmatch, IP = IPaddress[/netmask],
##    N = low[-high] number range, V= matching or compatible
##          values
## SERVICE: 'X' - Connection request; 'R' - lpr request from
##          remote host;
##    'P' - print job in queue; 'Q' - lpq request, 'M' - lprm
##          request;
##    'C' - lpc spool control request;
## NOTE: when printing (P action), the remote and job check
##          values
##    (i.e. - RUSR, JUSR) are identical.
## NOTE: the HOST, USER, SAMEUSER and SAMEHOST checks always
## succeed
##    when checking permissions for a spool queue;  they are
##          active only when
##    checking permissions of a spooled job.
##
## The UNIXSOCKET will match (true) when connection was made
##          over a UNIX
##    socket.
##
## The SAMEHOST match checks to see that one (or more) of the
##  IP addresses of the host originating a request is/are the
##  matches one or more of the IP addresses of the host whose
##  hostname appears in the control file.
## The SAMEHOST match checks to see that one (or more) of the
##  IP addresses of the host originating a request is/are the
##  matches one or more of the IP addresses of the server.
## FORWARD  is the same as NOT SAMEHOST, i.e. - request is
##  forwarded.
##
## The  special key letter=patterns searches the control file
## line starting with the (upper case) letter, and is usually
## used  with  printing  and  spooling  checks.  For example,
## C=A*,B* would check that the class information (i.e.- line
## in  the control file starting with C) had a value starting
## with A or B.
##
## A permission line consists of list of tests and a result
## value.
## If all of the tests succeed,  then a match has been found
## and the permission testing completes with the result value.
```

```
## You use the DEFAULT reserved word to set the default
## ACCEPT/DENY result.
## The NOT keyword will reverse the sense of a test.
##
## Each test can have one or more optional values separated by
## commas. For example USER=john,paul,mark has 3 test values.
##
## The Match type specifies how the matching is done.
## S = glob type string match OR </path
##      Format:  string with wildcards (*) and ranges
##               * matches 0 or more chars
##               [a-d] matches a or b or c or d
##      Character comparison is case insensitive.
##      For example - USER=th*s matches uTHS, This, This, Theses
##                    USER=[d-f]x matches dx, ex, fx
##      If the match is </path then the specified file is
##      opened and read, and the file contents are treated like
##      S type entries separated by whitespace
##
##
## IP = IP address and submask.  IP address must be in dotted
## form.
##         OR </path
##      Format: x.x.x.x[/y.y.y.y]  x.x.x.x is IP address
##              y.y.y.y is optional submask, default is
##              255.255.255.255
##      Match is done by converting to 32 bit x, y, and IP
##      value and using:
##          success = ((x ^ IP ) & y) == 0    (C language
##          notation)
##      i.e.- only bits where mask is non-zero are used in
##      comparison.
##      For example - REMOTEIP=130.191.0.0/255.255.0.0 matches
##      all address 130.191.X.X
##      If the match is </path then the specified file is
##      opened and read, and the file contents are treated like
##      S type entries separated by whitespace
##
## N = numerical range   -   low-high integer range.
##       Format: low[-high]
##       Example: PORT=0-1023 matches a port in range 0 - 1023
##       (privileged)
```

```
##
## The SAMEUSER and SAMEHOST are options that form values from
## information in control files or connections.  The GROUP
## entry searches the user group database for group names
## matching the pattern,  and then searches these for the user
## name.  If the name is found,  the search is successful.
## The SERVER entry is successful if the request originated
## from the current lpd server host.
##
## Note carefully that the USER, HOST, and IP values are based
## on values found in the control file currently being checked
## for permissions.  The REMOTEUSER, REMOTEHOST, and REMOTEIP
## are based on values supplied as part of a connection to the
## LPD server,  or on the actual TCP/IP connection.
##
## The LPC entry matches an LPC command.  For example LPC=topq
## would match when an lpc topq command is being executed.  You
## must still have the SERVICE=C entry to trigger this action.
##
## Note: the SERVICE=R and SERVICE=P both check the LPR actions
## of sending a job.  However, SERVICE=R does it when the job
## is being sent to the LPD server.  Some LPD (and LPR)
## implementations cannot handle a job being rejected due to
## lack of permissions,  and sit in an endless loop trying to
## resend the job.  This is the reason for the SERVICE=P check.
## You can accept the job for printing,  and then have the
## SERVICE=P check remove the job.
##
## NOTE: if you do not have an explicit ACCEPT SERVICE=P or
## DEFAULT ACCEPT action then your print jobs will be accepted
## and then quietly discarded.
##
## Example Permissions
##
## # All operations allowed except those specifically forbidden
## DEFAULT ACCEPT
##
## # Accept connections from hosts on subnet 130.191.0.0 or
## # from the server.
```

```
##    ACCEPT SERVICE=X REMOTEIP=130.191.0.0/255.255.0.0,\
##              128.0.0.0/8
## # from a named set of sites
##    ACCEPT SERVICE=X REMOTEHOST=engpc*
## # listed in the /etc/accepthost file
##    ACCEPT SERVICE=X REMOTEHOST=</etc/accepthost
##      - /etc/rejecthost contains list of entries separated
##        by whitespace.  For example:
##            10.0.0.0/8 128.0.0.0/8
##            192.168.10.1  192.168.10.2
##     # don't take them from this particular host
##    REJECT SERVICE=X REMOTEHOST=badhost.eng.com
## # Reject all others
##    REJECT SERVICE=X
##
## #Do not allow anybody but root or papowell on
## #astart1.astart.com or listed in the /etc/ok file
## #to use lpc commands:
##    ACCEPT SERVICE=C SERVER REMOTEUSER=root
##    ACCEPT SERVICE=C REMOTEHOST=astart1.astart.com \
##        REMOTEUSER=papowell,</etc/ok
##    /etc/ok has list of users:
##          root papowell nobody
##          user1 user2
##
## #Allow root on talker.astart.com to control printer hpjet
##    ACCEPT SERVICE=C HOST=talker.astart.com PRINTER=hpjet
##        REMOTEUSER=root
## #Reject all others
##    REJECT SERVICE=C
##
## #Do not allow forwarded jobs or requests
##    REJECT SERVICE=R,C,M FORWARD
##


## You can make sure that connections come from a privileged
## port.
## Default is to allow them from any port so that non-setuid
## programs
#  can do printing.
#  Totally RFC1179
```

```
#REJECT SERVICE=X NOT PORT=1-1023
#REJECT SERVICE=X NOT PORT=1-1023
#  Privileged
#REJECT SERVICE=X NOT PORT=721-731
#
# allow root on server to control jobs
ACCEPT SERVICE=C SERVER REMOTEUSER=root
# allow anybody to get server, status, and printcap
ACCEPT SERVICE=C LPC=lpd,status,printcap
# reject all others
REJECT SERVICE=C
#
# allow same user on originating host to remove a job
ACCEPT SERVICE=M SAMEHOST SAMEUSER
# allow root on server to remove a job
ACCEPT SERVICE=M SERVER REMOTEUSER=root
REJECT SERVICE=M
# all other operations allowed
DEFAULT ACCEPT
```

The /etc/lpd.conf file is used to configure the lpd service. A sample of
this file appears in the following listing:

```
# See "man lpd.conf" for a list of options you can set here.
#   check_for_nonprintable means the 'check_for_nonprintable'
#   option default value is on or 1
#
#   To set it to OFF or 0, change this to read:
#      check_for_nonprintable@
check_for_nonprintable@
client_config_file=/etc/lpd.conf
filter_ld_path=/lib:/usr/lib:/usr/X11R6/lib:/usr/local/lib
filter_path=/bin:/usr/bin:/usr/local/bin:/usr/sbin:/usr/local/
➥   sbin:/usr/lib/filters:/usr/X11R6/bin
mail_operator_on_error=root
pr=/usr/bin/pr
printcap_path=/etc/printcap
# If you distribute your printcap entries through NIS,
# use the following line instead:
#printcap_path=|/usr/lib/yp/match_printcap
printer_perms_path=/etc/lpd.perms
server_config_file=/etc/lpd.conf
```

```
server_user=lp
user=lp
group=lp
# If your printer doesn't print the job remove the "@" from the
# following line. (for example necessary for HP4M with a
# JetDirect Card)
send_data_first@
mc#0
send_try#0
max_connect_interval#10
```

Entries here affect such items as whether or not a banner will always be present by default, what the default job format is, the directory to use for temporary files, and so on.

Printing Utilities

A number of utilities exist to work with various components of the printing service. The first to examine is `lpc`—the line printer control program. This utility can be used on any printer defined in either the **printcap** or `lpd.conf` files. To see an extensive list of all the options it offers, first start `lpc` by entering the command at the command prompt, and then type **m** for the menu at the `lpc>` prompt if you are using LPRng, or a question mark (?) if you are using CUPS. You exit out of `lpc` by pressing **q** for quit.

The `lpq` utility is used to list jobs within the queue. Very similar to the status command within `lpc`, it gets its information directly from the daemon. Here's an example of the output that `lpq` shows:

```
Printer: printer@linux 'lpdfilter drv=upp method=auto color=yes'
 Queue: 2 printable jobs
 Server: pid 7855 active
 Unspooler: pid 7859 active
 Status: cannot open '192.168.0.101%9100' - 'Connection
➥refused', attempt 160, sleeping 10 at 14:49:57.897
 Rank   Owner/ID                 Class Job Files
➥Size Time
stalled(1726sec) root@linux+242    A   242 edul.txt
➥57486 07:31:01
2      root@linux+707             A   707 edul.txt
➥57486 14:17:08
```

The `lprm` utility is used to remove print jobs from the queue. When used, it sends a request to remove the jobs, based on job number. If no job number is given, it attempts to remove the last job you submitted. An example of this utility in operation is shown in Figure 9.11.

FIGURE 9.11
The `lprm` utility removes spooled jobs.

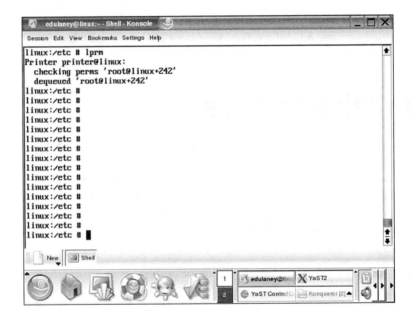

In this case, the most recent job submitted by the user has been removed. The `lprm` utility can be used with a username as an option to delete the jobs submitted by that user.

The `lpadmin` utility allows you to do most of the configuration you can do within YaST from the command line. Figure 9.12 shows all the options available with it.

A complement to this utility is `lpoptions`, which is used to modify network printers from the command line. Some of the options that can be used with it include:

▶ `-d` to set the default printer

▶ `-h` to specify the CUPS server

▶ `-p` to set the destination and instance

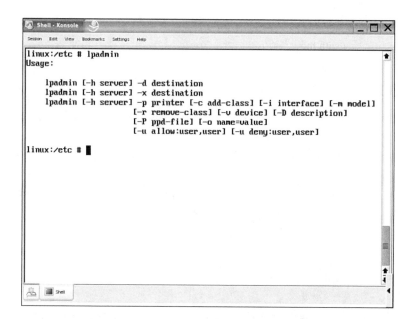

FIGURE 9.12
With `lpadmin`, you can modify printer settings from the command line.

If you are sharing your printer across the network, there are a few other files that can be helpful, although they are not utilities as such:

▶ /etc/hosts.lpd—This file holds the names of hosts that are allowed to access the printer.

▶ /etc/hosts.equiv—This file holds the name of hosts allowed to access this machine (not just the printer) as if they were local.

To enable and disable printing from the command line, you can use the /usr/bin/enable and /usr/bin/disable commands, respectively. Each command must be followed by the name of the printer for which you are enabling/disabling. If you want the printer to finish what is in its queue but not accept any additional jobs, you can use /usr/sbin/reject followed by the printer name (the opposite of which is /usr/sbin/accept).

The CUPS service can be stopped in two ways: using the command /etc/init.d/cups stop or rccups stop. The opposite of these actions is accomplished by using start in place of stop.

The lppasswd utility can be used to add a password to the CUPS Web Administration tools. If you enter the command by itself at the command line, you will be prompted to enter a password twice. The password you give must be at least 6 characters long and cannot contain your username; it must also contain at least one letter and number. Options that can be given at the command line are **-g** to specify a groupname, and **-a** or **-x** to specify a username. For the Webadmin tools, you need to run the following command:

```
lppasswd -g sys -a root
```

to create the **sys** group and root user. You will then be prompted for the password to use.

To access the Web Administration tools, simply access port 631 on the server. Figure 9.13 shows the opening screen that appears when you access this port. These tools allow you to remotely manage the printers and jobs as well as do administrative tasks such as add/manage classes, manage jobs, and add/manage printers.

FIGURE 9.13
The Webadmin tools can be accessed at port 631.

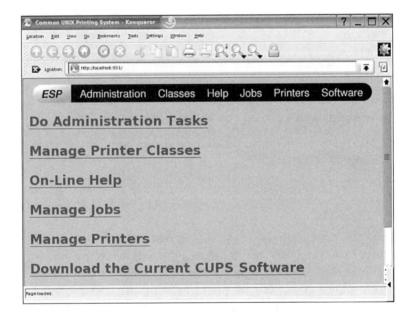

One last item of note is that the file **/var/log/cups/error_log** is where error messages for the CUPS daemon are written. The **access_log** shows all access to the service. Both can be useful in troubleshooting situations when you need to ascertain why a printer is unavailable.

Summary

This chapter focused on the topics you need to know about printing for the exam and print administration in general.

Command Summary

Table 9.1 lists the commands that were discussed in this chapter.

Commands for Print Management   **TABLE 9.1**

UTILITY	DEFAULT PURPOSE
lp	The original utility for submitting jobs to the print service
lpadmin	To work with printer configuration from the command line
lpc	The main utility for managing the print service
lpoptions	Tool to modify network printers from the command line
lppasswd	The utility for configuring authentication options for the Web Administration printing utilities
lpq	The primary tool for looking at contents and status of the print queue
lpr	An relative of lp, it allows you to submit jobs for printing
lprm	The utility used to remove print jobs
pr	A utility for processing files before sending them to the printer

Administrative Tasks Revisited

The words implying system administration first appeared in this book in the title of Chapter 5, "Basic Linux Administration." Truthfully, though, the topic of system administration is prevalent throughout this book. It is an administrators' exam that you are studying for—not one for programmers or developers.

This chapter looks at a number of topics, including package management and security. It covers the following course objectives:

1. Executing RPM Package Related Operations (3036)
2. Using the Basic Linux `mail` Command (3036)
3. Monitor Your SLES 9 System (3037)
4. Manage RPM Software Packages (3037)
5. Verify and Update Software Library Access (3037)
6. Manage the Kernel (3037)
7. Create a Security Concept (3038)
8. Limit Physical Access to Server Systems (3038)
9. Limit the Installed Software Packages (3038)
10. Ensure File System Security (3038)
11. Use ACLS for Advanced Access Control (3038)
12. Be Informed About Security Issues (3038)
13. Apply Security Updates (3038)
14. Add New Hardware to a SLES 9 System (3038)

Installing Software

Course Objective Covered

6. Manage the Kernel (3037)

There are several primary methods of software distribution within the Linux community. One is to use one of the package management systems, which we will look at later. The second is to use the compressed "tarball" file. The tarball is a single file containing a tar image of a set of files.

You know you are working with a tarball or compressed tarball because there is a `.tar` or `.tar.gz` on the end of the filename. For example, the following files are tarballs:

```
program-1-2-3.tar.gz
program-1-2-3.tar
```

But the following example is not:

```
program-1.2.3.rpm
```

To install a tarball, you must first identify the software you want to install, and obtain it from a provider. For example, to get **wumpus** from ftp.ccil.org, use **ftp** as shown in the following example:

```
ftp> bin
200 Type set to I.
ftp> get wumpus-1.3.tar.gz
local: wumpus-1.3.tar.gz remote: wumpus-1.3.tar.gz
227 Entering Passive Mode (192,190,237,102,12,145)
150 Opening BINARY mode data connection for wumpus-1.3.tar.gz
➥ (9293 bytes).
226 Transfer complete.
9293 bytes received in 0.207 secs (44 Kbytes/sec)
ftp>
```

This results in **wumpus-1.3.tar.gz** on your system, which must be uncompressed and then untarred. You can do this in one or two steps. The two-step approach, which has traditionally been used, involved uncompressing the file and then untarring the files. This is done using the following commands:

```
# gzip -d FILE
# tar xvf FILE
```

The first of these commands uncompresses the file, and the second performs the extraction. Because this has been such a common way of distributing software, the GNU version of `tar` included with Linux includes a feature to uncompress the archive and extract the files. This is done using the command:

```
# tar zxvf FILE
```

The `-z` option is used to filter the archive through `gzip`.   **NOTE**

The `v` option to `tar` lists all the files in the archive as they are extracted. If you prefer not to see the files listed, simply omit the `v`. The `x` informs `tar` to extract the files, and the `f` identifies the file to extract the files from:

```
# tar zxf wumpus*
# ls -l
total 42
drwxr-xr-x    5 edulaney    edulaney         1024 Nov 26
➥ 16:01 Desktop
-rw-r--r--    1 104         bin               359 Aug 20  1994
➥Makefile
-r--r--r--    1 104         bin               307 Apr 25  1994
➥READ.ME
-r--r--r--    1 104         bin             10084 Apr 25
➥   1994 superhack.c
-rw-rw-r--    1 root        root             9293 Nov 26 16:22
➥ wumpus-1.3.tar.gz
-r--r--r--    1 104         bin             17883 Apr 25  1994
➥wumpus.c
#
```

We have just extracted the files from the tarball. **wumpus** is simple in that it only involves a few files. We compile **wumpus** using the program **make**. Note that you must have the development tools installed in order to be able to compile any software on your system. The **make** command relies on a specification file to define what it needs to do. This is called a Makefile and is illustrated in the following code:

```
#
# Makefile for `Hunt the Wumpus' and `Superhack' games
#

CC=gcc
CFLAGS=-g
```

```
all: wumpus superhack

wumpus: wumpus.c
        $(CC) $(CFLAGS) wumpus.c -o wumpus

superhack: superhack.c
        $(CC) $(CFLAGS) superhack.c -o superhack

clean:
        rm -f wumpus wumpus.o superhack superhack.o TAGS

TAGS:
        etags wumpus.c

tar:
        tar -cvf wumpus.tar READ.ME Makefile wumpus.c
➥ superhack.c
#
```

This is a very simple Makefile, but it is suitable for our discussion. With the Makefile, some parameters or options may need to be changed to get the program compiled on your environment. The Makefile is structured with options, like CC=gcc, and with objects like all. The object all is dependent upon the objects wumpus and superhack.

We can see that the object wumpus is dependent upon the object wumpus.c. This tells make that to make the object all, it must first make the object wumpus. Compiling wumpus.c makes the object wumpus. Make performs the same process on the other objects all is dependent upon. The first object is typically the default. This means that typing make with no argument results in make building all. Typing make wumpus results in make building only the components to build wumpus:

```
# make
cc -g wumpus.c -o wumpus
cc -g superhack.c -o superhack
# ls -l
total 109
-rw-r--r--   1 104      bin           359 Aug 20  1994
➥Makefile
-r--r--r--   1 104      bin           307 Apr 25  1994
➥READ.ME
-rwxrwxr-x   1 root     root        35127 Nov 26 16:25
➥ superhack
-r--r--r--   1 104      bin         10084 Apr 25  1994
➥ superhack.c
```

```
-rwxrwxr-x      1 root      root        31460 Nov 26 16:25 wumpus
-rw-rw-r--      1 root      root         9293 Nov 26 16:22
➥ wumpus-1.3.tar.gz
-r--r--r--      1 104       bin         17883 Apr 25   1994
➥wumpus.c
#
```

We can now test **wumpus** by running the compiled program:

```
# ./wumpus
INSTRUCTIONS (Y-N)
?y
HUNT THE WUMPUS

YOU ARE IN ROOM 11
TUNNELS LEAD TO 10 12 19

SHOOT OR MOVE (S-M)
?
```

Typically, editing the Makefile is required to alter parameters like the C compiler to be used, or the path specifications to find programs. You may have to edit the libraries included during the compile. However, more complex software no longer relies on the user to edit the Makefile because there can be simply too many options to wrestle with, which has results in the development of **Configure**. Looking at a more complex situation, we want to install a version of Perl. We can download it from http://www.perl.com:

```
ftp> bin
200 Type set to I.
ftp> get perl-5.6.0.tar.gz
local: perl-5.6.0.tar.gz remote: perl-5.6.0.tar.gz
227 Entering Passive Mode (209,85,3,25,12,163).
150 Opening BINARY mode data connection for perl-5.6.0.tar.gz
  (5443601 bytes).
226 Transfer complete.
5443601 bytes received in 148 secs (36 Kbytes/sec)
ftp>
```

We again uncompress and unpack:

```
# tar zxf perl*
```

This gives us a new directory called **perl-x.x.x** where the x's are replaced by version numbers. In that directory you will find at least one command called `Configure`. This script is common to many GNU utilities and configures the software for the environment:

```
# ls -l Configure
-r-xr-xr-x    1 504        1001        346347 Mar 22  2000
➥ Configure
# ./Configure

Sources for perl5 found in "/home/edulaney/perl-5.6.0".

Beginning of configuration questions for perl5.

Checking echo to see how to suppress newlines...
...using -n.
The star should be here-->*

First let's make sure your kit is complete.  Checking...
Looks good...

This installation shell script will examine your system and ask
➥ you questions
to determine how the perl5 package should be installed. If
➥you get
stuck on a question, you may use a ! shell escape to
➥start a subshell or
execute a command.  Many of the questions will have default
➥ answers in square
brackets; typing carriage return will give you the default.

On some of the questions which ask for file or directory names
➥ you are allowed
to use the ~name construct to specify the login directory
➥ belonging to "name",
even if you don't have a shell which knows about that.
➥Questions where this is
allowed will be marked "(~name ok)".

[Type carriage return to continue]
```

The `Configure` script will prompt you for answers to some questions while figuring out the configuration of your system. After the questions are answered, you must run **make** to actually compile the software:

```
# make
`sh  cflags libperl.a miniperlmain.o`  miniperlmain.c
         CCCMD =  cc -DPERL_CORE -c -fno-strict-aliasing
```

```
➡-D_LARGEFILE_SOURCE -D
_FILE_OFFSET_BITS=64 -O2
...
#
```

Installation is accomplished using the command `make install`. This installs the binary and additional files into the places designated during the execution of `Configure`.

Shared Libraries

Course Objective Covered

5. Verify and Update Software Library Access (3037)

Most Linux programs make use of shared libraries. A shared library allows a program to be smaller and require less storage space because it pulls in the libraries it requires when it needs to. For example, if a program is dependent upon `libcrypt.a`, during compilation, all of the functions in `libcrypt.a` are included in the compiled binary. This is not efficient, because changes to `libcrypt.a` require the programs to be recompiled for the new changes to be included. By using shared libraries, as the library changes, the programs that depend upon that library can take advantage of the changes without the need to recompile.

Several commands are available to review the configuration of shared libraries on your system. These are `ldd` and `ldconfig`. `ldd` is used to see what shared libraries a program is dependent upon. To use it, supply a program name as an argument, for example

```
# ldd /usr/bin/perl
        libnsl.so.1 => /lib/libnsl.so.1 (0x4001e000)
        libdl.so.2 => /lib/libdl.so.2 (0x40035000)
        libm.so.6 => /lib/libm.so.6 (0x40038000)
        libc.so.6 => /lib/libc.so.6 (0x40057000)
        libcrypt.so.1 => /lib/libcrypt.so.1 (0x40175000)
        /lib/ld-linux.so.2 => /lib/ld-linux.so.2 (0x40000000)
#
```

The output of `ldd` informs us that `/usr/bin/perl` is dependent upon these shared libraries. As these shared libraries are updated, the new functionality or bug fixes are automatically available to the program, without the need for recompiling the software.

The `ldconfig` program is used to update and maintain the cache of shared library data and symbols for the `ld.so` dynamic linker. `ldconfig` checks the file `/etc/ld.so.conf` for information on the shared libraries, and also checks each file in the trusted directories, `/lib` and `/usr/lib`.

The `ldconfig` command must be run as root so that any updates to system files can be performed. The dynamic linker cache is found at `/etc/ld.so.cache` and is managed using `ldconfig`. You can rebuild the cache by running `ldconfig` with no options. This rebuilds the cache. You can review the current cache using the option -p:

```
# ldconfig -p | more
398 libs found in cache `/etc/ld.so.cache'
        libzvt.so.2 (libc6) => /usr/lib/libzvt.so.2
        libz.so.1 (libc6) => /usr/lib/libz.so.1
        libz.so (libc6) => /usr/lib/libz.so
        libxrx.so.6 (libc6) => /usr/X11R6/lib/libxrx.so.6
        libxrx.so (libc6) => /usr/X11R6/lib/libxrx.so
        libxmms.so.1 (libc6) => /usr/lib/libxmms.so.1
        libxml.so.1 (libc6) => /usr/lib/libxml.so.1
,,,
```

Here we see that there are 398 entries in the cache as reported by `ldconfig`. It is only necessary to use this command if a new shared library is installed. The new library is not used until `ldconfig` is run and the cache is rebuilt.

Package Management with Red Hat

Course Objectives Covered

1. Executing RPM Package Related Operations (3036)
4. Manage RPM Software Packages (3037)

Earlier in this chapter, we examined how to extract a tarball and build an application. Today, however, more and more software distribution in the Linux community is accomplished using packages. There are two principal methods of package management: the RPM or Red Hat package manager and the `dpkg` approach employed by Debian.

RPM, the Red Hat Package Manager, is an open system for the packaging and distribution of software in the Unix environment. Though most commonly used for Linux, RPM has been compiled and used on other Unix platforms also. RPM allows users to take source code and package it in source and binary form such that the programs can be easily tracked and rebuilt.

RPM also created and maintains a database of the packages and files to allow for the verification of the package, querying information about the packages and files, and the removal of those packages if desired.

The query options to RPM allow searches through the database for specific packages or files, including how to identify which package a file came from. The RPM files are themselves compressed images. These compressed images contain a custom binary header allowing for quick retrieval of information about the package and its contents.

The verification options allow the user to determine if portions of packages are missing. If so, the user can re-install the package, while maintaining any altered configuration files. RPM is an extremely powerful tool, and as such we will review some of its functionality. Specifically we will look at these aspects:

- ▶ Installing and removing software using RPM
- ▶ Verifying an RPM
- ▶ Querying an RPM
- ▶ Building an RPM

Installing and Removing Software Using RPM

The simplest method used to install software using RPM is with the command

```
rpm -i rpm-name.rpm
```

For example, to install the `foobar-2.3-8.i386.rpm` package, the command is

```
# rpm -i foobar-2.3-8.i386.rpm
```

This instructs `rpm` to read the RPM file, extract the files, and place them in the correct location as specified in the RPM file. Removing a package is accomplished with the following command:

```
rpm -e foobar
```

Both of these scenarios expect the RPM file to be local on your hard disk. Because we typically do not keep the RPM file after the software is installed, it is also possible to install direct from FTP if you know the source path, or URL, for the RPM file:

```
rpm -i ftp://ftp.some.site/pub/name.rpm
```

In the preceding example, rpm will use your network connection, retrieve the RPM file, and install the package.

These are simple examples demonstrating rpm's capabilities. Use the command rpm--help to see what capabilities your specific version of rpm has.

Verifying an RPM

rpm is used to also verify what packages are installed and what files are missing. This allows the administrator to query the system after a file or directory may have been accidentally erased. The following command verifies all of the packages installed on the system:

```
# rpm -Va
```

The verification process compares information about the installed files in the package with information about the files taken from the original package and stored in the rpm database. Among other things, verifying compares the size, MD5 sum, permissions, type, owner, and group of each file. Any discrepancies are displayed.

Querying a Package

The structure of the RPM files and database allows a package to be queried to determine information about the package, or to see which package a particular file belongs to. For example, to see what package a particular file belongs to, you must use the options -qf to rpm and specify the filename.

```
$ rpm -qf /sbin/insmod
mod-init-tools-3.0_pre10-37.16
$
```

In this case, the /sbin/insmod program is part of the mod-init-tools package.

You can also use the query options to rpm to print information about the module. For example, to see what information is available on the zip package you found on the Internet, use these options:

```
$ rpm -qpi zip-2.3-8.i386.rpm
Name         : zip           Relocations: /usr
Version      : 2.3           Vendor: Red Hat, Inc.
Release      : 8             Build Date: Thu 24 Aug 2000
➥ 11:16:53 AM EDT
Install date: (not installed)            Build Host:
➥porky.devel.redhat.com
Group        : Applications/Archiving    Source RPM:
➥ zip-2.3-8.src.rpm
Size         : 271467                         License:
➥ distributable
Packager : Red Hat, Inc. <http://bugzilla.redhat.com/bugzilla>
Summary      : A file compression and packaging utility
➥ compatible with PKZIP.
Description :
The zip program is a compression and file packaging utility.
➥Zip is
analogous to a combination of the UNIX tar and compress
➥ commands and
is compatible with PKZIP (a compression and file packaging
➥ utility for
MS-DOS systems).

Install the zip package if you need to compress files using
➥ the zip program.
```

You can also list the files in the package by changing the "I" option to the letter "l":

```
$ rpm -qpl zip-2.3-8.i386.rpm
/usr/bin/zip
/usr/bin/zipcloak
/usr/bin/zipnote
/usr/bin/zipsplit
/usr/share/doc/zip-2.3
/usr/share/doc/zip-2.3/BUGS
/usr/share/doc/zip-2.3/CHANGES
/usr/share/doc/zip-2.3/MANUAL
/usr/share/doc/zip-2.3/README
/usr/share/doc/zip-2.3/TODO
/usr/share/doc/zip-2.3/WHATSNEW
/usr/share/doc/zip-2.3/WHERE
/usr/share/doc/zip-2.3/algorith.txt
/usr/share/man/man1/zip.1.gz
$
```

With the basics of **rpm** handling covered, let's turn to a discussion of constructing a simple package.

Building RPMs

Building the RPM itself isn't hard, but it is best if you can get the source to build on its own. We are going to look at our **wumpus** tarball and build an RPM package with it.

To build the RPM, you need to perform the following steps:

1. Get the source code you are building the RPM for to build on your system.

2. Make a patch of any changes you had to make to the sources to get them to build properly.

3. Make a **spec** file for the package.

4. Make sure everything is in its proper place.

5. Build the package using RPM.

RPM requires the construction of a **spec** file, which includes information regarding the package, along with information on how to build it and a file list for all the binaries that are installed. The **spec** file is named according to a defined specification:

```
Package name—version number—release number . spec
```

That would be **wumpus-1.3-A.spec** for our **wumpus** example. This allows multiple versions of the same package—at least the **.spec** file remains intact. Here is a sample **spec** file:

```
$ more *.spec
summary: Hunt the wumpus
Name: wumpus
Version: 1.3
Release: A
Copyright: GPL
Group: Amusement/Games
Source: http://a-uRL-pointing-to-the-source
Patch:
Buildroot: /var/tmp/%name-buildroot

%description
This is a true implementation of the classic mainframe computer
➥ game, wumpus.
```

```
%prep
%setup -q
%patch -p1 -b .buildroot

%build
make RPM_OPT_FLAGS="$RPM_OPT_FLAGS"

%install
rm -rf $RPM_BUILD_ROOT
mkdir -p $RPM_BUILD_ROOT/usr/local/games
mkdir -p $RPM_BUILD_ROOT/usr/man/man1

install -s -m 755 eject $RPM_BUILD_ROOT/usr/local/games/wumpus

%clean
rm -rf $RPM_BUILD_ROOT

%files
%defattr(-,root,root)
%doc README TODO COPYING ChangeLog

/usr/local/games/wumpus

%changelog
* Sat Dec  2 15:24:30 EST 2000 Emmett Dulaney
➥ <edulaney@iquest.net>
- created RPM from wumpus tarball
$
```

As you see in the sample **spec** file, there is a common structure to the RPM header. The sections are explained in Table 10.1.

RPM Headers   **TABLE 10.1**

SECTION	DESCRIPTION
Summary	This is a one-line description of the package.
Name	This must be the name string from the rpm filename you plan to use.
Version	This must be the version string from the rpm filename you plan to use.
Release	This is the release number for a package of the same version.

Table 10.1 Continued

SECTION	DESCRIPTION
Copyright	This line tells how a package is copyrighted. You should use something like GPL, BSD, MIT, public domain, distributable, or commercial.
Group	This is a group that the package belongs to in a higher-level package tool or the Red Hat installer.
Source	This line points to the HOME location of the original source file. It is used if you ever want to get the source again or check for newer versions.
Patch	This is the place you can find the patch if you need to download it again.
Buildroot	This line allows you to specify a directory as the "root" for building and installing the new package. You can use this to help test your package before having it installed on your machine.
%description	It's not really a header item, but should be described with the rest of the header. You need one description tag per package and/or subpackage. This is a multi-line field that should be used to give a comprehensive description of the package.

The second section is the %prep section. Here the specifications to build the sources are defined. The %prep section contains a series of macros available to assist in the compilation and setup of the package. Each of these macros is listed in Table 10.2.

TABLE 10.2 %Prep **Macros**

MACRO NAME	DESCRIPTION
%setup	This macro unpacks the sources and enters the directory tree. The -q option sets the name of the directory tree to the defined %name.
%patch	This macro assists in applying the patches to the source.

Everything executed in the %setup and %patch sections, right up to the %build section, is executed using the shell. The %build section doesn't really have any macros, but is intended for you to put in commands specifically to build the software after you have extracted the source, patched it, and are in the source directory. Because the commands are also passed to the shell, any legal shell commands can be executed here.

With the `%build` complete, the next step is installation. There are no real macros in the `%install` section, but the commands to install the software are included for execution by the shell. If you are using a Makefile to build the software, you can either patch the Makefile to include a `make install` command, or install the files by hand in this section.

The `%clean` macro included in the **spec** file is used to ensure that there is a clean source tree for you to build into. Be advised—failing to check the directory you are in may result in the removal of your Linux operating systems because you may be in the / directory.

The RPM manager has no way of knowing what files are to be installed when the compilation of the source files is completed. The %Files section lists the binary files for installation, and the location they are installed in.

Finally, the `%changelog` section lists all of the changes made for each version and release of the package. Each change is started with an asterisk (*), and includes the date, your name, and your email address. The rest of the text is free-form, but should follow some coherent manner for readability.

With the **spec** file defined, we can now build the package.

Building a Package

We are required to have a properly defined build tree, which can be modified in the file `/etc/rpmrc` or `/ur/lib/rpm/rpmc`. This is a large and comprehensive set of information used for building packages. Most people use the `/usr/src` directory for installing their sources to build a package. When creating the source tree to build the package, you may need to create some directories including

- ▶ BUILD—Where `rpm` will build the package
- ▶ SOURCE—Where the source files are located
- ▶ SPECS—Where the **spec** files should go
- ▶ RPMS—Where `rpm` will put the binary RPM files after it builds them
- ▶ SRPMS—Where `rpm` will put the source RPMS

When this is done, compile the source and review it for the files that are installed, where they go, and what you had to do to compile, such as create a patch. With the compilation complete you are ready to build the RPM.

Using the **spec** file, you can try to build the package using the command

```
$ rpm -ba filename.spec
```

This creates the source and binary RPMs for your package. The easiest and best way to test it is to install it on a different system. Because you have just installed it on your own system, it will be difficult to know if the test was actually successful. Even if you remove the package, you might have missed a file in your file list and the package will not be completely removed. When the package is reinstalled, your system is complete, but the package is not. It is important to consider that while you are doing the following operation

```
$ rpm -ba package-name
```

most people will be executing

```
$ rpm -I package name
```

So it is important to not miss anything in the package build and install sections. Assuming you want to distribute your RPMs, you can upload the new RPM to many different sites.

Understanding the Linux Kernel

Course Objective Covered

6. Manage the Kernel (3037)

The kernel is a software component of the operating system that acts as the system supervisor. The kernel provides all system services to the applications and commands users execute. This includes allocation of CPU time, memory management, disk access, and hardware interfaces. Users are not typically aware of the kernel functions as they are hidden from their view by the applications, such as the shell, that the user interacts with. The system administrator becomes familiar with the kernel as he or she perform the jobs.

When a system administrator executes a command such as **ps**, the kernel accesses the system table to provide information regarding the currently running processes. More commonly, however, system administrators interact with the kernel to handle the installation of new hardware.

Kernel Modules

Unlike other Unix implementations, the Linux kernel makes use of loadable modules to add new features or support for specific hardware. This provides the administrators with the flexibility to reconfigure their systems as required. Typical Unix implementations require the administrator to build a new kernel whenever a change is required to the kernel. Although some changes do require building a new kernel, most do not.

Loadable modules are kernel components that are not directly linked or included in the kernel. The module developer compiles them separately and the administrator can insert or remove them into the running kernel. The scope of actual modules available has grown considerably and now includes filesystems, Ethernet card drivers, tape drivers, PCMCIA, parallel-port IDE, and many printer drivers. Using loadable modules is done using the commands listed in Table 10.3.

Loadable Module Commands   TABLE 10.3

COMMAND	DESCRIPTION
lsmod	List the loaded modules
insmod	Install a module
rmmod	Remove a module
modinfo	Print information about a module
modprobe	Probe and install a module and its dependents
depmod	Determine module dependencies

The commands affect the modules in the currently running kernel and will also review information available in the /proc filesystem. lsmod is used to list the currently loaded modules. The output of the command is

```
[root@server7 edulaney]# lsmod
Module                  Size  Used by
udf                    93700  0
parport_pc             41024  0
parport                44232  1 parport_pc
iptable_filter          7040  0
ip_tables              22400  1 iptable_filter
nls_iso8859_1           8320  0
snd_pcm_oss            65576  0
snd_pcm               112772  1 snd_pcm_oss
snd_page_alloc         16136  1 snd_pcm
```

```
snd_timer                  32132  1 snd_pcm
snd_mixer_oss              24448  1 snd_pcm_oss
snd                        70884  4 snd_pcm_oss,snd_pcm,snd
_timer,snd_mixer_oss
soundcore                  13536  1 snd
edd                        13720  0
joydev                     14528  0
sg                         41632  0
st                         44828  0
sr_mod                     21028  0
nvram                      13448  0
usbserial                  35952  0
ehci_hcd                   33412  0
uhci_hcd                   35728  0
intel_mch_agp              14352  1
agpgart                    36140  2 intel_mch_agp
ipv6                      276348  17
hw_random                   9620  0
evdev                      13952  0
thermal                    16648  0
processor                  21312  1 thermal
fan                         8196  0
button                     10384  0
battery                    12804  0
ac                          8964  0
af_packet                  26376  2
e100                       38400  0
mii                         9344  1 e100
usbcore                   116700  5 usbserial,ehci_hcd,uhci_hcd
subfs                      12160  1
nls_cp437                   9984  1
vfat                       19456  1
fat                        49824  1 vfat
nls_utf8                    6272  2
ntfs                       94352  1
dm_mod                     57472  0
ide_cd                     42628  0
cdrom                      42652  2 sr_mod,ide_cd
reiserfs                  263504  1
ata_piix                   11908  0
libata                     43648  1 ata_piix,[permanent]
sd_mod                     25088  0
scsi_mod                  118340  5 sg,st,sr_mod,libata,sd_mod
```

This is the same information that is displayed with another command, as
shown in the following example:

```
[root@server7 edulaney]# cat /proc/modules
udf 93700 0 - Live 0xe0d7a000
parport_pc 41024 0 - Live 0xe0ca3000
parport 44232 1 parport_pc, Live 0xe0ba4000
iptable_filter 7040 0 - Live 0xe0bda000
ip_tables 22400 1 iptable_filter, Live 0xe0ceb000
nls_iso8859_1 8320 0 - Live 0xe0cf7000
snd_pcm_oss 65576 0 - Live 0xe0d4d000
snd_pcm 112772 1 snd_pcm_oss, Live 0xe0d30000
snd_page_alloc 16136 1 snd_pcm, Live 0xe0cf2000
snd_timer 32132 1 snd_pcm, Live 0xe0cbe000
snd_mixer_oss 24448 1 snd_pcm_oss, Live 0xe0ce4000
snd 70884 4 snd_pcm_oss,snd_pcm,snd_timer,snd_mixer_oss,
 Live 0xe0cfb000
soundcore 13536 1 snd, Live 0xe0cdf000
edd 13720 0 - Live 0xe0cb9000
joydev 14528 0 - Live 0xe0bd5000
sg 41632 0 - Live 0xe0cd3000
st 44828 0 - Live 0xe0cc7000
sr_mod 21028 0 - Live 0xe0bce000
nvram 13448 0 - Live 0xe0bc9000
usbserial 35952 0 - Live 0xe0caf000
ehci_hcd 33412 0 - Live 0xe0bba000
uhci_hcd 35728 0 - Live 0xe0bb0000
intel_mch_agp 14352 1 - Live 0xe0b85000
agpgart 36140 2 intel_mch_agp, Live 0xe0b9a000
ipv6 276348 17 - Live 0xe0bdd000
hw_random 9620 0 - Live 0xe0b8a000
evdev 13952 0 - Live 0xe0906000
thermal 16648 0 - Live 0xe0b7f000
processor 21312 1 thermal, Live 0xe0b78000
fan 8196 0 - Live 0xe0b44000
button 10384 0 - Live 0xe0b35000
battery 12804 0 - Live 0xe0b30000
ac 8964 0 - Live 0xe0b2c000
af_packet 26376 2 - Live 0xe0b68000
e100 38400 0 - Live 0xe0b39000
mii 9344 1 e100, Live 0xe0b28000
usbcore 116700 5 usbserial,ehci_hcd,uhci_hcd,
 Live 0xe0b4a000
subfs 12160 1 - Live 0xe0b24000
nls_cp437 9984 1 - Live 0xe0b20000
```

```
vfat 19456 1 - Live 0xe0b1a000
fat 49824 1 vfat, Live 0xe0970000
nls_utf8 6272 2 - Live 0xe0901000
ntfs 94352 1 - Live 0xe0ae0000
dm_mod 57472 0 - Live 0xe0ad0000
ide_cd 42628 0 - Live 0xe0941000
cdrom 42652 2 sr_mod,ide_cd, Live 0xe0935000
reiserfs 263504 1 - Live 0xe097e000
ata_piix 11908 0 - Live 0xe08f6000
libata 43648 1 ata_piix,[permanent], Live 0xe0929000
sd_mod 25088 0 - Live 0xe08ee000
scsi_mod 118340 5 sg,st,sr_mod,libata,sd_mod,
 Live 0xe090b000
 [root@server7 edulaney]#
```

The output of lsmod includes some header text identifying the different columns of data. Column one specifies the module that has been loaded, column two is the size of the module in bytes, column three indicates the number of references to the module, and column four specifies the modules that call this module. For example, the nfs module is loaded. The lockd module, which is an element of nfs, is referenced by the nfs module.

Removing a module with rmmod requires that you specify the module to be removed.

The modinfo command is used to query information from the module file and report to the user. modinfo can be used to report

- ▶ The module author
- ▶ The module description
- ▶ The typed parameters the module accepts

Bear in mind that many modules do not report any information at all. If the module author does not provide the information when the module is developed, there is nothing for modinfo to report. You can use the -a option to get as much information as possible, but some modules will still report <none>.

The depmod and modprobe commands can also be used to load modules. Although the method previously reviewed can be tedious and frustrating, it is worthwhile to understand the relationships between the modules. depmod is used to determine the dependencies between modules.

The `/etc/modules.conf` file is a text-based file that can be used to store information that affects the operation of **depmod** and **modprobe**. By default, this is a zero size file in SLES 9, but the format of the file is shown here:

```
[root@server7 block]# cat /etc/conf.modules
alias scsi_hostadapter ncr53c8xx
alias eth0 tulip
alias parport_lowlevel parport_pc
pre-install plip modprobe parport_pc ;
echo 7 > /proc/parport/0/irq
pre-install pcmcia_core /etc/rc.d/init.d/pcmcia start
post-install supermount modprobe scsi_hostadapter
alias sound es1371
[root@server7 block]#
```

The `conf.modules` **file and** `modules.conf` **file are one and the same. Which one is used depends on the Linux vendor.**   **NOTE**

When modifying or reading the `/etc/modules.conf` file, remember:

- ▶ All empty lines and all text on a line after a # are ignored.
- ▶ Lines may be continued by ending the line with a backslash (\).
- ▶ The lines specifying the module information must fall into one of the following formats:

  ```
  keep

  parameter=value

  options module symbol=value ...

  alias module real_name

  pre-install module command ...

  install module command ...

  post-install module command ...

  pre-remove module command ...

  remove module command ...

  post-remove module command ...
  ```

In the preceding list, all values in the "parameter" lines will be processed by a shell, which means that "shell tricks" like wildcards and commands enclosed in back quotes can be used during module processing. For example

```
path[misc]=/lib/modules/1.1.5?
path[net]=/lib/modules/`uname -r`
```

These have the effect of values to the path to look for the system modules. Table 10.4 lists the legal/allowed parameters.

TABLE 10.4 **Allowed Configuration Parameters**

PARAMETER	DESCRIPTION
keep	If this word is found before any lines containing a path description, the default set of paths will be saved, and thus added to. Otherwise the normal behavior is to replace the default set of paths with those defined on the configuration file.
depfile=DEPFILE_PATH	This is the path to the dependency file created by depmod and used by modprobe.
path=SOME_PATH	The path parameter specifies a directory to search for the modules.
path[tag]=SOME_PATH	The path parameter can carry an optional tag. This tells us a little more about the purpose of the modules in this directory and allows some automated operations by modprobe. The tag is appended to the path keyword enclosed in square brackets. If the tag is missing, the tag misc is assumed. One very useful tag is boot, which can be used to mark all modules that should be loaded at boot time.
Options	Define options required for specific modules.
Alias	Provide an alternate to a module.
pre-install module command ...	Execute a command prior to loading the module.
install module command ...	Install the following module.
post-install module command ...	Execute a command after the module is loaded.
pre-remove module command ...	Execute a command prior to removing the module.

Table 10.4 Continued

PARAMETER	DESCRIPTION
remove module command ...	Remove the named module.
post-remove module command ...	Execute a command after the module has been removed.

If the configuration file /etc/conf.modules is missing, or if any parameter is not overridden, the following defaults are assumed:

```
depfile=/lib/modules/`uname -r`/modules.dep
path[boot]=/lib/modules

path[fs]=/lib/modules/`uname -r`
path[misc]=/lib/modules/`uname -r`
path[net]=/lib/modules/`uname -r`
path[scsi]=/lib/modules/`uname -r`
path[cdrom]=/lib/modules/`uname -r`
path[ipv4]=/lib/modules/`uname -r`
path[ipv6]=/lib/modules/`uname -r`
path[sound]=/lib/modules/`uname -r`

path[fs]=/lib/modules/default
path[misc]=/lib/modules/default
path[net]=/lib/modules/default
path[scsi]=/lib/modules/default
path[cdrom]=/lib/modules/default
path[ipv4]=/lib/modules/default
path[ipv6]=/lib/modules/default
path[sound]=/lib/modules/default

path[fs]=/lib/modules
path[misc]=/lib/modules
path[net]=/lib/modules
path[scsi]=/lib/modules
path[cdrom]=/lib/modules
path[ipv4]=/lib/modules
path[ipv6]=/lib/modules
path[sound]=/lib/modules
```

This explains why it is not necessary to have any of these entries in your /etc/modules.conf file.

All "option" lines specify the default options needed for a module. For example, if we must tell `modprobe` the option to use, we must define it in our `/etc/conf.modules` file. For example, when loading the `de620` module, we must do the following:

```
modprobe de620 bnc=1
```

And then we must add the following entry to the `/etc/conf.modules` file:

```
options de620 -o bnc=1
```

However, even though we specify them in this file, if the administrator runs `modprobe` himself, the options specified on the command line override those specified in the `/etc/conf.modules` file.

The alias lines are used to assign an alternate name to a module. Recalling the `/etc/conf.modules` file, we see this:

```
alias scsi_hostadapter ncr53c8xx
alias eth0 tulip
```

This establishes the alias `scsi_hostadapter` for the module `ncr53c8xx`, and `eth0` for the tulip module. This means we do not have to remember the actual module name, but address the module also through the alias.

When you use `modprobe`, it first examines the directory containing modules compiled for the current release of the kernel. If the module is not found there, `modprobe` will look in the directory containing modules for a default release. For example, we can determine the current release of the kernel with the command `uname -r`.

When installing a new Linux kernel, you should move the modules to a directory related to the release (and version) of the kernel you are installing. Then you should create a symbolic link from this directory to the "default" directory. Each time you compile a new kernel, the command `make modules_install` will create a new directory, but won't change the default. This is discussed later in the chapter during kernel construction.

Kernel Construction

Course Objective Covered

6. Manage the Kernel (3037)

The construction of a kernel is not required on a daily basis. It is typically needed to support the devices or services that must be included in the kernel. Newer kernels will have other improvements that may include better process management and improved speed and stability. Reconfiguration of the kernel does not necessarily mean a whole new version. There may be a series of updates and patches that you want to have included into the new kernel.

Creating the kernel, however, is not a trivial task. It requires you to have a strong knowledge of your system hardware and what services you need configured. You must have a C compiler and the appropriate libraries as recommended by the kernel source code. Generally, if you installed the kernel source code from your distribution CD, you will have the elements required.

Obtaining the Kernel Source Code

Even if you are only going to add a single new service to your kernel, it is advisable to get the most recent kernel source code from your Linux vendor. Alternatively, you can download the latest kernel sources from ftp.funet.fi or any number of locations that offer Linux mirrors. The kernel software is typically named `linux-x.y.z.tar.gz` where `x.y.z` is the version number. The highest number is the latest version, and is considered a test version. If you are expecting your system to be stable, don't use this one.

After you have retrieved the new source code, you must install and unpack it. If you are not using new source code, this is already done, provided you installed the Linux kernel source code from your distribution CD. Log in or `su` to `root`, and `cd` to `/usr/src`. If there is a `linux` directory there, you likely have the kernel source code installed.

If you have the disk space to spare and are installing a new kernel source tree, make sure the directory is named with the link-kernel version number. In this case, there is a link from `linux` to the existing source tree. If that is the case, you must remove the link in order to preserve your existing source. It is not recommended that you simply destroy the existing source tree, unless you are very short of disk space.

Configuring the kernel can be a tedious event depending upon the method you choose to accomplish it. `make config` executes a command-line–oriented view, where each question is asked and you respond to it. This is illustrated in the following example:

NOTE The following code displays assume that you are in the `/usr/src/linux` directory.

```
[root@server7 linux]# make config
rm -f include/asm
( cd include ; ln -sf asm-i386 asm)
/bin/sh scripts/Configure arch/i386/config.in
#
# Using defaults found in .config
#
*
* Code maturity level options
*
Prompt for development and/or incomplete code/drivers
⇥ (CONFIG_EXPERIMENTAL) [Y/n/?]
*
* Processor type and features
*
Processor family (386, 486/Cx486, 586/K5/5x86/6x86,
⇥Pentium/K6/TSC, PPro/6x86MX)
 [586/K5/5x86/6x86]
   defined CONFIG_M586
Maximum Physical Memory (1GB, 2GB) [1GB]
   defined CONFIG_1GB
Math emulation (CONFIG_MATH_EMULATION) [N/y/?]
```

Several other options are available if you installed X Window and TK or curses. The command make xconfig loads an X Window interface to choose the kernel configuration options.

This option provides a fully menu-oriented implementation, where you choose the kernel area you want to configure. When you select the given area, a second window opens, providing the selections for each configurable item.

For each configurable item, the options y, m, and n are available. Y means include support in the kernel. N means do not include support, and M, which is commonly seen on device drivers, indicates that the driver should be made and included as a loadable module. Loadable modules were discussed previously in this chapter, but these options provide a method of gaining great flexibility over the system without having to deal with extremely large kernels.

If you do not have X Window or TK installed, you can also choose to use the `curses` screen interface. `curses` is a language that allows you to graphically manipulate a display on the screen and make items such as menus. The command `make menuconfig` will create the `curses` program to provide a menu interface. Using either the X Window or `curses` interfaces has clear advantages—if you make a mistake it is very easy to go back and correct it.

As with the X Window interface, the administrator chooses, within the `curses` interface, the item he or she wants to configure. Then a second menu opens so that the administrator can make configuration choices.

The `make` command has another argument. You can also start the configuration process with the command `make oldconfig`, which instructs `make` to use the previously defined configuration. The previously defined configuration is stored in `/usr/src/linux/.config`.

The top-level dependency information to build the kernel is stored in `/usr/src/linux/.depend`. If neither of these files exists, you must use one of the previously described methods to generate one. The dependency file is created during the kernel build process.

Building the Kernel

With the configuration completed through `make config`, `make oldconfig`, `make menuconfig`, and or `make xconfig`, you can now proceed to actually build the kernel and associated modules. When the configuration scripts are finished, they tell you to create the dependencies using the command `make dep`.

During this process, the dependencies for the kernel code and associated modules are determined. This information is saved for the actual build process. This process does not in itself take very long.

The `make` command recognizes when the configuration and dependency components have not been completed. When they have been, simply running `make` in the `/sur/src/linux` directory will go through the generation of a new kernel. The exact amount of time this takes depends on the number of objects that must be built, and the speed of your processor.

When the compile finishes, you have built the kernel. This results in a kernel image located in `/usr/src/linux` and called `vmlinux`. However, you should create a compressed kernel image or a compressed disk image. The compressed kernel image, or `zImage`, is unused at system boot and automatically uncompressed. You create this image using the command `make` zImage. If you are doing this right after doing a `make`, the compile process moves along very quickly.

It may be necessary for you to rebuild the modules for the kernel because the new functionality you are adding may be related to a module. You must first boot with your new kernel (presented later in this chapter), and make sure it is operating correctly. When you are running on the new system, the process is essentially duplicated, except that the command for `make` is `make modules`. The rebuild process follows the source tree again and builds the module code that was not specified during the kernel build.

This process puts the newly created modules in the directory `/usr/src/linux/modules`. You can use them directly from that location, or you can execute `make modules_install`, which then copies them to `/lib/modules/<kernel-version>`.

Working with mail

Course Objective Covered

2. Using the Basic Linux `mail` Command (3036)

For an administrator, mail is important because a number of processes will send mail to you if there are problems with their execution. When you log in, a message appears indicating if you have any new messages that you have not read and you can access these messages by giving the command `mail`.

If you give this command when there is no mail waiting for you, a text message indicating that nothing is there will appear, as shown in Figure 10.1.

If there is mail waiting (spooled in `/var/mail`), it will be displayed, and the prompt will change to a question mark (?), as shown in Figure 10.2.

NOTE   Notice that in Figure 10.2, it is possible to check for mail for another user by using the -u option.

FIGURE 10.1
The mail command will indicate if no messages are queued.

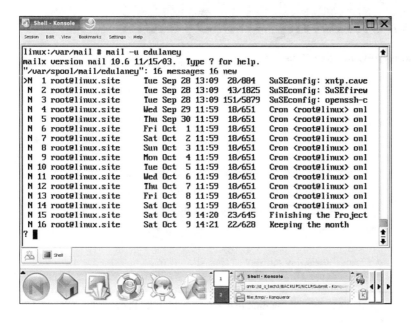

FIGURE 10.2
The mail utility shows the messages spooled up.

At the ? prompt, you can enter the following commands:

▶ D to delete messages

▶ E to edit messages

▶ F to see the headers of messages

- ▶ N to go to/type the next message
- ▶ R to reply to messages
- ▶ T to type messages
- ▶ U to undelete messages
- ▶ X or Q to quit

To send mail to someone from the command line, use the following command (where *name* is the user you want to send a message to):

```
$ mail name
```

A prompt appears asking for a subject. After you enter that (and press Enter), you can type as much of a message as you want. When you are finished with the message, press Ctrl+D at a blank line and "EOT" will appear indicating the End Of Transmission, and you will be returned to your usual prompt.

Monitoring the System

Course Objective Covered

3. Monitor Your SLES 9 System (3037)

It is important to be able to quickly identify the status of your server and know that it is working as it should. There are a number of ways you can identify this. Most often, you want to first know that the system booted properly. Boot messages are written to the /var/log/boot.msg file and can be read with the dmesg utility. Because the file is so large, it is often beneficial to pipe the output to more with the command

```
$ dmesg | more
```

This generates a display similar to that shown in Figure 10.3.

NOTE   You can also see this information using YaST, which is discussed in Chapter 12, "Working with YaST."

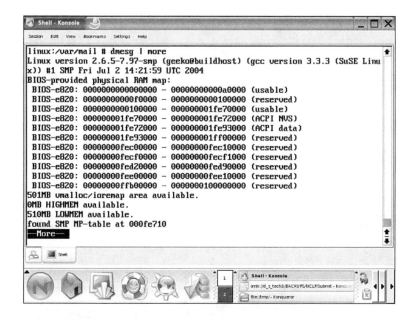

FIGURE 10.3
The dmesg utility shows the boot messages.

Hardware-related information is stored in temporary files beneath /proc and can be viewed from there. These files are shown in Figure 10.4, and most of the names telegraph the information they hold—dma, for example, holds information on the Direct Memory Access modules.

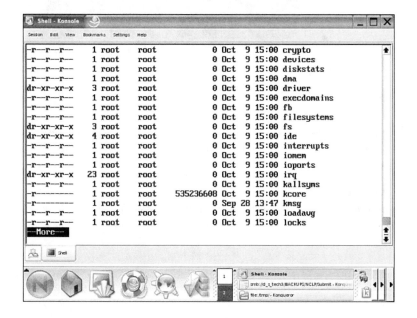

FIGURE 10.4
The /proc files identify hardware information.

The `hwinfo` utility can be used to see a list of information about the installed devices. If you use the `-log` option, you can specify a file for the information to be written to. The `hdparm` utility can be used to see and change hard disk parameters. There are a plethora of options available, and just entering `hdparm` without any other parameters will show those to you. The `lspci` utility can show information about the PCI buses, and is discussed in Chapter 13, "Other Items to Know."

The KDE System Guard can offer a quick snapshot of the system load and process table, as shown in Figure 10.5. This tool is started by choosing System from the main menu, then Monitor, and KDE System Guard.

FIGURE 10.5
The KDE System Guard offers a quick overview of the system.

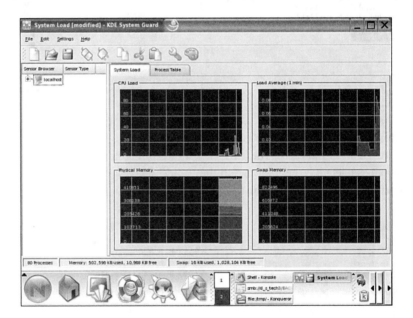

The KDE Info Center (System, Monitor, KDE Info Center) offers another view of all the hardware devices and configuration parameters, as shown in Figure 10.6.

The SuSEPlugger, shown in Figure 10.7, offers yet another way to access this information. This tool is started from the command line with the command `suseplugger`, and it is often already running as indicated by a small icon in your panel.

FIGURE 10.6
The KDE Info Center allows quick access to device parameters.

FIGURE 10.7
The SuSEPlugger offers another venue to hardware information.

Performing Administrative Security Tasks

Course Objectives Covered

7. Create a Security Concept (3038)

8. Limit Physical Access to Server Systems (3038)

9. Limit the Installed Software Packages (3038)

10. Ensure File System Security (3038)

11. Use ACLS for Advanced Access Control (3038)

12. Be Informed About Security Issues (3038)

13. Apply Security Updates (3038)

Common sense is always the guiding factor when applying security to a system, to a network, or to the Internet. If you apply no security whatsoever, you run the risk of someone accessing your data who otherwise should not. What they do with the data after they access it is anyone's guess: They can use it to underbid you or steal trade secrets, they can mischievously delete it, or they can alter it in a myriad of ways.

On the other hand, if you apply too much security to a system, you make it too difficult to use. For example, to prevent anyone from seeing the files on a system, simply unplug the system and then smash the hard drive with a hammer. Although no one would disagree that it is overkill, it accomplishes the purpose.

Somewhere between no security and total security resides a level of comfort that you must find and apply. That level depends on such factors as the value of the data you are securing, the type of access (local, remote, dial-in) that users utilize, and so on. That level of comfort can always be changing, as well being as acted upon by extraneous factors. For example, if you've just heard that another division in your company is having troubles with break-ins, you will want to increase your security, and so on.

Under all conditions, there are some common sense rules that should be applied:

> ▶ Secure the physical environment. If host machines are providing services and are not used by users sitting in front of them, there is no reason why those machines need to be sitting in the middle of the office.

Move those machines to secured wiring closets and reduce the risk of someone simply sitting down in front of them and accessing data.

▶ Pay attention to ambient factors. Data does not just get corrupted by users—it can get corrupted by system failures as well. To reduce system failures—and hence potential data corruption—pay attention to such items as proper electrical feeds (utilize an uninterruptible power supply—UPS), and don't run wiring over objects that can cause electro-mechanical interference (EMI) such as fluorescent lighting or electrical motors. Pay attention to moisture conditions, and so on.

▶ Before you install any software, verify that the software is clean. This can prevent you from adding rogue processes to a good machine. There are a number of ways in which you can attempt to do this: Verify the checksum to make certain no corruption occurred during downloading (and download only from trusted sites), list the contents of a package and verify it against what should be there, and so on. The best method, however, is to install the software on a standalone machine and verify it works as it should before installing it on a production machine.

▶ Require all users to use passwords and create a suitable password policy. Make sure those passwords are not just single characters (6–8 characters is a good minimum), and implement regular expirations. Remember that passwords are changed with the `passwd` command and you can disable accounts by adding characters to the user's entry in the `/etc/passwd` file.

▶ Utilize shadow entries for passwords. This applies to both users and groups. Shadowing merely moves the passwords from files that can be accessed by all users into files that can only be accessed by the root user and adds additional security.

▶ Routinely check the log files and make certain that only logins and logouts (which can be seen with `last`) are not suddenly showing odd times. If users start accessing the system at 3:00 in the morning when they have never done so before, be certain to follow up and verify that it is indeed that user who is accessing the system and not someone else. While on the subject, routinely check all log files—they are there for a purpose and they can alert you to situations you need to catch early on before they become uncontrollable.

▶ Disable *any* accounts that need not be in current use. This is true for both user and group accounts and provides one less door by which entry can be gained.

▶ Assign authentication to dial-in access. PPP is the most commonly used dial-in protocol on TCP/IP. It allows for authentication using PAP—the Password Authentication Protocol—which does not encrypt passwords and allows plain text to be sent—leaving the door open for anyone snooping to intercept. Thankfully, it also has the ability to authenticate with CHAP—Challenge Handshake Authentication Protocol—which encrypts the passwords and makes them much less valuable if intercepted.

▶ Use TCP wrappers to reduce the traffic that you are allowing to come in across the network. A wrapper (which works with the `/etc/hosts.deny` and `/etc/hosts.allow` files) is a rule determining who can come in. Using a wrapper, you can reduce the allowed hosts to only those that are local, or only rule out unknown hosts, or any other combination needed to meet your needs.

▶ Regularly run a check to see which files have permissions involving SGID or SUID. There should be an indisputable reason for their existence, or they should not exist at all. If a user cannot run a process as themselves, what level of comfort do you have giving them higher-level permissions to run jobs? What if the process should crash and they are left as that user?

▶ Related to the preceding one—always use the minimal user and group ownership for any file or daemon that runs with SUID or SGID permissions, respectively. If a daemon can function properly without being owned by root, that ownership change should be made.

▶ Use the secure shell (`ssh`) in place of `telnet` for remote logins. `telnet` (port 23) uses plain text passwords, whereas `ssh` (port 22) uses encryption and provides more security. `ssh` is not included with most releases, but can be easily found and downloaded from the Internet. OpenSSH is discussed in Chapter 11, "Networking Fundamentals."

▶ Use an appropriate `umask` value to make default permissions for newly created files and directories as minimal as possible.

The majority of these rules were discussed in the previous chapters, or constitute common sense. In the real world, and on the exam, always think through both the possibilities and the ramifications when considering adding security to a host or a network.

Working with iptables

Although it's somewhat of a generalization, it can be said that `ipfwadm` goes with the Linux kernel 2.0.x and previous, and `ipchains` replaced it in 2.2.x. Although `ipchains` is still available—and still in use in many locations—`iptables` basically superseded it as of 2.4.x.

`iptables` is a generic implementation of packet filtering that can function in both stateful and stateless modes. More information on `iptables` can be found in the tutorial at http://iptables-tutorial.frozentux.net/.

Host Security

The best way to secure a host is to know everything you can about it. When you set up a host to provide Web services, its purpose is to deliver Web content and pages to users. That host has no business providing DHCP addresses to clients—or even the ability to do so—in this situation.

The `/etc/inetd.conf` file holds a list of the services that will be started on a host when networking is started. Carefully audit this file on each host and verify that there is a legitimate need for each service that will start and that it will not jeopardize the system or the network by opening a door by which unwelcome guests can enter your site. Audit, as well, the log files created by the `syslogd` to see what services are starting and if they are encountering any problems forcing them to die off, restart, and so on.

You should, as an administrator, regularly keep track of security-related developments and problems as they occur in the world, and respond to them accordingly. For example, if your entire network is made up of the XYZ implementation of Linux and it is suddenly reported that versions of XYZ have a bug that provides an open door for anyone typing "wizard" at a login prompt, you had best know about the situation and formulate a plan of response quickly.

You can keep on top of security issues by monitoring your vendor's site as well as those of CERT (originally an acronym for Computer Emergency Response Team) at www.cert.org. Now a division of Carnegie Mellon Software Engineering Institute, CERT had 3,734 reported incidents in 1998. In 1999, that number almost tripled to 9,859. For 2003 (the last reporting period for which numbers are available for at press time), that number escalated to more than 137,000.

As the number of incidents reported has grown, so too has the number of vulnerabilities, and related statistics. If you suspect a problem on your own network and need to contact CERT, you can do so via email at cert@ cert.org, or through regular mail at

CERT Coordination Center
Software Engineering Institute
Carnegie Mellon University
Pittsburgh, PA 15213-3890

It is also highly recommended that you subscribe to the BUGTRAQ mailing list, which can be done by sending an email to listserv@securityfocus.com with a blank subject and in the body, indicate "SUBSCRIBE BUGTRAQ".

When security problems are found, the most common solution is an update of the affected binaries. These are almost always available at the vendor's site and you will want to obtain and install them immediately. The only way to deal with a threat is to eliminate it as expeditiously as possible.

NOTE Whenever you make any changes to the system, you should always fully document what you have done in a method that you can readily refer back to should unforeseen problems occur later. You should also do complete backups before making any major changes.

User-Level Security

If you give a user root-level permissions to the whole network, the scope of the damage they can cause is equal to that of the whole network. If you give the user very limited permissions to only one machine, the amount of potential damage he or she can cause is severely limited. Although this objective repeats everything else that has been discussed, it focuses on how to limit the user.

One of the main methods to limit the user is to use the rule of always granting them minimal permissions needed to do their job. It is always better to give someone not enough and then have to go back and give them a little more, than to give them too much and find out the hard way. At the risk of bordering on silliness, allow me to use an analogy.

If my five-year-old son wants to be able to drive, I can buy him a Power Wheels Jeep (a toy that runs on two six-volt batteries) for roughly the same money as I can buy a scrapped Oldsmobile Cutlass (a 20-year-old real car) from the auto salvage yard. When initially receiving the present, the five-year-old will be equally tickled with either one, and they both cost me the same. With the toy, he can sit low to the ground, drive about four miles per hour, and bounce off the garage door. With the real car, he can sit fairly high off the ground, drive about 80 miles an hour, and drive through the garage door and over anything that happens to get in his way.

No one would ever think of giving a real automobile to a five-year-old boy, but the analogy is not as far off the mark as it may seem. Far too many administrators err on the side of giving too much permission when creating new users. This most often occurs through group memberships, and is intended (by the administrators) to make the administrator's job easier by not having to respond to calls from users about being denied access to a file, directory, resource, and so on.

On the system, the equivalent to being able to drive through the garage door and everything in it is the ability to use the `rm` command meaning to delete only a few files and inadvertently using recursive commands to delete far too much. When that happens, the system administrator assuredly wishes she had given fewer permissions and had those actions denied.

It is also important to place other limits on the users as well. You can limit such things as

- ▶ The amount of storage space the users are allowed on the system. This is accomplished by implementing quotas.

- ▶ The processes they can run. The `ulimit -u` command is used to place restrictions on this, and will limit the maximum number of processes a single user can have at any one time.

- ▶ Their memory usage. The `ulimit -v` command will allow you to specify a maximum amount of virtual memory that is available to a shell.

The `ulimit` specifications should be placed in the `/etc/profile` to apply to all users.   **NOTE**

- ▶ The users' logins. The `/etc/securetty` file holds a list of all terminals from which the root user can log in. By default, every known terminal is listed here. You may want, taking into account security, to edit this file and remove some or most of the terminals from the list. The `/etc/usertty` (which does not exist by default) can be used to hold user restrictions. Within this file, you can specify allowed `tty`s and hosts on a per-user basis under the USERS section. The GROUPS section allows the same on a per-group basis, and a CLASSES section can define classes of `ttys` and hostname patterns. An example of this file would be

```
# cat /etc/usertty
USERS
evan   tty3
kristin   tty4 @152.12.14.0/255.255.255.0
#
```

This restricts **evan** to only being able to use **tty3**. It also restricts **kristin** to **tty4**, or a machine on the **152.12.14.x** network. To apply a restriction to all users, begin the line with an asterisk (*).

With `ulimit`, which was mentioned in several points in the preceding list, you can specify that values are either **H** (hard) or **S** (soft). If they are hard values, they can never be increased. If they are soft values—the default—they can be increased. Options that can be used with `ulimit` other than those already listed include

- ▶ -a to show all current limits

- ▶ -f to specify the maximum size of files created by a shell

- ▶ -t to specify the maximum CPU time that can be used (in seconds)

- ▶ -n for the maximum number of open files

NOTE On most Linux systems, the -n setting can be viewed but not set.

An example of the command in action follows:

```
# ulimit -a
core file size (blocks)   0
data seg size (kbytes)    unlimited
file size (blocks)        unlimited
max memory size (kbytes)  unlimited
stack size (kbytes)       8192
cpu time (seconds)        unlimited
max user processes        256
pipe size (512 bytes)     8
open files                1024
virtual memory (kbytes)   2105343
#
```

Adding Hardware

Course Objective Covered

14. Add New Hardware to a SLES 9 System (3038)

With the exception of monitoring, much of this chapter has focused on software issues. There are times when you need to add new hardware to a system as well. The installation of new hardware to SuSE is very straightforward, for in most instances the device is recognized (with Hotplug) and configuration begins immediately.

If the device you are adding is one that requires you to remove covers and cases, be sure to shut the system down and remove all power before so doing. If the device you are adding is one that will require networking, you can always change to runlevel 1, make the configuration changes, and then change back to your default runlevel—reinitiating everything in the process.

Lab Exercise 10-1: Evaluating and Correcting a Security Risk

In this exercise, you will work with the user account created when you manually added a new user at the end of Chapter 5. If you did not do that exercise, you must do so before you are able to complete this one.

Complete the following:

1. Look at the user manually added in the exercise at the end of Chapter 5 and contemplate what each of the fields symbolizes.

2. What you have done is added a user named **edulaney** who does not have a password—the first improper action.

3. The user added has the same user ID, group ID, and home directory as root (another no-no).

4. Remove the user by opening the file for editing:

   `vi passwd`

5. Move to the last line of the file and remove it:

   `yy`

6. Save the file:

   `{escape}`
   `:w`

7. Exit the file:

   `{escape}`
   `:q`

Summary

This chapter looked at a number of administrative tasks and what you need to know about them. It covered package and kernel management, as well as security and adding new hardware.

Command Summary

Table 10.5 lists the commands that were discussed in this chapter.

Linux Administration Commands in This Chapter **TABLE 10.5**

UTILITY	DEFAULT PURPOSE
depmod	Determines module dependencies
dmesg	Displays boot messages
dpkg	Debian package manager
gzip	Compress files
hdparm	Can be used to see and change hard disk parameters
hwinfo	Displays a list of information about an installed devices
insmod	Install a module
ldconfig	Updates and maintains the cache of shared library data and symbols for the dynamic linker
ldd	Shows what shared libraries a program is dependent upon
lsmod	List the loaded modules
lspci	Shows information about the PCI buses
mail	Checks to see if mail is queued
modinfo	Print information about a module
modprobe	Probe and install a module and its dependents
rmmod	Remove a module
rpm	Red Hat Package Manager
tar	Create and extract files known as tarballs
ulimit	Shows user limits currently imposed

Networking Fundamentals

This chapter focuses on the fundamentals of networking. In this chapter, you'll learn about the TCP/IP networking protocol and how to configure it. This chapter builds on those concepts, and you'll learn about some of the services that run on TCP/IP. When studying for the exam, it is important to have a broad knowledge of all the topics presented here.

This chapter covers the following course objectives:

1. Introduction to Network-Related Command Line Commands (3036)
2. Configure Your Network Connection (3037)
3. Configure and Manage Routes (3037)
4. Test the Network Interface (3037)
5. Configure Network File Systems (3037)
6. Manage Resources on the Network (3037)
7. Enable a Web Server (Apache) (3037)
8. Enable the Extended Internet Daemon (`xinetd`) (3037)
9. Enable an FTP Server (3037)
10. Understand the Linux Network Terms (3038)
11. Set Up Network Devices with the IP Tool (3038)
12. Save Device Settings to a Configuration File (3038)
13. Set Up Routing with the IP Tool (3038)
14. Save Routing Settings to a Configuration File (3038)
15. Configure Host Name and Name Resolution (3038)
16. Test the Network Connection with Command Line Tools (3038)

17. Deploy OpenLDAP on a SLES 9 Server (3038)

18. Configure an Apache Web Server (3038)

19. Configure a Samba Server as a File Server (3038)

TCP/IP Background

Course Objectives Covered

1. Introduction to Network-Related Command Line Commands (3036)

10. Understand the Linux Network Terms (3038)

The Transmission Control Protocol/Internet Protocol (TCP/IP) is an industry-standard suite of protocols designed to be routable and efficient. TCP/IP was originally designed as a set of wide area network (WAN) protocols for the purpose of maintaining communication links and data transfer between sites in the event of an atomic/nuclear war. Since those early days, development of the protocols has passed from the hands of the government and has been the responsibility of the Internet community for some time.

The evolution of these protocols from a small four-site project into the foundation of the worldwide Internet has been extraordinary. But despite more than 25 years of work and numerous modifications to the protocol suite, the inherent spirit of the original specifications is still intact. TCP/IP has the following advantages over other protocols:

▶ An industry-standard protocol. Because TCP/IP is not maintained or written by one company, it is not proprietary or subject to as many compatibility issues. The Internet community as a whole decides whether a particular change or implementation is worthwhile.

▶ A set of utilities for connecting dissimilar operating systems. Many connectivity utilities have been written for the TCP/IP suite, including the File Transfer Protocol (FTP) and Terminal Emulation Protocol (Telnet).

▶ A scalable, cross-platform client/server architecture. Consider what happened during the initial development of applications for the TCP/IP protocol suite. Vendors wanted to be able to write their own client/server applications, for instance, SQL Server and Simple Network Management Protocol (SNMP). The specification for how to write applications was also up for public perusal. Which operating systems would be included? Users everywhere wanted to be able to take advantage of the connectivity options promised through utilizing TCP/IP, regardless of the operating system they were currently running.

▶ Access to the Internet. TCP/IP is the de facto protocol of the Internet and allows access to a wealth of information that can be found at thousands of locations around the world. To connect to the Internet, though, a valid IP address is required.

The Four Layers of TCP/IP

TCP/IP maps to a four-layer architectural model. This model is called the Internet Protocol Suite and is broken into the Network Interface, Internet, Transport, and Application layers. Each of these layers corresponds to one or more layers of the OSI model, which it predates. The Network Interface layer corresponds to the Physical and Data Link layers. The Internet layer corresponds to the Network layer. The Transport layer corresponds to the Transport layer, and the Application layer corresponds to the Session, Presentation, and Application layers of the OSI model.

Each of the four layers of the model is responsible for all the activities of the layers to which it maps.

The Network Interface layer is responsible for communicating directly with the network. It must understand the network architecture being used, such as token-ring or Ethernet, and provide an interface allowing the Internet layer to communicate with it. The Internet layer is responsible for communicating directly with the Network Interface layer.

The Internet layer is primarily concerned with the routing and delivery of packets through the Internet Protocol (IP). All the protocols in the Transport layer must use IP to send data. The Internet Protocol includes rules for how to address and direct packets, fragment and reassemble packets, provide security information, and identify the type of service being used. However, because IP is not a connection-based protocol, it does not guarantee that packets transmitted onto the wire will not be lost, damaged, duplicated, or out of order. This is the responsibility of higher layers of the networking model, such as the Transport layer or the Application layer. Other protocols that exist in the Internet layer are the Internet Control Message Protocol (ICMP), Internet Group Management Protocol (IGMP), and the Address Resolution Protocol (ARP).

The Transport layer maps to the Transport layer of the OSI model and is responsible for providing communication between machines for applications. This communication can be connection-based or non-connection–based. The primary difference between these two types of communications is whether there is a mechanism for tracking data and guaranteeing the delivery of the data to its destination. Transmission Control Protocol (TCP) is the protocol used for connection-based communication between two machines providing reliable data transfer. User Datagram Protocol (UDP) is used for non-connection–based communication with no guarantee of delivery.

The Application layer of the Internet Protocol Suite is responsible for all the activities that occur in the Session, Presentation, and Application layers of the OSI model. Numerous protocols have been written for use in this layer, including Simple Network Management Protocol (SNMP), File Transfer Protocol (FTP), Simple Mail Transfer Protocol (SMTP), as well as many others.

The interface between each of these layers is written to have the capability to pass information from one layer to the other.

The interface between the Network Interface layer and the Internet layer does not pass a great deal of information, although it must follow certain rules. Namely, it must listen to all broadcasts and send the rest of the data in the frame up to the Internet layer for processing, and if it receives any frames that do not have an IP frame type, they must be silently discarded.

The interface between the Internet layer and the Transport layer must be able to provide each layer full access to such information as the source and destination addresses, whether TCP or UDP should be utilized in the transport of data, and all other available mechanisms for IP. Rules and specifications for the Transport layer include giving the Transport layer the capability to change these parameters or to pass parameters it receives from the Application layer down to the Internet layer. The most important thing to remember about all of these boundary layers is that they must use the agreed-upon rules for passing information from one layer to the other.

Primary Protocols

Six primary protocols are associated with TCP/IP:

- ▶ Transmission Control Protocol (TCP)
- ▶ User Datagram Protocol (UDP)

- ▶ Internet Protocol (IP)

- ▶ Internet Control Message Protocol (ICMP)

- ▶ Address Resolution Protocol (ARP)

- ▶ Internet Group Management Protocol (IGMP)

Transmission Control Protocol

The first protocol that lives in the Transport layer is the Transmission Control Protocol (TCP). This protocol is a connection-based protocol and requires the establishment of a session before data is transmitted between two machines. TCP packets are delivered to sockets or ports. Because TCP uses a connection between two machines, it is designed to verify that all packets sent by a machine are received on the other end. If, for some reason, packets are lost, the sending machine resends the data. Because a session must be established and delivery of packets is guaranteed, there is additional overhead involved with using TCP to transmit packets.

The TCP is a connection-based protocol that requires a connection, or session, between two machines before any data is transferred. TCP exists within the Transport layer, between the Application layer and the IP layer, providing a reliable and guaranteed delivery mechanism to a destination machine. Connection-based protocols guarantee the delivery of packets by tracking the transmission and receipt of individual packets during communication. A session is able to track the progress of individual packets by monitoring when a packet is sent, in what order it was sent, and by notifying the sender when it is received so that it can send more.

After the TCP session has been created, the machines begin to communicate just as people do during a phone call. In the example of the telephone, if the caller uses a cellular phone and some of the transmission is lost, the user indicates she did not receive the message by saying "What did you say? I didn't hear that." This indicates to the sender that he needs to resend the data.

During the initialization of a TCP session, often called the "three-way handshake," both machines agree on the best method to track how much data is to be sent at any one time, acknowledgment numbers to be sent upon receipt of data, and when the connection is no longer necessary because all data has been transmitted and received. It is only after this session is created that data transmission begins. To provide reliable delivery, TCP places packets in sequenced order and requires acknowledgments that these packets reached their destination before it sends new data. TCP is typically used for transferring large amounts of data, or when the application requires acknowledgment that data has been received. Given all the additional overhead information that TCP needs to keep track of, the format of a TCP packet can be somewhat complex.

TCP uses the concept of sliding windows for transferring data between machines. Sliding windows are often referred to in the Linux\Unix environment as streams. Each machine has both a send window and a receive window that it utilizes to buffer data and make the communication process more efficient. A window represents the subset of data that is currently being sent to a destination machine, and is also the amount of data that is being received by the destination machine. At first this seems redundant, but it really isn't. Not all data that is sent is guaranteed to be received, so the packets must be kept track of on both machines. A sliding window allows a sending machine to send the window data in a stream without having to wait for an acknowledgment for every single packet.

User Datagram Protocol

The second protocol that lives in the Transport layer is the User Datagram Protocol, or UDP. This protocol is a non-connection–based protocol and does not require a session to be established between two machines before data is transmitted. UDP packets are still delivered to sockets or ports, just as they are in TCP. But because UDP does not create a session between machines, it cannot guarantee that packets are delivered or that they are delivered in order or retransmitted if the packets are lost. Given the apparent unreliability of this protocol, some may wonder why a protocol such as UDP was developed.

Sending a UDP datagram has very little overhead involved. A UDP datagram has no synchronization parameters or priority options. All that exists is the source port, destination port, the length of the data, a checksum for verifying the header, and then the data.

There are actually a number of good reasons to have a transport protocol that does not require a session to be established. For one, very little overhead is associated with UDP, such as having to keep track of sequence numbers, Retransmit Timers, Delayed Acknowledgment Timers, and retransmission of packets. UDP is quick and extremely streamlined functionally; it's just not guaranteed. This makes UDP perfect for communications that involve broadcasts, general announcements to the network, or real-time data.

Another really good use for UDP is in streaming video and streaming audio. Not only does the unguaranteed delivery of packets enable more data to be transmitted (because a broadcast has little to no overhead), but also the retransmission of a packet is pointless, anyway. In the case of a streaming broadcast, users are more concerned with what's coming next than with trying to recover a packet or two that may not have made it. Compare it to listening to a music CD and a piece of dust gets stuck in one of the little grooves. In most cases, the omission of that piece is imperceptible; your ear barely notices and your brain probably filled in the gap for you anyway. Imagine instead that your CD player decides to guarantee the delivery of that one piece of data that it can't quite get, and ends up skipping and skipping indefinitely. It can definitely ruin the listening experience. It is easier to deal with an occasional packet dropping out to have as fulfilling a listening experience as possible. Thankfully, UDP was developed for applications to utilize in this very same fashion.

Internet Protocol

A number of protocols are found in the Internet layer, including the most important protocol in the entire suite, the Internet Protocol (IP). The reason that this is probably the most important protocol is that the Transport layer cannot communicate at all without communicating through IP in the Internet layer.

The most fundamental element of the IP is the address space that IP uses. Each machine on a network is given a unique 32-bit address called an Internet address or IP address. Addresses are divided into five categories, called classes, that are discussed later in this chapter.

IP receives information in the form of packets from the Transport layer, from either TCP or UDP, and sends out data in what are commonly referred to as datagrams. The size of a datagram is dependent upon the type of network that is being used, such as token-ring or Ethernet. If a packet has too much data to be transmitted in one datagram, it is broken into pieces and transmitted through several datagrams. Each of these datagrams has to then be reassembled by TCP or UDP.

Internet Control Message Protocol

Internet Control Message Protocol (ICMP) is part of the Internet layer and is responsible for reporting errors and messages regarding the delivery of IP datagrams. It can also send "source quench" and other self-tuning signals during the transfer of data between two machines without the intervention of the user. These signals are designed to fine-tune and optimize the transfer of data automatically. ICMP is the protocol that warns you when a destination host is unreachable, or how long it took to get to a destination host.

ICMP messages can be broken down into two basic categories: the reporting of errors and the sending of queries. Error messages include the following:

- ▶ Destination unreachable
- ▶ Redirect
- ▶ Source quench
- ▶ Time exceeded

ICMP also includes general message queries. The two most commonly used are the following:

- ▶ Echo request
- ▶ Echo reply

The most familiar tool for verifying that an IP address on a network actually exists is the Packet Internet Groper (PING) utility. This utility uses the ICMP echo request and reply mechanisms. The echo request is a simple directed datagram that asks for acknowledgment that a particular IP address exists on the network. If a machine with this IP address exists and receives the request, it is designed to send an ICMP echo reply. This reply is sent back to the destination address to notify the source machine of its existence. The PING utility reports the existence of the IP address and how long it took to get there.

Internet Group Management Protocol

Internet Group Management Protocol (IGMP) is a protocol and set of specifications that allows machines to be added and removed from IP address groups, utilizing the class D range of addresses. IP allows the assignment of class D addresses to groups of machines so that they may receive broadcast data as one functional unit. Machines can be added and removed from these units or groups, or be members of multiple groups.

NOTE Unicast messages are those sent to one host. Multicast messages are those sent to a number of hosts. Broadcast messages are those sent to all hosts. Understanding this distinction is helpful when discussing networking.

Address Resolution Protocol

Unless IP is planning to initiate a full broadcast on the network, it has to have the physical address of the machine to which it is going to send datagrams. For this information, it relies on Address Resolution Protocol (ARP). ARP is responsible for mapping IP addresses on the network to physical addresses in memory. This way, whenever IP needs a physical address for a particular IP address, ARP can deliver. But ARP's memory does not last indefinitely, and occasionally IP will ask for an IP address that is not in ARP's memory. When this happens, ARP has to go out and find one.

ARP is responsible for finding a map to a local physical address for any local IP address that IP may request. If ARP does not have a map in memory, it has to go find one on the network. ARP uses local broadcasts to find physical addresses of machines and maintains a cache in memory of recently mapped IP addresses to physical addresses. Although this cache does not last indefinitely, it enables ARP to not have to broadcast every time IP needs a physical address.

As long as the destination IP address is local, ARP simply sends a local broadcast for that machine and returns the physical address to IP. IP, realizing that the destination IP address is local, simply formulates the datagram with the IP address above the physical address of the destination machine.

Protocols and Ports

The Transport layer uses port numbers to transfer data to the Application layer. These ports allow a host to support and track simultaneous sessions with other hosts on the network. There are more than 65,000 definable ports, and Table 11.1 lists the most common assignments.

For the exam, be sure to memorize the ports that appear in Table 11.1.   **NOTE**

Port Numbers Used by the Common Services   **TABLE 11.1**

PORT	SERVICE	PURPOSE
20,21	FTP	Transfer files from one host to another
23	Telnet	Connect to a host as if on a dumb terminal for administrative purposes

Table 11.1   Continued

PORT	SERVICE	PURPOSE
25	SMTP	Simple Mail Transfer Protocol
53	DNS	Domain Name System
80	WWW	The World Wide Web service
110	POP3	The Post Office Protocol (version 3) for retrieving email
119	NNTP	The Network News Transfer Protocol
139	NetBIOS	Used to translate Windows-based names to IP addresses
143	IMAP	The Internet Mail Access Protocol, which can be used in place of POP3
161	SNMP	The Simple Network Management Protocol

The /etc/services file holds definitions for common ports. It is an ASCII file that maps text names to services. The Internet Assigned Numbers Authority (IANA) assigns lower number ports, but administrators may assign higher numbers freely.

TCP/IP Host Configuration

Course Objectives Covered

  2. Configure Your Network Connection (3037)

  16. Test the Network Connection with Command Line Tools (3038)

To configure TCP/IP on a host, you must know and configure three values. The three needed values are

  ▶ IP address

  ▶ Subnet mask

  ▶ Default gateway

NOTE Technically, you need to configure IP and subnet. Gateway is optional and only needed if you want to move off your subnet.

Each of these three values is examined in the following sections.

IP Address

Every host on a TCP/IP network must have a unique IP address. An IP address is made up of values from a 32-bit binary number. Because it is next to impossible to memorize 32-bit binary numbers, IP addresses are usually written in the form of four decimal number octets. The first octet identifies the "class" of address that it is, which determines the number of hosts available on the network as shown in Table 11.2.

Available Host IP Addresses   **TABLE 11.2**

CLASS	ADDRESS	NUMBER OF HOSTS AVAILABLE	DEFAULT SUBNET MASK
A	01-126	16,777,214	255.0.0.0
B	128-191	65,534	255.255.0.0
C	192-223	254	255.255.255.0
D	224-239	Used only for multicasting and cannot be assigned to individual hosts	
E	240-255	Reserved addresses that cannot be issued	

The first octet cannot be 127 because the address **127.0.0.1** is reserved for a loopback address to always signify the current host. Depending on the class, the second through fourth octets are used to identify the network and the host.

It is important to understand that the IP address must be unique within the realm of the network the host communicates with. If the host is connected only to three other machines, each of the three machines must have a unique value. If the host connects to the Internet, the address must be unique within the scope of the Internet.

Subnet Mask

The subnet mask, to oversimplify, tells whether the network has been subdivided into smaller networks, or all the hosts can be found on one wire. The default value is based on the class of the network as shown in Table 11.2. If you deviate from this value, you are divvying your possible hosts from one network to multiple networks. This allows you to better isolate and find your hosts, but the tradeoff is that you have fewer possible hosts available to use (a result of using up some of your binary numbers to signify the network and leaving fewer for the host). Table 11.3 illustrates this tradeoff.

TABLE 11.3   **Subnet Mask Values**

ADDITIONAL BITS REQUIRED	SUBNET ADDRESS	MAXIMUM NUMBER OF SUBNETS	MAXIMUM NUMBER OF HOSTS—C NETWORK	MAXIMUM NUMBER OF HOSTS—B NETWORK	MAXIMUM NUMBER OF HOSTS—A NETWORK
0	0	0	254	65,534	16,777,214
2	192	2	62	16,382	4,194,302
3	224	6	30	8,190	2,097,150
4	240	14	14	4,094	1,048,574
5	248	30	6	2,046	524,286
6	252	62	2	1,022	262,142
7	254	126	invalid	510	131,070
8	255	254	invalid	254	65,534

It is important to understand that when a subnet value is used, it limits the possible values that can be used for the IP address by taking away some of the bits (thus values) that could otherwise have been used. For example, if you have a class C address of 201.1.1, and are not subnetting, the values that can be used in the fourth field are 1–254 (made up of possible values from eight binary digits). On the other hand, if you are using a subnet of 192 (made by using two binary bits), six bits are left and you therefore have a maximum of 62 host addresses on two subnet ranges. The ranges that can be used are: 65–126 and 129–190.

Default Gateway

The default gateway is an optional field if you want to communicate beyond your subnet. It used to hold the IP address of the router. If a client connects to an ISP through a dial-up connection (such as a standalone Linux machine dialing from home), the ISP fills in the address here.

To summarize: The IP address must be unique for every host; all hosts on that subnet share the subnet value; and the default gateway is shared by every host that uses that router to get beyond the local network.

Supplying Values

The needed values for TCP/IP configuration can be entered manually each time you add a host to the network, or you can use the Dynamic Host Configuration Protocol (DHCP) service. With DHCP, you do not need to enter any values when adding new hosts to the network. A server hosting the DHCP Daemon (`dhcpd`) holds a range of addresses—known as a scope—and can "lease" IP addresses out to clients. The lease duration is configurable—from a short time period up to forever. So long as forever is not used, the client will regularly attempt to renew the lease it is using if possible. If the server does not hear it, the client will try again at regular intervals all the way up until the lease expires. When the lease expires, it goes back into the scope and the client must obtain another lease anew. After every expiration, when a client requests an address, it will always attempt to get the one it had the last time if it is available.

Other TCP/IP Configuration

Course Objectives Covered

  4. Test the Network Interface (3037)

 12. Save Device Settings to a Configuration File (3038)

 14. Save Routing Settings to a Configuration File (3038)

 15. Configure Host Name and Name Resolution (3038)

There are a number of configuration files and utilities to be aware of for the exam. The files to know are as follows:

▶ `/etc/HOSTNAME`—This file holds the name of the host and domain on a single line. If networking is not configured, the entry will read:
  `noname nodomain nowhere`

  On some implementations, this is `/etc/hostname`.

▶ `/etc/hosts`—This ASCII file is used to list IP addresses and text names. It can convert the test (host) names to the IP addresses on the network. This file is suitable for use only on small networks as it must exist on every host in the network and must constantly be updated when each host is added to the network. On large networks, you want to avoid using the **hosts** file and use the DNS (Domain Name System) service instead. DNS is discussed in the next chapter.

▶ /etc/sysconfig/network—This directory holds the configuration files for the known networks the host can communicate with. The following listing shows the default **config** file beneath this directory:

```
## Path:      Network/Hardware/Config
## Description:    Set some general network configuration
## Type:      string("","-","+")
## Default:      "+"
## ServiceRestart: network
#
# DEFAULT_BROADCAST is used when no individual BROADCAST
➥is
# set. It can get one of the following values:
# ""   : don't set a broadcast address
# "-" : use IPADDR with all host bits deleted
# "+" : use IPADDR with all host bits set
DEFAULT_BROADCAST="+"


## Type:      yesno
## Default:      yes
# sometimes we want some script to be executed after an
# interface has been brought up, or before an interface
# is taken down.
# default dir is /etc/sysconfig/network/if-up.d for
➥POST_UP
# and /etc/sysconfig/network/if-down.d for PRE_DOWN
GLOBAL_POST_UP_EXEC="yes"
GLOBAL_PRE_DOWN_EXEC="yes"


## Type:      yesno
## Default:      no
# If ifup should check if an ip address is already in use,
# set this to yes. Make sure that packet sockets
#(CONFIG_PACKET) are supported in the kernel,
# since this feature uses arping, which depends on that.
# Also be aware that this takes one second per interface;
# consider that when setting up a lot of interfaces.
CHECK_DUPLICATE_IP="no"


## Type:      yesno
## Default:      no
# Switch on/off debug messages for all network
# configuration stuff. If set to no
# most scripts can enable it locally with "-o debug".
DEBUG="no"
```

```
## Type:        yesno
## Default:     yes
# Should error messages from network configuration scripts
# go to syslog, or do
# you like them on stderr?
USE_SYSLOG="yes"


## Type:        yesno
## Default:     yes
# There are some services (ppp, ippp, dhcp-client, pcmcia,
# hotplug) that have to change the /etc/resolv.conf
# dynamically at certain times.  E.g. if ppp/ippp
# establishes a connection and is supplied by the peer
➥with
# a list of nameservers. Or pcmcia needs to set the
➥correct
# nameserver for the chosen configuration scheme. If you
# don't like these services to change
# /etc/resolv.conf at all, then set this variable to "no".
# If unsure, leave it at the default (which is "yes").
#
MODIFY_RESOLV_CONF_DYNAMICALLY="yes"


## Type:        yesno
## Default:     no
# Like MODIFY_RESOLV_CONF_DYNAMICALLY, except it modifies
# /etc/named.conf.
# If unsure, leave it at the default (which is "no").
#
MODIFY_NAMED_CONF_DYNAMICALLY="no"


# Handling of network connections
# ^^^^^^^^^^^^^^^^^^^^^^^^^^^^^^^^^^
# These features are designed for the convenience of the
# experienced user. If you encounter problems you don't
# understand then switch them off. That is the default.
# Please do not complain if you get troubles. But if you
# want help to make them smarter write to
# <http://www.suse.de/feedback>.


## Type:    yesno
## Default:    no
#
# If you are interested in the connections and nfs mounts
#  that use a network interface, you can set
```

```
# CONNECTION_SHOW_WHEN_IFSTATUS="yes".
# Then you will see them with 'ifstatus <interface>'
# (or 'ifstatus
# <config>')
# This one _should_ never harm ;)
#
CONNECTION_SHOW_WHEN_IFSTATUS="no"

## Type:     yesno
## Default:  no
#
# If an interface should be set down only if there are no
# active connections, then use CONNECTION_CHECK_BEFORE_
# IFDOWN="yes"
#
CONNECTION_CHECK_BEFORE_IFDOWN="no"

## Type:     yesno
## Default:  no
#
# If these connetions (without the nfs mounts) should be
# closed when
# shutting down an interface, set CONNECTION_CLOSE_BEFORE
#_IFDOWN="yes".
# WARNING: Be aware that this may terminate applications
# which need one of these connections!
#
CONNECTION_CLOSE_BEFORE_IFDOWN="no"

## Type:     yesno
## Default:  no
#
# If you are a mobile laptop user and like even nfs mounts
# to be closed when you leave your current workplace, then
# set CONNECTION_UMOUNT_NFS_BEFORE_IFDOWN="yes". This does
# only work if CONNECTION_CLOSE_BEFORE_IFDOWN="yes", too.
# WARNING: Be aware that this may terminate applications
# which use these nfs mounts as working directory. Be very
# careful if your home is mounted via nfs!!!
# WARNING: This may even lead to hanging ifdown processes
# if there are processes that could not be terminated. If
# you are using hotpluggable devices (pcmcia, usb,
# firewire), first shut them down before unplugging!
#
CONNECTION_UMOUNT_NFS_BEFORE_IFDOWN="no"
```

```
## Type:     yesno
## Default:    no
#
# If terminating processes that use a connection or nfs
# mount is not enough, then they can be killed after an
# unsuccesfull termination.
# If you want that set CONNECTION_SEND_KILL_SIGNAL="yes"
#
CONNECTION_SEND_KILL_SIGNAL="no"


## Type:         string
## Default:        ""
#
# Here you may specify which interfaces have to be up and
# configured properly
# after 'rcconfig start'. rcconfig will return 'failed' if
# any of these
# interfaces is not up. You may use interface names as
➥well
# but better use
# hardware descriptions of the devices (eth-id-
➥<macaddress>
# or eth-bus-... See
# man ifup for 'hardware description'). The network start
# script will wait for
# these interfaces, but not longer as set in
# WAIT_FOR_INTERFACES.
# You need not to add dialup or tunnel interfaces here,
# only physical devices.
# The interface 'lo' is always considered to be mandatory
# and can be omitted.
# If this variable is empty, rcnetwork tries to derive the
# list of mandatory
# devices automatically (try 'rcnetwork start -o debug')
MANDATORY_DEVICES=""


## Type:     integer
## Default:     20
#
# Some interfaces need some time to come up or come
# asynchronously via hotplug.
# WAIT_FOR_INTERFACES is a global wait for all mandatory
# interfaces in
# seconds. If empty no wait occurs.
```

```
#
WAIT_FOR_INTERFACES="20"

## Type:      yesno
## Default:    yes
#
# With this variable you can determine if the
# SuSEfirewall when enabled
# should get started when network interfaces are started.
FIREWALL="yes"

## Type:         string("off","guess","auto-off",
# "auto-manual","manual")
## Default:     "off"
#
# !!!This feature is still not implemented. Leave it
# to 'off'!!!
# What shall we do if there is no valid configuration?
# off:         do nothing, just fail
# guess:       try to guess the needed info (zeroconf)
# auto-off:    trigger automatic creation of a config
➡file;
# if that fails, do
#              nothing, just fail
# auto-manual: trigger automatic creation of a config
➡file;
#  if that fails, ask
#              user to provide configuration (via yast)
# manual:      ask user to provide configuration (via
➡yast)
# !!!This feature is still not implemented.
# Leave it to 'off'!!!
FAILURE_ACTION=off

## Type:        string
## Default:     "eth*[0-9]|tr*[0-9]|wlan[0-9]|ath[0-9]"
#
# Automatically add a linklocal route to the matching
# interfaces.
# This string is used in a bash "case" statement, so it
➡may
# contain '*', '[', ']'  and '|' meta-characters.
#
LINKLOCAL_INTERFACES="eth*[0-9]|tr*[0-9]|wlan[0-9]|ath[0-
➡9]"
```

▶ /etc/sysconfig/network/routes—This file is the configuration file
   used to hold routing information.

The following are the utilities to know for this exam, and system administration in general:

▶ arp—ARP, as a utility, can be used to see the entries in the Address
   Resolution table, which maps network card addresses (MAC addresses) to IP addresses. You can check to see if the IP addresses you
   believe should be in the table are there and if they are mapped to the
   computers they should be. Usually, you do not know the MAC
   addresses of the hosts on your network. However, if you cannot contact a host, or if a connection is made to an unexpected host, you can
   check this table with the ARP command to begin isolating which host
   is actually assigned an IP address.

▶ dig—This utility works with DNS (discussed later in this chapter) and
   looks up entries on DNS name servers. Following is an example of the
   output generated by the **dig** utility without any parameters:

```
; <<>> DiG 9.2.3 <<>>
;; global options:  printcmd
;; Got answer:
;; ->>HEADER<<- opcode: QUERY, status: NOERROR, id: 61821
;; flags: qr rd ra; QUERY: 1, ANSWER: 13, AUTHORITY: 0,
➥ADDITIONAL: 13
;; QUESTION SECTION:
;.                    IN    NS

;; ANSWER SECTION:
.              244262    IN    NS    L.ROOT-SERVERS.NET.
.              244262    IN    NS    M.ROOT-SERVERS.NET.
.              244262    IN    NS    I.ROOT-SERVERS.NET.
.              244262    IN    NS    E.ROOT-SERVERS.NET.
.              244262    IN    NS    D.ROOT-SERVERS.NET.
.              244262    IN    NS    A.ROOT-SERVERS.NET.
.              244262    IN    NS    H.ROOT-SERVERS.NET.
.              244262    IN    NS    C.ROOT-SERVERS.NET.
.              244262    IN    NS    G.ROOT-SERVERS.NET.
.              244262    IN    NS    F.ROOT-SERVERS.NET.
.              244262    IN    NS    B.ROOT-SERVERS.NET.
.              244262    IN    NS    J.ROOT-SERVERS.NET.
.              244262    IN    NS    K.ROOT-SERVERS.NET.
```

```
;; ADDITIONAL SECTION:
L.ROOT-SERVERS.NET.       330662   IN    A    198.32.64.12
M.ROOT-SERVERS.NET.       330662   IN    A    202.12.27.33
I.ROOT-SERVERS.NET.       330662   IN    A    192.36.148.17
E.ROOT-SERVERS.NET.       330662   IN    A
192.203.230.10
D.ROOT-SERVERS.NET.       330662   IN    A    128.8.10.90
A.ROOT-SERVERS.NET.       330662   IN    A    198.41.0.4
H.ROOT-SERVERS.NET.       330662   IN    A    128.63.2.53
C.ROOT-SERVERS.NET.       330662   IN    A    192.33.4.12
G.ROOT-SERVERS.NET.       330662   IN    A    192.112.36.4
F.ROOT-SERVERS.NET.       330662   IN    A    192.5.5.241
B.ROOT-SERVERS.NET.       330662   IN    A
192.228.79.201
J.ROOT-SERVERS.NET.       330662   IN    A    192.58.128.30
K.ROOT-SERVERS.NET.       330662   IN    A    193.0.14.129

;; Query time: 55 msec
;; SERVER: 192.168.0.1#53(192.168.0.1)
;; WHEN: Sun Oct  3 13:31:27 2004
;; MSG SIZE  rcvd: 436
```

▶ domainname—Similar to hostname, it shows the domain name used by the host.

▶ ethereal—This utility is not installed by default, but can be added to the system through YaST, as discussed in the next chapter. After ethereal has been added, it offers a graphical interface with which you can monitor network traffic. This same functionality is inherently available at the command line using the tcpdump utility.

▶ ftp—The File Transfer utility, operating on the File Transfer Protocol, is used to send files back and forth between a local and remote host.

▶ hostname—This simple utility shows the name of the host.

▶ ifconfig—This utility is used to configure the TCP/IP parameters on the command line. The syntax is: ifconfig interface options. Thus to configure the IP address of 201.13.12.65 for the first Ethernet card, the command would be ifconfig eth0 201.13.12.65, and this would use the default subnet mask. To do the same configuration with a subnet mask of 192, the command becomes: ifconfig eth0 201.13.12.65 netmask 255.255.255.192. Figure 11.1 shows an example of the output from the ifconfig utility.

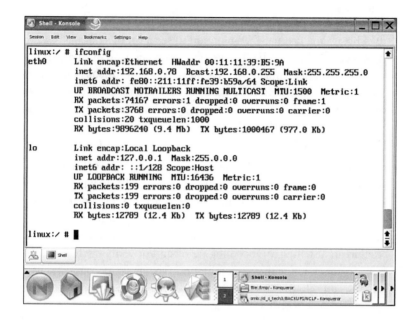

FIGURE 11.1
An example of
the output from
ifconfig.

▶ `ifup` and `ifdown`—These two utilities are used to start or stop a preconfigured network interface. To see the status (either started or stopped), you can use the `ifstatus` command. Figure 11.2 shows the options available with the latter command.

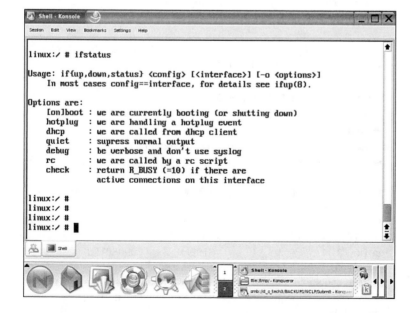

FIGURE 11.2
A number of
options are
available with
`ifstatus` and
its related
commands.

▶ netcat—This utility can be used to establish a connection between two hosts. You can use the -h option to see a list of all available parameters. The most basic operation, however, is to open a port on one host with a command such as netcat -l -p 16000, which puts port 16000 in listen mode. Following this, you establish a connection with that host on another by using the command netcat {hostname to connect to} 16000. The connection will stay established until you press Ctrl+C.

▶ netstat—This command shows the statistics of the TCP and UDP protocols. Executing netstat without switches displays protocol statistics and current TCP/IP connections. When you have determined that your base level communications are working, you will need to verify the services on your system. This involves looking at the services that are listening for incoming traffic and/or verifying that you are creating a session with a remote station. The netstat command will allow you to do this. The following listing is an example of the output generated by netstat without any options:

NOTE

To see the options available for netstat, as you do with most other utilities, use the -? option.

```
Active Internet connections (w/o servers)
Proto Recv-Q Send-Q Local Address   Foreign Address    State

tcp        0       0 linux.mshome.net:32833   D_S_Tech3.
➥m:netbios-ssn ESTABLISHED
tcp        0       0 linux.mshome.net:32832   D_S_Tech3.
➥m:netbios-ssn ESTABLISHED
tcp        1       0 localhost:filenet-rpc
➥localhost:svrloc          CLOSE_WAIT
Active UNIX domain sockets (w/o servers)
➥Proto RefCnt Flags        Type        State       I-Node
➥Path
unix  10      [ ]          DGRAM                   3608
➥/dev/log
unix  2       [ ]          DGRAM
➥3610    /var/lib/ntp/dev/log
unix  3       [ ]          STREAM      CONNECTED
➥2287641
 /tmp/ksocket-root/klauncherYc7nCa.slave-socket
unix  3       [ ]          STREAM      CONNECTED
➥2287640
```

```
unix   3        [ ]            STREAM     CONNECTED
➡2285303
➡ /tmp/.ICE-unix/dcop3558-1096404519
unix   3        [ ]            STREAM     CONNECTED
➡2285302
unix   3        [ ]            STREAM     CONNECTED
➡2285282
➡ /tmp/ksocket-root/konqueror9xiRhb.slave-socket
unix   3        [ ]            STREAM     CONNECTED
➡2285280
unix   3        [ ]            STREAM     CONNECTED
➡2285149
➡ /tmp/.ICE-unix/dcop3558-1096404519
unix   3        [ ]            STREAM     CONNECTED
➡2285148
unix   3        [ ]            STREAM     CONNECTED
➡2285147
➡ /tmp/ksocket-root/konquerorSYKnXa.slave-socket
unix   3        [ ]            STREAM     CONNECTED
➡2285146
unix   52       [ ]            STREAM     CONNECTED
➡2285141
➡ /tmp/.X11-unix/X0
unix   3        [ ]            STREAM     CONNECTED
➡2285140
unix   3        [ ]            STREAM     CONNECTED
➡2285084
➡ /tmp/ksocket-root/konquerorZ7Ffrc.slave-socket
unix   3        [ ]            STREAM     CONNECTED
➡2285083
unix   3        [ ]            STREAM     CONNECTED
➡2285067
➡ /tmp/.ICE-unix/dcop3558-1096404519
unix   3        [ ]            STREAM     CONNECTED
➡2285066
unix   3        [ ]            STREAM     CONNECTED
➡2285059
➡ /tmp/.ICE-unix/3614
unix   3        [ ]            STREAM     CONNECTED
➡2285058
unix   3        [ ]            STREAM     CONNECTED
➡2285055
➡ /tmp/.X11-unix/X0
unix   3        [ ]            STREAM     CONNECTED
➡2285054
unix   2        [ ]            DGRAM
➡2262685
```

unix	2	[ ]	DGRAM		226712
unix	3	[ ]	STREAM	CONNECTED	226678
unix	3	[ ]	STREAM	CONNECTED	226677
unix	3	[ ]	STREAM	CONNECTED	226676
unix	3	[ ]	STREAM	CONNECTED	226675
unix	3	[ ]	STREAM	CONNECTED	226674
unix	3	[ ]	STREAM	CONNECTED	226673
unix	3	[ ]	STREAM	CONNECTED	226672
unix	3	[ ]	STREAM	CONNECTED	226671
unix	3	[ ]	STREAM	CONNECTED	226670
unix	3	[ ]	STREAM	CONNECTED	226669
unix	3	[ ]	STREAM	CONNECTED	226668
unix	3	[ ]	STREAM	CONNECTED	226667
unix	3	[ ]	STREAM	CONNECTED	226666
unix	3	[ ]	STREAM	CONNECTED	226665
unix	3	[ ]	STREAM	CONNECTED	226664
unix	3	[ ]	STREAM	CONNECTED	226663
unix	3	[ ]	STREAM	CONNECTED	226662
unix	3	[ ]	STREAM	CONNECTED	226661
unix	3	[ ]	STREAM	CONNECTED	226660
unix	3	[ ]	STREAM	CONNECTED	226659
unix	3	[ ]	STREAM	CONNECTED	226658
unix	3	[ ]	STREAM	CONNECTED	226657
unix	3	[ ]	STREAM	CONNECTED	226656
unix	3	[ ]	STREAM	CONNECTED	226655
unix	3	[ ]	STREAM	CONNECTED	226654
unix	3	[ ]	STREAM	CONNECTED	226653
unix	3	[ ]	STREAM	CONNECTED	226652
unix	3	[ ]	STREAM	CONNECTED	226651
unix	3	[ ]	STREAM	CONNECTED	226650
unix	3	[ ]	STREAM	CONNECTED	226649
unix	3	[ ]	STREAM	CONNECTED	226648
unix	3	[ ]	STREAM	CONNECTED	226647
unix	3	[ ]	STREAM	CONNECTED	226646
unix	3	[ ]	STREAM	CONNECTED	226645
unix	3	[ ]	STREAM	CONNECTED	226644
unix	3	[ ]	STREAM	CONNECTED	226643
unix	3	[ ]	STREAM	CONNECTED	226642
unix	3	[ ]	STREAM	CONNECTED	226641
unix	3	[ ]	STREAM	CONNECTED	226640
unix	3	[ ]	STREAM	CONNECTED	226639
unix	3	[ ]	STREAM	CONNECTED	226638
unix	3	[ ]	STREAM	CONNECTED	226637
unix	3	[ ]	STREAM	CONNECTED	226636

```
unix  3        [ ]          STREAM      CONNECTED      226635
unix  3        [ ]          STREAM      CONNECTED      226634
unix  3        [ ]          STREAM      CONNECTED      226633
unix  3        [ ]          STREAM      CONNECTED      226632
unix  3        [ ]          STREAM      CONNECTED      226631
unix  3        [ ]          STREAM      CONNECTED      226630
unix  3        [ ]          STREAM      CONNECTED      226629
unix  3        [ ]          STREAM      CONNECTED      226628
unix  3        [ ]          STREAM      CONNECTED      226627
unix  3        [ ]          STREAM      CONNECTED      219952
➥ /tmp/.ICE-unix/dcop3558-1096404519
unix  3        [ ]          STREAM      CONNECTED      219951
unix  3        [ ]          STREAM      CONNECTED      219944
➥ /tmp/.ICE-unix/3614
unix  3        [ ]          STREAM      CONNECTED      219943
unix  3        [ ]          STREAM      CONNECTED      219940
➥ /tmp/.X11-unix/X0
unix  3        [ ]          STREAM      CONNECTED      219939
unix  3        [ ]          STREAM      CONNECTED      51613
➥ /tmp/.ICE-unix/dcop3558-1096404519
unix  3        [ ]          STREAM      CONNECTED      51612
unix  3        [ ]          STREAM      CONNECTED      51343
➥  /tmp/.X11-unix/X0
unix  3        [ ]          STREAM      CONNECTED      51342
unix  3        [ ]          STREAM      CONNECTED      8706
➥  /tmp/.ICE-unix/3614
unix  3        [ ]          STREAM      CONNECTED      8705
unix  3        [ ]          STREAM      CONNECTED      8700
➥  /tmp/.X11-unix/X0
unix  3        [ ]          STREAM      CONNECTED      8699
unix  3        [ ]          STREAM      CONNECTED      8698
➥  /tmp/.ICE-unix/dcop3558-1096404519
unix  3        [ ]          STREAM      CONNECTED      8697
unix  3        [ ]          STREAM      CONNECTED      8665
➥  /tmp/.ICE-unix/3614
unix  3        [ ]          STREAM      CONNECTED      8664
unix  3        [ ]          STREAM      CONNECTED      8643
➥  /tmp/.X11-unix/X0
unix  3        [ ]          STREAM      CONNECTED      8642
unix  3        [ ]          STREAM      CONNECTED      8641
➥  /tmp/.ICE-unix/dcop3558-1096404519
unix  3        [ ]          STREAM      CONNECTED      8640
unix  3        [ ]          STREAM      CONNECTED      8555
➥  /tmp/.ICE-unix/3614
unix  3        [ ]          STREAM      CONNECTED      8554
```

```
unix  3       [ ]              STREAM       CONNECTED      8548
➥    /tmp/.ICE-unix/3614
unix  3       [ ]              STREAM       CONNECTED      8547
unix  3       [ ]              STREAM       CONNECTED      8541
➥    /tmp/.ICE-unix/3614
unix  3       [ ]              STREAM       CONNECTED      8540
unix  3       [ ]              STREAM       CONNECTED      8515
➥    /tmp/.ICE-unix/3614
unix  3       [ ]              STREAM       CONNECTED      8514
unix  3       [ ]              STREAM       CONNECTED      8499
➥    /tmp/.X11-unix/X0
unix  3       [ ]              STREAM       CONNECTED      8498
unix  3       [ ]              STREAM       CONNECTED      8497
➥    /tmp/.ICE-unix/dcop3558-1096404519
unix  3       [ ]              STREAM       CONNECTED      8496
unix  3       [ ]              STREAM       CONNECTED      8493
➥    /tmp/.X11-unix/X0
unix  3       [ ]              STREAM       CONNECTED      8492
unix  3       [ ]              STREAM       CONNECTED      8491
➥    /tmp/.ICE-unix/dcop3558-1096404519
unix  3       [ ]              STREAM       CONNECTED      8490
unix  3       [ ]              STREAM       CONNECTED      8472
➥    /tmp/.X11-unix/X0
unix  3       [ ]              STREAM       CONNECTED      8471
unix  3       [ ]              STREAM       CONNECTED      8470
➥    /tmp/.ICE-unix/dcop3558-1096404519
unix  3       [ ]              STREAM       CONNECTED      8469
unix  3       [ ]              STREAM       CONNECTED      8465
➥    /tmp/.X11-unix/X0
unix  3       [ ]              STREAM       CONNECTED      8464
unix  3       [ ]              STREAM       CONNECTED      8462
➥    /tmp/.ICE-unix/dcop3558-1096404519
unix  3       [ ]              STREAM       CONNECTED      8461
unix  3       [ ]              STREAM       CONNECTED      8449
➥    /tmp/.ICE-unix/3614
unix  3       [ ]              STREAM       CONNECTED      8448
unix  3       [ ]              STREAM       CONNECTED      8423
➥    /tmp/.X11-unix/X0
unix  3       [ ]              STREAM       CONNECTED      8422
unix  3       [ ]              STREAM       CONNECTED      8421
➥    /tmp/.ICE-unix/dcop3558-1096404519
unix  3       [ ]              STREAM       CONNECTED      8420
unix  3       [ ]              STREAM       CONNECTED      8400
➥    /tmp/.ICE-unix/3614
unix  3       [ ]              STREAM       CONNECTED      8399
```

```
unix  3       [ ]           STREAM      CONNECTED    8387
➡   /tmp/.ICE-unix/3614
unix  3       [ ]           STREAM      CONNECTED    8386
unix  3       [ ]           STREAM      CONNECTED    8377
➡   /tmp/.X11-unix/X0
unix  3       [ ]           STREAM      CONNECTED    8376
unix  3       [ ]           STREAM      CONNECTED    8375
➡   /tmp/.ICE-unix/dcop3558-1096404519
unix  3       [ ]           STREAM      CONNECTED    8374
unix  3       [ ]           STREAM      CONNECTED    8368
➡   /tmp/.X11-unix/X0
unix  3       [ ]           STREAM      CONNECTED    8367
unix  3       [ ]           STREAM      CONNECTED    8366
➡   /tmp/.ICE-unix/dcop3558-1096404519
unix  3       [ ]           STREAM      CONNECTED    8365
unix  3       [ ]           STREAM      CONNECTED    8361
➡   /tmp/.X11-unix/X0
unix  3       [ ]           STREAM      CONNECTED    8360
unix  3       [ ]           STREAM      CONNECTED    8357
➡   /tmp/.ICE-unix/dcop3558-1096404519
unix  3       [ ]           STREAM      CONNECTED    8356
unix  3       [ ]           STREAM      CONNECTED    8341
➡   /tmp/.ICE-unix/3614
unix  3       [ ]           STREAM      CONNECTED    8340
unix  3       [ ]           STREAM      CONNECTED    8339
➡   /tmp/.ICE-unix/dcop3558-1096404519
unix  3       [ ]           STREAM      CONNECTED    8338
unix  3       [ ]           STREAM      CONNECTED    8335
➡   /tmp/.ICE-unix/3614
unix  3       [ ]           STREAM      CONNECTED    8334
unix  3       [ ]           STREAM      CONNECTED    8331
➡   /tmp/.X11-unix/X0
unix  3       [ ]           STREAM      CONNECTED    8330
unix  3       [ ]           STREAM      CONNECTED    8325
➡   /tmp/.ICE-unix/dcop3558-1096404519
unix  3       [ ]           STREAM      CONNECTED    8324
unix  3       [ ]           STREAM      CONNECTED    8319
➡   /tmp/.X11-unix/X0
unix  3       [ ]           STREAM      CONNECTED    8318
unix  3       [ ]           STREAM      CONNECTED    8312
➡   /tmp/ksocket-root/kdeinit__0
unix  3       [ ]           STREAM      CONNECTED    8311
unix  3       [ ]           STREAM      CONNECTED    8308
➡   /tmp/mcop-root/linux_site-0df3-4159ce2a
unix  3       [ ]           STREAM      CONNECTED    8307
```

```
unix   3       [ ]            STREAM      CONNECTED     8282
  ⟼   /tmp/.X11-unix/X0
unix   3       [ ]            STREAM      CONNECTED     8281
unix   3       [ ]            STREAM      CONNECTED     8280
  ⟼   /tmp/.ICE-unix/dcop3558-1096404519
unix   3       [ ]            STREAM      CONNECTED     8279
unix   3       [ ]            STREAM      CONNECTED     8178
  ⟼   /tmp/.X11-unix/X0
unix   3       [ ]            STREAM      CONNECTED     8177
unix   3       [ ]            STREAM      CONNECTED     8156
  ⟼   /tmp/.X11-unix/X0
unix   3       [ ]            STREAM      CONNECTED     8155
unix   3       [ ]            STREAM      CONNECTED     8154
  ⟼   /tmp/.ICE-unix/dcop3558-1096404519
unix   3       [ ]            STREAM      CONNECTED     8153
unix   3       [ ]            STREAM      CONNECTED     8134
  ⟼   /tmp/.ICE-unix/dcop3558-1096404519
unix   3       [ ]            STREAM      CONNECTED     8133
unix   3       [ ]            STREAM      CONNECTED     8129
unix   3       [ ]            STREAM      CONNECTED     8128
unix   2       [ ]            DGRAM                     7999
unix   3       [ ]            STREAM      CONNECTED     7936
  ⟼   /tmp/.X11-unix/X0
unix   3       [ ]            STREAM      CONNECTED     7414
unix   2       [ ]            DGRAM                     6991
unix   2       [ ]            DGRAM                     6476
unix   2       [ ]            DGRAM                     6125
unix   2       [ ]            DGRAM                     5541
unix   2       [ ]            DGRAM                     5431
```

▶ ping—This utility will send echo messages to a host to see if it is reachable. If it is, the ICMP protocol on the remote host will echo the response. If it is not reachable, the resulting error message will indicate that. Figure 11.3 shows the results of pinging a host.

▶ route—This utility is used to see and configure routing. If you give the route command with no parameters, it displays the current routing table. This command is discussed further in the "Configuring Routes" section that follows.

▶ **tcpdump**—This command-line utility allows you to monitor network traffic and analyze packets flowing through an interface in promiscuous mode. The `-i` option is used to specify an interface. The command `tcpdump -i eth0`, for example, turns on promiscuous mode for the first Ethernet interface and immediately begins displaying data to the terminal until you break out of it. The `-c` option can be used to specify that you only want to listen to a certain number of packets. `tcpdump -i eth0 -c 32`, for example, will display the output for the next 32 packets and then exit. At the end of the display, it will report how many packets were captured, how many were received by filter, and how many were dropped by the kernel.

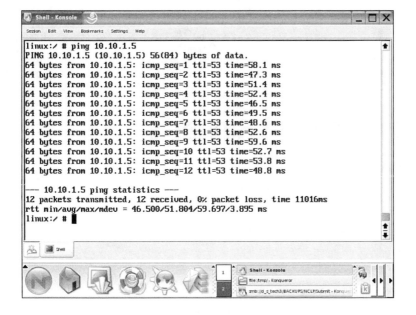

FIGURE 11.3
Packets are successfully reaching the host.

▶ **telnet**—Allows you to establish a connection with a remote host. This is often used for administrative purposes.

▶ **traceroute**—This is a much-enhanced version of the **ping** utility, and is used in place of it. Not only will it show that the remote host is reachable, but also it shows the path that was taken to reach the host. Figure 11.4 shows the utility interacting with the same host that was pinged in Figure 11.3; now it is possible to see the number of hops necessary in order to reach that host.

FIGURE 11.4
The traceroute
utility shows how
the host is
reached.

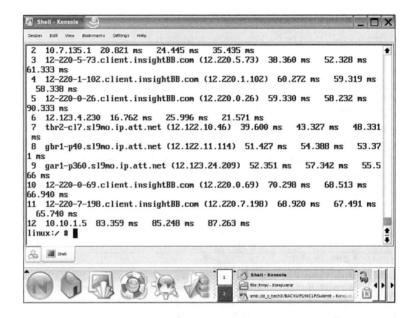

FIGURE 11.4
The traceroute
utility shows how
the host is
reached.

Configuring Routes

Course Objective Covered

3. Configure and Manage Routes (3037)

Three types of routes exist to help IP packets make their way to their final destination:

▸ Host routes

▸ Network/gateway routes

▸ Default routes

The purpose behind any route is to point the way for the data to find its target, and the tool to use with routes is simply the **route** utility. To add a route, use the **route add** command. To delete a route, use the **route del** command.

Figure 11.5 shows the simplest display possible—this example is on a server that has no routes configured but is able to communicate across the network.

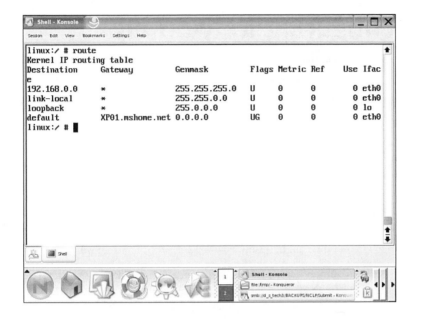

FIGURE 11.5
An example of the output from route.

Figure 11.6 shows the options available with the route utility.

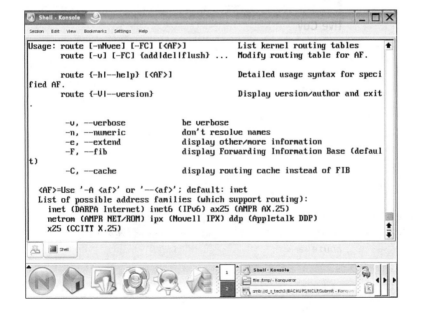

FIGURE 11.6
The route utility offers a number of options.

Configuring Networking Services

Course Objective Covered

8. Enable the Extended Internet Daemon (xinetd) (3037)

Within Linux, there is a superdaemon known as init, which is responsible for bringing up the services required at specific runlevels and maintaining the integrity of the system. The init daemon will start and stop other daemons such as the system logger (syslogd), the swapper (kswapd), and so on. One of the daemons it starts is a superdaemon over networking services: xinetd (also known as the extended Internet Services Daemon).

The xinetd daemon is a replacement for inetd that offers a vast improvement in security. The configuration options are now modularized. For the exam, you need to know that this daemon is a replacement for inetd and can be downloaded from a number of sites and used in place of the original.

NOTE   As a general rule, any process with a last character of "d" is a daemon.

When started, the xinetd looks at its configuration file, /etc/xinetd.conf, and determines from it what additional services it is responsible for. By default, this file exists on every host whether it is used or not: If it is not used, most of the lines are commented out. Following is an example of the default file:

```
#
# xinetd.conf
#
# Copyright (c) 1998-2001 SuSE GmbH Nuernberg, Germany.
# Copyright (c) 2002 SuSE Linux AG, Nuernberg, Germany.
#

defaults
{
    log_type        = FILE /var/log/xinetd.log
        log_on_success = HOST EXIT DURATION
    log_on_failure   = HOST ATTEMPT
#       only_from        = localhost
```

```
        instances       = 30
   cps         = 50 10

#
# The specification of an interface is interesting, if we
# are on a firewall.
# For example, if you only want to provide services from
# an internal network interface, you may specify your
# internal interfaces IP-Address.
#
#    interface     = 127.0.0.1

}


includedir /etc/xinetd.d
```

Notice that this file has the ability to call settings from other files and need not be self-contained. If you change any of the settings in this file, you must restart the **xinetd** before the changes will be recognized. There are a number of ways to do this—including rebooting the system, starting and stopping networking, and so on. The simplest way of doing so, however, is to kill the **xinetd** daemon with

`/etc/rc.d/xinetd restart`

or

`/etc/rc.d/xinetd reload`

Then the daemon will restart—rereading the configuration file when it does.

More information on the daemon can be found at http://www.xinetd.org/. The HowTo can be found at http://www.debianhowto.de/howtos/en/xinetd/c_xinetd.html.

The /etc/services File

This file was mentioned earlier in this chapter, but its real usefulness is that it is checked to determine what port a particular service is to use. This ASCII file exists on every host by default, and divides the entries into three fields:

▶ Service—Whatever name also appears in the `/etc/inetd.conf` file.

▶ Port—What port to use.

▶ Alias(es)—These are optional and constitute other names the service is known as.

Here's an example of the first few lines of the file on a standard host:

```
#
# Network services, Internet style
#
# Note that it is presently the policy of IANA to assign a
# single well-known port number for both TCP and UDP;
# hence, most entries here have two entries even if the
# protocol doesn't support UDP operations.
#
# This list could be found on:
#          http://www.iana.org/assignments/port-numbers
#
# (last updated 2004-02-12)
#
# The port numbers are divided into three ranges: the Well
# Known Ports, the Registered Ports, and the Dynamic and/or
# Private Ports.
#
# The Well Known Ports are those from 0 through 1023.
#
# The Registered Ports are those from 1024 through 49151
#
# The Dynamic and/or Private Ports are those from 49152
# through 65535
#
#
### UNASSIGNED PORT NUMBERS SHOULD NOT BE USED.  THE IANA
# WILL ASSIGN THE NUMBER FOR THE PORT AFTER YOUR
# APPLICATION HAS BEEN APPROVED ###
#
#
# WELL KNOWN PORT NUMBERS
#
# The Well Known Ports are assigned by the IANA and on most
# systems can only be used by system (or root) processes or
# by programs executed by privileged users.
#
# Ports are used in the TCP [RFC793] to name the ends of
# logical connections which carry long term conversations.
# For the purpose of providing services to unknown callers,
# a service contact port is defined.  This list specifies
```

```
# the port used by the server process as its contact port.
# The contact port is sometimes called the "well-known
# port".
#
# To the extent possible, these same port assignments are
# used with the UDP [RFC768].
#
# The range for assigned ports managed by the IANA is
# 0-1023.
#
# Port Assignments:
#
# Keyword         Decimal     Description           References
# -------         -------     -----------           ----------
#               0/tcp     Reserved
#               0/udp     Reserved
#                           Jon Postel <postel@isi.edu>
tcpmux          1/tcp     # TCP Port Service Multiplexer
tcpmux          1/udp     # TCP Port Service Multiplexer
#                           Mark Lottor <MKL@nisc.sri.com>
compressnet     2/tcp     # Management Utility
compressnet     2/udp     # Management Utility
compressnet     3/tcp     # Compression Process
compressnet     3/udp     # Compression Process
#                           Bernie Volz <VOLZ@PROCESS.COM>
#               4/tcp     # Unassigned
#               4/udp     # Unassigned
rje             5/tcp     # Remote Job Entry
rje             5/udp     # Remote Job Entry
#                           Jon Postel <postel@isi.edu>
#               6/tcp     # Unassigned
#               6/udp     # Unassigned
echo            7/tcp     Echo
echo            7/udp     Echo
#                           Jon Postel <postel@isi.edu>
#               8/tcp     # Unassigned
#               8/udp     # Unassigned
discard         9/tcp     # Discard
discard         9/udp     # Discard
#                           Jon Postel <postel@isi.edu>
#               10/tcp    # Unassigned
#               10/udp    # Unassigned
systat          11/tcp    users    # Active Users
systat          11/udp    users    # Active Users
#                           Jon Postel <postel@isi.edu>
```

```
#                12/tcp    # Unassigned
#                12/udp    # Unassigned
daytime          13/tcp    # Daytime (RFC 867)
daytime          13/udp    # Daytime (RFC 867)
#                          Jon Postel <postel@isi.edu>
#                14/tcp    # Unassigned
#                14/udp    # Unassigned
netstat          15/tcp    # Unassigned [was netstat]
#                15/udp    # Unassigned
#                16/tcp    # Unassigned
#                16/udp    # Unassigned
qotd             17/tcp    quote     # Quote of the Day
qotd             17/udp    quote     # Quote of the Day
#                          Jon Postel <postel@isi.edu>
msp              18/tcp    # Message Send Protocol
msp              18/udp    # Message Send Protocol
#                          Rina Nethaniel <---none--->
chargen          19/tcp    # Character Generator
chargen          19/udp    # Character Generator
ftp-data         20/tcp    # File Transfer [Default Data]
ftp-data         20/udp    # File Transfer [Default Data]
ftp              21/tcp    # File Transfer [Control]
fsp              21/udp    # File Transfer [Control]
#                          Jon Postel <postel@isi.edu>
ssh              22/tcp    # SSH Remote Login Protocol
ssh              22/udp    # SSH Remote Login Protocol
#                          Tatu Ylonen <ylo@cs.hut.fi>
telnet           23/tcp    # Telnet
telnet           23/udp    # Telnet
#                          Jon Postel <postel@isi.edu>
#                24/tcp    any private mail system
#                24/udp    any private mail system
#                          Rick Adams <rick@UUNET.UU.NET>
smtp             25/tcp    mail        # Simple Mail Transfer
smtp             25/udp    mail        # Simple Mail Transfer
#                          Jon Postel <postel@isi.edu>
#                26/tcp    # Unassigned
#                26/udp    # Unassigned
nsw-fe           27/tcp    # NSW User System FE
nsw-fe           27/udp    # NSW User System FE
#                          Robert Thomas <BThomas@F.BBN.COM>
#                28/tcp    # Unassigned
#                28/udp    # Unassigned
msg-icp          29/tcp    # MSG ICP
msg-icp          29/udp    # MSG ICP
```

```
#                       Robert Thomas <BThomas@F.BBN.COM>
#           30/tcp      # Unassigned
#           30/udp      # Unassigned
msg-auth    31/tcp      # MSG Authentication
msg-auth    31/udp      # MSG Authentication
#                       Robert Thomas <BThomas@F.BBN.COM>
#           32/tcp      # Unassigned
#           32/udp      # Unassigned
dsp         33/tcp      # Display Support Protocol
dsp         33/udp      # Display Support Protocol
#                       Ed Cain <cain@edn-unix.dca.mil>
#           34/tcp      # Unassigned
#           34/udp      # Unassigned
#           35/tcp      any private printer server
#           35/udp      any private printer server
#                       Jon Postel <postel@isi.edu>
#           36/tcp      # Unassigned
#           36/udp      # Unassigned
time        37/tcp      # Time
time        37/udp      # Time
#                       Jon Postel <postel@isi.edu>
rap         38/tcp      # Route Access Protocol
rap         38/udp      # Route Access Protocol
#                 Robert Ullmann <ariel@world.std.com>
rlp         39/tcp      # Resource Location Protocol
rlp         39/udp      # Resource Location Protocol
#           Mike Accetta <MIKE.ACCETTA@CMU-CS-A.EDU>
#           40/tcp      # Unassigned
#           40/udp      # Unassigned
graphics    41/tcp      # Graphics
graphics    41/udp      # Graphics
name        42/tcp      # Host Name Server
name        42/udp      # Host Name Server
nameserver  42/tcp      # Host Name Server
nameserver  42/udp      # Host Name Server
nicname     43/tcp whois    # Who Is
nicname     43/udp whois    # Who Is
mpm-flags   44/tcp      # MPM FLAGS Protocol
mpm-flags   44/udp      # MPM FLAGS Protocol
mpm         45/tcp      # Message Processing Module
 [recv]
mpm         45/udp      # Message Processing Module
 [recv]
mpm-snd     46/tcp      # MPM [default send]
mpm-snd     46/udp      # MPM [default send]
```

```
#                        Jon Postel <postel@isi.edu>
ni-ftp          47/tcp  # NI FTP
ni-ftp          47/udp  # NI FTP
#                        Steve Kille <S.Kille@isode.com>
auditd          48/tcp  # Digital Audit Daemon
auditd          48/udp  # Digital Audit Daemon
#                        Larry Scott <scott@zk3.dec.com>
tacacs          49/tcp  # Login Host Protocol (TACACS)
tacacs          49/udp  # Login Host Protocol (TACACS)
#                       Pieter Ditmars <pditmars@BBN.COM>
re-mail-ck      50/tcp  # Remote Mail Checking Protocol
re-mail-ck      50/udp  # Remote Mail Checking Protocol
#                        Steve Dorner <s-dorner@UIUC.EDU>
la-maint        51/tcp  # IMP Logical Address Maintenance
la-maint        51/udp  # IMP Logical Address Maintenance
#                        Andy Malis <malis_a@timeplex.com>
xns-time        52/tcp  # XNS Time Protocol
xns-time        52/udp  # XNS Time Protocol
#                   Susie Armstrong <Armstrong.wbst128@XEROX>
domain          53/tcp  # Domain Name Server
domain          53/udp  # Domain Name Server
#                        Paul Mockapetris <PVM@ISI.EDU>
xns-ch          54/tcp  # XNS Clearinghouse
xns-ch          54/udp  # XNS Clearinghouse
#                   Susie Armstrong <Armstrong.wbst128@XEROX>
isi-gl          55/tcp  # ISI Graphics Language
isi-gl          55/udp  # ISI Graphics Language
xns-auth        56/tcp  # XNS Authentication
xns-auth        56/udp  # XNS Authentication
#                   Susie Armstrong <Armstrong.wbst128@XEROX>
#               57/tcp  any private terminal access
#               57/udp  any private terminal access
#                        Jon Postel <postel@isi.edu>
xns-mail        58/tcp  # XNS Mail
xns-mail        58/udp  # XNS Mail
#                   Susie Armstrong <Armstrong.wbst128@XEROX>
#               59/tcp  any private file service
#               59/udp  any private file service
#                        Jon Postel <postel@isi.edu>
#               60/tcp  Unassigned
#               60/udp  Unassigned
ni-mail         61/tcp  # NI MAIL
ni-mail         61/udp  # NI MAIL
#                        Steve Kille <S.Kille@isode.com>
acas            62/tcp  # ACA Services
```

```
acas             62/udp   # ACA Services
#                         E. Wald <ewald@via.enet.dec.com>
whois++          63/tcp   # whois++
whois++          63/udp   # whois++
#                      Rickard Schoultz <schoultz@sunet.se>
covia            64/tcp   # Communications Integrator (CI)
covia            64/udp   # Communications Integrator (CI)
#                      Dan Smith <dan.smith@den.galileo.com>
tacacs-ds        65/tcp   # TACACS-Database Service
tacacs-ds        65/udp   # TACACS-Database Service
#                         Kathy Huber <khuber@bbn.com>
sql*net          66/tcp   # Oracle SQL*NET
sql*net          66/udp   # Oracle SQL*NET
#                      Jack Haverty <jhaverty@ORACLE.COM>
bootps           67/tcp   # Bootstrap Protocol Server
bootps           67/udp   # Bootstrap Protocol Server
bootpc           68/tcp   # Bootstrap Protocol Client
bootpc           68/udp   # Bootstrap Protocol Client
#                 Bill Croft <Croft@SUMEX-AIM.STANFORD.EDU>
tftp             69/tcp   # Trivial File Transfer
tftp             69/udp   # Trivial File Transfer
#                         David Clark <ddc@LCS.MIT.EDU>
gopher           70/tcp   # Gopher
gopher           70/udp   # Gopher
#                  Mark McCahill <mpm@boombox.micro.umn.edu>
netrjs-1         71/tcp   # Remote Job Service
netrjs-1         71/udp   # Remote Job Service
netrjs-2         72/tcp   # Remote Job Service
netrjs-2         72/udp   # Remote Job Service
netrjs-3         73/tcp   # Remote Job Service
netrjs-3         73/udp   # Remote Job Service
netrjs-4         74/tcp   # Remote Job Service
netrjs-4         74/udp   # Remote Job Service
#                         Bob Braden <Braden@ISI.EDU>
#                75/tcp   any private dial out service
#                75/udp   any private dial out service
#                         Jon Postel <postel@isi.edu>
deos          76/tcp   # Distributed External Object Store
deos          76/udp   # Distributed External Object Store
#                      Robert Ullmann <ariel@world.std.com>
#                77/tcp   any private RJE service
#                77/udp   any private RJE service
#                      Jon Postel <postel@isi.edu>
vettcp           78/tcp   # vettcp
vettcp           78/udp   # vettcp
```

Novell Certified Linux Professional Study Guide

```
#              Christopher Leong <leong@kolmod.mlo.dec.com>
finger         79/tcp    # Finger
finger         79/udp    # Finger
#                   David Zimmerman <dpz@RUTGERS.EDU>
http           80/tcp    # World Wide Web HTTP
http           80/udp    # World Wide Web HTTP
www            80/tcp    # World Wide Web HTTP
www            80/udp    # World Wide Web HTTP
www-http       80/tcp    # World Wide Web HTTP
www-http       80/udp    # World Wide Web HTTP
#                  Tim Berners-Lee <timbl@W3.org>
hosts2-ns      81/tcp    # HOSTS2 Name Server
hosts2-ns      81/udp    # HOSTS2 Name Server
#                  Earl Killian <EAK@MORDOR.S1.GOV>
xfer           82/tcp    # XFER Utility
xfer           82/udp    # XFER Utility
#              Thomas M. Smith <Thomas.M.Smith@lmco.com>
mit-ml-dev     83/tcp    # MIT ML Device
mit-ml-dev     83/udp    # MIT ML Device
#                       David Reed <--none--->
ctf            84/tcp    # Common Trace Facility
ctf            84/udp    # Common Trace Facility
#                  Hugh Thomas <thomas@oils.enet.dec.com>
mit-ml-dev     85/tcp    # MIT ML Device
mit-ml-dev     85/udp    # MIT ML Device
#                       David Reed <--none--->
mfcobol        86/tcp    # Micro Focus Cobol
mfcobol        86/udp    # Micro Focus Cobol
#                  Simon Edwards <--none--->
#              87/tcp    any private terminal link
#              87/udp    any private terminal link
#                  Jon Postel <postel@isi.edu>
kerberos       88/tcp    # Kerberos
kerberos       88/udp    # Kerberos
#                  B. Clifford Neuman <bcn@isi.edu>
su-mit-tg      89/tcp    # SU/MIT Telnet Gateway
su-mit-tg      89/udp    # SU/MIT Telnet Gateway
#                  Mark Crispin <MRC@PANDA.COM>
########### PORT 90 also being used unofficially by
# Pointcast #########
dnsix          90/tcp    # DNSIX Securit Attribute Token Map
dnsix          90/udp    # DNSIX Securit Attribute Token Map
#                       Charles Watt <watt@sware.com>
mit-dov        91/tcp    # MIT Dover Spooler
mit-dov        91/udp    # MIT Dover Spooler
```

```
#                          Eliot Moss <EBM@XX.LCS.MIT.EDU>
npp              92/tcp    # Network Printing Protocol
npp              92/udp    # Network Printing Protocol
#                          Louis Mamakos <louie@sayshell.umd.edu>
dcp              93/tcp    # Device Control Protocol
dcp              93/udp    # Device Control Protocol
#                          Daniel Tappan <Tappan@BBN.COM>
objcall          94/tcp    # Tivoli Object Dispatcher
objcall          94/udp    # Tivoli Object Dispatcher
#                          Tom Bereiter <--none--->
supdup           95/tcp    # SUPDUP
supdup           95/udp    # SUPDUP
#                          Mark Crispin <MRC@PANDA.COM>
dixie            96/tcp    # DIXIE Protocol Specification
dixie            96/udp    # DIXIE Protocol Specification
#            Tim Howes <Tim.Howes@terminator.cc.umich.edu>
swift-rvf  97/tcp    # Swift Remote Virtural File Protocol
swift-rvf  97/udp    # Swift Remote Virtural File Protocol
#                          Maurice R. Turcotte
#            <mailrus!uflorida!rm1!dnmrt%rmatl@uunet.UU.NET>
tacnews          98/tcp    # TAC News
tacnews          98/udp    # TAC News
#                          Jon Postel <postel@isi.edu>
metagram         99/tcp    # Metagram Relay
metagram         99/udp    # Metagram Relay
#            Geoff Goodfellow <Geoff@FERNWOOD.MPK.CA.US>
newacct          100/tcp   # [unauthorized use]
hostname         101/tcp   # NIC Host Name Server
hostname         101/udp   # NIC Host Name Server
#                          Jon Postel <postel@isi.edu>
iso-tsap         102/tcp   # ISO-TSAP Class 0
iso-tsap         102/udp   # ISO-TSAP Class 0
#                 Marshall Rose <mrose@dbc.mtview.ca.us>
gppitnp      103/tcp   # Genesis Point-to-Point Trans Net
gppitnp      103/udp   # Genesis Point-to-Point Trans Net
acr-nema   104/tcp   # ACR-NEMA Digital Imag. & Comm. 300
acr-nema   104/udp   # ACR-NEMA Digital Imag. & Comm. 300
#                          Patrick McNamee <--none--->
cso              105/tcp   # CCSO name server protocol
cso              105/udp   # CCSO name server protocol
#                 Martin Hamilton <martin@mrrl.lut.as.uk>
csnet-ns         105/tcp   # Mailbox Name Nameserver
csnet-ns         105/udp   # Mailbox Name Nameserver
#                 Marvin Solomon <solomon@CS.WISC.EDU>
3com-tsmux       106/tcp   # 3COM-TSMUX
```

```
3com-tsmux      106/udp     # 3COM-TSMUX
#                           Jeremy Siegel <jzs@NSD.3Com.COM>
#                   James Rice <RICE@SUMEX-AIM.STANFORD.EDU>
```

At more than 12,000 lines in length, it is not possible to print the entire list-ing for the file, but the lines shown should give you a good feel for what is there. It is important to know that the ports appearing by default in the file are *common port* assignments for those services. An administrator can change the port a service is using for security, or other purposes. This still allows the service to run, but now requires the user using it to know of—and specify—the new port.

One of the best examples of this is the www service, which runs on port 80, by default. If you make a website available to the world, using the Fully Qualified Domain Name (FQDN) of www.ds-technical.com, then anyone in the world can enter that address and reach your site by making a call to port 80. On the other hand, if you want the site to be up, and accessible from anywhere, yet only used by your employees in the outback, you can move the www service to one not being used by anything else—15000 for example. Now, anyone entering www.ds-technincal.com will still be hitting port 80, and unable to find the www service there. Your employees will use www.ds-technincal.com:15000 and be able to operate as they would at a regular website.

Network Access

You can limit access to your network host to explicitly named machines via the use of either a hosts.allow file or a hosts.deny file, both of which reside in the /etc directory. The syntax within these files is the same:

daemon: group

They either limit who is allowed in (to those specifically named in the .allow file) or limit who cannot come in (to those specifically named in the .deny file). The use of such variables as ALL to indicate all services or ALL EXCEPT to indicate all but a particular service is allowed in both files.

By default, both files exist on a host, though their lines are commented out. To recap

- ▶ hosts.allow is used to specifically list the names of other hosts that can access this machine through any of the /usr/sbin/tcpd services.

- ▶ hosts.deny is used to specifically list the names of other hosts that cannot access this machine through the /usr/sbin/tcpd services.

Working with LDAP

Course Objective Covered

17. Deploy OpenLDAP on a SLES 9 Server (3038)

Lightweight Directory Access Protocol (LDAP) is used to make access to directory services possible. OpenLDAP is the most popular implementation of LDAP for the Linux environment, and it allows you to organize entries into a hierarchical tree with all the expected objects—distinguished names, relative distinguished names, and so on.

Object classes within LDAP are defined in schema files, which can be found in `/etc/openldap/schema` and contain these classes:

- ▶ `Root`—The root of the directory tree
- ▶ `c`—Countries
- ▶ `o`—Organizations
- ▶ `oou`—Organizational units
- ▶ `*dc`:—Domain components

Complete administration information for OpenLDAP can be found at http://www.openldap.org in the Admin Guide and the Quick Start Guide. For this exam, know that the configuration files are beneath `/etc/openldap` and the two primary files are

- ▶ `slapd.conf`—The main configuration file
- ▶ `ldap.conf`—The default configuration for the clients

Working with Apache

Course Objectives Covered

7. Enable a Web Server (Apache) (3037)

18. Configure an Apache Web Server (3038)

Apache is a World Wide Web server to Linux in the same way that Internet Information Server is a WWW server for Windows NT/2000 and Windows Server 2003. You can devote years to learning the intricacies of this service.

Although Apache is included with most Linux implementations, including SuSE, you can obtain documentation and any newer versions of it that become available from www.apache.org.

The primary daemon running Apache is `httpd` and it, like the others, is started by the `inetd` when networking begins. If you want Apache to start automatically when the system is booted, you need to add it to the default runlevel's directory.

The exam objective specifies the need to know how to manage the `httpd` *files*, which is an important point because in the newest versions of Apache, there is only one configuration file—`/etc/apache2/httpd.conf`. In older versions, `httpd.conf` looked for additional values in two other files:

- ▶ `access.conf` allowed certain pages of the website to be restricted to individual users or groups.
- ▶ `srm.conf` specified the root directory for the website.

The default directory now being examined for data files with Apache is `/srv/www/htdocs`. This is the directory that the user will first enter when giving the address of the server at an `http://` prompt. The default file looked for, and loaded, in this directory is `index.html`.

Other configuration files to know beneath `/etc/apache2` are

- ▶ `default-server.conf`—The default Web server settings. These are overwritten by settings in all other files.
- ▶ `error.conf`—This file allows you to configure what should happen upon an error.
- ▶ `listen.conf`—The configuration file for the port to be used by Apache (80 is the default).
- ▶ `server-tuning.conf`—Fine-tuning parameters for the server. Under almost all circumstances, the defaults are fine.
- ▶ `ssl-global.conf`—This file allows you to configure the Secure Socket Layer (SSL) configuration.
- ▶ `uid.conf`—This file defines the user and group ID that will be used by the anonymous user accessing Apache.
- ▶ `vhost.d`—A subdirectory that holds the configuration files for virtual hosts.

If you make changes to the configuration file(s), and need those changes read immediately, you can kill the `httpd` with `kill -1|SIGHUP` to force rereading the files upon restart. You can also use the commands `rcapache2 stop` and `rcapache2 start` to stop and start the service, respectively.

One important consideration when using Apache, or any Web server, is that you need to verify valid entries in the `/etc/services` file for www services.

Working with NFS, smb, and nmb

Course Objectives Covered

5. Configure Network File Systems (3037)

6. Manage Resources on the Network (3037)

19. Configure a Samba Server as a File Server (3038)

These objectives addresses sharing. The three subcomponents of this topic have only a passing familiarity with each other, but all fall within the broad category of file/directory sharing.

NFS

NFS is the Network File System, and the way in which partitions are mounted and shared across a Linux network. NFS falls into the category of being a Remote Procedure Call (RPC) service. NFS utilizes three daemons— `nfsd`, `portmap`, and `rpc.mountd`—and loads partitions configured in the `/etc/exports` file. This file exists on every host, by default, but is empty. Within this file, you must specify the partition to be shared and the rights to it.

The NFS server can be started with the `/etc/init.d/nfsserver start` command and the daemons `rpc.nfsd` and `rpc.mountd` are spawned. `rpc.nfsd` is the service daemon, although `rpc.mountd` acts as the mount daemon.

Problems with NFS generally fall into two categories: errors in the `/etc/exports` listings (fixed by editing and correcting them) or problems with the daemons. The most common problem with the daemons involves their not starting in the correct order. The `portmap` daemon must begin first, and is the only daemon needed on a host that accesses shares but does not offer any.

NOTE　Shares can also be manually mounted, using the mount **command.**

NIS

The Network Information Service (NIS) acts as a giant phone book, or Yellow Pages, to resources distributed across the network. NIS acts so much like a directory, in fact, that most of the files and utilities begin with the letter **yp** as a carryover from when it was known as that. The three components of NIS are

▶ Master server—There must be at least one running the **ypserv** program and holding the configuration files.

▶ Slave servers—These are optional and not used in small networks. When used, they act as intermediaries on behalf of the master server in processing requests.

▶ Clients—These run the **ypbind** program and retrieve data from the server.

An NIS network is organized into domains with the /etc/defaultdomain file defining the domain and /etc/yp.conf holding the server address. Common resources mapped with NIS include user information (/etc/passwd), group information (/etc/group), and services (/etc/services), though you can add many more.

There are a number of utilities to know to work with NIS:

▶ **ypdomainname** shows the name of the NIS domain.

▶ **ypmatch** queries the key field of a map and shows the results.

▶ **yppasswd** changes the user password on the NIS server.

▶ **yppoll** shows the ID number of the NIS map.

▶ **ypwhich** shows the NIS server the client uses.

SMB

SMB stands for Server Message Block and is the protocol used for sharing resources on a Microsoft Windows-based network (Windows 95, Windows 98, Windows NT, Windows 2000, and so on). The resources shared can be directories, printers, or other devices. In order for Linux to access shared resources on a Windows-based network (we will use NT as an example), it is necessary to have Linux communicating via the same SMB protocol.

Unfortunately, the SMB protocol is not native to many implementations of Linux; however, it can be added through the use of other products. The most popular product, and the one the exam focuses on for this purpose, is Samba. Samba is a free program that can be found at www.samba.org (from which you must first choose your country).

Samba makes the Linux host an SMB client using values found in the /etc/samba/smb.conf file. When the Linux host is installed and configured (providing permissions are adequate), it can access any shared SMB resources on the NT network: directory, printer, and so on.

Though the concept is the same, when you configure the shares, you must config-ure them separately. Printer shares are configured by setting up a path to the resource, whereas directory shares are configured using *settings*.

NOTE

When the objects can be reached, they are mounted to make them accessi-ble, and you use them as if they resided locally.

SMB support is native to SuSE, and you can access shared resources through SuSE without needing to do anything further, as shown in Figure 11.7.

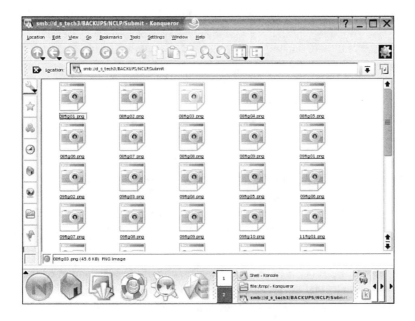

FIGURE 11.7
SMB support is included in SuSE.

NMB

In the Windows-based world, NetBIOS names are often used to identify computers. Although using SMB allows Linux computers to share files, communicating with those resources if NetBIOS names are used is not possible without something to resolve the names. That is where NMB comes into play. The NetBIOS Message Block allows Linux to identify the resources on Windows-based networks by the names that they are known as on those resources.

Samba includes both the `smbd` daemon and `nmbd` daemon to allow resources to be referenced and accessed. Users on the Windows systems will be able to click on their Network Neighborhood icon and see the resources there that exist on Linux machines as if they were on fellow Windows-based systems.

The `smb.conf` file is used for configuration of all Samba parameters including those for the NMB daemon.

Working with DNS

Course Objective Covered

15. Configure Host Name and Name Resolution (3038)

To understand the Domain Name System (DNS), you must first grasp the concept of name resolution and why it is important. It is probably safe to say that it is difficult for most people to remember a large number of 32-bit binary numbers. This is a shame in many ways, for it is by utilizing unique 32-bit binary numbers that every host on the Internet is able to differentiate itself one from another. Converting it to a decimal number helps a bit, but not much.

The simplest solution is to use a Fully Qualified Domain Names (such as www.ds-technical.com). Because the host name closely resembles the company name, the odds are much better that you will be able to memorize this entity than if it were a digital number or binary number. What is needed is a means to translate the text into the digital number.

There are two ways of resolving host names to IP addresses: using the host file or DNS. The one issue you must keep in mind is that in all cases, the resolution is to IP addresses—as they are the unique values that truly identify the site/host. Regardless of the resolution method implemented, all resolution is done by applications and occurs at the seventh layer (Application) of the OSI model.

Using the hosts Files

Many years ago (when TCP/IP was new), networks were small—consisting of only a handful of hosts at each site. There may have been dozens of users accessing the network, but they were doing so as dumb terminals connected to a host. The majority of the user's work would be done on one host, with an occasional need to interact with another host—send email to another user, access a file, and so on.

In those days—and in that environment if it still exists today—using /etc/hosts files is ideal for name resolution. hosts files are static, ASCII-text files that must reside on each host, and hold the information needed to resolve names in the form of columns. An example of a hosts file would be

```
#This is an example to show how the HOSTS file works
#the name of this host is Muncie, and need not be listed here
192.168.14.10 Yorktown
192.168.14.11 Daleville Chesterfield
192.168.14.12 Anderson
192.168.14.13 Lapel #Pendleton
192.168.14.14 Noblesville Westfield Carmel
192.168.14.15 Rosston
192.168.14.16 Lebanon
```

Because hosts files are ASCII text files, they can be created and edited with any text editor. The pound sign (#) is used as a comment character and causes the line to be ignored from the location where the character is found to the end of the line. In the preceding example, the first two lines are all comment and completely ignored for purposes of resolution; in the sixth line, the name Pendleton is also ignored.

Whether the entries in the hosts **file are case sensitive or not is dependent on the operating system in question. On Linux and Unix, the entries are case sensitive, whereas on Windows NT 4.0, Windows 2000, and Windows Server 2003, the entries are not case sensitive.** **NOTE**

Each line of the file can contain up to 255 characters and there can be an unlimited number of lines within the file. The first column of each line is the IP address of the host. Whitespace must follow that to separate the columns and can be either a space or a tab—these delimiters must be used to separate subsequent columns as well. The second—and all subsequent—columns are text names associated with that IP address (the host names).

In the example shown, a user could specify that they want to telnet to 192.168.14.10 by using that IP address, or by specifying "Yorktown". The HOSTS file would be used to translate the text name "Yorktown" into 192.168.14.10 and the connection results would be the same: This is the only host name associated with this host. In the case of the host 192.168.14.14, it can be referred to by three names—"Noblesville", "Westfield", and "Carmel".

Because the HOSTS file must reside on every host, the file on each host should be slightly different. In the preceding example, the file is from the host Muncie, and need not contain a reference to itself (though the existence of such a reference would do no real harm). On host Anderson, it need not have a reference to itself, but must have a reference to Muncie, as the following example shows:

```
#This is an example to show how the HOSTS file works
#the name of this host is Anderson, and need not be listed here
192.168.14.9 Muncie
192.168.14.10 Yorktown
192.168.14.11 Daleville Chesterfield
192.168.14.13 Lapel #Pendleton
192.168.14.14 Noblesville Westfield Carmel
192.168.14.15 Rosston
192.168.14.16 Lebanon
```

This means that every time a new host is added to the network, you must update the hosts file on each host, or they will not be able to access the new system. This restriction severely limits the usage of this method of name resolution to small networks that do not change often. On the positive side, their implementation is accepted by every operating system capable of running TCP/IP.

Also worthy of note: The file is always read sequentially from the top to the bottom—or until a resolution is found. To speed up your resolution: Comment lines should be moved to the bottom of the file to prevent their being obtrusively in the way each time the file is read, and the most commonly accessed hosts should be placed at the top of the file so that their matches are found quickly. It is also extremely important that duplicate host names not appear within the file. Consider the following file:

```
#This is an example to show how the HOSTS file works
#the name of this host is Muncie, and need not be listed here
```

```
192.168.14.10 Yorktown
192.168.14.11 Daleville Chesterfield
192.168.14.12 Anderson
192.168.14.13 Lapel #Pendleton
192.168.14.14 Noblesville Westfield Carmel
192.168.14.15 Rosston
192.168.14.16 Lebanon
192.168.14.17 Carmel
```

Because the file is read sequentially from top to bottom, all attempts to access the host named "Carmel" will always take the user to **192.168.14.14** and never to **192.168.14.17**. If the order of the lines is reduced on another host, a user will always get to the latter host there, and not the former. This can cause havoc in many ways, so be careful in order to avoid duplicate name entries.

Moving Up to DNS

In the early days of the Internet, a single **hosts** file was routinely updated and downloaded to all hosts for name resolution. However, the major problem with the **hosts** file method of resolution is that it must exist on every host, and changes must be made to every copy to take effect.

DNS—Domain Name Service/Server—solves this problem for large networks. Instead of putting an ASCII file locally for every host to use, the hosts access a server to do the name resolution for them. First introduced in 1984, DNS allows the host names to reside in a database that can be distributed among multiple servers. The distribution decreases the load on any one server and allows for more than one point of administration. It also allows the database size to be virtually unlimited because more servers can be added to handle additional parts of the database.

Configuring a client to use DNS is simply a matter of supplying it with the IP address of the server offering this service. On operating systems such as Linux, the DNS server can be specified in the ASCII file **resolv.conf** found in the **/etc** directory. A sample of this file follows:

```
### BEGIN INFO
#
# Modified_by:   dhcpcd
# Backup:        /etc/resolv.conf.saved.by.dhcpcd
# Process:       dhcpcd
# Process_id:    1630
# Script:        /sbin/modify_resolvconf
```

```
# Saveto:
# Info: This is a temporary resolv.conf created by
# service dhcpcd.
# The previous file has been saved and will be
# restored later.
#
# If you don't like your resolv.conf to be changed, you
# can set MODIFY_{RESOLV,NAMED}_CONF_DYNAMICALLY=no. This
# variables are placed in /etc/sysconfig/network/config.
#
# You can also configure service dhcpcd not to modify it.
#
# If you don't like dhcpcd to change your nameserver
# settings
# then either set DHCLIENT_MODIFY_RESOLV_CONF=no
# in /etc/sysconfig/network/dhcp, or
# set MODIFY_RESOLV_CONF_DYNAMICALLY=no in
# /etc/sysconfig/network/config or (manually) use dhcpcd
# with -R.  If you only want to keep your searchlist, set
# DHCLIENT_KEEP_SEARCHLIST=yes in
# /etc/sysconfig/network/dhcp or
# (manually) use the -K option.
#
### END INFO
search mshome.net
nameserver 192.168.0.1
```

DNS Structure

The hierarchical name system is assembled in a tree-type structure that very closely resembles a directory structure, much like one we would find in eDirectory, NDS, AD, or LDAP. To use an analogy, you can have a file called WARRANTY.DOC in C:\ and another file called WARRANTY.DOC in C:\DOCS\REFRIGERATOR. With a non-tree structure, you would only be able to have one file by that name, whereas the tree structure allows you to have multiples and to interpret each one as existing on its own. In a network using DNS, you can have more than one server with the same name, as long as each is located in a different path.

Resolution is done through the use of a combination of domains and host-names into Fully Qualified Domain Names—FQDNs. The domain can be one of several possibilities, the most common of which are

▶ com—Commercial enterprise

▶ edu—Educational institution

- ▶ gov—Government
- ▶ mil—Military
- ▶ net—Network provider
- ▶ org—Organization/original/not-for-profit

All of these domains are representative of entities within the United States. If the entity resides outside the United States, the domain becomes an abbreviation (typically two letters) for the host country. Although there are dozens of such abbreviations, some of those most frequently used include

- ▶ au—Australia
- ▶ de—Germany
- ▶ es—Spain
- ▶ fr—France
- ▶ il—Israel
- ▶ pr—Puerto Rico
- ▶ su—Soviet Union
- ▶ uk—United Kingdom
- ▶ us—United States

The hostname can be only the name of the host to contact or can include subdomains as well. For example, www.ds-technical.com is considered a Fully Qualified Domain Name (FQDN) for it includes the parent domain and subdomain (ds-technical.com), and the host portion (www).

---

www can also indicate the server to access, as well as the service. **NOTE**

An FQDN of kristin.ds-technical.com contains additional information. Although the domain stays the same (.com), it must now find the network ds-technical, and then the host kristin beneath that.

Always read an FQDN from right to left when breaking it into components. **NOTE**

DNS Zones

With the enormous number of hosts and sites on the Internet, it is not possible for a single server to hold all the address resolutions needed regardless of the capabilities of the database. Instead of a single server, DNS resolution for the Internet is performed by a number of servers, each responsible for a zone.

By using multiple servers/multiple zones, the load and the administrative burden of managing the database are diffused. Administrators manage only the DNS database records stored in their zones—which can be any portion of the domain name space. For each zone, there is a primary server—responsible for all updates—and one or more secondary servers. Any changes made to the zone file must be made on the primary server as the zone file on the secondary server(s) is a read-only copy. Zones are copied from the primary to the secondary name servers through replication (also known as zone transfer).

NOTE Another benefit of multiple zones is that smaller amounts of information are replicated than would be necessary if the domain records were located in only one zone file.

In addition to primary and secondary servers, there are also servers known as caching-only servers. A caching-only DNS Server doesn't have a zone file, and its only function is to make DNS queries, return the results, and cache the results. Although primary and secondary servers always have a file locally, when a caching-only server first starts, it has no stored DNS information, and it builds this information over time when it caches results of queries made after the server starts.

NOTE The ideal implementation for a caching-only server is in a situation where there is a slow WAN link because entire zone files don't need to be transferred. When a query is made, only one record is sent and not the full zone file. All future queries for the same information are resolved locally from the cache—eliminating the need to go across the WAN link.

DNS Records

Each record within the DNS zone file consists of a number of entries. The entries are also known as *resource records*, and can vary ever so slightly, but the following sections examine the most common record types.

SOA Record

Every database file starts with an Start Of Authority (SOA) record. This record identifies the zone and contains a number of other parameters, including

- ▶ Source host—The name of the primary server (with the read/write copy of the file)

- ▶ Contact email—Email address for the administrator of the file

- ▶ Serial number—The incrementing version number of the database

- ▶ Refresh time—The delay in seconds that secondary servers wait before checking for changes to the database file

- ▶ Retry time—The time in seconds a secondary server waits before another attempt if replication fails

- ▶ Expiration time—The number of seconds on secondary servers before the old zone information is deleted

- ▶ Time to live (TTL)—The number of seconds a caching-only server can cache resource records from this database file before discarding them and performing another query

NS Record

The Name Server record simply specifies the other name servers for the domain, or maps a domain name to that of the primary server for the zone.

A Record

The Address record holds the IP address of the name.

CNAME Record

The Canonical Name record is an alias field allowing you to specify more than one name for each TCP/IP address. For example, the CNAME record for ftp.ds-technical.com would indicate that it is an alias for kristin. ds-technical.com.

Using CNAME records, you can combine an FTP and a Web server on the same host.   **NOTE**

MX Record

The Mail Exchanger record specifies the name of the host that processes mail for this domain.

HINFO Record

The Host Record is the record that actually specifies the TCP/IP address for a specified host. All hosts that have static TCP/IP addresses should have an entry in this database.

PTR Record

Pointer records are used for reverse lookup entries. They specify the IP address in reverse order and the corresponding host name.

Utilities to Use with DNS

Any application—`telnet`, `ping`, and so on—can resolve addresses for host names simply by querying the address of the DNS server specified on the client. If the DNS server specified does not have a resolution for the address, it will query another DNS server based on the specified domain given in the FQDN. Applications that are capable of this silent resolution are known as resolvers.

The `hostname` command returns the name of the current host. The `nslookup` command is used to query DNS and find IP resolution. When first initiated, `nslookup` begins an interactive session and shows the DNS server's name and IP address. Commands that can be given are as follows:

```
NAME               - print info about the host/domain NAME using
➡ default server
NAME1 NAME2        - as above, but use NAME2 as server
help or ?          - print info on common commands
set OPTION         - set an option
    all                - print options, current server and host
    [no]debug          - print debugging information
    [no]d2             - print exhaustive debugging
➡information
    [no]defname        - append domain name to each query
    [no]recurse        - ask for recursive answer to query
    [no]search         - use domain search list
    [no]vc             - always use a virtual circuit
    domain=NAME        - set default domain name to NAME
    srchlist=N1[/N2/.../N6] - set domain to N1 and search
➡ list to N1,N2, etc.
    root=NAME              - set root server to NAME
    retry=X                - set number of retries to X
    timeout=X              - set initial time-out interval
➡ to X seconds
    type=X                 - set query type
```

```
➥ (ex. A,ANY,CNAME,MX,NS,PTR,SOA,SRV)
   querytype=X         - same as type
   class=X             - set query class
➥ (ex. IN (Internet), ANY)
   [no]msxfr           - use MS fast zone transfer
   ixfrver=X           - current version to use in IXFR
➥ transfer request
server NAME    - set default server to NAME, using current
➥ default server
lserver NAME   - set default server to NAME, using
➥initial server
finger [USER]  - finger the optional NAME at the current
➥ default host
root           - set current default server to the root
ls [opt] DOMAIN [> FILE] - list addresses in DOMAIN
➥ (optional: output to FILE)
   -a          - list canonical names and aliases
   -d          - list all records
   -t TYPE     - list records of the given type
➥ (e.g. A,CNAME,MX,NS,PTR etc.)
view FILE           - sort an 'ls' output file and
➥view it with pg
exit           - exit the program
```

For example, if you enter an FQDN, **nslookup** shows the IP address of the given site or host.

In SLES 9 nslookup **is deprecated for** dig, **which was discussed earlier in this chapter. You should know both utilities.** **NOTE**

In addition to resolving a host name to an IP address, you can also resolve an IP address to a host name through a process known as reverse lookup. Whereas an FQDN starts with the specific host and then the domain, an IP address starts with the network ID and then the host ID. Because you want to use DNS to handle the mapping, both must go the same way, so the octets of the IP address are reversed. That is, **148.53.66.7** in the inverse address resolution is **7.66.53.148**.

Now that the IP address is reversed, it is going the same way as an FQDN and you can resolve the address using DNS. To do so, you need to create a zone based on address class—for example, in the address **148.53.66.7**, the portion that was assigned to the site by the governing committee is **148.53** (and for **204.12.25.3** it is **204.12.25**). Given this, simply create a zone in

which these numbers are reversed and to which you add the records
in-addr.arpa—that is, 53.148.in-addr.arpa or 25.12.204.
in-addr.arpa, respectively. These zones can be copied from their
respective primary servers.

Working with OpenSSH

Course Objective Covered

9. Enable an FTP Server (3037)

A File Transfer Protocol (FTP) server can be established to allow users to
transfer files between their host and the server. This can be done on an
anonymous user basis, or you can require users to authenticate by giving
their username and password.

There are a great many FTP server packages available, but the one Novell
prefers to focus upon is PureFTPd. Although not installed by default, it is
included with the SLES 9 packages and can be installed at any time (the
package name is pure-ftpd).

After PureFTPd has been installed, you can configure the anonymous home
directory in /srv/ftp and tweak the settings in pure-ftpd.conf for your
environment.

As something of an alternative to FTP, SSH (Secure Shell) is a protocol suite
intended to add security to otherwise non-secure standard utilities.
OpenSSH is a free, open source implementation of the SSH suite.

OpenSSH is a replacement for telnet (as well as FTP and related utilities)
that is included standard with some Linux implementations, and available
for all others. Because of the weaknesses inherent in both telnet and FTP,
the implementation of OpenSSH is one of the first steps to undertake in any
attempt to harden the operating system.

As a generalization, OpenSSH encrypts all traffic and includes tunneling and
authentication. This makes it much more secure than the older remote connection utilities that sent plain text, or unencrypted, passwords.

OpenSSH uses the sshd daemon and includes a set of utilities. Quoting
from the OpenSSH site (http://www.openssh.org):

> The OpenSSH suite includes the ssh program which replaces rlogin and
> telnet, scp which replaces rcp, and sftp which replaces ftp. Also

included is `sshd` which is the server side of the package, and the other basic utilities like `ssh-add`, `ssh-agent`, `ssh-keysign`, `ssh-keyscan`, `ssh-keygen` and `sftp-server`. OpenSSH supports SSH protocol versions 1.3, 1.5, and 2.0.

OpenSSH is primarily developed by the OpenBSD Project, and its first inclusion into an operating system was in OpenBSD 2.6. The software is developed outside the USA, using code from roughly 10 countries, and is freely useable and re-useable by everyone under a BSD license.

For the exam, the primary thing to know is the names of the replacement utilities (and those they replace). There are three options that can be used with `scp`:

- ▶ `-B` repeats the same password when copying multiple files.
- ▶ `-p` preserves time stamps and file permissions.
- ▶ `-r` recursively copies a tree.

The syntax for the command is

```
scp <-b|-p|-r> <source file> <destination file>
```

Thus to copy from the remote server to the local host, an example would be

```
scp -p poweredge:/data/dulaney/anderson.txt
➥/data/scott/indiana.txt
```

To do it in reverse—copy the file from the local host to the remote—the command would become

```
scp -p /data/scott/indiana.txt
➥poweredge:/data/dulaney/anderson.txt
```

Working with the IP Tool

Course Objectives Covered

11. Set Up Network Devices with the IP Tool (3038)

13. Set Up Routing with the IP Tool (3038)

SuSE includes the `ip` utility to let you see and change the current network configuration. Though the options offered are many, the choices are very simplistic as shown in Figure 11.8.

FIGURE 11.8
The choices
offered by ip are
simple and easy
to understand.

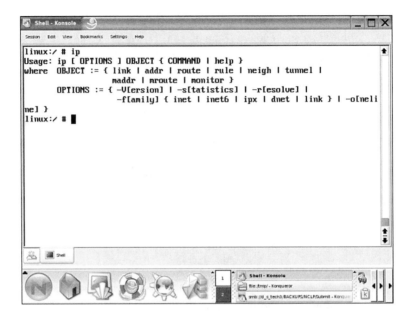

To see the current configuration, the command **ip address show** is used, as shown in Figure 11.9. Compare what is shown in Figure 11.9 with the output of the **ifconfig** command shown in Figure 11.1, and you will see that they are identical.

FIGURE 11.9
The ip tool can
be used to see
the current con-
figuration.

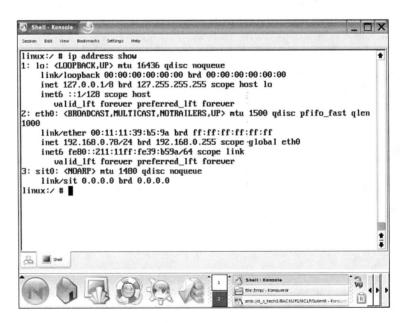

Substituting **add** for **show**, you can add to the settings, and using **del** allows you to delete existing settings.

The command **ip link show** will show the hardware address of every Ethernet device, as shown in Figure 11.10.

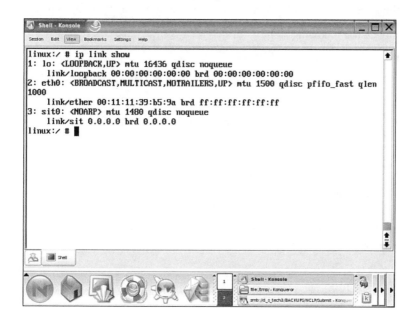

FIGURE 11.10
The **ip** tool can be used to see hardware addresses.

To work with the routing table, use the following commands:

- ▶ **ip route show** to see the current routing table
- ▶ **ip route add** to add a route
- ▶ **ip route add default** to add a default route
- ▶ **ip route delete** to delete a route

Tunnel interfaces take the form sit*x* **where** *x* **is a number (**sit **is short for Simple Internet Transition).** sit0 **is used as a generic route between IPv4 and IPv6.**

NOTE

Lab Exercise 11-1: Verifying Your Host Information

In this exercise, you will examine the networking information for your host.

Complete the following steps:

1. Log in as root.

2. Open a command-line window, if you are not automatically taken to one.

3. Check the configuration of the current network interface card:

   `ifconfig`

4. Look at the current host name:

   `hostname`

5. See which services currently are available and/or in use:

   `netstat -a`

Lab Exercise 11-2: Create an Entry in the hosts File

In this exercise, you will add a fictitious entry in the /etc/hosts files.

Complete the following steps:

1. Log in as root.

2. Open a command-line window, if you are not automatically taken to one.

3. Change to the /etc directory:

   ```
   cd /etc
   ```

4. Add a line to the end of the hosts file that gives this machine an alias equal to that of the loopback address:

   ```
   cat >> hosts
   127.0.0.1 willpassthisexam
   ^d
   ```

5. Verify that the address resolution works by sending five pings to the new alias:

   ```
   ping willpassthisexam -c 5
   ```

Lab Exercise 11-3: Identifying Running Network Services

In this exercise, you will look to see which services are running on a host.

Complete the following steps:

1. Log in as root.

2. Open a command-line window, if you are not automatically taken to one.

3. Change to the /etc directory:

   cd /etc

4. Look at the first few lines of services running:

   netstat -a | more

5. Look in the Local Address column to see which services are running. Some of the services appear as names—such as "www." Others appear as numbers. The translation is done by entries in the /etc/services file.

6. Pick an entry that appears in alphabetic form and verify which port it is running on. The following uses finger as an example:

   grep finger services

   The returned result should show that it is running at the default port of 79.

7. Pick a port number from the netstat output that does not show up as an alphabetic entry and verify that it is not in the /etc/services file. The following example uses the entry 6971:

   six document grep 6971 services

Summary

This chapter focused on the fundamentals of networking, and in particular TCP/IP. After providing background information on the protocol suite, the chapter examined the process of configuring the suite. This chapter also looked at a number of network services that are available for Linux. The discussion began by looking at the daemons that are in charge of networking—inetd and xinetd—and then turned to such services as Apache, NFS, and DNS before looking at OpenSSH.

Command Summary

Table 11.5 lists the commands that were discussed in this chapter.

Commands in This Chapter	**TABLE 11.5**

UTILITY	DEFAULT PURPOSE
arp	Shows the entries in the Address Resolution table
dig	Shows DNS entries
domainname	Displays the domain name used by the host
ftp	A utility for transferring files between hosts
ifconfig	Displays the TCP/IP configuration parameters
ifdown	Stops a preconfigured network interface
ifup	Starts a preconfigured network interface
ifstatus	Displays the status of a preconfigured network interface
netstat	Displays network status information
ping	Displays echo messages to show whether or not a host can be reached
route	Displays the routing table
telnet	A utility for establishing a connection with a remote host
traceroute	Displays the route taken to reach a remote host

Working with YaST

One of the primary features differentiating SuSE from other implementations of Linux is its inclusion of YaST (Yet Another Setup Tool). This one-stop tool provides a convenient interface to virtually every aspect of system administration. The latest versions of SuSE—including SLES 9—ship with the second version of this tool—YaST2.

This chapter looks at that tool and a sampling of the administrative tasks that you can do with it. It covers the following course objectives:

1. Introduction to YaST2 (3036)
2. Managing User Accounts with YaST2 (3036)
3. Understanding the YaST2 Software Management Feature (3036)
4. Obtaining Hardware Configuration Information from YaST2 (3036)
5. Managing the Network Configuration Information from YaST2 (3036)
6. Manage Software Updates with YaST Online Update Server (YOU) (3037)
7. Enable Remote Administration with YaST (3037)
8. Configure Security Settings with YaST (3038)

Introducing YaST

Course Objective Covered

1. Introduction to YaST2 (3036)

The YaST tool is available in SuSE as both a command-line interface and an X Window application. The command-line interface, regardless of which version of YaST you are running, is an **ncurses** application. When YaST is run as an X Window application, the appearance can differ based on whether you are using the first or second version of the tool—the first is **ncurses**-based, and the second (YaST2) is **Qt**-based. Because YaST2 ships with SLES 9, this discussion focuses on that version of the tool.

NOTE

ncurses **and** QT **are two programming languages used for drawing graphics on the terminal. There are a number of other plug-ins that programmers can use, but these are two of the most common.**

The purpose of this tool is to provide a one-stop interface to most of the tasks an administrator must work with on a regular basis. Although the appearance of the text mode differs from that of the graphical mode, all the choices are available in both interfaces.

Figure 12.1 shows the text-mode version of the tool upon startup (you start it by typing **yast** on the command line).

FIGURE 12.1
The startup view of YaST2 in text mode.

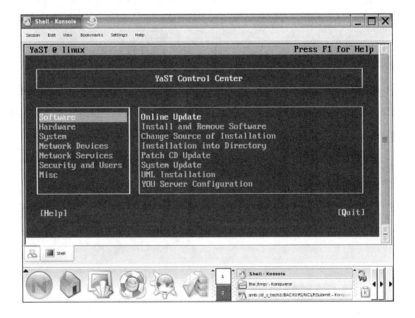

From the command line, you can type

yast -h

to see the help information available. You can also type

`yast -1`

to view a list of all available modules.

In text mode, you can navigate through the menus and choices by using the arrow keys (up and down), and the Tab key to move between boxes (Alt+Tab moves you from window to window). You can also use the space-bar to highlight items and Enter to choose them. You can press F9 to quit, and F1 to bring up help (as shown in Figure 12.2).

FIGURE 12.2
Help is available in the text mode by pressing F1.

You can start the graphical mode by typing **yast2** at the command line, or by simply choosing it from the KDE menu choices. Figure 12.3 shows the startup view of this interface.

Within the graphical interface, you navigate by using the mouse. You first click on a category within the left frame, and then choose an item from the right frame. You can also click on the Search button and enter a keyword to find.

FIGURE 12.3
The startup view
of YaST2 in
graphical mode.

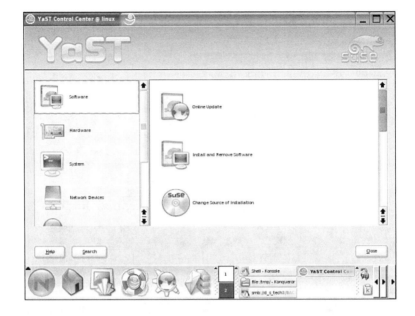

Working with Users

Course Objective Covered

2. Managing User Accounts with YaST2 (3036)

To work with users in the YaST tool, first choose Security and Users from
the left frame. This brings up a number of choices in the right frame:

- ▶ CA Management
- ▶ Edit and Create Groups
- ▶ Edit and Create Users
- ▶ Firewall
- ▶ Import Common Server Certificate
- ▶ Security Settings
- ▶ VPN

Choose the Edit and Create Users choice and a screen similar to that shown
in Figure 12.4 appears.

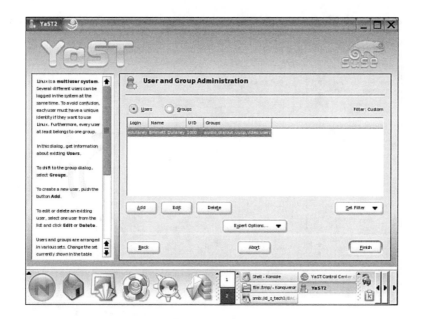

FIGURE 12.4
Users and groups can be added and altered from the User and Group Administration module.

You can also start YaST with the user account module loaded by typing yast2 **users at the command line.**

From this menu, you can add, delete, or edit a user. The Expert Options button is used to set defaults that will apply to newly created accounts, and the Set Filter button lets you choose what you want displayed—local users are the default, but you can also choose system users, or customize the display.

To edit a user, click the Edit button. A dialog similar to that shown in Figure 12.5 appears. Here you can change any of the settings that exist for that user.

If you click Details, you can see and change such values as the user ID, home directory, shell, and so on. Figure 12.6 shows the variables present in the Details settings.

FIGURE 12.5
The Edit button can change any of the parameters set for a user.

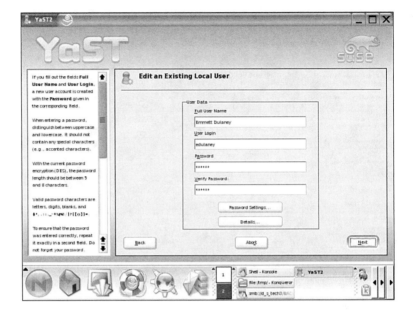

FIGURE 12.6
All values for the user can be changed.

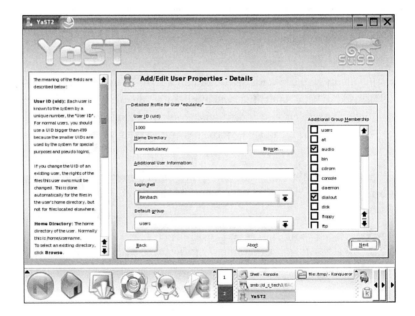

Conversely, clicking on Password Settings, shown in Figure 12.5, allows you to set password expiration and other variables as shown in Figure 12.7.

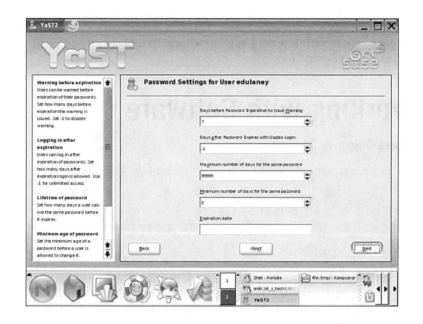

FIGURE 12.7
Password configuration parameters can be displayed and changed.

Groups are added and edited in the same way as users. Figure 12.8 shows the main menu for groups, with System groups filtered and the Expert Options expanded.

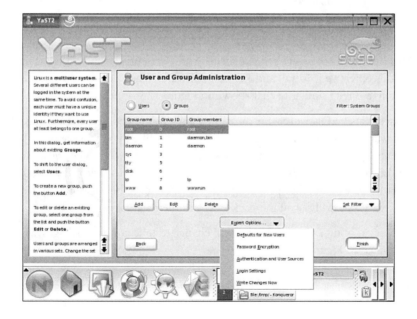

FIGURE 12.8
You can add, edit, and delete groups in the same way as you do with users.

NOTE You can also start YaST with the group account module loaded by typing yast2 groups **at the command line,**

Working with Software

Course Objective Covered

3. Understanding the YaST2 Software Management Feature (3036)

When you choose Software in the opening left frame of the YaST2 window, as shown in Figure 12.3, a number of choices appear on the right:

- ▶ Online Update
- ▶ Install and Remove Software
- ▶ Change Source of Installation
- ▶ Installation into Directory
- ▶ Patch CD Update
- ▶ System Update
- ▶ UML Installation
- ▶ YOU Server Configuration

Most of these choices are self-explanatory, and the one you should focus on for this objective is Install and Remove Software. When you choose this option, a screen similar to that shown in Figure 12.9 appears.

Notice that the Filter drop-down menu allows you to choose what packages you want to see. If you choose Selections as your filter, you will see only the installed packages. If you choose Package Groups, you will see all software on the installation media. If you choose Search, you can specify where you want to look for another package. Lastly, if you choose Installation Summary, you will see all the packages with their status marked.

Choose an option and the display will change to reflect those packages, as illustrated in Figure 12.10.

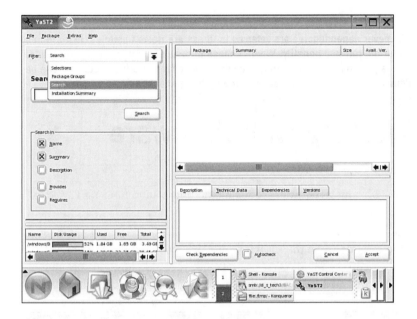

FIGURE 12.9
You can add and remove software easily.

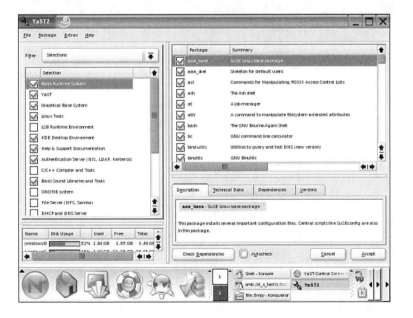

FIGURE 12.10
You can see what is installed and choose what you want to add or delete.

Click on a package until the action you want appears, and then click the Accept button. As needed, you will be prompted to insert media.

NOTE Whenever dependencies are referred to, these are items (modules) that are needed for the full functionality. When a check of dependencies is done, an examination is performed to see if all the needed components are installed. This can be done manually, or automatically by the system (autocheck).

Working with Hardware

Course Objective Covered

4. Obtaining Hardware Configuration Information from YaST2 (3036)

The YaST tool provides a simple interface to hardware configuration. Simply choose Hardware in the left frame, and then choose the object you want to configure in the right. As an example, Figure 12.11 shows the opening of the configuration options for the Graphics Card and Monitor module.

FIGURE 12.11
You can change hardware settings through YaST2.

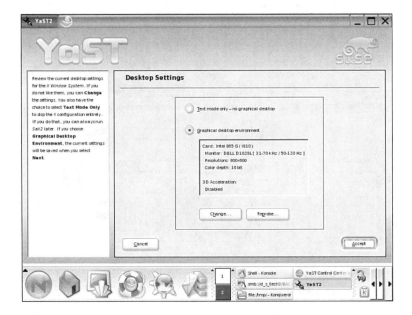

Choosing Change would open the correct module to allow you to configure the monitor and graphics card.

Before making any changes, however, it is highly recommended you choose the Hardware Information option. This allows you to see the current settings of your devices, as shown in Figure 12.12.

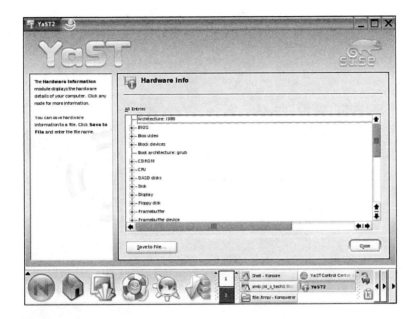

FIGURE 12.12
Hardware Information shows the current settings.

Working with Networks

Course Objective Covered

5. Managing the Network Configuration Information from YaST2 (3036)

To obtain networking configuration information, first choose Network Devices in the left pane. Choices in the right pane can include

- ▶ DSL
- ▶ Fax
- ▶ ISDN
- ▶ Modem
- ▶ Network Card
- ▶ Phone Answering Machine

For the purpose of this discussion, choose Network Card. This will bring up the screen shown in Figure 12.13.

Novell Certified Linux Professional Study Guide

FIGURE 12.13
Current settings
for the network
cards.

Devices already configured will appear in the bottom pane (Change), and
new entries can be added at the top (Configure). Choosing Change first
brings up the screen shown in Figure 12.14. Notice that you can add, edit,
and delete from here.

FIGURE 12.14
You can change
the network card
settings.

Choosing a new card (Configure) brings up the manual configuration dialog box shown in Figure 12.15.

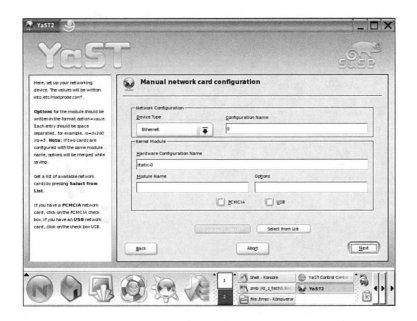

FIGURE 12.15
Adding a new
card manually.

Choices you have to make when configuring a card manually include whether to use DHCP or manually assign an IP address, subnet mask, and other networking values that were discussed in Chapter 11, "Networking Fundamentals."

Working with YOU

Course Objective Covered

6. Manage Software Updates with YaST Online Update Server (YOU) (3037)

The YaST Online Update (YOU) server is a giant step forward for Linux networks. It allows you to create a local server that holds updates rolled out to clients across your network. By centralizing the updates, it allows you to reduce the need (and traffic) of updating every host individually. Choosing Software in the left pane of YaST and YOU Server Configuration in the right pane starts configuration of the YOU server. This brings up the display shown in Figure 12.16.

NOTE

You can also start YaST with this module loaded by typing `yast2 you_server` at the command line.

FIGURE 12.16
The opening
screen of YOU
configuration.

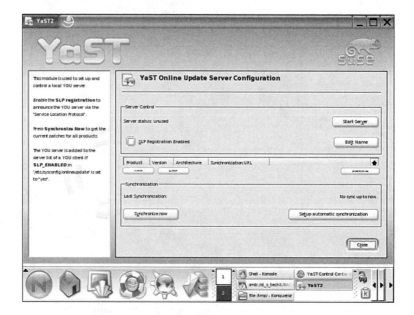

Notice that the YOU server uses SLP (Service Location Protocol)—this must be enabled to work properly. You start the server by clicking Start Server and the server status should change to indicate that it is running. You can get the current patches for all products by clicking on the Synchronize Now button.

NOTE

Clients can connect to the YOU server by simply going to the KDE desktop and selecting the YaST icon, giving the root password, and choosing Online Update from the Software menu. Alternatively, it is possible to type `sux -` and give the root password at a terminal window, and then type `yast2 online_update`.

After the session is established, you can configure the client and see information about the latest update(s).

Working with Remote Administration

Course Objective Covered

7. Enable Remote Administration with YaST (3037)

When you click the Network Services option in the left pane of YaST, a number of choices appear on the right. Among those choices is one for Remote Administration, as shown in Figure 12.17.

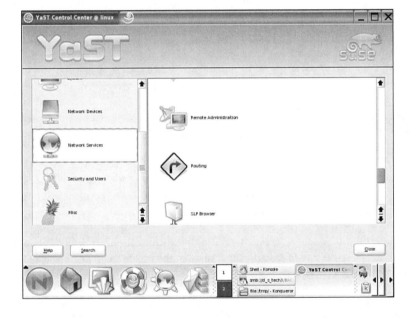

FIGURE 12.17
The Remote Administration module allows you to configure your server.

The choices here are remarkably simple—either to allow remote administration or not (the default). These two choices are depicted in Figure 12.18.

You can also start YaST with this module loaded by typing `yast2 remote` at the command line.

 NOTE

After you choose to enable remote administration, display manager must be restarted. The server can now be accessed and remotely administered.

FIGURE 12.18
Click the Allow
Remote
Administration
radio button to
enable remote
administration.

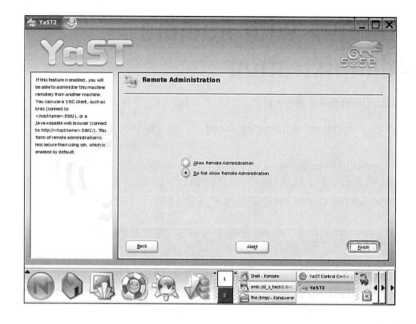

To administer it remotely, enter the following in a browser (replace *host* with the IP address of your server): **http://*host*:5081**

A Virtual Network Session (VNS) window will open and you will be prompted for a username and password. At the prompt for these items, you can click the Administration button instead and YaST will be initiated (requiring you to enter the root password).

> **NOTE**
>
> **Should it be necessary to restart your X session, the** rcxdm restart **command will do the trick for you.**

Working with Security Settings

Course Objective Covered

8. Configure Security Settings with YaST (3038)

Just as YaST can be used for all other aspects of configuration, it can also provide an interface to your security settings. To reach this module, choose Security and Users in the left pane, and Security Settings in the right pane. The module shown in Figure 12.19 will appear.

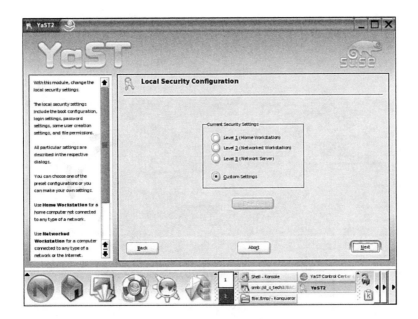

FIGURE 12.19
Security settings
within YaST.

The four settings that appear on this menu are

▶ Level 1 (Home Workstation)—This is the lowest level of security that
you can apply and should not be used in a business setting.

▶ Level 2 (Networked Workstation)—This is a moderate level of security
and should be considered the minimum setting for a business.

▶ Level 3 (Network Server)—A high level of security recommended for
servers.

▶ Custom Settings—The default.

You can choose any of the predefined roles and choose Details to tweak any
individual settings. Alternatively, you can stick with the default of Custom
Settings, and then click Next to see all the options that are available. The
first screen that appears allows you to set password settings, and the next,
shown in Figure 12.20, shows boot settings.

Following boot settings, you configure login settings, then parameters to
affect newly added users and groups. Lastly, miscellaneous settings allow
you to configure the user who runs **updatedb** (either nobody or root), and
the settings on file permissions. You can choose from three possible file permission settings:

▶ Easy—The majority of configuration files can be read by users.

▶ Secure—Only root can read system files like `/var/log/messages`.

▶ Paranoid—Access rights are the most restrictive possible.

FIGURE 12.20
Configure the
default boot
settings.

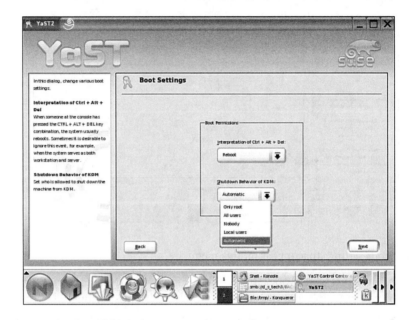

You can see the individual settings for each of these levels by going to `/etc` and looking at `permissions.easy`, `permissions.secure`, and `permissions.paranoid`. There are around 850 lines in each file.

Summary

This chapter focused on the graphical side of Linux and examined how YaST (Yet Another Setup Tool) makes SuSE stand out from the rest of the pack. Using this tool, you can perform most administrative functions without needing to fumble for the command-line syntax in order to accomplish the task.

## CHAPTER 13

Other Items to Know

As with most certification exams, there are a few topics in the courses corresponding to the study for this exam that do not fall nicely into a major category. Some of them are minor topics that are just useful to know, and others are important enough that the psychometricians will expect you to be familiar with them. Regardless of their context or reason for being here, this chapter represents a potpourri of topics and covers the following course objectives:

1. Accessing and Using `man` Pages (3036)
2. Using `info` Pages (3036)
3. Accessing Release Notes and White Papers (3036)
4. Using GUI-based Help in the Linux System (3036)
5. Finding Help on the Web (3036)
6. Finding Files on Linux (3036)
7. Schedule Jobs (3037)
8. Automate Data Backups with `cron` (3038)
9. Understand the Basics of C Programming (3038)
10. Understand the GNU Build Tool Chain (3038)
11. Understand the Concept of Shared Libraries (3038)
12. Perform a Standard Build Process (3038)
13. Monitor the Operating System (3038)
14. Monitor the File System (3038)

Using Local Documentation

Course Objectives Covered

1. Accessing and Using man Pages (3036)

2. Using info Pages (3036)

3. Accessing Release Notes and White Papers (3036)

4. Using GUI-based Help in the Linux System (3036)

A number of methods are available in all implementations of Linux for finding help on the operation of utilities. Additionally, many vendors add their own documentation and/or utilities for simplifying the process. In this section, we will look at these common utilities:

▶ man

▶ --help

▶ info

The man Utility

The man (as in manual) utility dates back to the early days of Unix. Using whatever page utility is defined in the user's environmental variables for PAGER, it displays document files found beneath the subdirectories included in the MANPATH variable. The PAGER variable is usually equal to less on SuSE, but can also be equal to more. The MANPATH variable usually includes /usr/share/man, /usr/local/man, /usr/X11R6/man, and /opt/gnome/share/man, but can include others as well.

Although there are a number of directories beneath /usr/share/man, the main ones—and their purpose—include the directories listed in Table 13.1.

TABLE 13.1   Subdirectories of /usr/share/man

SUBDIRECTORY	DESCRIPTIONS CONTAINED WITHIN
man1	Shell utilities/user commands
man2	System calls
man3	libc calls
man4	/dev descriptions
man5	/etc and other configurable files (such as protocols)

Table 13.1   Continued

SUBDIRECTORY DESCRIPTIONS CONTAINED WITHIN

SUBDIRECTORY	DESCRIPTIONS CONTAINED WITHIN
man6	Games
man7	Linux system files, conventions, and so on
man8	Root user/system administration utilities

When you enter the command to display a manual page (man), these subdirectories are searched until the first match is found. For example, if you entered the following command

```
man nice
```

The directories would be searched until the first match of a manual page describing **nice** is found. When the manual page is found, it is displayed using the utility specified by the **PAGER** variable. An example of the output follows (line numbering has been added to aid the discussion):

```
1.   NICE(1)                  User Commands                  NICE(1)

2.   NAME
3.   nice--run a program with modified scheduling priority

4.   SYNOPSIS
5.   nice [OPTION] [COMMAND[ARG]...]

6.   DESCRIPTION
7.   Run COMMAND with an adjusted scheduling priority. With no
8.   COMMAND, print the current scheduling priority. ADJUST is
a.   by default. Range goes from -20 (highest priority) to
9.   19 (lowest).

10.   -n, --adjustment=ADJUST
11.   increment priority by ADJUST first

12.   --help display this help and exit

13.   --version
14.   output version information and exit

15.   AUTHOR
16.   Written by David MacKenzie.

17.   REPORTING BUGS
```

18.   Report bugs to <bug-coreutils@gnu.org>.

19.   COPYRIGHT
20.   Copyright © 2004 Free Software Foundation, Inc.
21.   This is free software; see the source for copying condi-
22.   tions. There is NO warranty; not even for
➥MERCHANTABILITY
23.   or FITNESS FOR A PARTICULAR PURPOSE.

24.   SEE ALSO
25.   The full documentation for nice is maintained as a
➥Texinfo
26.   manual. If the info and nice programs are properly
27.   installed at your site, the command

28.   info coreutils nice

29.   should give you access to the complete manual.

30.   nice 5.2.1   June 2004   NICE(1)

The nice utility is pretty straightforward and does not have an unlimited
number of options, and thus makes it a good choice for dissecting as an
example of the output available from man. Using the more or less utilities to
display the page (whichever is defined by the PAGER variable), you can move
through the documentation in a number of ways after the first screen
appears, as shown in Table 13.2.

TABLE 13.2 **Navigating with the** more **and** less **Utilities**

KEY COMBINATION	MOVEMENT
Enter	Scroll down the next line
Spacebar	Scroll down the next page
b	Scroll up to the previous page
q	Quit
/	Search forward for the first page containing specified text
?	Search backward for the first page containing specified text
N	Move to the next occurrence of a string after a search
Shift+N	Move to the previous occurrence of a string after a search
PageDown	Scroll half a screen forward

Table 13.2 Continued

KEY COMBINATION	MOVEMENT
PageUp	Scroll half a screen back
End	Move to the end of the page
Home	Move to the beginning of the page

Let's examine the actual display: Line 1 gives the name of the utility and the parentheses identify what subdirectory the documentation is coming from. In this case, the 1 indicates that it is a shell utility or user command that the documentation was found for and displayed. If there is documentation for other entities named "nice" as well, they will not be displayed, as the default action is to only display the first entity found.

To see if there is more than one set of documentation on the system by the same name, you can use the `whatis` command:

```
$ whatis nice
nice (1)     - run a program with modified scheduling priority
nice (2)     - change process priority
nice (1p)    - invoke a utility with an altered nice value
nice (3p)    - change the nice value of a process
$
```

In this case, it turns out that there is another set of documentation for `nice` under `man2` and more under `1p` and `3p` as well. The list displayed comes from a `whatis` database. To see the second set of documentation instead of the first, the command would be

```
man 2 nice
```

This command specifies that you want the documentation for `nice` from the `man2` directory (3 would be used for `man3`, 4 for `man4`, and so on).

Other lines of the manual file begin sections for Name, Synopsis, Description, and Options, respectively. Based on the complexity of the utility and other features, there can also be sections for See Also, Diagnostics, Files, Bugs, and History and Author.

The third line is a short synopsis in and of itself of what the utility does, and matches the line returned by the `whatis` utility. Other lines describe the options that can be used and go into more detail on the workings of each.

Various options that can be used with man (which could be ascertained with the command man man) include

▶ -a to display all pages matching the text given and not quit after the first (matches are not found using the whatis database but by checking the subdirectories).

▶ -k to show all the manual pages with the same name (as found in the whatis database) and not stop after displaying the first. This differs from -K in that the former searches the entire page, and -k only searches the header.

▶ -M to specify the path to check (versus all subdirectories of /usr/man).

▶ -P to specify a different pager to use. The default in SLES 9 is less, but you can change that with this option. Whatever you specify here will override the setting that exists for the $PAGER variable.

Using --help

As was shown in the manual entry for nice, with many utilities/commands, you can follow the name of the utility with --help. This will provide very terse online help for the utility, showing syntax only, for example:

```
$ nice --help
Usage: nice [OPTION]... [COMMAND [ARG]...]
Run COMMAND with an adjusted scheduling priority.
With no COMMAND, print the current scheduling priority.  ADJUST
➡is 10
by default.  Range goes from -20 (highest priority) to 19
➡(lowest).

 -ADJUST                      increment priority by ADJUST first
 -n, --adjustment=ADJUST   same as -ADJUST
     --help                   display this help and exit
     --version                output version information and exit

Report bugs to <bug-coreutils@gnu.org>
$
```

This is a much abbreviated version of only some of the manual entry (syntax only). Whether or not the help is there in this manner depends on the programmer creating the utility. Most of the newer (and GNU) utilities/ commands do include the --help option, but it is far from a standard and rare with older utilities, and rarely available with applications.

Getting Info

The info utility can be used to display documentation on the GNU utilities. The syntax is either

info

or

info {utility name}

If the utility is called with no utility name following, it shows a main menu screen similar to the one shown in Figure 13.1.

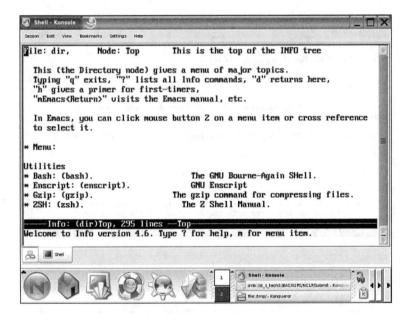

FIGURE 13.1
The opening of the info menu.

As the display states, you are really looking at the top (head) of a file named dir. This file contains a list of all the utilities for which the info command works, broken into sections (Miscellaneous, GNU file utilities, programming languages, and so on). Following each asterisk is the name of the item and within each set of parentheses is the text you would type to see the entry for that item. For example, to see the info for Bash, at the command line you would type

```
$ info bash
```

Within the menu, you can also press "m" to bring up a menu prompt, and then type the shortcut string ("bash" in this case). The first screen lists the commands to know for navigating within the tool (h, d, and so on) and their functions. The down arrow is used to scroll through the list one line at a time, and the Enter key selects that entry and shows you the information on it. The files are in hypertext format, so more often than not, making one selection will lead you to another menu.

To illustrate, you can use the down arrow to scroll through the list to this line:

```
* Gzip:(gzip).          The gzip command for compressing files.
```

Then when you press Enter, the menu of options specific to gzip will come up, as shown in Figure 13.2.

FIGURE 13.2
The info display for the gzip utility.

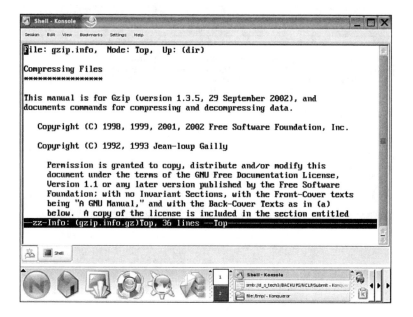

From here, you would make your selection and choose to read the information relevant to what you are attempting to accomplish. Pressing q will quit, or pressing d will take you back to the main menu.

NOTE   Notice the two empty colons following each choice on the gzip submenu. This means that you cannot type "info" followed by any shortcut text to arrive at that location. Very rarely is shortcut text available for use on anything but the main menu.

Other key combinations that work within `info` are summarized in Table 13.3. Just as files for the manual documentation reside beneath `/usr/share/man`, the files for the `info` utility reside beneath `/usr/share/info`.

Navigating Within `info`   **TABLE 13.3**

KEY COMBINATION	MOVEMENT
Spacebar, PageDown	Scroll down the next page
Backspace, PageUp	Scroll up to the previous page
q	Quit
B	Place cursor at beginning of `info` page
E	Place cursor at end of `info` page
Tab	Move cursor to next reference
Enter	Move to beneath the current reference (select this choice)
N	Move to the next `info` page at the same level
P	Move to the previous `info` page at the same level
U	Move one level higher
L	Move to the last text displayed
S	Search
H	Help
?	Show a summary of commands

Other Local Documentation

There are other locations where information can be found, and other utilities that serve limited purposes within this scope. Two utilities to be aware of are

- ▶ `whereis`
- ▶ `apropos`

The `whereis` utility will list all the information it can find about locations associated with a file, including `man` documentation (if any). For example

```
$ whereis nice
nice: /usr/bin/nice /usr/share/man/man1/nice.1.gz
```

```
/usr/share/man/man2/nice.2.gz
...
$
```

The search is limited to specific directories only. The first listing, in this case, is of the binary itself, and the other two are the **man** entries. If no **man** entry exists, nothing will be shown there, and if there are source files or related files, they will be shown. For example

```
$ whereis info
info: /usr/bin/info  /usr/share/info
...
$
```

The **apropos** utility uses the **whatis** database to find values and returns the short summary information about the listing seen earlier with **whatis**. The difference is that it scans the database and reports all matches—not just exact matches—to the utility name:

```
$ apropos nice
CGI::Pretty (3pm)      - module to produce nicely formatted HTML
➥code
snice (1)              - send a signal or report process status
nice (1p)              - invoke a utility with an altered nice
➥value
nice (3p)              - change the nice value of a process
renice (8)             - alter priority of running processes
English (3pm)          - use nice English (or awk) names for
➥ugly punctuation
➥ variables
renice (1p)            - set nice values of running processes
getpriority (3p)       - get and set the nice value
nice (1)               - run a program with modified scheduling
➥priority
nice (2)               - change process priority
setpriority (3p)       - get and set the nice value
$
```

Other locations where you can find documentation such as white papers and release notes locally include the subdirectories beneath /usr/share/doc. This directory contains a number of subdirectories, and the key ones for you to know are the following:

- ▶ howto—This directory holds subdirectories with descriptions of how to do tasks.

- ▸ `manual`—Contains the SLES administration manual, usually in both PDF and HTML formats.

- ▸ `packages`—The documentation for packages is located beneath subdirectories under here.

- ▸ `release-notes`—Contains HTML and RTF versions of the release notes.

Other local documentation that exists is dependent upon vendor applications installed. Always look under packages first to see if the information on them is located there. In many applications, you can press F1 to obtain help as well.

SuSE includes a HelpCenter that can also be used to obtain help from within the graphical interface. This is indicated by the lifesaver icon on the desktop (in the KDE panel). Clicking on this brings up the HelpCenter main screen shown in Figure 13.3.

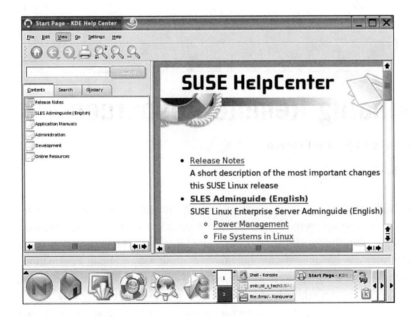

FIGURE 13.3
The SuSE HelpCenter offers help for common problems.

You can use the search feature to find information, or click through the Contents or Glossary to find what you are looking for.

Within the KDE browser, you can also use the help features through HTML links. To read the `man` page for `nice`, for example, enter this address:

```
man:nice
```

This will bring up the display shown in Figure 13.4.

FIGURE 13.4
You can access the same help features through the browser.

Finding Remote Resources

Course Objective Covered

5. Finding Help on the Web (3036)

In addition to the resources available locally, numerous other resources are also available across the Internet. These resources can be divided into two categories: websites and newsgroups. The former provide static information that may change daily or infrequently, but allow you to obtain information without providing any specific interaction. Newsgroups, on the other hand, consist of ongoing threads of communication between individuals who decide to participate. You can post a question specific to your situation in a newsgroup and (hopefully) have it answered by one or more knowledgeable individuals attempting to help. You would never use a newsgroup to post a common question to which the answer could easily be found elsewhere.

Table 13.4 lists sites that provide Linux or utility-oriented resources. As the Internet is a constantly changing entity, it is possible that in the future not all sites listed here will still exist, or that newer/better sites will come into being: Never underestimate the power of a good search engine in informing you of both.

Linux or Utility-Oriented Resources

TABLE 13.4

CATEGORY	SITE	DESCRIPTION
Documentation	www.kde.org	The organization behind the KDE interface
Documentation	www.tldp.org	Linux Documentation Project (LDP)—invaluable for finding HOWTO information
Documentation	www.linuxlookup.com	LinuxLookup—HOWTOs and reviews
Kernel	www.kernel.org	For all matters related to the kernel
News	www.linux.com	Linux.com
News	www.linux.org	Linux Online
News	www.linuxplanet.com	LinuxPlanet
Security	www.cert.org	Tracking of bugs/viruses
Security	www.securityfocus.com	Security issues
Vendor	www.suse.com	SuSE

Even though the site may be for a software vendor, or for a version of Linux other than what you are running, you should never dismiss checking the site. The simple reason for this is that many of the Linux sites post FAQs and help files for the operating system in general in addition to promoting their products.

The following newsgroups can be invaluable aids in solving specific problems you may be experiencing. The wonderful thing about newsgroups is that most of the time their names are self-explanatory, and this can prevent you from posting a question in the wrong location:

- ▶ comp.os.linux.advocacy
- ▶ comp.os.linux.announce.html
- ▶ comp.os.linux.answers
- ▶ comp.os.linux.development.apps
- ▶ comp.os.linux.development.system

▶ comp.os.linux.hardware

▶ comp.os.linux.misc

▶ comp.os.linux.networking

▶ comp.os.linux.setup

▶ comp.os.linux.x

There are also Linux mailing lists you can subscribe to in order to see mail threads on particular topics. To subscribe, send a message to majordomo@vger.rutgers.edu with the topic "subscribe" and the name of the mailing list from the following list. Again, the names are self-explanatory:

▶ linux-admin

▶ linux-alpha

▶ linux-apps

▶ linux-c-programming

▶ linux-config

▶ linux-doc

▶ linux-kernel

▶ linux-laptop

▶ linx-newbie

▶ linux-sound

▶ linux-standards

Working with KFind

Course Objective Covered

6. Finding Files on Linux (3036)

Chapter 4, "Working with Files," introduced a number of utilities that can be used to find files on a system. In addition to this, we have already examined whereis—one of the more useful tools available. There is one more tool to look at that can help you find what you are looking for: KFind.

The KFind utility provides a graphical version of find. You can start it by choosing Find Files in the KDE menu, or choosing Tools from the

Konqueror menu and then choosing Find File. Regardless of how you start it, the screen shown in Figure 13.5 appears.

FIGURE 13.5
You can look for files graphically with KFind.

All regular expressions and wildcards are supported and the results are shown in the bottom frame, as shown in Figure 13.6.

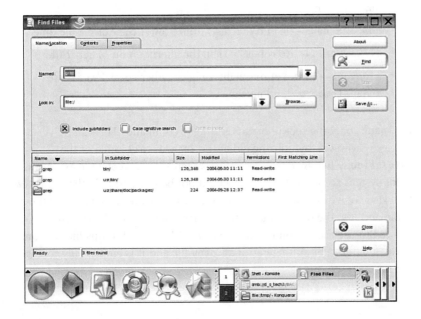

FIGURE 13.6
The results of searching for entries matching "grep" in KFind.

Scheduling Jobs for Later

Course Objectives Covered

7. Schedule Jobs (3037)

8. Automate Data Backups with `cron` (3038)

Quite often there are jobs that can run in your absence, but which need to run either at odd hours, or with a fair amount of frequency. If you have a job that needs to run one time, and it is convenient to run it when you are not around, you can schedule it using the **at** command. If you have a job that runs with any degree of frequency (once a month every month, once a week, and so on), you can schedule it with `cron`.

Using at

The **at** command allows you to schedule a job to run *at* a specified time. The syntax is simple:

```
at {time}
```

The time can be specified in a great many ways. Here are some examples:

- ▶ `17:31`—To run the command at 5:31 in the afternoon.

- ▶ `now`—To run now.

- ▶ `now + 5 days`—To run five days from now at the exact same time.

- ▶ `17:31 Mar 14`—To run at 5:31 in the afternoon on March 14th.

- ▶ `midnight`—To run at midnight tonight. Other special words are `today`, `tomorrow`, and `noon`.

By default, only the root user can use the **at** command. This can be changed, however, by utilizing either the `/etc/at.allow` file or the `/etc/at.deny` file. By default, on most systems the `at.deny` file exists and holds system accounts that a user should not be using. If only the `at.allow` file exists, only users who are listed within that file are allowed to use the **at** command. On the other hand, if the `at.deny` file exists, all users are allowed to use the **at** command except those listed within this file. To complicate matters a bit, if there is an `at.deny` file and it is empty, only root can use it.

When you give the **at** command and the time, the prompt changes to the **PS2** prompt (>, by default), and you can enter as many commands as you want to run at that time. When you are finished, press Ctrl+D to return to the **PS1** prompt.

Jobs that are spooled for future execution can be listed with either this command:

```
at -l
```

or

```
atq
```

Individual users will see only their own entries, whereas the root user can see all. In reality, the listings are text files stored beneath **/var/spool/atjobs**. These text files hold a copy of environment information that applied when the user created the job, as well as the commands within the job itself. Prior to execution, the command can be stopped with either of the following commands and the job number:

```
at -d
```

or

```
atrm
```

When a job is spooled, there is a file representing it with a very odd name (cryptic format) beneath **/var/spool/atjobs**. An example of the filename would be **a000010011756e1**, and its contents (which you must be root to see) would look like this:

```
#!/bin/sh
# atrun uid=0 gid=0
# mail     root 0
umask 22
LESSKEY=/etc/lesskey.bin; export LESSKEY
NNTPSERVER=news; export NNTPSERVER
INFODIR=/usr/local/info:/usr/share/info:/usr/info; export
INFODIR
MANPATH=/usr/share/man:/usr/local/man:/usr/X11R6/man:/opt/gnome/
➥share/man;
export MANPATH
KDE_MULTIHEAD=false; export KDE_MULTIHEAD
HOSTNAME=linux; export HOSTNAME
GNOME2_PATH=/usr/local:/opt/gnome:/usr; export GNOME2_PATH
XKEYSYMDB=/usr/X11R6/lib/X11/XKeysymDB; export XKEYSYMDB
```

```
GPG_AGENT_INFO=/tmp/gpg-vNNZtn/S.gpg-agent:6965:1; export
➥GPG_AGENT_INFO
HOST=linux; export HOST
PROFILEREAD=true; export PROFILEREAD
HISTSIZE=1000; export HISTSIZE
XDM_MANAGED=/var/run/xdmctl/xdmctl-:0,rsvd,method=classic;
➥export XDM_MANAGED
STYLE=keramik; export STYLE
GTK2_RC_FILES=/etc/opt/gnome/
➥gtk-2.0/gtkrc:/opt/gnome/share/themes/Geramik/
gtk-2.0/gtkrc:/root/.gtkrc-2.0keramik:/
➥root/.kde/share/config/gtkrc;
export GTK2_RC_FILES
GTK_RC_FILES=/etc/opt/gnome/gtk/gtkrc:/opt/gnome/share/themes/
➥Geramik/gtk/gtkrc
:/root/.gtkrc-keramik:/root/.kde/share/config/gtkrc; export
➥GTK_RC_FILES
WINDOWID=46137351; export WINDOWID
KDEHOME=/root/.kde; export KDEHOME
QTDIR=/usr/lib/qt3; export QTDIR
XSESSION_IS_UP=yes; export XSESSION_IS_UP
KDE_FULL_SESSION=true; export KDE_FULL_SESSION
JRE_HOME=/usr/lib/java/jre; export JRE_HOME
USER=root; export USER
XCURSOR_SIZE=; export XCURSOR_SIZE
LS_COLORS=no=00:fi=00:di=01\;34:ln=00\;36:pi=40\;33:so=01\;35:do
➥=01\;35:bd=40\
;33\;01:cd=40\;33\;01:or=40\;31:ex=00\;32:\*.cmd=00\;32:\*.exe=0
➥1\;32:\*.com=01
\;32:\*.bat=01\;32:\*.btm=01\;32:\*.dll=01\;32:\*.tar=00\;31:\*.
➥tbz=00\;31:\
*.tgz=00\;31:\*.rpm=00\;31:\*.deb=00\;31:\*.arj=00\;31:\*.taz=00
➥\;31:\*.lzh=00\
;31:\*.zip=00\;31:\*.zoo=00\;31:\*.z=00\;31:\*.Z=00\;31:\*.gz=00
➥\;31:\*.bz2=00\
;31:\*.tb2=00\;31:\*.tz2=00\;31:\*.tbz2=00\;31:\*.avi=01\;35:\*.
➥bmp=01\;35:\
*.fli=01\;35:\*.gif=01\;35:\*.jpg=01\;35:\*.jpeg=01\;35:\*.mng=0
➥1\;35:\*.mov=01
\;35:\*.mpg=01\;35:\*.pcx=01\;35:\*.pbm=01\;35:\*.pgm=01\;35:\*.
➥png=01\;35:
\*.ppm=01\;35:\*.tga=01\;35:\*.tif=01\;35:\*.xbm=01\;35:\*.xpm=0
➥1\;35:\*.dl=01\
;35:\*.gl=01\;35:\*.aiff=00\;32:\*.au=00\;32:\*.mid=00\;32:\*.mp
➥3=00\;32:\
*.ogg=00\;32:\*.voc=00\;32:\*.wav=00\;32:; export LS_COLORS
OPENWINHOME=/usr/openwin; export OPENWINHOME
```

```
XNLSPATH=/usr/X11R6/lib/X11/nls; export XNLSPATH
HOSTTYPE=i386; export HOSTTYPE
KDEROOTHOME=/root/.kde; export KDEROOTHOME
SESSION_MANAGER=local/linux:/tmp/.ICE-unix/7018; export
➥SESSION_MANAGER
PAGER=less; export PAGER
LD_HWCAP_MASK=0x20000000; export LD_HWCAP_MASK
KONSOLE_DCOP=DCOPRef\(konsole-7053,konsole\); export
➥KONSOLE_DCOP
MINICOM=-c\ on; export MINICOM
DESKTOP_SESSION=custom; export DESKTOP_SESSION
PATH=/sbin:/usr/sbin:/usr/local/sbin:/root/bin:/usr/local/bin:/
➥usr/bin:
/usr/X11R6/bin:/bin:/usr/games:/opt/gnome/bin:/opt/kde3/bin:
/usr/lib/java/jre/bin; export PATH
CPU=i686; export CPU
JAVA_BINDIR=/usr/lib/java/jre/bin; export JAVA_BINDIR
KONSOLE_DCOP_SESSION=DCOPRef\(konsole-7053,session-1\); export
➥KONSOLE_DCOP
SESSION
INPUTRC=/etc/inputrc; export INPUTRC
PWD=/etc; export PWD
XMODIFIERS=@im=local; export XMODIFIERS
JAVA_HOME=/usr/lib/java/jre; export JAVA_HOME
TEXINPUTS=::/root/.TeX:/usr/share/doc/.TeX:/usr/doc/.TeX:/root/.
➥TeX:
/usr/share/doc/.TeX:/usr/doc/.TeX; export TEXINPUTS
SHLVL=2; export SHLVL
HOME=/root; export HOME
LESS_ADVANCED_PREPROCESSOR=no; export LESS_ADVANCED_PREPROCESSOR
OSTYPE=linux; export OSTYPE
LS_OPTIONS=-a\ -N\ --color=tty\ -T\ 0; export LS_OPTIONS
no_proxy=localhost; export no_proxy
XCURSOR_THEME=crystalwhite; export XCURSOR_THEME
WINDOWMANAGER=/usr/X11R6/bin/kde; export WINDOWMANAGER
GTK_PATH=/usr/local/lib/gtk-2.0:/opt/gnome/lib/gtk-2.0:/
➥usr/lib/gtk-2.0;
 export GTK_PATH
LESS=-M\ -I; export LESS
MACHTYPE=i686-suse-linux; export MACHTYPE
LOGNAME=root; export LOGNAME
LC_CTYPE=en_US.UTF-8; export LC_CTYPE
PKG_CONFIG_PATH=/opt/gnome/lib/pkgconfig; export PKG_CONFIG_PATH
LESSOPEN=lessopen.sh\ %s; export LESSOPEN
USE_FAM=; export USE_FAM
ACLOCAL_PATH=/opt/gnome/share/aclocal; export ACLOCAL_PATH
```

```
INFOPATH=/usr/local/info:/usr/share/info:/usr/info; export
➥INFOPATH
LESSCLOSE=lessclose.sh\ %s\ %s; export LESSCLOSE
G_BROKEN_FILENAMES=1; export G_BROKEN_FILENAMES
JAVA_ROOT=/usr/lib/java; export JAVA_ROOT
COLORTERM=; export COLORTERM
OLDPWD=/usr/share/zoneinfo; export OLDPWD
cd /etc || {
     echo 'Execution directory inaccessible' >&2
     exit 1
}
/home/edulaney/myexample
```

All of this is necessary just to run a one-line command—/home/edulaney/myexample. Notice how all relevant information about the user has been placed here: User ID, environmental variables, and so on. This prevents a user from running a command through at that he or she would not have access and permissions to run otherwise. The very last line is the command to run: It is always recommended that the full path be given as there is no relative path for the service that runs the command.

A few other options exist with at: -m to mail the user when the job is done, and -f to feed the lines into at from a file. There is also an alias for the command called batch. The batch utility works exactly the same except that it only runs the processes when system utilization is low.

One thing to keep in mind about at jobs that is worth repeating—they are good for running one time. If you had to schedule a dozen jobs every day, and they were the same jobs, it would become time-consuming to do so because there is no trace of them to resurrect after they have finished executing. If you need to run jobs more than once, you will want to avoid the at jobs, and investigate the uses of cron.

Working with cron

As has been stated, cron is used to run commands at an interval, and that can be any type of interval. With cron, a file of times/commands named crontab (as in cron table) is read to find what must be run when. By default, every user can have his or her own crontab file. The default changes, however, if there is a /etc/cron.allow or /etc/cron.deny file. In the presence of the cron.allow file, only those users who appear within the file can create crontab files. In the presence of a cron.deny file, all users can use crontabs except those whose names appear within the file. The two files are optional and mutually exclusive: You would never have both on the same system.

To see if there is a current `crontab` file, a user uses this command:

```
crontab -l
```

To remove it, they would use the `-r` option:

```
crontab -r
```

To edit it, they would use the `-e` option:

```
crontab -e
```

For the root user to see other user's files, such as for `larry`, he would use this option:

```
crontab -u larry -l
```

There is one entry per line in the file, and each line consists of six fields. The six fields are separated by whitespace. The first time you look at such a file, it will look like a garbled mess. To understand what you are seeing, remember that there are six fields:

1. Minutes (0–59)
2. Hours (0–23)
3. Day of month (1–31)
4. Month (1–12)
5. Day of week (0=Sunday, 6=Saturday)
6. Command to run

Here's an illustration:

```
$  pwd
/home/edulaney
$ cat example
logger This is running every five minutes after the hour
$
$ crontab -l
no crontab for edulaney
$ crontab -e
```

This opens a blank file within the editor.   **NOTE**

```
5 * * * * /home/edulaney/example
```

This exits the editor.

This sets the shell script (which logs an entry to /var/log/messages) to run every five minutes after the hour, regardless of the hour (*), the day of the month (*), the month (*), or the day of the week (*). Within each of the fields, the asterisk means all, and the following list shows other possible parameters:

▶ A number means only when there is a match (such as the 5 in the example).

▶ A hyphen can indicate an inclusive range of numbers, for example 1-10.

▶ A comma can separate numbers, for example: 1,10.

Some examples of specifications are shown in Table 13.5.

TABLE 13.5 **Examples of cron Entries**

SYNTAX	RESULT
1 12 * * *	12:01 every day of the year
15 18 1 * *	6:15 in the evening on the first day of each month
1,16,31,46 * * * *	Every 15 minutes
30 0,12 * * *	12:30 in the morning and afternoon
20 10 31 10 *	Only on October 31st at 10:20
1 6 * * 1-5	At 6:01 every weekday morning

The cron daemon, started by init, wakes up once a minute to look for jobs that are set to execute. The jobs are held in the spooler (/var/spool/cron), and come from the user crontabs or /etc/crontab. The at jobs are executed by the at daemon (atd) on most systems (on others, atrun is started routinely by the cron daemon to look for at jobs).

Programming 101

Course Objectives Covered

9. Understand the Basics of C Programming (3038)

10. Understand the GNU Build Tool Chain (3038)

11. Understand the Concept of Shared Libraries (3038)

12. Perform a Standard Build Process (3038)

Don't let the objectives in this section fool you or scare you. This exam is aimed at system administrators, not developers or programmers. At the same time, Novell wants you to know something about the development process so that you can communicate effectively, and that is truly where these four objectives enter the picture.

You need to know that Linux, like Unix before it, is written mainly in C or C++, both of which are compiler languages. This means the applications must be compiled before they can be run—unlike scripts, which were discussed in Chapter 6, "Shells, Scripting, Programming, and Compiling." The advantages of a compiler language are that execution is fast and it is possible to create add-ons such as drivers. The compiler for C used by Linux is gcc—the Gnu C Compiler. gcc is installed by default in SuSE, and most other Linux implementations.

The GNU Build Process consists of the following steps:

1. Use the configure utility to prepare a build. This is essentially the startup file to begin configuration for the build.

2. Use the make utility to create (compile) the source code. Depending on the size of the package, this could take anywhere from a few seconds to a considerable amount of time to complete.

3. Use make install to actually install the compiled program. Running this command installs all the package components in their default directories.

4. Install required packages.

It is highly recommended that you read through the man pages for configure and make to familiarize yourself with their basic functionality.

Know that a Linux distribution (any Linux distribution) has hundreds of package files. A package file can contain anywhere from one program file to hundreds or thousands of them.

Shared libraries are used so that applications that perform common functions do not need to have those functions embedded within each of them. The shared library consists of the shared object and a header file.

To put everything together, the following represents the steps to a standard build process for the `xpenguins` game:

1. Extract the source archive: **tar xzf xpenguins-2.2.tar.gz**
2. Change to the source directory: **cd xpenguins-2.2/**
3. Run the configuration script: **./configure**
4. Start the compilation: **make**
5. Install the program: **make install**

At the risk of redundancy, it is worth pointing out again that the administrators' exam does not expect you to be a programmer. You do not need to know how to code in C. You do, however, need to know the steps given here for a standard build process.

Monitoring SLES

Course Objectives Covered

13. Monitor the Operating System (3038)
14. Monitor the File System (3038)

When everything is up and running as it should be, the challenge becomes to stay on top of it and proactively spot—and respond to—potential problems before they become real ones. This is accomplished through monitoring, and two key elements to monitor are the operating system and the filesystem.

Chapter 5, "Basic Linux Administration," discussed configuring system logs and the `syslog` daemon—`syslogd`. Be sure to remember that this daemon is configured with the `/etc/syslog.conf` file and remember how to use the `logrotate` command. Not found in Chapter 5, but worth knowing, is the `lspci` utility. This tool will list all devices connected through the PCI bus.

Following is an example of the output from this command:

```
# lspci
0000:00:00.0 Host bridge: Intel Corp. 82865G/PE/P DRAM
➥Controller/Host-Hub Interface (rev 02)
0000:00:02.0 VGA compatible controller: Intel Corp. 82865G
➥Integrated Graphics Device (rev 02)
0000:00:1d.0 USB Controller: Intel Corp. 82801EB/ER
➥(ICH5/ICH5R) USB UHCI #1 (rev 02)
0000:00:1d.1 USB Controller: Intel Corp. 82801EB/ER
➥(ICH5/ICH5R) USB UHCI #2 (rev 02)
0000:00:1d.2 USB Controller: Intel Corp. 82801EB/ER
➥(ICH5/ICH5R) USB UHCI #3 (rev 02)
0000:00:1d.3 USB Controller: Intel Corp. 82801EB/ER
➥(ICH5/ICH5R) USB UHCI #4 (rev 02)
0000:00:1d.7 USB Controller: Intel Corp. 82801EB/ER
➥(ICH5/ICH5R) USB2 EHCI Controller (rev 02)
0000:00:1e.0 PCI bridge: Intel Corp. 82801BA/CA/DB/EB/ER Hub
➥interface to PCI Bridge (rev c2)
0000:00:1f.0 ISA bridge: Intel Corp. 82801EB/ER (ICH5/ICH5R)
➥LPC Bridge (rev 02)
0000:00:1f.1 IDE interface: Intel Corp. 82801EB/ER (ICH5/ICH5R)
➥Ultra ATA 100 Storage Controller (rev 02)
0000:00:1f.2 IDE interface: Intel Corp. 82801EB (ICH5) Serial
➥ATA 150 Storage Controller (rev 02)
0000:00:1f.3 SMBus: Intel Corp. 82801EB/ER (ICH5/ICH5R) SMBus
➥Controller (rev 02)
0000:01:01.0 Multimedia audio controller: Creative Labs SB
➥Audigy LS
0000:01:08.0 Ethernet controller: Intel Corp. 82562EZ 10/100
➥Ethernet Controller (rev 02)
#
```

Another handy utility is `siga`, which stands for System Information Gathering. This tool will read both configuration files and diagnostic output of some tools and then save the results in two files: `/tmp/siga/siga.txt` and `/tmp/siga/siga.html`. The `w3m` browser is automatically opened after completion of the utility and the `html` file displayed (see Figure 13.7), but you can also view the text file to sift through the information in any way you want.

FIGURE 13.7
The results of
siga are divided
into categories.

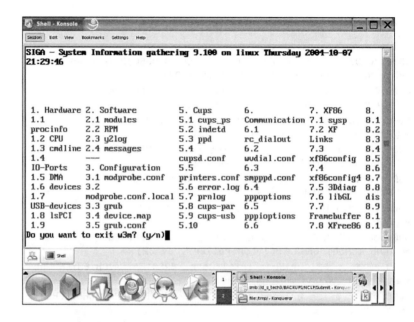

The text file can be quite large—in excess of 9,000 lines—but it can provide an excellent baseline file to compare what is happening now with what is happening over time.

To monitor the filesystem, there are three utilities you should be aware of:

- df—The disk free utility was discussed in Chapter 8, "Working with Filesystems."

- lsof—Used to list open files.

- fuser—Can be used to monitor user access to files.

If you give the command lsof by itself—with no parameters—all open files will be displayed and the list will be in the thousands on a normal server. The -p option can be used to specify a process ID number that will limit the display to only the open files associated with that process ID. Figure 13.8, for example, shows only the open files associated with the root user.

The fuser utility works as the converse to lsof. Instead of showing the open files associated with a process, this tool shows the processes associated with a file. Figure 13.9 shows the options available with this utility.

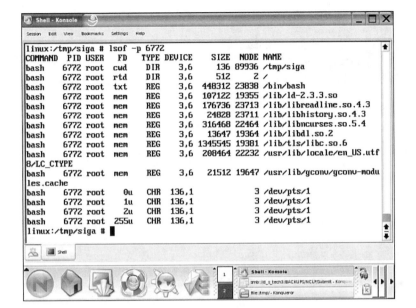

FIGURE 13.8
The open files in use by the root user.

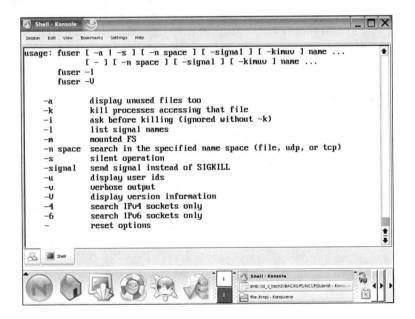

FIGURE 13.9
A number of options are available with fuser.

Figure 13.10 shows a simple example of using fuser to find out who is logged in by looking to see who is accessing the /bin/bash shell.

FIGURE 13.10
The results of
finding who
is using
/bin/bash.

Together these tools can help you keep track of information related to the operating system and filesystem status. By proactively monitoring, you can look for problems and react to them quickly.

Summary

You've spent enough time reading. This chapter wrapped up the meat of the book by looking at some miscellaneous topics that did not fit well in other chapters. You are now ready to take what you've learned and work through the sample practicum in the following chapter. As much fun as the reading has been, there is absolutely no tool that can prepare you for the exam as well as experience. Spend as much time as you can with the operating system and learn as much about it as you can before signing up for the exam. Then walk into the testing center with an air of confidence, and you'll be well on your way to walking out with NCLP on your resume.

Command Summary

Table 13.6 lists the commands that were discussed in this chapter.

Commands for This Chapter **TABLE 13.6**

UTILITY   DEFAULT PURPOSE

UTILITY	DEFAULT PURPOSE
apropos	Returns a short summary of information from whatis
at	Allows you to schedule a job to run *at* a specified time
crontab	Interacts with the cron files to create jobs that run at later times
fuser	Used to monitor user access to files
info	Shows the help information available on a command
KFind	A graphical version of find
lsof	Lists open files
lspci	Lists all devices connected through the PCI bus
man	Displays the manual pages for a command, utility, or file
whatis	Returns information about the utility or command
whereis	Lists all information it can find about locations associated with a file

Sample Practicums

The reading is over. Now it is time to take what you learned from the chapters of this book and apply it to problem solving. One of the underlying principles of learning is known as Bloom's Taxonomy. To oversimplify, one of the things this principle states is that there are various levels of understanding. At the bottom there is only knowledge—being able to recite facts and figures—and higher up there is the ability to apply that knowledge.

The CLP exam is not a knowledge-level exam—it does not ask you who Linux is named after and offer four multiple-choice answers. The CLP exam is a practicum-based test asking you to complete a series of tasks.

What follows are two sample practicums. At this point, you should be able to work through these tasks without referring to this book or any other help source. Use your ability to do so as a guide to how prepared you are for the real exam. If you have no problems breezing through, you should consider scheduling an exam. On the other hand, if you get stuck, or need to look up information, more studying should be undertaken.

Practicum One

You are the head Linux administrator for a medium-sized company. A new server has been ordered and has just arrived with only a base installation. This server will be used at a remote office manned primarily by the sales department. You need to configure this server to do the tasks for which it was purchased.

The server will need to function according to the requirements given in Table 14.1.

TABLE 14.1 **Server Requirements**

SPECIFICATION	DETAILS
SLES 9 Server Name	Pearson-SLES
Static IP Address Configuration	Use an IP address of 192.168.0.78, a subnet mask of 255.255.255.0, and a default router address of 192.168.0.1.
DNS Server Address	The server should obtain this address dynamically.
Server Services	The server should have the following services: Apache Web Server Samba

You need to create a new group—**SALES**—on the server and add five users to the system and to this group. The users you need to create are shown in Table 14.2.

TABLE 14.2 **Members of the SALES Group**

USERNAME	ATTRIBUTES	VALUE
Mpurcell	Full Name Shell Password	Matt Purcell /bin/bash Windsor
Jwatson	Full Name Shell Password	Jenny Watson /bin/ksh Supreme
Kdulaney	Full Name Shell Password	Kristin Dulaney /bin/bash Smooth
Mberson	Full Name Shell Password	Margaret Berson /bin/csh Canadian
Warrenw	Full Name Shell Password	Warren Wyrostek /bin/bash Beverage

The server needs to be configured to have three physical volumes of 5GB each (for a total of 15GB). Apache should be configured to allow symbolic links and it should be running. Samba should be installed and configured as a workgroup with the name **PEARSON-WKGRP**.

Practicum Two

You are the senior Linux administrator for a technical solutions company. One of your customers has ordered a new SuSE Enterprise Linux Server 9 system to be configured at your location and then transported to them. Another administrator has already installed the operating system and added some applications that are standard for your company. You must now configure and tweak it.

The server will regularly run a number of unattended jobs as root. The appropriate configuration file should be edited to include entries for those processes shown in Table 14.3. All entries should run and write any output (standard or error) to /dev/null.

Processes to Run Automatically **TABLE 14.3**

PROCESS	FREQUENCY
/usr/local/bin/oriontest.sh	Every 5 minutes starting on the hour
/usr/local/bin/suf.sh	Every 15 minutes starting on the hour
/usr/local/bin/use.sh	Every 10 minutes, starting at 5 minutes past the hour
/usr/local/bin/orionrestart.sh	6:30 in the morning on Sunday, Tuesday, Thursday, and Saturday

You also need to configure the system according to the settings listed in Table 14.4.

System Configuration Settings and Changes **TABLE 14.4**

ENTITY	NEW VALUE
Newly created files	All newly created files should have default permissions on them set to rw-rw-r--.
/home/jackson	The owner on all files beneath this directory should be changed from jackson to syed. Additionally, the group associated with all files beneath this directory should be changed from users to root.
/bin/zcat	Create a link to this file in the home directory of the root user. The name of the link should be viewer.

Table 14.4   Continued

ENTITY	NEW VALUE
Users	Add two new users to the system: `wintel` and `omni`. The UID of `wintel` should be 1010 and of `omni` 1011. The password settings for each account should be such that they must be changed in 90 days. Additionally, all passwords should be in the `/etc/shadow` file as opposed to `/etc/passwd`.
Initial Runlevel	Set the initial runlevel of the system to the custom setting of 4.
Static IP Address Configuration	Use an IP address of `192.168.10.7`, a subnet mask of `255.255.255.0`, and a default router address of `192.168.10.101`.
Documentation	Add an entry to the end of `/var/log/messages` that the system has been configured on this date.

Summary

Looking at this type of scenario can be overwhelming. Before you do anything, take a deep breath and then break the items down into tasks. Remember that SuSE has a wonderful advantage over other implementations of Linux in its inclusion of YaST.

Being able to pass the sample practicum is not a guarantee of readiness for the actual exam, but it does provide a measurement tool to allow you to gauge your own ability to work through a server's configuration with a handful of details.

I wish you the best.

INDEX

Symbols

A

D